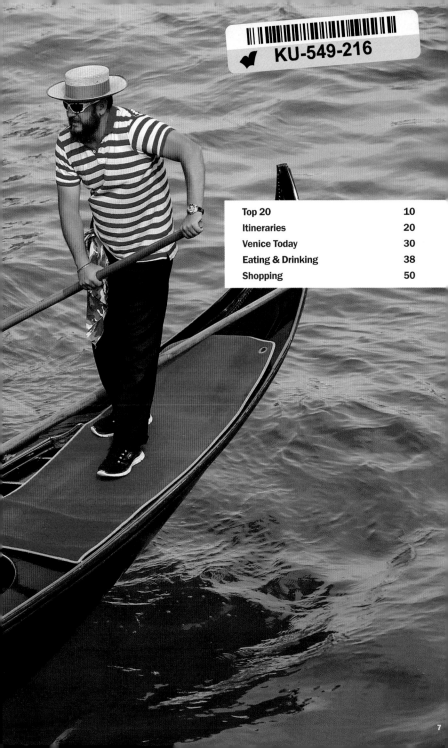

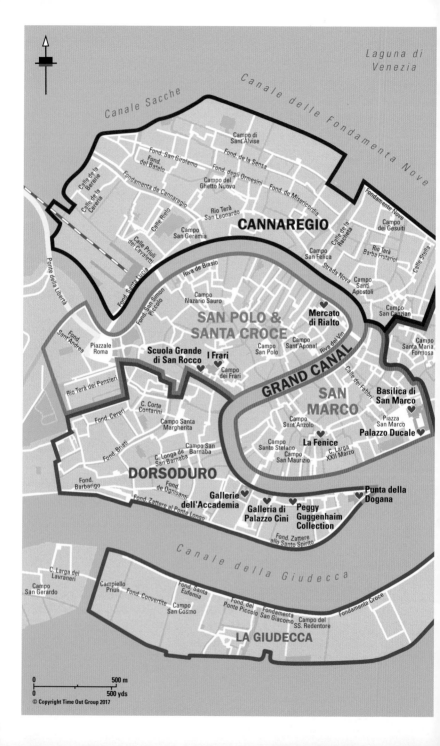

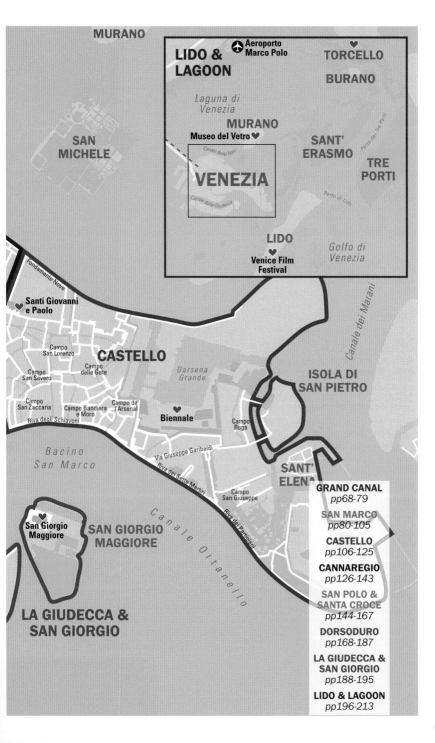

MURANO

LIDO & LAGOON

✈ Aeroporto Marco Polo

TORCELLO

BURANO

Laguna di Venezia

MURANO
Museo del Vetro ♥

SANT' ERASMO

TRE PORTI

Porto dei Tre Porti

SAN MICHELE

VENEZIA

Canale delle Navi

Canale della Giudecca

Porto di Lido

LIDO ♥
Venice Film Festival

Golfo di Venezia

Fondamente Nove

Santi Giovanni e Paolo ♥

Campo San Lorenzo

CASTELLO

Campo San Severo

Campo delle Gate

Darsena Grande

Canale dei Marani

ISOLA DI SAN PIETRO

Campo San Zaccaria

Campo Bandiera e Moro

Campo de l'Arsenal

Biennale ♥

Campo Ruga

Riva degli Schiavoni

Bacino San Marco

Via Giuseppe Garibaldi

Riva dei Sette Martiri

Campo San Giuseppe

Riva dei Partigiani

SANT' ELENA

San Giorgio Maggiore ♥

SAN GIORGIO MAGGIORE

Canale Ortanello

LA GIUDECCA & SAN GIORGIO

9

Top 20

Art, churches, palaces, gondolas, markets and more

01

Basilica di San Marco *p86*

A heart-stopping sight lording it over piazza San Marco, the basilica of St Mark is equally magical inside where acres – literally – of glistening golden mosaic follow the sinuous curves of its domes. From the upstairs museum, where the four bronze horses are displayed, to the gem-encrusted Pala d'Oro, it's all wondrous.

02

I Frari *p162*

A remarkable repository of fine art, this huge hangar-like church is dominated by Titian's glorious *Assumption of the Virgin,* swirling heavenwards wrapped in her scarlet gown and blue cape. Also here is a *Madonna and Child with saints* by Giovanni Bellini, arguably one of his greatest works, and Titian's magnificent *Madonna di Ca' Pesaro.*

03

Mercato di Rialto *p149*

Venetians stock up each morning (Mon-Sat) at the north-west foot of the Rialto Bridge, where stalls are piled high with fruit and vegetables, and – in the Pescaria – slimy, slithering creatures of the deep, many of which you'll be hard-pressed to identify. With its Grand Canal frontage, this must surely count as one of the world's most atmospheric shopping venues.

04

La Fenice *p247*

Venice's opera house is a gem – and one with a long season of top-rate operas and concerts. If you can't catch a performance, there are guided tours of the building, offering a chance to see the gilded, stuccoed extravaganza of the auditorium and the state-of-the-art backstage areas.

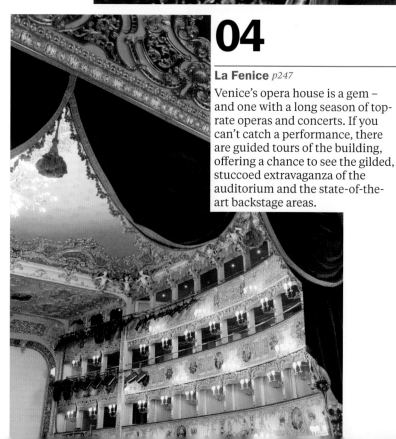

05

Gallerie dell'Accademia *p180*

One of the world's great galleries, the Accademia expanded into neighbouring premises in 2015, giving curators a chance to pull some forgotten treasures out of storage, and arrange familiar masterpieces in a more effective way. From the stiff icon-like first stirrings of Venetian art to the greats of the Renaissance, they're all here, in all their glory.

06

Gondolas *p63*

Eight varieties of tree, 280 pieces of wood, one expensive ride – but gliding beneath Venice's bridges, along its quiet canals, with just the splash of the single oar as it propels you through the labyrinth in this oh-so-Venetian craft is certainly a unique experience.

07

Palazzo Ducale (Doge's Palace) *p92*

This iconic building was where Venice wielded its power and displayed its might, in public rooms designed to instil shock and awe, and with artworks to drive the Serene Republic's self-important message home. Meeting halls, private apartments, torture rooms and prison cells – they're all here in the fulcrum of power.

08

Torcello *p212*

'Mother and daughter, you behold them both in their widowhood: Torcello and Venice', wrote John Ruskin. A powerful player well before Venice proper, the island of Torcello today is picturesquely forlorn and almost uninhabited. Only a cathedral with remarkable mosaics, a little museum and a pretty round church remain as testimonies to its more important former self.

09

Punta della Dogana *p185*

The stunning makeover by Japanese archi-star Tadao Ando of the Serene Republic's bonded customs warehouse at the southern end of the Grand Canal, facing across the water to St Mark's square, is worth a visit simply for the spaces. But there's also a chance to see a selection from French tycoon Francois Pinault's contemporary art collection too.

10

Traditional bacari *p41*

The *ombra*, a small, cheap glass of wine is one of the best examples of the tourist/local contrast in Venice. To experience it in its most salt-of-the-earth form, head to a traditional *bacaro*, such as Da Lele (see *p167*). It opens at dawn but there's no coffee machine: just alcohol. Unadorned and always busy, it's the epitome of hard-working Venice – the flip side of the city's finery and pomp.

11

La Biennale *p121*

Officially the name of Venice's massive arts umbrella organisation, 'La Biennale' is used to refer to unmissable contemporary art (odd years) and architecture (even years) bonanzas that draw the world's finest practitioners, and its cognoscenti, for shows that last through the summer months – offering a chance to get inside the otherwise-shut Arsenale and the Biennale gardens (*see p118*).

12

Rowing regattas *p71*

Voga all Veneta is an essential part of Venetian life, with over 100 rowing events taking place each year. These range from the serious and ceremonial Regata Storica to the jolly Vogalonga, in which a multicoloured jumble of craft and rowers go on a madcap race around the city.

13

Santi Giovanni e Paolo *p111*

Once the final resting place for Venice's rulers, there are 25 doges buried in this huge church. But there are also artworks by Giovanni Bellini, Lorenzo Lotto and Paolo Veronese, as well as some very fine sculpture by the Lombardo family.

14

Scuola Grande di San Rocco *p166*

Tintoretto made the interior of this *scuola* his life's work: 50 dramatic paintings are spread across three rooms and along the walls of the staircase. Look out too for the intriguing wooden sculptures by Francesco Pianta.

15

Murano glass *p204*

Murano glass played a major role in the development of this trading city and remains one of the most popular and sought-after – yet misunderstood – Venetian products. Just beware cheap imitations from the Far East...

16

16

Carnevale *p231*

It may be a 1970s reincarnation of long-dead Venetian merry-making but it's no less exceptional for all that: for two weeks in the run-up to Lent, Venice shrugs off its winter lethargy and fills with masked-and-costumed revellers who flock for a programme of events that grows by the year.

17

Galleria Palazzo Cini *p186*

Tiny, well-hidden Galleria Cini glows with calm Madonnas on gilded backgrounds, and unsettles you as the eyes of its beautiful portraits follow you around the room. It's low-key by Venetian standards, but displays some wonderful art from Ferrara and Florence.

18

San Giorgio Maggiore *p195*

Occupying a piece of prime real estate directly across the water from the Doge's Palace, this most elegant of churches was designed by the great Renaissance architect Palladio. There are artworks to admire, by Tintoretto *et al*, but San Giorgio's biggest draw is its belltower, with spectacular views over Venice and far beyond.

19

Peggy Guggenheim Collection *p183*

Charmingly unfinished Grand Canal-side Palazzo Venier dei Leoni was the home of eccentric millionairess Peggy Guggenheim who brought her extraordinary collection of modern art (and artists) with her to the lagoon city in 1949. With garden, café and fascinating artworks, it's little wonder this is Venice's third-most-visited sight.

20

Venice Film Festival *p236*

Movie world A-listers, razzmatazz, hordes of paparazzi and furious bustle: you'd barely recognise Venice's sleepy seaside Lido island for those ten days in August-September when the Film Festival comes to town. The world's oldest – though no longer its most cutting edge – the Venice event (unlike many others) still offers the public a good chance to see the films on show.

COME
HERE, YOU

Get to know the Venice attractions
with pulling power, and book them
for less with Time Out.

Itineraries

Make the most of every moment with a tailored travel plan

ESSENTIAL WEEKEND

Venice in two days
Budget €265 per person
Getting around Vaporetti and lots of walking

▶ *Budgets include transport, meals and admission prices, but not accommodation or shopping.*

Basilica di San Marco

DAY 1

Passing through and anxious to get the city's major sights under your belt? Much is possible in a single day, as long as you set off early and have laid the groundwork with some pre-booking. If you're here for two days, day 1 of our itinerary makes an excellent introduction to the city, while day 2 takes you deeper into *La Serenissima*.

Morning

St Mark's Basilica (*see p86*) doesn't open to tourists until 9.30 or 9.45am, so book your entry in advance for a €2 fee, but arrive earlier to stroll around the (relatively) uncrowded *piazza* and admire the architecture before entering. If you need refreshment, note that a coffee consumed at a café table in piazza San Marco may be the most expensive hot beverage of your life: drunk standing at the counter inside it costs a fraction of the price. Once inside the basilica, take time to climb up to the **Museo Marciano** in the loggia to see the famous bronze horses and enjoy the sweeping view of St Mark's square from the balcony.

Gallerie dell'Accademia

A visit to the **Doge's Palace** (see p92) next door is essential to understand the mighty machinery of the Venetian state, and to get to grips with some seriously large-scale art.

From the San Zaccaria stop, take a vaporetto to the Palanca stop, admiring Palladio's splendid churches of **San Giorgio Maggiore** (see p195) and **Redentore** (see p193) en route.

Afternoon

For lunch, grab a quick plate of excellent seafood at one of the canal-side tables at **Alla Palanca** (see p193). Then sail back to Zattere and head for the **Gallerie dell'Accademia** (see p180), Venice's foremost treasure trove for the grand masters of classical art. If, on the other hand, your preference is for something more up to date, head for the charming **Peggy Guggenheim Collection** (see p183), with its fine displays of modern art.

Take the route through campo San Barnaba to **campo Santa Margherita** and refresh yourself in one of the many café-bars in this hopping square, before continuing on to the vast **Frari** church (see p162) for another art feast.

Evening

Backtrack just a little for your evening *aperitivo* to friendly **Estro Vino e Cucina** (see p178). Once you settle down here, you may opt to eat as well. But if you have the strength, take vaporetto 1 at San Tomà and steam along the Grand Canal, with the city bathed in sunset light, to the **ponte di Rialto** (see p74). Watching the evening draw in from the top of the bridge may be a cliché, but it's undeniably romantic. There are eateries for all budgets on both sides of the bridge.

Estro Vino e Cucina

Murano glass

Museo Ebraico

DAY 2

Morning

Explore further afield today, starting off at the magnificent church of **Santi Giovanni e Paolo** (*see p111*), perhaps with a cappuccino stop at a pavement table at **Rosa Salva** right next door.

A stroll along the lovely lagoon-side walkway will take you to the Fondamenta Nove vaporetto stop for the quick hop across to **Murano** (*see p202*). Ignore anyone trying to lure you into a glass showroom along the sniper's alley of shops. These peddle anything from stunning Murano creations to cheap tat imported from the other side of the globe. Head instead for the **Museo del Vetro** (*see p205*) for a fine introduction to Venice's long glass-making tradition. (Alternatively, you can leave the vaporetto at **San Michele** island (*see p202*) and languish among the famous graves of the city's picturesque cemetery.)

Afternoon

Back at Fondamenta Nove, weave your way to **Alla Frasca** (*see p142*) for lunch in a delightful campo. You'll need all your orienteering skills to get from here to the **Madonna dell'Orto** (*see p140*), where huge works by Tintoretto dominate the church. The artist is buried here too. Now wend your way south into the **Ghetto** (*see p137*) where the **Museo Ebraico** (*see p139*) charts the long history of Venice's Jewish community.

From the Guglie stop, take vaporetto 4.1 up the final reaches of the Grand Canal, under the **Ponte della Costituzione** (aka Pwonte di Calatrava after its controversial Catalan designer), through what counts as Venice's industrial wasteland and on to **Palanca**, on the Giudecca island.

Evening

There are few finer places in the world to watch the sun set than at the **Skyline Bar** (*see p193*) on the roof of the Molino Stucky Hilton. From Palanca – or indeed from any of the stops along the Giudecca if you feel like a stroll – vaporetto 4.1 continues on to **San Zaccaria. CoVino** (*see p124*) is a smart stop for a gourmet dinner, but be sure to book ahead.

FAMILY DAY OUT

Travelling with tots or teens

Budget €250 for a family of four

Getting around Much of your travelling will be done on foot. After the fifth stepped bridge of the morning, that pushchair may not seem like a great idea: consider bringing a child backpack or resign yourself to endless carrying/dawdling. Children under the age of six travel free on the public transport system; from ten onwards, they pay the same as adults. Visitors aged six to 29 can purchase a Rolling Venice card (€6 through www. veneziaunica.it) for reduced-price transport and museum entry. *Traghetti* are a cheap and cheerful way for kids to experience the canals without you having to shell out for a gondola.

Venice is a wonderland: a citywide playground of hidey-holes and creepy corners, with water where the streets should be and a vast stone menagerie of fantastic beasts and improbable monsters. However, you may need to adopt some special strategies to avoid sightseeing saturation with tinies. Keep dim (if art-filled) churches as refuges in moments of over-heating, and enliven interminable (if fascinating) galleries with the occasional game of I-spy. Plan your day to allow plenty of time for enjoying the city's ice-cream shops and for leaning over its 350-odd bridges watching the delivery boats put-put gently by. Teens may be inveigled into a Venetian frame of mind with a pre-emptive gift of Cornelia Funke's novel *The Thief Lord*. Terry Jones' *Nicobobinus* and Anthony Horowitz's *Scorpia* both begin with exciting scenes set in Venice.

Murano

DENONTIE SECRET
CONTRO CHI OCCVLT
GRATIE ET OFFICI
Ō COLLVDERĀ PER
NASCON DER LA VE
RENDITA Ō ESSI

Doge's Palace

Morning

A view over the city is a good place to begin a day's exploration. Give the over-subscribed campanile in St Mark's Square a miss, and take a vaporetto from the San Zaccaria stop to **San Giorgio** (*see p188*). The bird's-eye view from the tower is arguably better: you're one wide canal away from the main island, and so the whole sweep of the city is laid out before you, bisected by the backwards-S-shaped Grand Canal. On a clear day, you can see the faraway peaks – at times snow-covered – of the Dolomites.

Head back to San Zaccaria and turn left along the **Riva degli Schiavoni** promenade to the lagoon-facing façade of the **Doge's Palace** (*see p92*). (Note en route that the final bridge you cross gives a fine view to the Bridge of Sighs.) Stop at the third column from the palace's corner for the most famous Venetian game of all. Stand with your back touching the column and try to walk around it, all the way. Can you do it without slipping off the shoe-eroded edge of the marble pavement?

In **piazza San Marco**, on the north side of the basilica, crouch two little red marble lions, their backs worn smooth by generations of small bottoms: if you're longing for a photo of your child astride the symbol of St Mark – Venice's patron saint – this is the place.

Afternoon

Grabbing a slab of pizza is often a good lunch option, though the big, noisy **Alla Basilica** (*see p115*) diner right behind St Mark's Basilica also provides a (relatively) cheap lunch for starving children.

A ten-minute stroll north east of the piazza, the **Scuola di San Giorgio degli Schiavoni** (*see p106*) is a charming place to introduce children to the allure of Venetian painting. In the first years of the 16th century, artist Vittore Carpaccio was commissioned to decorate this social centre for Slav residents with stories from the lives of Dalmatian saints. Look out for St George rescuing the lovely princess of Trebizond from the fiery dragon; St Jerome looking bewildered as his fellow monks scarper at the sight of a cuddly lion, and 12-year-old St Tryphon banishing a cheeky-looking basilisk-devil that had possessed the emperor's daughter. There are infinite engaging details in Carpaccio's dreamy world.

If it's all going well and you feel you can risk a little more art, check out the series of 18th-century scenes of Venetian life by Gabriel Bella at the nearby **Fondazione Querini Stampalia** (*see p112*). Between serious processions and doges going about their official duties are football matches, ice-skating parties on the frozen lagoon, bear- and bull-baiting fixtures and the unusual 'sport' of head-butting cats to death.

If, on the other hand, a change of tack is needed, head south-east for the **Museo Storico Navale** (*see p156*), containing models of Venetian ships from mighty galleons to the Doge's magnificent gilded *Bucintoro* barge. Its annexe, the **Padiglione delle Navi**, has full-size (real) gondolas, fishing boats, naval vessels and racing boats.

Padiglione delle Navi

Evening

You're far enough east now to collapse in some greenery, either in the *giardini* off via Garibaldi or – slightly further away – those in Sant'Elena. Both come with swings and slides and shady tree cover. If you make it to Sant'Elena, the **Vincent Bar** (*see p125*) serves good café-style meals at outside tables from which you can watch your offspring play in the park. Nearer to via Garibaldi, **Dai Tosi** (*see p124*) offers good pizza and much else.

Riva degli Schiavoni

onte della Costituzione

BUDGET BREAK

For the euro-conscious visitor
Budget €25 per person
Getting around Walking

▶ *Budgets include transport, meals and admission prices, but not accommodation or shopping.*

Venice is an expensive holiday destination: there's no getting away from that. Approach it like a Venetian, though, and prices come down. Remember, too, that just wandering around and wondering at this unique city costs nothing at all.

Morning

For a very special take on **St Mark's Basilica** (*see p86*), enter by the piazza dei Leoncini door and attend the sung mass at 9am. You can't wander around – you're there for the service – but craning up at those acres of shimmering mosaic as the music drifts over you is unique. And it's free.

In calle degli Albanesi, just behind the basilica, grab a restorative cappuccino at **Da Bonifacio** (*see p116*) – in Italy, sitting down to consume your coffee costs more, but there's no danger of that here as there's nowhere to sit – before heading to the nearby church of **San Zaccaria** (*see p114*) with its Tintoretto, its Tiepolo and its marvellous *Madonna and Four Saints* by Giovanni Bellini – all for free.

Sacra conversazione, San Zaccaria

Afternoon

As you wiggle your way north to campo Santi Giovanni e Paolo, pick up the ingredients for a picnic. You can eat it on the canal-side steps opposite the entrance to the massive church. To see the interior of **Santi Giovanni e Paolo** (*see p111*) you'll be charged €2.50 – a small price for all those fine doges' tombs and great art. Next door at the **Scuola Grande di San Marco** (*see p115*), on the other hand, you can see the magnificent halls and the intriguing collection of historical medical-related artefacts – this medical science museum is located inside the city's hospital – for free.

Further west near the Rialto Bridge, the **Fondaco dei Tedeschi** (*see p101*) is a luxury shopping mall with little to entice the visitor on a tight budget. But if you can time your stopover here for just before sunset, climb to the rooftop viewing platform for an utterly magnificent and utterly gratis panorama over the city centre.

Scuola Grande di San Marco

Grand Canal at dusk

Alla Ciurma

Evening

Shun the Fondaco's ground-floor bar if you want to save your *centesimi* and cross the Rialto bridge to **Al Mercà** (*see p150*). This hole-in-the-wall purveyor of snacks and drinks serves great spritzes at €2.50. One or two of these, consumed among the crowd of happy *aperitivo*-drinkers who fan out to occupy the campo, will set you up nicely for your evening meal. If you're not too late you might squeeze into **Alla Ciurma** (*see p150*) and eat a meal's-worth of delicious *cicheti* (bar snacks), but the place closes at 9pm: remember, to eat cheaply in Venice, be prepared to eat standing up and eat early.

TRAILING TINTORETTO

Follow in the footsteps of Venice's master colourist
Budget €65 per person
Getting around Walking and one vaporetto ride

Jacopo Robusti – aka Tintoretto – rarely left the city and painted furiously during the whole of his long life (1519-1594). The results are everywhere.

Morning

The **Gallerie dell'Accademia** (*see p180*) is a good place to start. It provides an overview of Tintoretto's works, and allows visitors to compare and contrast this master with his friends and rivals, including Titian and Veronese.

Heading west, Tintoretto's *Last Supper* in the church of **San Trovaso** (*see p176*) includes a tavern scene so realistic that you might be moved to replicate it at the **Cantinone Già Schiavi** (*see p186*) opposite, over a light lunch.

Cantinone Già Schiavi

Santa Maria dell Orto

Evening

With some expert map-reading, continue east to **Bar Puppa** (*see p143*). This unassuming little bar serves seriously good spritz, excellent *cicheti* (bar snacks) and huge plates of very good pasta at prices that are well below Venetian norms.

Afternoon

Brace now for Tintoretto's *pièce de résistance*, the **Scuola di San Rocco** (*see p166*), which lies a short walk north. On and off for 23 years, Tintoretto continued to add to this overwhelming array of biblical scenes. After so much canvas, your head may be reeling and you may well need a rest, a stiff drink or just a change of scenery.

At San Tomà, take the number 1 vaporetto up the canal to San Marcuola, then strike off north to the **Madonna dell'Orto** (*see p140*). This was the artist's parish church; as well as many major artworks, his grave is also here. The Robusti family home was nearby, at Cannaregio 3399 on the fondamenta dei Mori. A plaque marks the place. Next door at 4100, at what was his workshop, is the **Bottega del Tintoretto** (www.tintorettovenezia.it) studio, which runs printing courses and stages exhibitions. On the parallel canal to the south, you'll pass the **Scuola della Misericordia** – now an art restoration centre. It was here that Tintoretto spread the largest canvas ever painted and created his *Paradise*, which is now in the Doge's Palace.

Scuola Grande di San Rocco

When to Visit

Venice by season

Off-seasons in Venice seem to have become more of a myth than a real thing. Visitors – both foreign and Italian – flock to this city all year round, due to its pervasive charm, history and culture, often overlooking the oppressive humidity in summer and the frigid temperatures in winter. However, there are still some (ever dwindling) periods that are less crowded and make for a more fulfilling experience.

Spring

February is **Carnevale** month (see p231), so be prepared to wear a costume and embrace the mayhem in the streets. Venice is also a popular destination on Valentine's Day, so if you prefer to avoid the crowds, try the period after Carnevale and before Easter. You may get deals on hotels and airfares at this time, but pack an umbrella and warmish clothes, as the weather will be wet and nights can be cold. May is a gorgeous month to visit – you'll get sunshine and a clear atmosphere, which make strolling through the city pure bliss. However, if you want to avoid the worst of the crowds, don't visit over the first weekend in May.

Summer

June to August is when four elements combine to create arguably the worst time to visit: excessive humidity (and mosquitoes), intense heat, huge crowds and high prices. Some days may be hazy, while others will be punctuated by heavy showers. The tiny alleys (*calli*) can get clogged with people, making it difficult to circulate in the most popular areas of the city, notably around the Rialto Bridge and St Mark's

Carnevale

Dance Biennale

Regata Storica

square. Note too, that 15 August is **Ferragosto** (see p232), a national Italian holiday when Venetians tend to leave town, meaning that many authentic shops and eateries are closed. During the **Venice Biennale** (see p230) and the **Venice Film Festival** (see p236) prices inflate even more; queues for water taxis are long, and fares prohibitively expensive. But if glitz and glam are your thing, it's worth the hassle.

Autumn

Due to its mild temperatures, September is becoming a favourite month to be in Venice, and events such as the **Regata Storica** (see p233) draw thousands of curious onlookers to the shores of the canals. October can also be a good time to stroll through the city with fewer tourists, but you should expect changeable weather. By November, *acqua alta* (high-water flooding) is common and tends to frighten off visitors. However, the combination of thick fog and flooded streets creates an eerie and enchanting atmosphere that will appeal to many – just be sure to pack your wellies. And don't miss the celebration of **Festa della Madonna della Salute** (see p233).

Winter

December is usually crowded, especially for the **Christmas holidays** (23 December to 6 January; see p233). At the beginning of the year, temperatures tend to drop, sometimes below freezing, so consider warming yourself up with a cup of hot chocolate, or some grappa.

Venice Today

Unique city, unique issues

'One day the tourists will travel here by boat to peer down into the waters, and they will see pillars and columns and marble far, far beneath them.' So wrote Daphne du Maurier in a fit of romantic gloom, and though the city is still keeping its head above water, multiple threats to Venice's unique fabric remain. If instances of *acqua alta* (high water: more than 80 centimetres at the Punta della Salute) have in fact declined in recent years – 100 in 2016, as against 155 in 2013 – huge strains continue to be placed on it by a cocktail of extreme vulnerability to the elements, foundations rocked by motorised boat traffic and the passage of giant cruise ships, and visitor numbers wildly out of proportion to the city's size and declining population. Successive administrations adopt stop-gap measures but little in the way of comprehensive policy.

High water in plazza San Marco

Beset by problems, or creating its own?

In the corner of a pharmacy window in campo San Bartolomeo (or San Bortolo, as Venetians know it), hidden away among stacks of female hygiene products, a small digital clock beams out a sequence of red numbers. At the time of writing, the clock reads 54,579, but the number has been steadily declining since it was installed a few years ago. It bears witness to the relentless decline of the city's inhabitants, whose number dropped from 76,000 in 1991 to 65,000 in 2001 and has kept on falling steadily.

In June 2006, British economist John Kay provoked outrage among Venetians when he argued that 'Venice is already a theme park... The economics of the city are the economics of Yosemite and Disneyland, not the economics of Bologna or Los Angeles.'

This is, to some extent, a gross over-simplification. But lose yourself in the St Mark's square maelstrom, or wander across the Rialto Bridge. You may find yourself wondering if there's a single Venetian left, and asking what are these mounds of the tackiest possible souvenirs doing in one of the world's most perfectly preserved treasure troves?

Is it inertia, or are the city fathers actively encouraging the kind of hit-and-run tourism in which droves of day-trippers are herded into the most heavily touristic spots in the *centro storico*, never ploughing any more back into the local economy than the price of a plastic gondola? Even those visitors who choose to bed down in *La Serenissima* stay for an average of 2.5 nights, against a considerably healthier average in Rome of 3.5 nights.

Cynics might say that this state of affairs suits Venetians, for whom St Mark's square is a no-go area, and who know alternative routes to just about everywhere: predictable madding crowds confined to easily avoidable areas means they can get on with life.

The locals are adept at avoiding the droves of day-trippers who clog thoroughfares around St Mark's square.

No Grandi Navi!

Vast cruise ships are a controversial feature of the Venice lagoon

On Sunday afternoons, the stretch of water in front of the Doge's Palace is a disheartening sight. One gigantic cruise ship after another sets off along the Giudecca Canal and across the Bacino di San Marco towards the northern Adriatic: a surreal procession of jarring mastodons dwarfing historic architectural landmarks which moments before had seemed so perfect in their peerless setting.

Venetians rail against these giants of the seas desecrating their lagoon, and countless dramatic photos in the world's press make the senselessness of it clear to all. But if cruise ships have been passing by here for decades – parading a toy-town Venice before decks packed with oblivious passengers – and no solution has been found, there must be a reason. Conflicting interests and big bucks could well be at the bottom of it.

When it comes down to it, the 1.8 million visitors that more than 520 ships brought into the tiny *centro storico* in 2015 were a small percentage of a total 25 million tourists who pounded Venice's narrow streets that year; housed, fed and entertained on board, they brought relatively little income to Venetian traders. The environmental damage to the city's fragile ecosystem was immense, as was the danger of a rogue captain capsizing his vessel against an iconic landmark. But around 4,000 people are employed by Venice's cruise ship passenger terminal, which generates some €220 million annually: the powers that be are loath to mess with so many voters and so much money.

Into this sticky morass in 2017 waded native Venetian Pino Musolino, the new, young head of the North Adriatic port authority whose experience has taken him to fill prestigious posts in the far larger ports of Antwerp and Singapore. He has talked of shifting cruise ship operations to Marghera on the mainland, and halting the unseemly parade through the heart of the lagoon city. It remains to be seen whether he can overturn the status quo.

Venice lives on tourism but considers its visitors annoying obstacles; its beauty is unimaginable but quality control is lacking. It's a theme park without the irony and a museum without sufficient true connoisseurs. Over 1,000 years as one of Europe's great powers has left it unable to face up to handling its insignificance.

Similarly, it struggles to deal with environmental problems that have existed for as long as the city itself. The MOSE moveable flood barrier scheme, intended to block excessive flow through the three exits from the lagoon to the sea, is set to be inaugurated in 2018 (but don't hold your breath). The project has drawn fierce criticism for the damage ecologists claim it could cause to the lagoon's fragile ecosystem. It has also absorbed vital funds that would otherwise go to Insula, the publicly owned company responsible for dredging canals, repairing and raising pavements and ensuring that the foundations of this waterlogged city remain sufficiently intact to keep the miracle of urban planning well above the waves. Beset by technical and legal woes, the battle for and against MOSE is equalled only by the wrangling over the passage of immense cruise ships, which do inestimable damage to the lagoon's fragile ecosystem as they dwarf the Doge's Palace and the Giudecca Canal (*see p33* No Grandi Navi!) in a parade buoyed up by economic interests.

The passage of immense cruise ships does inestimable damage to the lagoon's fragile ecosystem as they dwarf the Doge's Palace and the Giudecca Canal

Meanwhile, on *terraferma*

Beyond island Venice is another world again, that of the Veneto region. While *La Serenissima* continues to hold the world in her thrall, the *terraferma* side of the lagoon has come quietly but steadily into its own. Besides being one of Italy's biggest economic success stories, it now has a burgeoning tourist industry as well. In a region that ranks among Italy's most-visited, 17.25 million people, including 11.2 million non-Italians, checked into a hotel here in 2015, spending a total of 63.26 million nights; admittedly, 8.65 million of these people (including 6.53 million non-Italians) headed for Venice and its province, but Verona clocked up a healthy 4.2 million.

Any success that Venice and the Veneto have experienced has been recent. Venice had slipped far into decline before the city capitulated to Napoleon's troops in 1797. Under Austrian rule (1815-66) it was relegated to the status of a picturesque, inconsequential backwater. But if the city suffered, the fate of its former mainland territories was even worse: with no industry to speak of, and agriculturally

Inevitably, the burgeoning tourist industry has led to mass production of once-prized Venetian crafts.

backwards, the Veneto ran the semi-feudal South a close race for the title of Italy's own Third World. Between 1876 and 1901, almost 35 per cent of the 5.2 million desperate Italians who sought a better life abroad fled from the crushing poverty of the Veneto and the neighbouring Friuli region.

Industrialisation in Venice's mainland Porto Marghera between and after the wars shifted the more impoverished sectors of the population from agricultural to urban areas. But poverty remained. In 1961, 48 per cent of homes in the north-east had no running water, 72 per cent were without a bathroom and 86 per cent had no central heating.

What the people of the Veneto did have, however, was a deep-rooted attachment to their traditional crafts, and a cussedness of character unmatched anywhere else in Italy. In the past, both had proved detrimental: when captains of heavy industry sought meek vassals to man the furnaces, many of the natives of the Veneto who protested were forcibly deported to populate Fascist new towns in the malarial swamps south of Rome.

Across the lagoon, there is heavy industry at Porto Marghera.

Things can only get better

It was not, in fact, until the 1970s that north-eastern determination came into its own. With industrial downscaling all the rage, those family-run workshops that had ridden out the bad times gradually became viable business concerns. Giuliana Benetton's knitting machine gave birth to a global clothing empire centred in Treviso; Leonardo del Vecchio's metalworking lessons in an orphanage spawned Luxottica, the world's biggest spectacle frame-maker, based in Belluno; and Ivano Beggio progressed from tinkering with bikes in his father's cycle shop in Noale to running Aprilia, one of Europe's largest manufacturers of motorcycles and scooters. Through the mid to late 1990s a third

The people of the Veneto have a deep-rooted attachment to their traditional crafts, and a cussedness of character unmatched anywhere else in Italy

of the country's huge balance of trade surplus was generated in the north-east. In 1997, local industrialists boasted that the unemployment rate had fallen to zero; in 2007, it stood at 3.3 per cent, well below the national average of 6.1 per cent. By mid-2013, unemployment in the Veneto region had leapt to 7.5 per cent – still well below the national average of 12.7 per cent.

The 21st century has seen a tarnishing of the Veneto's Midas touch. The competitive edge for exports created by a weak lira was lost with the introduction of the euro. Crippling labour costs have forced many businesses to relocate eastwards; a manpower shortfall was bridged by hiring immigrant workers, resulting in an unprecedented ethnic potpourri. Learning to live with social and cultural differences is one of the biggest challenges the famously insular Veneto must face today.

The post-war parabola experienced by island Venice was, if anything, bleaker. As *terraferma* became industrialised, workers looked across the water for employment. Realising that housing on the mainland was cheaper, drier and easier to park in front of, they moved out in an exodus that brought the resident population of island Venice plunging from around 175,000 in 1951 to little more than 54,000 today.

For an area of 5.17 square kilometres (3.2 square miles), however, that's still a respectable figure. Few such small cities, moreover, can lay claim to a population comprising gondoliers, mask-makers, glass-blowers, fishermen, monks, nuns, musicians, artists, writers, architects, historians, academics, restoration experts and many of Italy's rich and famous. Add to that a sizeable student population, a dedicated group of expats and part-time residents and the result is a solid base of 'locals' that gives Venice its distinct flavour. Here is a 'real' city where dogged residents are prepared to persevere – despite exorbitant prices, grocers' shops turning

There are initiatives underway to keep Venice above water, both literally and figuratively

Venice's population has fallen from 175,000 in 1951 to little more than 54,000 today. Nevertheless there is a solid base of 'locals' that give Venice its distinct flavour.

into mask shops, and the chance that *acqua alta* may cause irreparable damage to their carpets.

And there are initiatives under way to keep Venice above water – both literally and figuratively – in the 21st century. For every headline-grabbing problem project – such as the 'tower of light' skyscraper project on the mainland (www.palaislumiere.eu) planned by Venetian exile Pierre Cardin, but thankfully shelved in 2013 – others carry on with no fanfare and much success. Take Insula (www.insula.it), for example: a consortium that has worked its way around Venice since 1997, dredging clogged canals, removing hundreds of thousands of cubic metres of mud, and rebuilding footpaths in a quiet but vital maintenance programme.

On the mainland, too, things are on the move. Among the high-tech businesses attracted to the rapidly developing Science and Technology Park at the northern end of Porto Marghera is a nanotechnologies laboratory that makes Venice a world leader in the field.

Work goes quietly on to keep Venice above water. Here, repairs are being made to a house's foundations.

The hidden city

Dazzled, disorientated and besieged by pigeons, the average visitor to *La Serenissima* may not even realise that a traipse from St Mark's to the Rialto tells them as much about the city as a guided tour of the Tower of London or a lift to the top of the Empire State Building tell about London and New York. Much of Venetian life takes place behind closed doors, concealed from the casual observer.

An isolated culture, hedged about by water, one that remained an independent republic for over a millennium, one that once lorded it over the entire Mediterranean, cannot be easily penetrated by an outsider, although everyone and anyone is welcome to try. Otherwise, feel free to simply sit back and enjoy the show.

Eating & Drinking

If seafood is your thing, the lagoon city is the place for you

An average 70,000 visitors rush through Venice each day, and the majority of the city's restaurants operate with these diners in mind: clearly, there's little real incentive to shoot for culinary excellence when you can be certain that 95 per cent of your guests will drop in once and once only.

But a discerning, faithful clientele of residents keeps standards high in a selection of mainly well-hidden establishments. Seek these out, and you'll eat very well indeed. In most cases, it will cost you more than elsewhere in Italy – Venice simpy isn't cheap – but you'll have the satisfaction of eating in the local tradition and rubbing shoulders with spirited Venetians rather than frazzled tourists.

Making sense of Venice's hostelries

Venice boasts the usual panoply of *ristoranti*, *trattorie* and *osterie*, but it is the humble neighbourhood *bacaro* (*see right* Traditional bacari) that is the salvation of the Venetian dining scene. These establishments serve cheap wine and tapas-like snacks called *cicheti* from dawn to dusk to a loyal local clientele. From creamed cod (*baccalà mantecato*) to meatballs, to sardines stewed in onion (*sarde in saor*), to tiny stuffed peppers, there is a huge selection, to be eaten one at a time or piled on to a plate to make what can add up to a pretty full meal. However, except where you can perch on a bar stool or occupy any front-of-house accommodation, this is actually on-the-hoof food: the proper tables are for proper diners, opting for the full pasta-plus-main meals that will appear from a kitchen hidden away behind.

Cicheti are charged individually – anything between €1.50 and €3 is normal, depending on what you choose. So a well-filled plate can cost €10 or less. Sitting down for a proper meal in the same hostelry, however, may cost €30 or more (sometimes much more) a head. To complicate

In the know
Restaurant price codes

We use the following price codes for restaurant listings throughout the guide; they represent the average cost of one main dish (*secondo*).

€ = under €10

€€ = €10-25

€€€ = €25-40

€€€€ = over €40

❤ Best tastes of Venice

Antiche Carampane *p153*
A simple, timeless classic.

Al Portego *p115*
Feast on some of Venice's best cicheti.

Alle Testiere *p115*
Hidden seafood gem.

Anice Stellato *p142*
Venetian classics in a lively setting.

Italians are assiduous frequenters of their local café for morning cappuccino.

💜 Traditional bacari

With their blackened beams and rickety wooden tables, *bacari* (emphasis on the first syllable) are local bars, often hidden down backstreets or in quiet campielli. These establishments – **Al Portego** (*see p115*), **Ca' d'Oro** (*see p130*), **All'Arco** (*see p150*), **Alla Ciurma** (*see p150*) and **Bottega ai Promessi Sposi** (*see p135*) are fine examples – serve alcohol and snacks (*cicheti; see p40*) to market traders, workers and students from early morning onwards, and cater for Venetians on a *giro di bacari* (pub crawl) at aperitivo time. They may have a dark room out the back with scant seating, but dominating the front of the premises is a high glass-fronted bar counter piled with *cicheti*. The drink of choice is the *ombra*, a small glass of house wine (*see p46* In the know), which is usually priced at around €1, but you'll find beer and spirits, too. The most famous and most down-to-earth of Venice's bacari is **Da Lele** (*see p167*), situated near Piazzale Roma in the back streets of Santa Croce. A drink here – don't ask for a coffee as it isn't served – will give you an unrivalled insight into local workaday Venice.

Cicheti

arrangements still further, many clients will just be here for a drink: they're generally the ones chatting, glass in hand, in the *calle* outside.

At the higher end of Venice's dining scene, *trattorie* and *ristoranti* function much as in the rest of Italy, the difference being that their prices tend to be higher than elsewhere. Between the two comes the trap that many visitors fall into: the hostelry catering only to the tourist horde. You can eat exceptionally well in the lagoon city... as long as you avoid anything with a *menu turistico* in several languages and a determined enticer at the door. Pay for the best, or seek out some dark *bacaro*: anything else will not be authentically Venetian.

Etiquette

In more rustic eateries, menus are often recited out loud; waiters are used to doing off-the-cuff English translations, though these can be a

Steer well clear of restaurants that employ sharply dressed waiters to persuade passing tourists to come in for a meal.

little approximate. If you are unsure of the price of something you have ordered, always ask.

If there is a printed menu, note that fish is often quoted by weight – generally by the *etto* (100 grammes). Steer well clear of restaurants – mainly around San Marco – that employ sharply dressed waiters to stand outside and persuade passing tourists to come in for a meal: an immediate recipe for rip-off prices. Always ask for a written *conto* (bill) at the end of the meal, as it is, in theory, illegal to leave the restaurant without one.

Finally, bear in mind that there are two timescales for eating in Venice. The more upmarket restaurants follow standard Italian practice, serving lunch from around 1pm to 3pm and dinner from 7.30pm until at least 10pm. But *bacari* and neighbourhood *trattorie* tend to follow Venetian workers' rhythms, with lunch running from midday to 2pm and dinner from 6.30pm to 9pm, although a newer generation places its emphasis more on food than on drinking-with-snacks, and keeps on cooking until 10pm or 10.30pm. As a rule, though, if you want to eat cheaply, eat early.

As a rule if you want to eat cheaply in Venice, eat early

The islands of the lagoon provide delicious fresh vegetables, including *fiori di zucca* and *castraure*.

Venetian Menu

Choosing what to eat

Antipasti (starters)

The dozens of *cicheti* that are served from the counters of the city's traditional *bacari* (*see p41*) are essentially antipasti; the choice may include: *baccalà mantecato* – stockfish beaten into a cream with oil and milk, often served on grilled polenta; *bovoleti* – tiny snails cooked in olive oil, parsley and garlic; *carciofi* – artichokes, even better if they are *castrauri* (baby artichokes); *canoce* (or *cicale di mare*) – mantis shrimps; *folpi/folpeti* – baby octopus; *garusoli* – sea snails; *moleche* – soft-shelled crabs, usually deep-fried; *museto* – a boiled pork brawn sausage, generally served on a slice of bread with mustard; *nervetti* – boiled veal cartilage; *polpette* – deep-fried spicy meatballs; polenta – yellow or white cornmeal mush, served either runny or in firm sliceable slabs; *sarde in saor* – sardines marinated in onion, vinegar, pine nuts and raisins: *schie* – tiny grey shrimps, usually served on a bed of soft white polenta; *seppie in nero* – cuttlefish in its own ink; *spienza* – veal spleen, usually served on a skewer; *trippa e rissa* – tripe cooked in broth.

Primi (first courses)

Bigoli in salsa – fat spaghetti in an anchovy and onion sauce; *gnocchi con granseola* – potato gnocchi in spider-crab sauce; pasta... *e ceci* – pasta and chickpea soup; ... *e fagioli* – pasta and borlotti bean soup; spaghetti... *alla busara* – in anchovy sauce; ... *al nero di seppia* – in squid-ink sauce; ... *con caparossoli/vongole veraci* – with clams; *risotto di zucca* – pumpkin risotto.

Secondi (main courses)

In addition to the antipasti mentioned above, you may find: *anguilla* – eel; *aragosta/ astice* – spiny lobster/lobster; *branzino* – sea bass; *cape longhe* – razor clams; *cape sante* – scallops; *cernia* – grouper; *coda di rospo* – anglerfish; *cozze* – mussels; *granchio* – crab; *granseola* – spider crab; *orata* – gilt-headed bream; *rombo* – turbot; *pesce San Pietro* – John Dory; *pesce spada* – swordfish; *sogliola* – sole; *tonno* – tuna; *vongole/ caparossoli* – clams.

Meat eaters are less well catered for in Venice; local specialities include: *fegato alla veneziana* – veal liver cooked in onions; *castradina* – a lamb and cabbage broth.

Dolci

Venice's restaurants are not the best place to feed a sweet habit – with a few exceptions, there are far more tempting pastries to be found on the shelves of the city's *pasticcerie*. The classic end to a meal here is a plate of *buranei* – sweet egg biscuits – served with a dessert wine such as Fragolino. Then it's quickly on to the more important matter of which grappa to order.

Granchio served at Riviera *p174*

What's on the plate?

If you want to eat well, eat local. Venice may be the most tourist-infested of Italian cities, but it has a long and glorious culinary tradition based on fresh seafood, game and vegetables, backed up by northern Italy's three main carbohydrate fixes: pasta, risotto and polenta.

Eating like the locals requires a certain spirit of open-minded experimentation. Not everybody has eaten *granseola* (spider-crab) before, or *garusoli* (sea snails) or *canoce* (mantis shrimps), but Venice is definitely the place to try these marine curios – as well as market garden rarities like *castraure* (baby artichokes) and *fiori di zucca* (courgette flowers). A writhing, glistening variety of seafood swims from the morning stalls of the Rialto and Chioggia markets into restaurant kitchens; it's not always cheap, but for dedicated pescivores, there are few better stamping grounds in the whole of Italy.

Cicheti and wine

The once-strong creative tradition with meat – especially the more unmentionable parts – is kept alive in a couple of restaurants and one marvellous *trattoria*, **Dalla Marisa** (*see p142*); it can also be found in bar-counter *cicheti* (tapas-style snacks) like *nervetti* (veal cartilage) and *cotechino* (spicy pig's intestine parcels filled with various cuts of pork).

Canoce

There are still very few dedicated veggie restaurants in the city, but Venetian cuisine relies heavily on seasonal vegetables, so it is quite easy to eat a vegetarian meal. *Secondi* are often accompanied by a wide selection of grilled vegetables: aubergine, courgette, tomato or radicchio.

Pizzerie

Like all major Italian cities, Venice has its fair share of pizza joints, though the standard is not particularly high. Still, prices in *pizzerie* remain reasonably low, which makes them a good standby for a carbohydrate-and-protein

Cotechino

injection between more expensive restaurant meals. In the rest of Italy, *pizzerie* are generally open only in the evening; tourist demand, though, means that almost all Venetian pizza emporia serve the doughy discs at lunchtime too. Note that beer, rather than wine, is the traditional accompaniment to pizza.

Cafés and bars

Italians are assiduous frequenters of their local café for morning cappuccino and of their favourite bar for evening *aperitivi* (in fact, one establishment may answer all their needs: the terms bar and café are generally interchangeable, and most venues are multi-purpose).

Venice's uniqueness extends into many unexpected spheres – eating and drinking included. Take, for example, the all-day bar. Unassuming places such as **Da Lele** (*see p167*) or **Alla Ciurma** (*see p150*) open their doors around 6am. But you'll search in vain for a coffee machine: market traders or workers arriving from the mainland drop by

In the know
Un' ombra de vin

The origin of the expression *un' ombra de vin* ('a shade of wine') is contested, but the most popular theory is that, in days of yore, innkeepers and travelling wine merchants would avoid the heat by peddling their wares in the shade of churches and belltowers, periodically relocating as the sun moved across the sky.

The terms bar and café are pretty well interchangeable. At *aperitivo* time, locals flock to *bacari* or *enoteche*.

at sunrise for their first (alcoholic) drink of the day. It keeps – they'll tell you –the damp out of your bones. *Aperitivi*, on the other hand, are quite likely to be consumed in a *pasticceria* (cake shop), with some fruity, creamy pastry concoction as a chaser.

Venice contributes its own specialities to the standard Italian routines for breakfast, light snacks, pastries and alcoholic beverages: the *ombra* (*see below*) and the spritz (*see p47*). Also flowing freely into Venetian glasses are prosecco, the bubbly white wine made in the hills of the Veneto region, and *spento*, a bubble-free version of the same wine.

In a city where everything seems to cost over the odds, a small glass of wine (*un'ombra*) costs anything from Da Lele's ridiculous 60c to around €1.50. And in all but the smartest bars, the ubiquitous spritz comes in at €2.50. Or rather, it does when consumed standing. It's true anywhere in Italy that a surcharge is applied to café/bar prices when you consume sitting at a table. But Venice takes this rule much further.

Café etiquette

The practice in Italian bars is to decide what you want, pay at the till in advance, then display your receipt when you order at the counter. If you return to the same establishment sufficiently often to be considered a regular, you can pay afterwards. Anything ordered at the counter must be consumed at the counter. Sitting down incurs a surcharge: the privilege of occupying a table will push your bill up a little in smaller places but jaw-droppingly in, say, piazza San Marco – especially in the evening, when palm court orchestras are playing. Cautionary tales of tourists paying €50 for a glass of mineral water may be apocryphal, but they give the general idea: don't expect much (if any) change from a €10 note.

In the know
Coffee

Venice's relationship with coffee is a long and significant one. The city's very first *bottega del caffè* opened in 1683 in piazza San Marco. By the late 18th century, as many as 24 coffee shops graced this square alone. Don't even think of ordering a Frappuccino in Venice (at the time of writing, there are no Starbucks here anyway). Instead, go for a cappuccino, caffè latte, or try one of these:

caffè espresso

caffè americano espresso diluted with hot water, served in a larger cup

caffè corretto espresso with a shot of alcohol (usually grappa)

caffè doppio double espresso

caffè lungo espresso made with slightly more water

caffè macchiato espresso with just a dash of milk

macchiatone cappuccino with less milk

decaffeinato any of the above drinks but without the buzz

▶ *Many bars that stay open late and/or host live music performances are listed in the Nightlife chapter (see pp238-243).*

The routine changes in traditional *bacari*, where you generally order your drink, then begin dipping into the array of *cicheti* (snacks) on the counter. Most bar staff have an uncanny gift for keeping track of who eats what, and totting up your bill at the end. But it's polite to remember how much you've consumed in order to help them with their calculations.

Spritz, Venice's favourite fizzy beverage

It's difficult to avoid spritz in Venice: before lunch, early evening, after dinner – just about any time, in fact, you'll find crowds outside Venetian bars, glasses of amber-orange liquid in hand. But despite its jaunty hue and party-fun flavour, spritz comes in varying degrees of dangerous.

The origins of this ubiquitous drink are as obscure as its 'real' recipe. Perhaps invented by Venice's Austrian occupiers in the 19th century (they couldn't take the strength of local wines, one story goes, and so ordered it watered down), a classic version calls for one part prosecco, one part bitters and one part sparking seltz water, with a slice of orange and some ice to finish off the job.

It's quite normal these days to find common or garden mineral water being used instead of the far more carbonated seltz soda; and white wine often replaces prosecco, making it altogether a less tingling experience.

The real threat to navigation comes from your choice of bitter. When ordering, you can specify spritz all'Aperol (11% proof), with the very Venetian Select (14%) or with Campari (20+%). Whatever version you choose, a generous glass will cost somewhere between €2.50 and €3.50 in all but the most high-end bars.

What to drink (and eat) when

The Venetian day begins at the local bar with a cappuccino and brioche (pronounced the French way), preferably one baked on the

Cicheti menu. Most bar staff have an uncanny gift for keeping track of who eats what.

Despite its jaunty hue and party-fun flavour, spritz comes in varying degrees of dangerous.

premises. Sweet things are consumed at other times too: many *pasticcerie* (cake shops) serve coffee and alcoholic beverages.

Gelato is an all-day stop-gap, indulged in by everyone during the hotter months. Quality varies greatly from place to place. A foolproof test of any shop is to eyeball the tub of banana ice-cream – if it's grey in colour, you know it's the real deal: bright yellow screams that the ice-cream's been made from a mix. Recent years have seen the spread – much to Venetians' indignation – of gastronomic chains using high-quality ingredients (*see p178* **Grom** and *p160* **Majer**), which, though a reliable fallback, lack a certain local feel and individual character.

The best offer an enormous selection of top-quality wines by the glass. Most have snacks, but in some you can pile your plate so high you may decide to skip the restaurant entirely.

The quality of gelato varies greatly from place to place and national chains may lack the character of independent or local *gelaterie*.

Many *pasticcerie* (cake shops) serve coffee and alcoholic beverages.

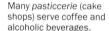

Wines of North-east Italy
The best tastes of the region

The wine-growing area that stretches from the Veneto north-east to Friuli is, after Tuscany and Piedmont, one of Italy's strongest: even in Venice's humbler establishments, the house wine is often surprisingly refined and locals are proud of it.

The grape-growing area is divided into two regions, the Veneto and Friuli-Venezia Giulia. The latter has the strongest reputation, mostly centred on the Collio and Colli Orientali appellations. This pair of appellations can be confusing. The names Collio and Colli Orientali don't tell you what you're getting in the glass: they are umbrella affairs. You might order a Colli Orientali tocai friuliano, or refosco; or a Collio merlot, or sauvignon.

The Veneto region is coming on, too. Long considered good only for full-bodied red Amarone and Valpolicella, the region is undergoing an image makeover, thanks to energetic winemakers who use local grape varieties like corvina and garganega to turn out some fine and complex reds. Even Soave has come good in the hands of producers like Pieropan or Inama. The Veneto is also home to Italy's favourite fizz, prosecco.

The following are the wines you are most likely to find in wine bars and *bacari*.

Red

Cabernet: When Venetians ask for a glass of cabernet, they generally mean cabernet franc. A staple of the Veneto's upland wine enclaves, the grape yields an honest, moreish red with an unmistakable grassy aroma. For Veneto area cabernets, look out for Mattiello, Costozza and Cavazza. In Friuli, cabernet sauvignon and cabernet franc have a foothold. Russiz Superiore and La Boatina make some of the best.

Raboso: The classic Venetian winter-warming red, raboso is rough, acidic, tannic and lacking in pretension. The best kind is served from a huge demijohn in your local *bacaro*.

Refosco: A ruby-red with hints of grass and cherries, locals like to keep this variety to themselves. Try the meaty version produced by Dorigo.

Valpolicella, Recioto della Valpolicella & Amarone: Standard Valpolicella suffers from overstretched DOC boundaries and overgenerous yields. But the best, bottled as Valpolicella classico or Valpolicella superiore, can be very good. Amarone and Recioto, the area's two famous passito wines, are made from partially dried Valpolicella grapes. Recioto is the sweet version, Amarone the dry. The best producers include Allegrini (Recioto), Bussola, Cantina Sociale Valpolicella, Corte Sant'Alda, Dal Forno, Masi (Amarone), Quintarelli (Amarone), Viviani and Zenato.

White and sparkling

Soave and Recioto di Soave: In the Soave classico area, a few winemakers are showing that this blend of garganega and trebbiano is capable of great things: look out in particular for Pieropan's La Rocca or Calvarino selections. In the 1980s, a few producers revived the tradition of Recioto di Soave, a dessert wine made from raisinised garganega grapes. The best producers include Anselmi, Ca' Rugate, Gini, Inama, Pieropan and Suavia.

Friulian whites: The Collio and Colli Orientali appellations turn out some of Italy's most graceful white wines. Four varietals dominate: sauvignon (the Ronco delle Mele cru produced by Venica & Venica is to die for); pinot bianco; pinot grigio; and tocai friuliano (a dry summery white). Producers who do great things with two or more of these varietals include Ascevi, Castello di Spessa, Collavini, Dorigo, Gravner, Humar, Jermann, Kante, Keber, Le Vigne di Zamò, Livio Felluga, Marco Felluga, Miani, Pecorari, Polencic, Primosic, Princic, Puiatti, Rodaro, Ronco dei Tassi, Ronco del Gelso, Ronco del Gnemiz, Russiz Superiore, Schioppetto, Scubla, Toros, Venica & Venica, Villa Russiz and Volpe Pasini. Other white varieties grown in these areas include chardonnay and ribolla gialla, a local grape that makes for fresh and lemony wines. Finally, there is Picolit, the hugely expensive Italian take on Sauternes, made from partially dried grapes.

Prosecco di Conegliano and Valdobbiadene: The classic Veneto dry white fizz, prosecco comes from vineyards around Valdobbiadene and Conegliano, in the rolling hills north of Treviso. The most highly prized (and expensive) version of prosecco is known as Cartizze. A more rustic, unfizzy version – known as prosecco spento or simply spento – is served by the glass in *bacari*. The best producers include Bisol, Bortolomiol, Col Vetoraz, Le Colture, Nino Franco and Ruggeri & Co.

Shopping

Masks, lace and glassware abound, but practical goods can be harder to track down

Venice was once the crossroads between East and West, and merchants from all over Europe met those from the Levant here to trade throughout the city. Exotic spices and raw silks were among the goods imported from distant lands and sold by shrewd Venetian merchants, though humble salt was also a major player in Venetian trade. One of the most important events in Renaissance Venice was La Sensa fair (*see p230*), which lasted a fortnight and was particularly popular for purchasing wedding trousseaux.

Traders of different nations each had their *fondaco* (alternatively spelt *fontaco* or *fondego*), a warehouse-cum-lodging. So successful in their business – and so desirous of making an impression – were the German traders in Venice that their Fondaco dei Tedeschi (*see p75*) was bedecked with frescoes by Titian and Giorgione.

T Fondaco dei Tedeschi *p101*

What to buy and where to buy it

The sumptuous brocades and damasks (*see p53*), Burano lace (*see p209*) and Murano glassware (*see p204*) still produced and found in the city are all legacies of *La Serenissima*'s thriving commerce. Though the prices of such authentic Venetian-made goods can be prohibitive, a recent resurgence of local artisans – shoemakers, jewellers, carpenters, mask makers and blacksmiths – has led to slightly more competitive rates, and has helped to keep traditional techniques alive.

The **Mercerie** – the maze of crowded, narrow alleyways leading from piazza San Marco to the Rialto – and the streets known collectively as the **Frezzeria**, which wind between La Fenice and piazza San Marco, have been the main retail areas in this city for the past 600 years or so. The densest concentration of big-name fashion outlets can be found around the calle larga XXII Marzo, just west of the piazza, where the top names such as Prada, Fendi, Versace and Gucci have all stacked their boutiques.

Devotees of kitsch should not miss the stalls and shops near the train station (*see p54*

Signor Blum *p179*

Murano glass

Material Makers

How sumptuous fabrics became and remained a hallmark of the city

The fact that rich-hued brocades – from luscious silks to sad nylon rip-offs – adorn thousands of Venetian hotel rooms does not signal lack of imagination on the part of local interior designers. The choice, in fact, reflects a traditional craft that dates back to the 13th century, or perhaps earlier.

It was *La Serenissima*'s privileged trading position with the Orient and its close links with Byzantium that provided the initial impetus. Venetian merchants filled the holds of their ships with the raw materials – cotton and silk – on their return to Venice from the great trading centres of the eastern Mediterrean. It may have been weavers from Byzantium who first showed the Venetians how to make fabric. But craftsmen brought from Lucca, an earlier Italian centre of textile excellence, also played a part. By the 14th century, Venice's fabrics – from cheap low-grade cottons to the most luxurious of heavy silks – had become highly sought-after commodities around Europe and the Levant. If Venice had become an international byword for unimaginable richness, it was in large part due to its textiles.

Today, the lagoon city is more commonly associated with lace, but this is misleading: far more fabric is now produced in and around Venice than lace. Manufacturers of the very finest materials are household names with top designers everywhere.

Rubelli (Palazzo Corner Spinelli, San Marco 3877, campiello del Teatro, 041 241 7329,

www.rubelli.com) has been weaving in the Veneto since 1835: its fabrics grace the La Fenice opera house (see *p247*) and all rooms of the Gritti Palace hotel (see *p291*). Its magnificent textile archive goes back far further than the company's own history, however, with examples of Venetian and many other fabrics dating from the 15th century onwards. It can be visited by appointment.

The **Bevilacqua** dynasty has operated in Venice for more than two centuries and some of its output is still produced on the original looms in its workshop in the Santa Croce district (Santa Croce 1320, campiello de la Comare, 041 721 566, www.luigi-bevilacqua. com). The shop at the same location sells fabric, household and apparel accessories and textile-related books, as well as holding the company's huge archive. There's more Bevilacqua fabrics, and homewares made with it, at the Bevilacqua shops near San Marco (see *p98*).

Spanish fashion designer-cum-polymath **Mario Fortuny** (see *p194*) opened his textile factory in a former convent on the Giudecca island in 1921, installing machinery specially designed by him that is still in use and remains a closely guarded secret. The factory's showroom can be visited, however: it positively glows with the colours emanating from the massive bolts of glorious fabrics that line the walls.

Bevilacqua

Station shopping), where plastic gondolas, illuminated gondolas, flashing gondolas, musical gondolas and even gondola cigarette lighters reign supreme.

For more tasteful souvenirs, Venice's glass, lace, fabrics and handmade paper are legendary – as are the much cheaper made-in-Taiwan substitutes that are passed off as the genuine article by unscrupulous traders. Sticking to the outlets listed in this guide will help you to avoid unpleasant surprises.

The steady demographic drop has led to the demise of 'everyday' shops: bread, fruit and veg, milk and meat are increasingly difficult to get hold of. And while new supermarkets have opened around the city and on the Giudecca, the flipside of this is the threat they pose to the livelihood of the few remaining greengrocers, bakers and butchers. This said, a string of daily and weekly food markets (*see p56*) takes place throughout the city and on neighbouring islands, meeting the locals' basic needs.

Opening hours and tax rebates

Most food shops are closed on Wednesday afternoons, while some non-food shops stay shut on Monday mornings. During high season (which in Venice includes Carnevale in February/March, Easter, the summer season from June to October and the four weeks

In the know
Station shopping

If you've failed to pick up souvenirs and gifts, and you get to the station with time to kill, you have two options. With your back to the station turn left down the tourist-tack-alley lista di Spagna for blinking *gondole* and glass animals. Or stay in the station itself – perhaps with a detour off to the adjoining Palazzo Compartimentale on the right – for a shiny new development of international-brand stores, plus a restaurant and café (see p135) that's a great spot for filling up as you arrive or depart.

According to Trenitalia (Italian railways) figures, Venice's Santa Lucia station sees 30 million arrivals and departures each year, making it one of Italy's busiest rail hubs. So the rather quaint old-fashioned hall that had greeted visitors until 2013 was somewhat outdated. The new selection of 37 shops ranges from Muji and Mango to pizza chain Spizzico, make-up purveyors Kiko and, just in case you need an elegant notebook for your Venice jottings, Moleskine. Shops are open from 8am to 10pm daily.

Masks

Versace boutique

leading up to Christmas) many shops abandon their lunchtime closing and stay open all day, even opening on Sundays.

It pays to be sceptical about the hours posted on the doors of smaller shops: opening times are often dictated by volume of trade or personal whim. If you want to be sure of not finding the shutters drawn, call before you set out.

Incomprehensibly – given that summer is Venice's busiest season – some shops close for holidays in August, but the majority of these are smaller ones that cater more to residents than tourists, such as *tabacchi*, photocopying centres or dry cleaners.

If you are not an EU citizen, remember to keep your official receipt (*scontrino*) as you are entitled to a rebate on IVA (sales tax) paid on purchases of personal goods costing more than €154, as long as they leave the country unused and are bought from a shop that provides this service. Make sure that there is a sign displayed in the window and also ask for the form that you'll need to show at customs upon

Gucci bags

♥ Best fashion

L'O.FT *p100*
Funky specs and accessories.

Banco Lotto № 10 *p125*
High fashion behind bars.

Attombri *p151*
Magnificent jewellery at the foot of Rialto.

departure. For more information about customs, see the Italian government website (www.agenziadogane.gov.it) for info in English.

For obvious reasons, which relate primarily to lack of space, Venice is not shopping-centre friendly, with the exception of **T Fondaco dei Tedeschi** (at the luxury end of the market, *see p101*) and **Santa Lucia station** (*see p54* Station Shopping). If you are looking for a mall to fill all your needs, you'll have to journey to the mainland. The Centro Barche in Mestre offers everything from H&M to Feltrinelli International bookstore.

Markets

As befits a city that was once at the centre of a bustling trade in goods from around the world, Venice boasts a wide selection of daily and weekly markets, selling everything from tacky fridge magnets to pungent creatures of the lagoon. On market day, locals will come out of the woodwork, wheelie carts in hand, and gather to share news and stock their pantries. The historic **Rialto markets** (*see p149*) are by

Venice is not shopping-centre friendly, with the exception of T Fondaco dei Tedeschi (see p101).

far the most visually stunning, but you need to go further afield to get a taste of day-to-day local life. Head to Sacca Fisola on Giudecca on a Friday morning, for example, and even a native Italian speaker will struggle to understand the meticulously coiffed elderly locals as they argue with the greengrocer in thick Venetian dialect. At the other end of Giudecca, on Thursday mornings, the enterprising inmates of the women's prison sell organic vegetables from their 'Garden of Marvels' (*see p192*), while boats piled high with fruit and veg make for unusual market stalls in via Garibaldi and fondamenta Gherardini.

The city's markets (see www.veneziaunica.it/en/content/markets for further details) have received a boost in recent years by the 'zero kilometre' movement, which calls for food miles to be kept to a minimum – a trend increasingly supported by restaurants serving only lagoon produce, and by eco-friendly cooperatives such as iSapori (www.isaporidisanterasmo.com), which delivers seasonal vegetables from the island of Sant'Erasmo (specialities include the distinctive purple artichoke) to various pick-up points across the city, and Valle Sacchetta e Sacchettina (www.pescherieonline.it), which exports fish all over Europe.

♥ **Best food & drink**

Drogheria Mascari *p151*
A treasure trove of spices and dry goods.

Panificio Volpe Daniele *p139*
The best Jewish pastries.

Viziovirtù *p117*
A cornucopia of chocolate delights.

SHOPPING

Tobacco shop

Rialto market *p1..*

Explore

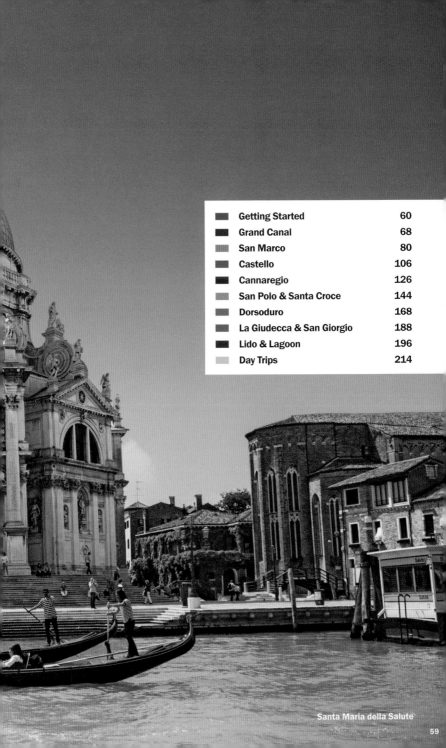

Santa Maria della Salute

Getting Started

First encountered at a distance, mediated through the beautifying camera lens, many of the world's great cities are a let-down when you get there. But not Venice. Nobody can come here without some idea of what to expect. The surprise is that it's true. The streets really are full of water – everywhere. The *palazzi* really do have a fairy-tale quality. And it's not just a matter of a carefully preserved little tourist centre surrounded by the usual high-rise flats and car parks; the *whole* of Venice is the centre.

Then there are the highlights. The **Basilica di San Marco** (*see p86*) is one of Christendom's greatest churches; the **Gallerie dell'Accademia** (*see p180*) contain an unparalleled section of Renaissance art; and the **Rialto** is a powerful symbol of mercantile energy as well as a fine bridge. But Venice is much more than this, and the best way to get an impression of its full diversity is to leave the main routes.

With its double topography of streets and canals, Venice provides a challenge even to the most skilled map-readers. But when you do lose your bearings, don't be alarmed: the *calli* will close in around you; you'll come to innumerable dead ends and find yourself returning inexplicably to the same (wrong) spot over and over again. But eventually you'll hit a busy thoroughfare

❤ **Best viewpoints**

Campanile di San Marco *p85*
Jaw-dropping 360-degree view of Venice in its entirety.

Campanile di San Giorgio Maggiore *p195*
Great views and fewer crowds.

Campanile di Santa Maria Assunta, Torcello *p213*
Deep in the Venice lagoon, with shoals, mudflats and meadows.

Fondaco dei Tedeschi *p101*
Head to the terrace to see the Rialto bridge and Grand Canal.

Loggia dei Cavalli *p89*
Up close and personal with the bronze horses overlooking St Mark's Square.

Scala Contarini del Bòvolo *p102*
Red roofs and belltowers from an iconic spiral staircase.

View from the Campanile di San Marco

💙 Gondolas

The Venetian style of rowing, in which the rower stands up, facing in the direction of travel, is known as *voga alla veneta*. Venetians find it difficult to understand why anybody would row any other way: the standing position allows one to put all one's force behind the stroke; facing forwards is also a major aid to navigation.

There are various types of *voga alla veneta*: team rowing is one (*see p71* Rowing regattas); the impressive solo, cross-handed, two-oar method known as *voga alla valesana* is another. But the most famous type is the *voga ad un solo remo*, as practised by Venetian gondoliers. It may look effortless, but the single-oar scull is one of the most difficult rowing strokes of all.

Most other forms of rowing rely on pairs of oars, whose equal and opposite forces keep the boat travelling in a straight line. The gondolier, on the other hand, only ever puts his oar in the water on the right side of the boat – where it rests in a *forcola*, an elaborate walnut-wood rowlock. Pushing on the oar (*premer* in Venetian dialect) has the obvious effect of making the gondola – or the bumbler sandolo, which is what most beginners train in – turn to the left. The trick consists in using the downstroke (*la stalìa*), during which the oar stays in the water, to correct the direction. Of course, if the check were equal to the push, the boat would go nowhere; it is the ability to correct the boat's course with almost minimal resistance that marks out the experienced rower from the beginner. It has been calculated that a gondolier uses up no more energy rowing a half-ton, 65-foot gondola with three passengers than the average person expends in walking.

Such ingenious efficiency made the gondola the most effective form of transportation in Venice for centuries, although its shape and appearance have evolved considerably over time. Originally an ornately gilded and covered craft, the classic gondola of today is painted entirely black and is exposed to the elements. A gondola comprises about 280 pieces of wood made from eight types of tree, including durmast, spruce and cherry.

The bottom is flat to allow it to navigate shallow waters. The prow, which resembles a comb, stabilizes the boat; its six prongs symbolize the six *sestieri*, or districts, and what looks like a butcher's cleaver at its top actually represents the cap worn by the doge. The creation of a gondola requires the collaboration of different artisans, who are also in charge of carving the oars and rowlock. The Squero di San Trovaso in Dorsoduro (*see p187*) is one of very few active gondola *squeri* or shipyards that survive in Venice today.

While gondola rides remain popular among tourists, they can be underwhelming for the price. A 30-minute ride costs €80 during the day and €100 at sunset for up to six people, but it's common to hear of gondoliers fleecing unwitting travellers. If you decide to hop on, be sure to confirm all fees with the gondolier before boarding, and be prepared to fork out extra for music. A more economical and authentic alternative exists in the form of *traghetti*, slightly larger craft manned by two gondoliers, that are used to ferry pedestrians across the Grand Canal. The cost for tourists is €2. As the local population plummets, so the regular *traghetti* routes are disappearing and run less frequently; your safest bet is at the Rialto Market.

If you fancy trying *voga alla veneta* for yourself, you can sign up for a lesson, combined with a tour, with www.veniceonboard.it and www.rowvenice.org. The latter all-female outfit also offers the 'Chicchetto Row', which combines a rowing lesson with food and drink in local *bacari*. Don't alienate your trainer by clamouring to be let loose on the Grand Canal, which is strictly for experts; lessons tend to take place on calmer – if somewhat less picturesque – stretches of water, such as the channel that runs alongside the railway bridge. And never wear gloves, not even in winter; hand on wood is the first commandment of *voga alla veneta*; you'll wear the blisters with pride for weeks afterwards.

▶ *For further details of official gondola stops and fares, see p297 Getting Around.*

or the Grand Canal and a vaporetto stop. Until that happens, enjoy the feel of village Venice – or, more appropriately, island Venice. The city is made up of over 100 islands, and every one has something – magnificent or quaint, historic or charming – to offer.

Venice is divided into six *sestieri* (*see p262* Venice's Sestieri). They are worth getting to grips with, first and foremost because all addresses include the *sestiere* name. Cradled by the lower bend of the Grand Canal is the *sestiere* of **San Marco**, the heart of the city; east of here is **Castello**, one of the most lived-in areas; extending to the west and north is **Cannaregio**, whose western stretches are among the most peaceful parts of Venice. To the west of the Rialto Bridge is **San Polo**, bristling with churches; north of that is **Santa Croce**, short on sights but not on atmosphere; while further south is **Dorsoduro**, one of the city's most elegant and artsy districts, with its wide Zattere promenade looking across to the long residential island of the **Giudecca** – the honorary seventh *sestiere*. Bear in mind that you may need more than an address to get to where you're going. Houses are counted by *sestiere* rather than by street, so don't be surprised if the number goes into the thousands. To complicate matters further, Venetians are not overly creative when it comes to street names, which are often linked to local trades or religious superstition (for instance, there's more than one 'baker street', *calle del Forno*, in each *sestiere*).

❤ Best places to escape the crowds

Giudecca *p188*
The picturesque working-class island just south of Venice proper.

San Francesco della Vigna *p112*
A little-visited campo, with an imposing church and two extraordinary cloisters.

San Lazzaro degli Armeni *p200*
This peaceful Armenian monastery is a 20-minute boat ride from San Marco.

Santa Marta *p172*
Hang out with locals and students in western Dorsoduro.

San Pietro in Castello *p123*
Venice's former cathedral is located far from the centres of political power.

Sant'Erasmo *p211*
An island of vegetable gardens, military ruins and famed cuisine.

In the know
Behind the scenes

Gain an insight into the inner workings of this watery city at www.venicebackstage.org, which has diagrams and cutaway drawings of Venice's unique mechanisms, from foundations to phone lines, sewage to the electricity grid.

Churches

Venice began life as a host of separate island communities, each clustered around its own parish church. The bridges came later. Like many more recent visitors to the city, Napoleon thought there were far too many churches; during his brief rule (*see p265*) he cleared away a good 40 or so, but there are still well over 100 of them left, containing inestimable artistic treasures.

Most of the major churches have reliable opening times; hours in minor churches depend on the goodwill or whim of the priest or sacristan. It's well worth exploring these too, since there's not a single one that does not contain some item of interest, whether it be a shrivelled relic or a glowing Madonna with *bambino*. In general, early morning and late afternoon are the best times for church-crawling. But it's best never to pass an opportunity by: if you see one open without a service under way, go in and poke around. No Sunday opening times are given in listings for churches that open only for Mass.

Passes

The most comprehensive pass is the **Venezia Unica City Pass** (*see p306*), which combines admission to sights with public transport and other services. Note that the passes detailed below can be included as part of a Venezia Unica City Pass package.

The museums around piazza San Marco (but not the paying parts of the basilica) can only be visited with one of these museum passes:

Musei di Piazza San Marco
Valid for three months, with one visit to each of the sights covered; costs €19 (€12 reductions, under-5s free). Covers Doge's Palace (*p92*), Museo Correr (*p90*), Museo Nazionale Archeologico (*p91*) and Biblioteca Marciana (*p91*).

Museum Pass
Valid for six months, with one visit to each museum covered; costs €24 (€18 reductions, under-5s free). Covers the sights listed above plus Ca' Rezzonico (*p175*), Casa di Carlo Goldoni (*p152*), Ca' Pesaro (*p155*), Museo del Vetro (*p205*), Museo del Merletti (*p210*), Museo di Storia Naturale (*p119*) and Palazzo Mocenigo (*p156*).

Passes can be bought at the sights themselves (not all accept credit cards), by phone (041 4273 0892) or online (www. visitmuve.it).

Palazzo Grimani & Ca' d'Oro
If you're planning to visit both Palazzo Grimani (*see p112*) and the Ca' d'Oro (*see p130*), save money with a cumulative ticket, which costs €11.50 (€7.50 reductions). There may be a surcharge if either or both places are staging special exhibitions. If you purchase your ticket in situ, you must pay cash; if you book them beforehand (through the call centre 041 520 0345 or the websites of either) you can pay with most major credit cards.

Chorus
There are around 140 churches in Venice proper and on the lagoon islands – an immense repository of artistic and architectural wonders. Of these, 18 belong to the Chorus organisation and charge an entry fee that is ploughed back into church upkeep. A €12 pass (€8 students with ID under 29; €20 family ticket for two adults with two children; under-12s free), purchasable at the churches themselves or online through www.veneziaunica.it, gets you into all of the Chorus churches. Tickets for each church individually cost €3. For further information, see www. chorusvenezia.org.

Transport

Venice is a boat-bound city, from the plodding *vaporetto* line 1, avoided by all but the laziest Venetians but brimming with tourists as it wends its scenic way down the Grand Canal, to the faster and sleeker *motoscafi* that set a speedy course from the station to the Lido and back. Services run with a reasonably high frequency day and night, and a boat trip can be an excellent way to see the city and get to grips with its layout. Vaporetto tickets and passes can be purchased from authorised retailers, from ticket machines, at VeneziaUnica agencies and at larger vaporetto stops. For more on transport options and pricing, *see p296*.

Vaporetto stop

Walk Like a Venetian

Pavement politics

With their unique transport situation, Venetians have developed a particular etiquette for getting around on foot, with clear rules depending on the particular weather conditions.

In general, 'traffic' tends to flow in lanes (keep to the right) with potential for passing: a quick acceleration to the left with a polite '*permesso*' will get you past those in front. Locals take a dim view of anyone stopping in narrow alleyways or on busy bridges to gawp or – worse still – spread out their picnics. Pull off well to the side or into a quiet side-street to consult a map or admire a building. Be adventurous and explore remoter districts if you want to avoid the high-season all-day-long traffic jam clogging the main arteries of the city, especially those near San Marco and Rialto.

Acqua alta (high water) presents other problems. Except in truly exceptional cases, all this means is that a couple of inches of water laps into the lowest parts of the city for an hour or two, then recedes. As the water rises, sirens sound five ten-second blasts two hours before the tide's high point. During the *acqua alta* season (September to April), trestles and wooden planks are stacked up along flood-prone thoroughfares, ready to be transformed into raised walkways. Venetians caught out by the rising water without wellies wait their turn patiently, then proceed slowly but surely. They expect tourists to do the same, or risk an angry telling-off.

Pedestrian etiquette extends beyond the walkways. The streets may be waterlogged, but they continue to function as a municipal road network; locals are understandably peeved if tourists doing Gene Kelly impersonations prevent them from reaching their destination dry. Remember, too, that during *acqua alta* you can't see where the pavement stops and the canal begins. Maps posted at vaporetto stops show flood-prone areas; if you don't want to get your feet wet, stick to higher ground or sit out those damp hours in your hotel room or a bar.

To see if you'll be facing this challenge, go to www.comune.venezia.it and click on '*previsione maree*' for tide forecasts. Anything over 80 centimetres means that low-lying areas, such as piazza San Marco, will be submerged.

October *acqua alta* (high water) in piazza San Marco

Grand Canal

The Grand Canal is Venice's high street, and although the craft caught up in today's waterborne traffic jams carry more tourists than exotic luxury goods arriving from around the Mediterrean and beyond, this mighty thoroughfare still provides a superb introduction to the city, telling you more about the way Venice works – and has always worked – than any historical tome.

Every family of note had to have a *palazzo* along the three and a half kilometre (two-mile) sweep from the railway station to San Marco, and this was not just for social cachet. The *palazzi* are undeniably splendid but they were first and foremost solid commercial enterprises, and their designs are as practical as they are eye-catching.

Most of the notable buildings on the canal were built between the 12th and 18th centuries. When a family decided to rebuild a *palazzo*, they usually maintained the same basic structure – for the good reason that they could use the same foundations. This resulted in some interesting style hybrids: the Grand Canal offers many examples of

❤ Don't miss

1 Ca' d'Oro *p75*
Gloriously ornate Gothic.

2 Ponte della Costituzione *p72*
The newest bridge.

3 Ponte di Rialto *p74*
Simple, effective and very mercantile.

4 Palazzo Venier del Leoni *p79*
Charmingly incomplete.

5 Santa Maria della Salute *p79*
Queening it over the Grand Canal.

View of the Grand Canal
from the Accademia bridge

Grand Canal

palazzi in which Veneto-Byzantine or Gothic features are incorporated into the Renaissance or Baroque.

Each *palazzo* typically had a main water-entrance opening on to a large hall with storage space on either side; a *mezzanino* with offices; a *piano nobile* (main floor – sometimes two in grander buildings) consisting of a spacious reception hall lit by large central windows and flanked on both sides by residential rooms; and a land entrance at the back. Over the centuries, architectural frills and trimmings were added, but the underlying form was stable – and, as always in Venice, it is form that follows function.

Many names recur in descriptions of the most notable *palazzi* for the simple reason that families expanded, younger sons inheriting as well as older ones. Compound names indicate that the *palazzo* passed through various hands over time. Originally the term '*palazzo*' was reserved for the Doge's Palace. Other *palazzi* were known as Casa ('house') or Ca' for short: this is still true of some of the older ones, such as Ca' d'Oro (*see p130*).

In the know
Getting around

This chapter deals mainly with canal-side *palazzi*. Churches and museums facing on to the canal are covered elsewhere in the guide (cross references are given). It follows the Grand Canal east from piazzale Roma and the train station towards St Mark's Square. Vaporetto stops on the north and east banks of the canal are shown in magenta; those on the south and west banks are shown in blue. For full details of vaporetti routes, tickets and fares, *see p295* Getting Around.

💜 Rowing regattas

The sight of a flotilla of boats being rowed full tilt across the lagoon or down the Grand Canal may well be the highlight of your stay as well as being evidence of the Venetian love of messing about in boats.

There are 120 'serious' fixtures on the lagoon during the rowing season from April to September, plus more to accompany every big Venetian feast day, including Carnevale (*see p231*), Festa della Sensa (*see p230*) and Il Redentore (*see p232*). The Regata delle Befane (*see p233*) is a light-hearted affair, but others are hard-fought battles between the city's famously excellent rowers displaying their own particular style of forward-facing rowing, known as Voga alla Veneta.

The most sumptuous of all the Venetian regattas, however, is the **Regata Storica** (www.regatastoricavenezia.it) on the first Sunday in September. This event begins with a procession of ornate boats down the Grand Canal, rowed by locals in 16th-century costume. The procession is followed by four races: one for young rowers, one for women, one for rowers of *caorline* – long canoe-like boats in which the prow and the stern are identical – and the Flast, the most eagerly awaited, featuring two-man sporting *gondolini*. The finish is at the sharp curve of the Grand Canal between Palazzo Barbi and Ca' Foscari: here, the judges sit in an ornate raft known as the *machina*, where the prize-giving takes place. Seating for spectators is on floating platforms near Campo San Polo (tickets for non-residents €60; €30 reductions; book well in advance).

More riotously jolly is the **Vogalonga** (041 521 0544/www.vogalonga.com), which takes place on a Sunday in May or early June and is open to anyone with a boat and an oar. For this one chaotically colourful day, Venetians protest against motorboats by boarding any kind of rowing craft and following a 30-km (18-mile) route through the lagoon and along the city's two main canals. They are joined in this annual free-for-all on the water by a host of out-of-towners and foreigners. Boats set off from the Canale di Guidecca, off Punta della Dogana, at 9am.

Vogalonga

The Bucintoro at the Regata Storica

Ferrovia–San Marcuola

Next to the train station, at the foot of the Ponte degli Scalzi is the fine Baroque façade of the **Gli Scalzi** church (*see p131*).

Unusually narrow **Palazzo Flangini** is a 17th-century building by Giuseppe Sardi. It owes its shape to the simple fact that the family's money ran out. Just before the wide Cannaregio Canal is the church of **San Geremia**; from the Grand Canal, the apse of the chapel of Santa Lucia is visible.

Standing with its main façade on the Cannaregio Canal is **Palazzo Labia**, the 18th-century home of the seriously rich Labia family. The story goes that parties ended with the host throwing his gold dinner plates into the canal to demonstrate his wealth; the servants would then be ordered to fish them out again. The building is now the regional headquarters of the RAI (the Italian state broadcaster). It contains suitably sumptuous frescoes by Tiepolo, which are opened very occasionally to the public.

San Geremia

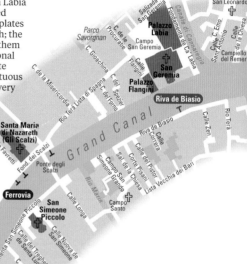

Piazzale Roma–Riva di Biasio

The first notable sight is the new bridge over the Grand Canal, linking the car park to the train station. Officially named the **Ponte della Costituzione**, it is still known to most Venetians as Ponte Calatrava, after its designer, the Spanish architect-superstar Santiago Calatrava. Its single, elegantly curving arch is constructed of steel, and the pavement is in the traditional Venetian materials of glass and Istrian stone.

Before the Scalzi Bridge is the church of **San Simeone Piccolo**, with its high green dome and Corinthian portico. For those arriving in Venice it's a picturesque introduction to the city.

The **Ponte degli Scalzi**, which leads across to the station, was built in stone by Eugenio Miozzi in 1934.

Fondaco dei Turchi

San Marcuola–Ca' d'Oro

The next building of note is **Palazzo Vendramin Calergi**, an impressive Renaissance *palazzo* designed by Mauro Codussi in the first decade of the 16th century. It uses his characteristic arched windows incorporating twin smaller arches; porphyry insets decorate the façade. Wagner died here in 1883. It now houses the **Venice Casinò**. From here, a fairly uneventful stretch ends at the **Ca' d'Oro**.

Ca d'Oro

Riva di Biasio–San Stae

Just before the rio del Megio stands the **Fondaco dei Turchi**, a 19th-century reconstruction of the original Veneto-Byzantine building, which was leased to Turkish traders in the 17th century as a residence and warehouse. Some of the original material was used but the effect as a whole is one of pastiche. Once lived in by the poet Torquato Tasso, it's now the **Museo di Storia Naturale** (*see p156*).

The **Depositi del Megio** (state granaries) have a battlemented, plain-brick façade. The sculpted lion is a modern replacement of the original, destroyed at the fall of the Republic.

The church of **San Stae** (*see p158*) has a Baroque façade by Domenico Rossi, with exuberant sculpture.

San Stae–Rialto Mercato

On the rio di Ca' Pesaro, and with a magnificent side wall curving along the canal in gleaming marble, is **Ca' Pesaro** (*see p155*), a splendid example of Venetian Baroque by Longhena.

After two smaller palazzi stands the **Palazzo Corner della Regina**, with a rusticated ground floor featuring grotesque masks, some just above water level. It was built for a branch of the Corner family, who were descended from Caterina Cornaro, Queen of Cyprus; Caterina was born in an earlier house on the site. The present *palazzo* dates from the 1720s and is home to the **Fondazione Prada** (fondazioneprada.org).

Just before the Rialto Mercato vaporetto stop, is the covered fish market, or **Pescaria** (*see p149*), which has occupied this site since the 14th century. The current neo-Gothic construction was built in 1907, replacing an iron one.

Rialto Mercato–San Silvestro

Next to the vaporetto stop is the longest façade on the Grand Canal, belonging to Sansovino's **Fabbriche Nuove**, built in 1554-56; it is now houses the Court of Assizes. Just beyond this stands the **Fabbriche Vecchie** by Scarpagnino, built after a fire in the early 16th century. The streets around have been the commercial centre of the city since the late 11th century (*see p149*).

Before the Rialto bridge, the **Palazzo dei Camerlenghi** (1523-25) is built around the curve of the canal; the walls lean noticeably. It was the headquarters of the Venetian Exchequer, with a debtors' prison on the ground floor. The **Ponte di Rialto**, squeaky clean after a recent restoration, was built in 1588-92, to a design by aptly named Antonio Da Ponte. Until the 19th century, it was the only bridge over the Grand Canal. It replaced a wooden one, which can be seen in Carpaccio's painting of *The Miracle of the True Cross* in the Accademia (*p180*). Designs by Michelangelo, Vignola, Sansovino and Palladio were rejected. Da Ponte's simple but effective project eventually went ahead, probably because it kept the utilitarian features of the previous structure, with its double row of shops. The bridge thus acts as a continuation of the market at its foot.

Ponte di Rialto

San Silvestro–San Tomà

Beyond the San Silvestro vaporetto stop are a few houses with Veneto-Byzantine windows and decorations, including **Ca' Barzizza**, one of the earliest Byzantine houses in Venice. Before the rio San Polo is the 16th-century **Palazzo Cappello Layard**, once the home of Sir Henry Austen Layard, archaeologist and British ambassador to Constantinople. **Palazzo Pisani Moretta** is a large, Gothic 15th-century building, often hired out for parties.

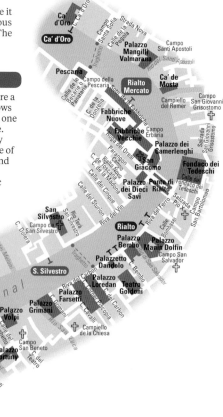

Ca' d'Oro–Rialto

The **Ca' d'Oro** (*see p130*) is the most gorgeously ornate Gothic building on the Grand Canal. Yet it is now sober compared with its original appearance, when its decorative features were gilded or painted in ultramarine blue and cinnabar red. It has an open loggia on the *piano nobile*, like the Doge's Palace, but unlike any other post-Byzantine *palazzo*.

Just before the rio dei Santi Apostoli is **Palazzo Mangilli Valmarana**, built in 1751 for Joseph Smith, the British consul, who amassed the huge collection of Canaletto paintings that now belongs to the Queen.

Beyond the rio dei Santissimi Apostoli stands the **Ca' da Mosto**, once the site of the Leon Bianco (white lion) Hotel. This is one of the earliest Veneto-Byzantine *palazzi* on the Grand Canal. It still has three of the original five arches of its water-entrance and a long array of Byzantine arches on the first floor.

At the foot of the Rialto bridge is the **Fondaco dei Tedeschi**, a huge residence-cum-warehouse leased to the German community from the 13th century onwards. The present building was designed by Spavento and Scarpagnino in 1505-08 after a fire. The façade once had glorious frescoes by Titian and Giorgione – now in a sad state of repair in the Ca' d'Oro gallery (*see p130*). The Fondaco, formerly the main post office, has recently been transformed into a shiny new luxury shopping complex, offering a stunning view from the roof (*see p101*).

Next to the Rialto vaporetto stop is **Palazzo Manin Dolfin**, with a portico straddling the *fondamenta*. The façade is by Sansovino (late 1530s); the rest was rebuilt by Ludovico Manin, the forlorn last doge of Venice (*see p265*). It now belongs to the Bank of Italy.

Rialto–Sant'Angelo

Palazzetto Dandolo is a Gothic building that appears to have been squeezed tight by its neighbours. Enrico Dandolo, the blind doge who led the ferocious assault on Constantinople in 1204 (*see p259*) was born in an earlier *palazzo* that stood on this site.

Palazzo Farsetti and **Palazzo Loredan** are Veneto-Byzantine buildings that now house the city hall and various municipal offices. Though heavily restored, these two adjoining *palazzi* are among the few surviving examples of the 12th-century Venetian house, with its first-floor polyforate window.

Palazzo Grimani is one of the largest *palazzi* on the Grand Canal. Its creator, Michele Sanmicheli, was famous for his military architecture, and this building is characteristically massive and assertive. The Grimani family were nouveaux riches, and wanted each one of their windows to be larger than the front door of the *palazzo* that used to stand opposite.

Seven *palazzi* further on, before the rio Michiel, stands the pink **Palazzo Benzon**, home of Countess Marina Querini-Benzon, a great society figure at the end of the 18th century. Byron was charmed by her when she was already in her sixties. She inspired a popular song, '*La biondina in gondoleta*', which the gondoliers used to sing before international tourism imposed the Neapolitan '*O' Sole Mio*'.

Just before the Sant'Angelo vaporetto stop is the small-scale **Palazzo Corner-Spinelli**, built in the last decade of the 15th century by Mauro Codussi. It is one of the most beautiful early Renaissance buildings in Venice, with a rusticated ground floor, elegant balconies and the characteristic double-arched windows.

Palazzo Loredan

San Tomà–Ca' Rezzonico

South of San Tomà, **Palazzo Balbi** (1582-90), whose obelisks are an indication that an admiral lived here, is the seat of the Veneto Regional Council. Looking down the rio Ca' Foscari behind Palazzo Balbi, you can see the archways of the city's fire station. (Further west, rio Ca' Foscari becomes the rio Novo, a canal dug in the 1930s to provide a short cut to the car park and station; traffic rocked the foundations of the buildings along the canal, so public transport stopped using the rio Novo in the 1980s.) Between the fire station and Palazzo Balbi is a minor building, on a site once scheduled to hold Frank Lloyd Wright's Centre for Foreign Architectural Students. In the end, his designs were judged too radical for so conspicuous a spot.

Just beyond the rio Ca' Foscari come three magnificent mid 15th-century Gothic *palazzi*. The first and largest is **Ca' Foscari**. It was here that Henry III of France was lavishly entertained in 1574 – so lavishly that his reason seems to have been knocked permanently askew. Doge Francesco Foscari died here of a broken heart after being ousted from office. It is now the headquarters of Venice's Università Ca' Foscari.

The next two buildings comprise the **Palazzi Giustinian**. Wagner stayed in one of them in the winter of 1858-59, composing part of *Tristan und Isolde*; the horn prelude to the third act was inspired by the mournful cries of the gondoliers.

Ca' Rezzonico (*see p175*) is a Baroque masterpiece by Longhena, begun in 1667 for the Bon family, then sold to the Rezzonico family. Robert Browning died here, while staying with his profitably married but otherwise talentless son Pen, who bought the *palazzo* with his wife's money. Later guests included Whistler and Cole Porter. The building now contains the Museum of 18th-century Venice. Just after the Ca' Rezzonico stop is the 15th-century **Palazzo Loredan**.

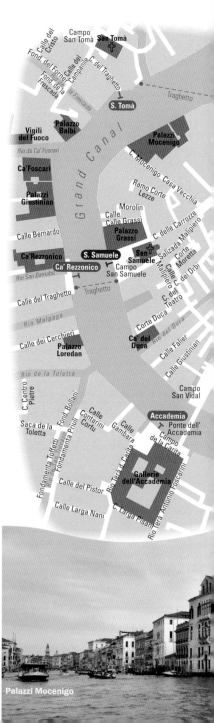

Ca' Foscari

Palazzi Mocenigo

Sant'Angelo–San Samuele

A little beyond the traghetto station for San Tomà stand the four **Palazzi Mocenigo**, with blue and white poles in the water. The central double *palazzo* (16th century) was where Byron and his menagerie of foxes, monkeys and dogs lived in 1818-19; he wrote to a friend: 'Venice is not an expensive residence... I have my gondola and about 14 servants... and I reside in one of the Mocenigo palaces on the Grand Canal; the rent... is two hundred a year (and I gave more than I need have done).'

Just before the San Samuele vaporetto stop is heavy, grey-white **Palazzo Grassi** (*see p101*), designed by Giorgio Massari. This was the last of the great patrician *palazzi*, built in 1748-72 when the city was already in terminal decline. Acquired by Fiat in the 1980s, it was sold again in 2005 to French magnate Francois Pinault and functions as a gallery.

San Samuele–Giglio

A short way beyond the stop, the **Ca' del Duca** incorporates, in one corner, a part of the rusticated base and columns of a palace that Bartolomeo Bon was going to build for the Cornaro family. In 1461, the site was bought by Francesco Sforza, Duke of Milan, and Bon's project was never completed.

Ca' Rezzonico

Palazzo Grassi

San Samuele–Giglio (continued)

Immediately beyond the Ponte dell'Accademia is the 16th-century **Palazzo Franchetti** and two **Palazzi Barbaro**. The first one – 15th-century Gothic, with a fine but battered Renaissance water-entrance – still partly belongs to the Curtis family, who played host to Henry James. The building was the model for Milly Theale's *palazzo* in *The Wings of the Dove*.

Bashful **Casetta delle Rose** is set back behind its own small trellised garden. Canova had a studio here, and novelist Gabriele D'Annunzio once stayed in the house. Another Grand Canal garden flanks the *casetta* to the right.

The massive rusticated ground floor of the **Palazzo Corner della Ca' Grande** (now

the Prefecture) was commissioned in 1537 from Sansovino for Giacomo Cornaro, and built after 1545. Never one to mince words, Ruskin called it 'one of the worst and coldest buildings of the central Renaissance'.

Giglio–San Marco Vallaresso/Giardinetti

The church of **Santa Maria del Giglio** (*see p104*) lies north of the vaporetto stop. Next along the Grand Canal is the 15th-century Gothic façade of **Palazzo Gritti**, now one of Venice's poshest hotels (*see p291*). Three *palazzi* further on is **Palazzo Contarini Fasan**, traditionally, but quite arbitrarily, known as Desdemona's House.

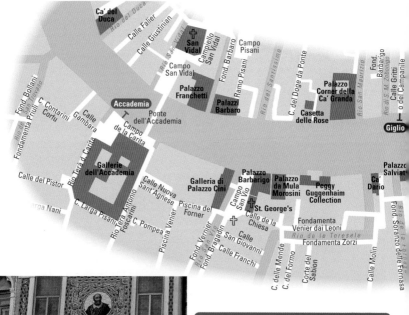

Accademia–Salute

The **Gallerie dell'Accademia** (*see p180*), once the church and monastery of Santa Maria della Carità, holds an unrivalled collection of Venetian art. Crossing the canal from here is the wooden **Ponte dell'Accademia**; the 'temporary' bridge from 1932 was rebuilt in 1984.

After the Accademia comes Galleria Palazzo Cini (*see p186*) and campo San Vio. In the corner is the Anglican church of **St George** (*see p180*). To one side of the campo is the 16th-century **Palazzo Barbarigo**, with eye-catching but tacky 19th-century mosaics. Next is the pretty Gothic **Palazzo Da' Mula**.

Palazzo Da Mula Morosini

Just before the rio di San Moisè is the **Europa & Regina Hotel**. It was once the home of Kay Bronson, an American society hostess whose hospitality was much appreciated by Henry James. Next door is the 17th-century **Palazzo Treves de Bonfilio**. The last notable building is **Ca' Giustinian**, built in the late Gothic style of the 1470s, and once a hotel where Verdi, Gautier, Ruskin and Proust stayed. George Eliot's honeymoon here was ruined when her husband fell (or threw himself) off the balcony into the Grand Canal. Recently restored, it houses the offices of the Biennale (*see p251*). At the corner of calle Vallaresso is **Harry's Bar** (*see p104*), the near-legendary Venetian watering hole, founded by Arrigo Cipriani senior in the 1930s.

Punta della Dogana

[Map with labels:]

Giardinetti Reali

Harry's Bar

Calle Valaresso

Calle del Ridotto

Calle dei XII Martiri

Rio di San Moisè

Ca' Giustinian

S. Marco Giardinetti

S. Marco Vallaresso

Calle C. Barozzi

Corte Barozzi

Calle del Traghetto

Campiello Contarini

Europe & Regina Hotel

Palazzo Treves de Bonfilio

Rio delle Ostreghe

Rio di San Moisè

Campo del Traghetto

Palazzo Contarini Fasan

Palazzo Gritti

Traghetto

Traghetto

Grand Canal

Salute

Abbazia di San Gregorio

Fondamenta Salute

Fondamenta Salute

Campo della Salute

Dogana da Mar

Punta della Dogana

Calle dell'Abazia

C. del Bastion

San Gregorio

Santa Maria della Salute

Pinacoteca Manfrediniana

Calle Lanza

Calle dell'Abazia

Calle di Mezo

Rio Terà dei Catecumeni

Rio Terà del Spezier

Rio Terà ai Saloni

A little beyond that is the single-storey **Palazzo Venier dei Leoni**. Work ground to a halt in 1749 when the family opposite objected to their light being blocked by such a huge pile. Art collector Peggy Guggenheim lived here from 1949 to 1979. The building now contains the **Peggy Guggenheim Collection** (*see p183*).

Next-but-one comes the pure, lopsided charm of the Renaissance **Ca' Dario**, built in the 1470s, perhaps by Pietro Lombardo, with decorative use of coloured marbles and chimney pots. Venetians say the *palazzo* is cursed; certainly the list of former owners who have met a sticky end is impressive. Beyond, **Palazzo Salviati** is a 19th-century

building with gaudy mosaics advertising the products of the Salviati glass works.

The former abbey of **San Gregorio** –now a luxury hotel – is the last building before the Salute stop, with a fine 14th-century relief of St Gregory over a Gothic doorway.

In a triumphant position, at the opening of the Grand Canal, stands the wonderfully curvy church of **Santa Maria della Salute** (*see p182*). Baldassare Longhena's audacious Baroque creation (1671) took 50 years to build. Beyond the church is the Patriarchal Seminary, which houses the **Pinacoteca Manfrediniana** art collection.

The right bank ends at **Punta della Dogana** with its complex of customs-related buildings which now house a major contemporary art gallery (*see p185*). The **Dogana da Mar** (Customs House, 1677), with its tower, gilded ball and weathervane figure of Fortune, affords a spectacular view out across the Bacino di San Marco towards the Lido.

San Marco

Piazza San Marco, Napoleon said, is the 'drawing room of Europe' – an acute observation. It may not be homely, but it is a supremely civilised meeting place. At times it appears that much of Europe's population is crammed into this great square and the pulsating shopping streets around it.

Three main thoroughfares link the key points of this neighbourhood: one runs from piazza San Marco to the Rialto Bridge; one from the Rialto to the Accademia bridge; and another from the Accademia back to piazza San Marco. For a respite from the jostling crowds, wander off these routes; even in this most tourist-packed *sestiere* you can always find little havens of Venetian calm in the narrow *calli* that wind their way off the beaten track.

❤ **Don't miss**

1 Basilica di San Marco *p86*
Arguably one of the greatest churches in Christendom.

2 Palazzo Ducale *p92*
The hub of Venetian power and magnificence.

3 Campanile *p85*
The view from the bell-tower in Piazza San Marco is peerless.

4 Gran Caffè Quadri *p97*
The ultimate gourmet blow-out.

5 Calle delle Botteghe *p101*
Galleries and a jumble of fascinating shops.

6 La Fenice *p247*
Top-notch opera in an over-the-top setting.

SAN MARCO

Restaurants

1. Gran Caffè Quadri
2. Osteria San Marco

Cafés, bars & gelaterie

1. Bacarando in Corte dell'Orso
2. Caffè Florian
3. Caffetteria Doria
4. Fiore
5. Harry's Bar
6. Marchini Time
7. L'Ombra del Leone
8. Rosa Salva

Shops & services

1. Alberto Bertoni – Libreria
2. Araba Fenice
3. Arcobaleno
4. Bevilacqua
5. Bugno Art Gallery
6. Caterina Tognon
7. Chiarastella Cattana
8. Cristina Linassi
9. Daniela Ghezzo Segalin Venezia
10. Diesel
11. Ebrû
13. Galerie Bordas
14. L'Isola – Carlo Moretti
15. L'O.FT
16. Ottica Carraro Alessandro
17. Paropàmiso
18. Pot-Pourrì
19. Rizzo Regali
20. Studium
21. T Fondaco dei Tedeschi
22. Trois
23. Venetian Dreams
24. Venetia Studium

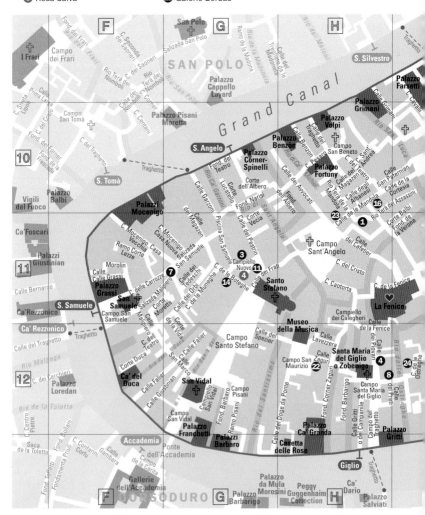

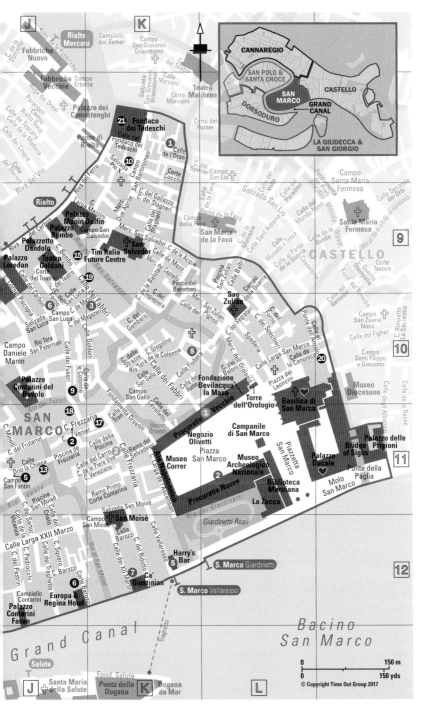

PIAZZA SAN MARCO & AROUND

► *Vaporetto San Marco Vallaresso or San Zaccaria.*

In magnificent piazza San Marco, Byzantine rubs shoulders with Gothic, late Renaissance and neoclassical. The Venetians have always kept the square clear of monuments (on occasion stooping to mendacity to do so – as with the monument to **Bartolomeo Colleoni**, *see p110*). This is typical of Venice, where individual glory always plays second fiddle to the common weal.

The north side of the square dates from the early 16th century. Its arches repeat a motif suggested by an earlier Byzantine structure (seen in Gentile Bellini's painting *Translation of the Relics of the Cross* in the Accademia; *see p180*). Here resided the procurators of St Mark's, who were in charge of maintaining the basilica – hence the name of this whole wing, the **Procuratie Vecchie**. At its eastern end is the **Torre dell'Orologio** (*see p97*).

Construction of the **Procuratie Nuove**, opposite, went on for most of the first half of the 17th century, to designs by Vincenzo Scamozzi. Napoleon joined the two wings at the far end – not for the sake of symmetry, but in order to create the ballroom that was lacking in the Procuratie Nuove, which had become the imperial residence. So, in 1807, down came Sansovino's church of San Geminiano and up went the **Ala Napoleonica**, which now houses the **Museo Correr** (*see p90*).

The **Campanile** (*see p85*) and **Basilica di San Marco** (*see p86*) close off the square in all its splendour to the east.

North of the basilica lies the **piazza dei Leoncini**, a small square named after two small marble lions rubbed smooth by generations of children's bottoms. The large *palazzo* at the far end of the square is the 19th-century residence of the patriarch (cardinal) of Venice.

Between the basilica and the lagoon, the **Piazzetta San Marco** is the real entrance to Venice, defined by two free-standing columns of granite. What appears to be a winged lion on top of the eastern column is in fact a chimera from Persia, Syria or maybe China; the wings and book are Venetian additions. St Theodore, who tops the other column, was Venice's first patron saint. The man who erected the columns in the 12th century asked for the right to set up gambling tables between them. The authorities agreed, but soon put a damper on the jollity by using the pillars to string up criminals. Superstitious locals still avoid walking between them.

Foreign visitors used to disembark here, and were dazzled by the pomp and

---

❤ Time to eat & drink

A taste of history
Caffè Florian *p98*

Venetian pastries at their best
Rosa Salva *p100*

A classic culinary luxury
Gran Caffè Quadri *p97*

❤ Time to shop

Venetian textiles fit for a king
Bevilacqua *p98*

Funky specs
L'O.FT *p100*

Luxury mall in a historical setting
T Fondaco dei Tedeschi *p101*

Beaded delights
Venetian Dreams *p103*

Piazza San Marco

Sights & museums

♥ Campanile di San Marco

San Marco, piazza San Marco. Vaporetto San Marco Vallaresso or San Zaccaria. **Open** *Nov-Mar 9.30am-5.30pm daily. Apr 9am-5.30pm daily. May-Sept 8.30am-9pm daily.* **Admission** *€8.* **No cards.** *Map p82 L11.*

At almost 99m (325ft), the Campanile is the city's tallest building, originally built between 888 and 912. Its present appearance, with the stone spire and the gilded angel on top, dates from 1514. In July 1902 it collapsed, imploding in a neat pyramid of rubble; the only victim was the custodian's cat. It was rebuilt exactly 'as it was, where it was', as the town council of the day promised. The Campanile served both as a watchtower and a bell tower. It provided a site for public humiliations: people of 'scandalous behaviour' were hung in a cage from the top. More wholesome fun was provided by the *volo dell'anzolo* (flight of the angel), when an *arsenalotto* (shipwright) would slide down a rope strung between the Campanile and the Palazzo Ducale at the end of Carnevale. The flight is still re-enacted today. Holy Roman Emperor Frederick III rode a horse to the top of the original in 1451; these days visitors take the lift. The view is superb, taking in the Lido, the whole lagoon and (on a clear day) the Dolomites in the distance. Sansovino's little Loggetta at the foot of the tower, which echoes the shape of a Roman triumphal arch, was also rebuilt using bits and pieces found in the rubble.

▶ *For an eye-to-eye view of the Campanile, climb up the Torre dell'Orologio, see p97.*

magnificence. The area directly in front of the Palazzo Ducale (**Doge's Palace**; *see p92*) corresponded to a modern-day parliamentary lobby. Known as the *broglio*, it was the place where councillors conferred and connived (hence the term 'imbroglio'). Opposite the palace stands the **Biblioteca Marciana** *(see p91)*, now the main city library.

West of the Piazzetta are the **Giardinetti Reali** (Royal Gardens), created by the French. The dainty neoclassical coffee house by Gustavo Selva is now a tourist information office. By the San Marco Vallaresso vaporetto stop is **Harry's Bar** *(see p104)*, the city's most famous watering hole, founded in the 1920s and made legendary by Ernest Hemingway, Orson Welles and a bevvy of other famous drinkers.

Heading east from the Piazzetta, you will cross the **ponte della Paglia** (Bridge of Straw). If you can elbow your way to the side of the bridge, there is a photo-op view of the **ponte dei Sospiri** (Bridge of Sighs). From the Bridge of Straw there is also a superb view of the Renaissance façade of the Palazzo Ducale.

Campanile

SAN MARCO

❤ Basilica di San Marco

*San Marco, piazza San Marco (041 270 8311, www.basilicasanmarco.it). Vaporetto San Marco Vallaresso or San Zaccaria. **Open** Basilica, Chancel & Pala d'Oro, Treasury 9.30am-5pm Mon-Sat; 2-4.30pm Sun. Loggia & Museo Marciano 9.45am-4.45pm daily. **Admission** Basilica free. Chancel & Pala d'Oro €2. Treasury €3. Loggia & Museo Marciano €5. No cards. **Map** p82 L11.*

▶ *To skip the huge queues that form at the basilica entrance at busy times, you can book your visit (€2 fee) through www. venetoinside.com. Large bags or rucksacks must be deposited (free) in a building in calle San Basso, off the piazzetta dei Leoncini. The basilica is open for mass and private prayer from 7am to 11.45am, and 5pm to 7.30pm, with entrance from the piazzetta dei Leoncini door.*

Often seen as the living testimony of Venice's links with Byzantium, St Mark's Basilica is also an expression of the city's independence. In the Middle Ages any self-respecting city state had to have a truly important holy relic. So when two Venetian merchants swiped the body of

St Mark (though some historians believe they got Alexander the Great's remains by mistake, a theme developed by Steve Berry in his 2007 novel *The Venetian Betrayal*) from Alexandria in 828, concealed from prying Muslim eyes under a protective layer of pork, they were going for the very best – a gospel writer, and an entire body at that. Fortunately, there was a legend (or one was quickly cooked up) that the saint had once been caught in the lagoon in a storm, and so it was fitting that this should be his final resting place. The Venetians were traders, but they never looked askance at a bit of straightforward looting as well. The basilica – like the city as a whole – is encrusted with trophies brought back from Venice's greatest spoliatory exploit, the Sack of Constantinople in 1204, during the free-for-all that went under the name of the Fourth Crusade.

The present basilica is the third on the site. It was built mainly between 1063 and 1094, although the work of decoration continued until the 16th century. The church became Venice's cathedral only in 1807, ten years after the fall of the Republic; until then the bishop exerted his authority

Western façade

The Tetrarchs

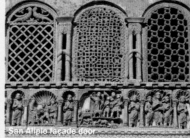
San Aliplo façade door

from San Pietro in Castello (*see p123*). Being next door to the Palazzo Ducale, Venice's most important church was associated with political as much as spiritual power. Venetians who came to worship here were very aware that they were guests of the doge, not the pope.

Exterior

The first view of the basilica from the western end of piazza San Marco is an unforgettable experience. It's particularly impressive in the evening, when the mosaics on the façade glow in the light of the setting sun (as they are mostly 17th- and 18th-century replacements, the distance improves them). The façade consists of two orders of five arches, with clusters of columns in the lower order; the upper arches are topped by fantastic Gothic tracery. The only original mosaic (c1260) is the one over the northernmost door, *The Translation of the Body of St Mark to the Basilica*, which is the earliest known representation of the church. Of curiosity value is the 17th-century mosaic over the southernmost door, which shows the body of St Mark being filched from Alexandria and the Muslims reeling back in disgust from its pork wrapping. The real treasures on show are the sculptures, particularly the group of three carved arches around the central portal, a Romanesque masterpiece. The inner curve of the outer arch is the liveliest, with its detailed portrayals of Venetian trades, arts, crafts and pastimes. The upper order, with fine 14th-century Gothic sculpture by the Dalle Masegne brothers and later Tuscan and Lombard sculptors, can be seen from the Loggia.

Visible through the doors, the **narthex** (covered porch) has an opus sectile marble floor; a small lozenge of porphyry by the central door is said to mark the spot where the Emperor Barbarossa paid homage to Pope Alexander III in 1177. The influence of Islamic art comes through in the few remaining grilles that cover the wall niches where early doges were buried. Above, a series of 13th-century mosaics in the Byzantine style shows Old Testament scenes.

The **south façade**, towards the Palazzo Ducale, was the first side seen by visitors arriving by sea and is thus richly encrusted with trophies proclaiming *La Serenissima's* might. There was a ceremonial entrance to the basilica here as well, but this was blocked by the construction of the **Zen Chapel** (*see p88*) in the 16th century. At the corner by the Doge's Palace stand the **Tetrarchs**, a fourth-century porphyry group of four conspiratorial-looking kings. These come from Constantinople and are usually accepted as representing Diocletian and his Imperial colleagues. However, popular lore has it that they are four Saracens turned to stone after an attempt to burgle the Treasury.

The two free-standing pillars in front of the Baptistry door, with Syrian carvings from the fifth century, come from Acre in modern-day Israel, as does the stumpy porphyry column on the corner, known as the **Pietra del Bando**, where official decrees were read.

The **north façade**, facing piazzetta dei Leoncini, is also studded with loot, including the carving of 12 sheep on either side of a throne bearing a cross, a seventh-century Byzantine work. Note the beautiful 13th-century Moorish arches of the **Porta dei Fiori**, which enclose a Nativity scene.

Interior

A lifetime would hardly suffice to see everything contained in this cave of wonders. The lambent interior exudes splendour and mystery, even when bursting with tourists. The basilica is Greek cross in form, surmounted by five great 11th-century domes. The surfaces are totally covered by more than four square kilometres (1.5 square miles) of mosaics, the result of 600 years of labour. The finest pieces, dating from the 12th and 13th centuries, are the work of Venetian craftsmen influenced by Byzantine art but developing their own independent style. The chapels and Baptistry were decorated in the 14th and 15th centuries; a century later, replacements of earlier mosaics were made using cartoons by such artists as Titian and Tintoretto. However, most of these later mosaics are flawed by the attempt to achieve the three-dimensional effects of Renaissance painting.

In the apse, *Christ Pantocrator* is a 16th-century reproduction of a Byzantine original. Beneath, in what may be the oldest mosaics in the church, are four

♥ Basilica di San Marco *continued*

saint-protectors of Venice: Nicholas, Peter, Mark and Hermagoras. The central **Dome of the Ascension**, with its splendidly poised angels and apostles, dates from the early 13th century. The Passion scenes on the west vault (12th century) are a striking blend of Romanesque and Byzantine styles. The **Pentecost dome** (near the entrance) was probably the first to be decorated; it shows the *Descent of the Holy Spirit*. Four magnificent angels hover in the pendentives.

In the **right transept** is the *Miraculous Rediscovery of the Body of St Mark*: this refers to an episode that occurred after the second basilica was destroyed by fire, when the secret of the whereabouts of the body was lost. The Evangelist obligingly opened up the pillar where his sarcophagus had been hidden (it's just opposite and is marked by an inlaid marble panel). Notice, too, the gorgeous 12th-century marble, porphyry and glass mosaics on the floor.

Baptistry & Zen Chapel

The Baptistry contains the Gothic tomb of Doge Andrea Dandolo and some interesting mosaics, including an image of Salome dancing. In the adjoining Zen Chapel is the bronze 16th-century tomb of Cardinal Zen (a common Venetian surname). The baptistry and chapel are very rarely open.

Chancel & Pala d'Oro

The Chancel is separated from the body of the church by the **iconostasis** – a red marble rood screen by the Gothic sculptors Jacobello and Pier Paolo Dalle Masegne, with fine statues of the Madonna, the apostles and St George. Access to the Chancel is via the **San Clemente chapel** to the right, with a mosaic showing merchants Rustico di Torcello and Buono di Malamocco, apparently about to FedEx the body of St Mark to Venice. St Mark's sarcophagus is visible through the grate underneath the altar. It was moved here from the 11th-century crypt in 1835; the crypt remains a popular venue for society weddings, though it's closed to the rest of us.

The indigestibly opulent **Pala d'Oro** (Gold Altar-piece) is a Byzantine work and, for a change, was acquired honestly. It was made in Constantinople in 976 on the orders of Doge Pietro Orseolo I and further enriched in later years with amethysts, emeralds, pearls, rubies, sapphires and topaz, topped off with a Gothic frame and resetting in 1345. It's a worldly corner of the church, this. Set in the frame of the curving sacristy door are bronze busts of its maker, Sansovino, and his friends, Titian and Aretino, who helped to get him out of prison in 1545. Aretino was a poet and playwright who moved to Venice in 1527 after scandalising Rome with his Lewd Sonnets. A great satirist and hedonist,

Pentecost dome

Iconostasis in the presbyterium

he is said to have died laughing at a filthy joke about his sister.

The **left transept** contains the **chapel of the Madonna Nicopeia** (the Victory Bringer), named after the tenth-century icon on the altar, another Fourth Crusade acquisition. The **St Isidore chapel** beyond, with its 14th-century mosaics of the life of the saint, is reserved for private prayer and confessions, as is the adjacent Mascoli chapel. The altarpiece in this chapel, featuring Saints Mark and John the Evangelist with the Virgin between them, is a striking piece of Gothic statuary. The chapel's mosaics, dating from 1430-50, have a definite Renaissance look to them. They are mostly by Michele Giambono, although some of the figures have been attributed to Jacopo Bellini and to the Florentine Andrea del Castagno, who was in Venice in 1432.

Loggia & Museo Marciano

Of all the pay-to-enter sections of the basilica, the **Loggia dei Cavalli** is definitely the most worthwhile – and it's the only part of the church you can visit on Sunday morning. Up a narrow stairway from the narthex are the **bronze horses** that vie with the lion of St Mark as the city's symbol; here, too, is Paolo Veneziano's exquisite Pala Feriale, a painted panel that was used to cover the Pala d'Oro on weekdays. The Loggia also provides a marvellous view over the square.

The original bronze horses are now kept indoors. They were among the many treasures brought back from the Sack of Constantinople, where they had stood above the city's Hippodrome. For many years they were attributed to a Greek sculptor of the fourth century BC, but the idea that they may be a Roman work of the second century AD has recently come into favour: the half-moon shape of their eyes is said to have been a Roman characteristic. They were at first placed in front of the Arsenale (*see p118*), but in around 1250 were moved to the terrace of the basilica.

In 1797 it was Napoleon's turn to play looter; the horses did not return to Venice from Paris until after his defeat at Waterloo. Apart from the parentheses of the two World Wars, when they were put away in safe storage, they remained on the terrace until 1974, when they were removed for restoration. Since 1982 they have been on display inside the basilica, with exact but soulless copies replacing them outside.

Treasury

This contains a hoard of exquisite Byzantine gold and silver plunder – reliquaries, chalices, candelabras. If you can stand the glitter, the highlights are a silver perfume censer in the form of a church and two 11th-century icons of the Archangel Michael.

Fondazione Bevilacqua la Masa

Exhibition space San Marco 71C, piazza San Marco (041 523 7819, www.bevilacqualamasa. it). Vaporetto San Marco Vallaresso. **Open** *(during exhibitions only) 10.30am-5.30pm Wed-Sun.* **Map** *p82 L10.*

The Fondazione Bevilacqua la Masa was founded more than a century ago by Duchess Felicita Bevilacqua La Masa, who left her palace of Ca' Pesaro (*see p155*) to the city in order to give local artists a space in which to explore new trends. This institution is very active in organising exhibitions, collaborating with the Arts and Design faculty of the IUAV (Venice's architecture university), and with other organisations working to foster new art in Italy. There are talks, performances, an archive and an artist-in-residence programme. The annual *esposizione collettiva* is dedicated to artists based in the Veneto area under the age of 30. The address given above is the main exhibition space; offices are at Dorsoduro 2826, fondamenta Gherardini (041 520 7797).

Museo Correr, Museo Archeologico & Biblioteca Marciana

San Marco 52, piazza San Marco/ sottoportego San Geminiano (041 240 5211, correr.visitmuve.it). Vaporetto San Marco Vallaresso. **Open** *10am-7pm daily.* **Admission** *€20, €13 reductions (with Palazzo Ducale. See p65 Passes).* **Map** *p82 K11.*

These three adjoining museums are all entered by the same doorway, which is situated beneath the Ala Napoleonica at the western end of piazza San Marco.

Museo Correr

The Museo Correr is dedicated to the history of the Republic. Based on the private collection of Venetian nobleman Teodoro Correr (1750-1830), it has gems – including some very fine artworks – enough to elevate it well beyond mere curiosity. The museum is housed in the Ala Napoleonica, the wing

that closes off the narrow western end of the *piazza*, and in a constantly expanding area of the Procuratie Nuove. Napoleon demolished the church of San Geminiano, which faced off across the *piazza* to the basilica, in order to make way for his exercise in neoclassical regularity, complete with that essential imperial accessory, a ballroom. It is through this ballroom that you enter the Museo Correr today. At the far end, in a secluded niche, stands an unlabelled statue (1811). This is the city's hated conqueror, Napoleon.

The route now leads through nine rooms that made up the suite occupied by Sissi, aka Empress Elizabeth of Austria, wife of Franz Joseph I. In fact the beautiful, tragedy-prone Sissi spent no more than a few months here, in 1861-62, but the stuccos and fittings – including beautiful textile reproductions by Rubelli (*see p53 Material Makers*) – faithfully reflect the decor of the period.

Passing through the pretty oval 'everyday dining room', the spirit of these same years continues in Rooms 4 and 5, dedicated to the beautiful if icy sculpture of Antonio Canova, whose first Venetian commission – the statue of Daedalus and Icarus displayed here – brought him immediate acclaim. Some of the works on display are Canova's plaster models rather than his finished marble statues.

From Room 6, the historical collection – which occupies most of the first floor of the Procuratie Nuove building – documents Venetian history and social life in the 16th and 17th centuries through displays of globes, lutes, coins and robes. Room 6 is devoted to the figure of the doge. Room 11 has a collection of Venetian coins, plus Tintoretto's fine *St Justine and the Treasurers*. Beyond are rooms dedicated to the Arsenale (*see p118*), a display of weaponry and some occasionally charming miniature bronzes.

Beyond Room 15 lies the nine-room Wunderkammer, charmingly laid out in a style inspired by the 18th-century passion for eclectic collecting. Curators went through the Museo Correr's store rooms, dusting off and restoring a few real gems, including a couple of early works by Vittore Carpaccio, and a remarkable portrait of dashing 16th-century mercenary Ferrante d'Avalos, formerly attributed to Leonardo da Vinci – an attribution once rubbished but now being reconsidered. Other rooms contain exquisite painted china produced for the Correr family, Renaissance bronzes and ivory carvings. In the final room of the Wunderkammer is the first-ever print of Jacopo de' Barbari's 1500 intricate bird's-eye view map of Venice, along with the original matrices in pear wood. This

Salone da ballo, Museo Correr

extraordinary woodcut is so finely detailed that every single church, *palazzo* and well-head in the city is clearly portrayed.

Stairs from the next room lead up to the Quadreria picture gallery – one of the best places to get a grip on the development of Venetian painting between the Byzantine stirrings of Paolo Veneziano and the full-blown Renaissance story-telling of Carpaccio. Rooms 25 to 29 are dedicated to Byzantine and Gothic painters; note Veneziano's fine *St John the Baptist* in Room 25 and the rare allegorical fresco fragments from a 14th-century private house in Room 27. Room 30 fast-forwards abruptly with the macabre, proto-Mannerist *Pietà* (c.1460) of Cosmè Tura. The Renaissance gets into full swing in Room 34 with Antonello da Messina's *Pietà with Three Angels*, haunting despite the fact that the faces have nearly been erased by cack-handed restoration. The Bellinis get Room 36 to themselves. The gallery's most fascinating work, though, must be Vittore Carpaccio's *Two Venetian Noblewomen* – long known erroneously as *The Courtesans* – in Room 38. These two bored women are not angling for trade: they're waiting for their husbands to return from a hunt. This was confirmed when *A Hunt in the Valley* (in the Getty Museum in Los Angeles) was shown to be this painting's other half.

Back downstairs, the historical collection continues with rooms dedicated to the Bucintoro (state barge), festivities, trade guilds and fairground trials of strength. The atmosphere gets neoclassical again along the corridor to the exit, café and gift shop which is lined with reliefs by Canova.

Museo Archeologico

This collection of Greek and Roman art and artefacts is interesting not so much for the individual pieces as for the light they cast on the history of collecting. Assembled mainly by Cardinal Domenico Grimani and his nephew Giovanni, the collection is a discerning 16th-century humanist's attempt to surround himself with the classical ideal of beauty. Highlights are the original fifth-century BC Greek statues of goddesses in Room 4, the Grimani Altar in Room 6, and the intricate cameos and intaglios in Room 7. Room 9 contains a fine head of the Emperor Vespasian. Room 20 has a couple of Egyptian mummies.

Biblioteca Marciana/Libreria Sansoviniana

In 1468, the great humanist scholar Cardinal Bessarion of Trebizond left his collection of Greek and Latin manuscripts to the state. Venice didn't get round to constructing a proper home for them until 1537. Jacopo Sansovino, a Florentine architect who

had settled in Venice after fleeing from the Sack of Rome in 1527, was appointed to create the library, a splendid building right opposite the Doge's Palace. With this building, Sansovino brought the ambitious new ideas of the Roman Renaissance to Venice. He also appealed to the Venetian love of surface decoration by endowing his creation with an abundance of statuary. His original plan included a barrel-vault ceiling. This collapsed shortly after construction, however, and the architect was immediately clapped into prison. His rowdy friends Titian and Aretino had to lobby hard to have him released.

The working part of Venice's main library is now housed inside La Zecca (*see p97*) and contains approximately 750,000 volumes and around 13,500 manuscripts, most of them Greek.

The main room has a magnificent ceiling, with seven rows of allegorical medallion paintings, produced by a number of Venetian Mannerist artists as part of a competition. Veronese's *Music* (sixth row from the main entrance) was awarded the gold chain by Titian. Beyond this is the anteroom, in which a partial reconstruction has been made of Cardinal Grimani's collection of classical statues, as arranged by Scamozzi (1596). On the ceiling is *Wisdom*, a late work by Titian. Don't miss Fra Mauro's map of the world (1459), a fascinating testimony to the great precision of Venice's geographical knowledge, with surprisingly accurate depictions of China and India.

There are occasional free guided tours in English; call 041 240 5211 for information.

▶ *For information on use of the library, see p302.*

bas-relief, Biblioteca Marciana

💙 Palazzo Ducale (Doge's Palace)

*San Marco 1, piazzetta San Marco (041 271 5911, bookings 041 4273 0892, www. visitmuve.it). Vaporetto San Marco Vallaresso or San Zaccaria. **Open** 8.30am-7pm daily. Tours (book at least 2 days in advance) 9.55am, 10.45am, 11.35am daily. **Admission** €20, €13 reductions (with Museo Correr, Museo Archeologico, Biblioteca Marciana), see p65 Passes. Audio guides €5. Tours €20, €14 reductions. **Map** p82 M11.*

An unobtrusive side door halfway down the right wall of the nave in San Marco leads straight into the courtyard of the **Palazzo Ducale** (Doge's Palace). Today's visitors take a more roundabout route, but that door is a potent symbol of the entwinement of Church and state in the glory days of *La Serenissima*. If the basilica was the Venetian Republic's spiritual nerve centre, the Doge's Palace was its political and judicial hub. The present site was the seat of ducal power from the ninth century onwards, though most of what we see today dates from the mid 15th century. Devastating fires in 1574 and 1577 took their toll, but after much heated debate it was decided to restore rather than replace – an enlightened policy for the time.

The palace is the great Gothic building of the city, but is also curiously eastern in style, achieving a marvellous combination of lightness and strength. The ground floor was open to the public; the work of government went on above. This arrangement resulted in a curious reversal of the natural order. The building gets heavier as it rises: the first level has an open arcade of simple Gothic

arches, the second a closed loggia of rich, ornate arcading. The top floor is a solid wall broken by a sequence of Gothic windows. Yet somehow it doesn't seem awkward.

The **façade** on the Piazzetta side was built in the 15th century as a continuation of the 14th-century waterfront façade. On the corner by the **ponte di Paglia** (Bridge of Straw) is an exquisite marble relief carving, the *Drunkenness of Noah*, from the early 15th century, while on the **Piazzetta corner** is a statue of Adam and Eve from the late 14th century. The capitals of the pillars below date from the 14th to the 15th centuries, although many of them are 19th-century copies (some of the originals are on display inside the palace).

The **Porta della Carta** (Paper Gate – so called because this was where permits were checked), between the palace and the basilica, is a grand piece of florid Gothic architecture and sculpture (1438-42) by Bartolomeo and Giovanni Bon. The statue of Doge Francesco Foscari and the lion is a copy dating from 1885; French troops smashed the original when they occupied the city in 1797.

Behind the palace's fairy-tale exterior the complex machinery of empire whirred away with assembly-line efficiency. Anyone really interested in the inner workings of the Venetian state should take the 90-minute **Itinerari Segreti tour**. This takes you into those parts of the palace that the official route does not touch: the cramped wooden administrative offices; the stark chambers of the **Cancelleria**

Palazzo Ducale

Column detail

Porta della Carta

Segreta, where all official documents were written up in triplicate by a team of 24 clerks; the chamber of the three heads of the Council of Ten, connected by a secret door in the wooden panelling to the **Sala del Consiglio dei Dieci**, and the torture chambers beyond. The tour ends up in the **leads** – the sweltering prison cells beneath the roof from which Casanova staged his famous escape (probably by bribing the guard, though his own account was far more action hero) – and among the extraordinary beams and rafters above the Sala del Maggior Consiglio (*see p95*).

Following reorganisation, the main visit – for which an audio guide is recommended – now begins at the **Porta del Frumento** on the lagoon side of the palace. The **Museo dell'Opera**, just to the left of the ticket barrier, has the best of the 14th-century capitals from the external loggia; the ones you see outside are mostly copies.

In the main courtyard stands the **Arco dei Foscari** – another fine late-Gothic work, commissioned by Doge Francesco Foscari in 1438, when Venice was at the height of its territorial influence. It was built by Antonio Bregno and Antonio Rizzo. Rizzo also sculpted the figures of Adam and Eve (these too are copies; the originals are in the first-floor *liagò*), which earned him gushing accolades and led to his appointment as official architect in 1483, after a disastrous fire. Rizzo had time to oversee the building of the overblown **Scala dei Giganti** (where doges were crowned) and some of the interior before he was found to have

embezzled 12,000 ducats; he promptly fled, and died soon after.

The official route now leads up the ornate **Scala d'Oro** staircase by Jacopo Sansovino, with stuccoes by Vittoria outlined in 24-carat gold leaf.

First floor: Doge's apartments

The doge's private life was entirely at the service of *La Serenissima* and even his bedroom had to keep up the PR effort. These rooms are occasionally closed or used for temporary exhibitions; when open, the **Sala delle Mappe** (also known as the Sala dello Scudo) merits scrutiny. Here, in a series of 16th-century maps, is the known world as it radiated from Venice. Just to the right of the entrance is a detailed map of the New World with Bofton (Boston) and Isola Longa (Long Island) clearly marked. Further on, seek out Titian's well-hidden fresco of St Christopher (above a doorway giving on to a staircase): it took the artist a mere three days to complete.

Second floor: State rooms

This grandiose series of halls provided steady work for all the great 16th-century Venetian artists. Titian, Tintoretto, Veronese, Palma il Vecchio and Jacopo Bassano all left their mark, though the sheer acreage that had to be covered, and the subjects of the canvases – either allegories or documentary records of the city's pomp and glory – did not always spur them to artistic heights.

Sala del Collegio

💙 Palazzo Ducale *continued*

Paradise (Tintoretto c1588)

The **Sala delle Quattro Porte** was where the Collegio – the inner cabinet of the Republic – met before the 1574 fire. After substantial renovation it became an ambassadorial waiting room, where humble envoys could gaze enviously at Andrea Vicentino's portrayal of the magnificent reception given to the young King Henry III of France in 1574. The **Anticollegio**, restored in part by Palladio, has a spectacular gilded stucco ceiling, four Tintorettos and Veronese's blowsy *Rape of Europa*.

Beyond here is the **Sala del Collegio**, where the inner cabinet convened. The propaganda paintings on the ceiling are by Veronese; note the equal scale of the civic and divine players, and the way both Justice and Peace are mere handmaidens to Venice herself. But for real hubris, stroll into the Sala del Senato, where Tintoretto's ceiling centrepiece shows *The Triumph of Venice*. Here the Senate debated questions

of foreign policy, war and commerce, and heard the reports of Venetian ambassadors. Beyond again are the **Sala del Consiglio dei Dieci** and the **Sala della Bussola**, where the arcane body set up to act as a check on the doge considered matters of national security. In the former, note Veronese's ceiling panel, *Juno Offering Gifts to Venice*. By the time this was painted in 1553, the classical gods had started to replace St Mark in Venice's self-aggrandising pantheon. The itinerary continues through an armoury.

First floor: State rooms

The **Sala dei Censori** leads down to a *liagò* (covered, L-shaped loggia), which gives on to the **Sala della Quarantia Civil Vecchia** (the civil court) and the **Sala del Guariento**. The latter's faded 14th-century fresco of *The Coronation of the Virgin* by Guariento (for centuries hidden behind Tintoretto's

Paradiso in the Sala del Maggior Consiglio) looks strangely innocent amid all this worldly propaganda. The shorter arm of the *liagò* has the originals of Antonio Rizzo's stylised marble sculptures of Adam and Eve from the Arco dei Foscari.

Next comes the **Sala del Maggior Consiglio** – the largest room in the palace. This was in effect the Republic's lower house, though this council of noblemen had fairly limited powers. Before the fire of 1577 the hall had been decorated with paintings by Bellini, Titian, Carpaccio and Veronese. When these works went up in smoke, they were replaced by less exalted ones, with one or two exceptions. Tintoretto's *Paradise*, on the far wall, sketched out by the 70-year-old artist but completed after his death in 1594 by his son Domenico, is liable to induce vertigo, as much for its theological complexity as its huge scale. In the ceiling panels are works by Veronese and Palma il Giovane; note too the frieze of ducal portraits made by Domenico Tintoretto and assistants; the black veil marks where Marin Falier's face would have appeared had he not unwisely conspired against the state in 1356.

On the left side of the hall, a balcony gives a fine view over the southern side of the lagoon. A door leads from the back of the hall into the **Sala della Quarantia Civil** and the large **Sala dello Scrutinio**, where the votes of the Maggior Consiglio were counted; the latter is flanked by vast paintings of victorious naval battles, including a dramatic *Conquest of Zara* by Jacopo Tintoretto and *Battle of Lepanto* by Andrea Vicentino.

Criminal courts & prisons

Backtracking through the Sala del Maggior Consiglio, a small door on the left leads past the Scala dei Censori to the **Sala della Quarantia Criminale** – the criminal court. The room next door retains some of the original red and gold leather wall coverings. Beyond this is a small room that has been arranged as a gallery, with Flemish paintings from Cardinal Grimani's collection.

The route now leads over the **Bridge of Sighs** to the **Prigioni Nuove**, where petty criminals were kept. Lifers were sent down to the waterlogged *pozzi* (wells) in the basement of the *palazzo* itself. By the 19th

century most visitors were falling for the tour-guide legend that, once over the Bridge of Sighs, prisoners would 'descend into the dungeon which none entered and hoped to see the sun again', as Mark Twain put it. But when this new prison wing was built in 1589, it was acclaimed as a paragon of comfort; in 1608 the English traveller Thomas Coryat remarked, 'I think there is not a fairer prison in all Christendom.'

Some of the cells have their number and capacity painted over the door; one has a trompe l'œil window, drawn in charcoal by an inmate. On the lowest level is a small exercise yard, site of an unofficial tavern. Up the stairs beyond is a display of Venetian ceramics found during excavations, and more cells, one with cartoons and caricatures left by 19th-century internees. Back across the Bridge of Sighs, the tour ends on the lower floor in the Avogaria – the offices of the clerks of court. Next to this a bookshop has been set up, with a good selection of works on Venice.

▶ *For a primer on Venice's convoluted system of government, see p96 Machinery of State.*

Bridge of Sighs

Machinery of State

Navigating the corridors of power

The longevity of the Venetian republic was due, to a large extent, to a finely honed system of checks and balances that kept the powerful merchant aristocracy closely involved in the machinery of state without allowing any one person or dynasty to lord it over the others. Rules, numbers and duties changed. At the end of the 13th century, what had started out as something close to a democracy became an oligarchy, with only the members of the 200-odd powerful clans included in the Libro d'oro (Golden Book) eligible for office. Later, anyone with the necessary funds could buy into the machinery of state. The main ruling bodies were:

Collegio dei savi
College of Wise Men – a group of experts, elected by the Senato, who staffed special committees to oversee all aspects of internal, marine and war policy.

Consiglio dei dieci
Council of Ten – appointed by the Senato, the council's extensive network of spies brought any would-be subversives to a closed-door trial, in which defence lawyers were forbidden. In time, the increasingly powerful Consiglio dei dieci would have the Inquisition to assist it in its task.

Il doge
The Duke – elected for life in a complicated, cheat-proof system of multiple ballots, the sumptuously robed Duke of Venice was glorious to behold. He could not, however, indulge in business of his own, receive foreign ambassadors alone, leave Venice without permission, or accept personal gifts. If his city state tired of him, he could be deposed. With the doge's extended family banned from high office for the term of his reign, many doges hailed from less politically adept clans. Most were very old by the time they donned the *biretta*, the distinctive horned hat – the average age of doges between 1400 and 1570 was 72. However, the doge was the only official privy to all state secrets and eligible to attend all meetings of state organs; he could, if he played his cards right, have a determining effect on Venetian policy.

Maggior consiglio
Great Council – the Republic's parliament – made up of all voting-age males from the clans that were included in the Libro d'oro – which elected (and provided the candidates for) most other state offices, including that of the doge.

Minor consiglio
Lesser Council – elected by and from the Maggior consiglio, this six-man team advised – or kept tabs on – the doge.

Pien collegio
Full College – made up of the Minor consiglio and the Collegio dei savi, this became Venice's real government, eventually supplanting the Senato.

Quarantie
The three supreme courts; the 40 members were chosen by the Senato.

Senato
Senate – known until the late 14th century as the Pregadi, the Senato was the upper house of the Venetian parliament; by the 16th century it had some 300 members.

Serenissima signoria
Most Serene Lordships – the Minor consiglio, the heads of the three Quarantie courts and the doge; this body was vested with ultimate executive power.

Consiglio dei dieci (Council of Ten)

Negozio Olivetti

*San Marco 101, piazza San Marco (041 522 8387, www.negoziolivetti.it). Vaporetto San Marco Vallaresso or San Zaccaria. **Open** Nov-Mar 10.30am-5.30pm Tue-Sun. Apr-Oct 10.30am-6.30pm Tue-Sun. **Admission** €8; €4 reductions. **No cards**. **Map** p82 K10.*

Snatched back from neglect by the admirable FAI – Italy's equivalent of the UK's National Trust – this former showroom for the Olivetti business machines company was given a Modernist makeover in the mid 1950s by architect Carlo Scarpa. Clean and linear, and dramatically lit by hidden natural light sources, the showroom is a gem. The floor in particular, with its inlaid coloured glass tessera, is superb. *See p273* Scarpa in Venice.

Torre dell'Orologio

*San Marco 147, piazza San Marco (bookings 041 4273 0892, torreorologio.visitmuve.it/en/home). Vaporetto San Marco Vallaresso or San Zaccaria. **Open** Guided tours in English 10am, 11am Mon-Wed; 2pm, 3pm Thur-Sun. **Admission** €12; €7 reductions. **Map** p82 L10.*

Note that there is no lift and the stairs are steep and narrow. The clock tower can *only* be visited on a tour, which can be booked at the Museo Correr (*see p90*), online, or by calling the number given above.

The clock tower, designed by Maurizio Codussi, was built between 1496 and 1506; the wings were an addition, perhaps by

Torre dell'Orologio

Pietro Lombardo. Above the clock face is the Madonna. During Ascension week and at Epiphany, the Magi come out and bow to her every hour, in an angel-led procession. At other times of year the hours and minutes are indicated in Roman and Arabic numerals on either side of the Madonna; this feature dates from 1858 – one of the earliest examples of a digital clock. On the roof, statues of two burly Moors, made of gunmetal and cast in 1497, strike the hour. Another Moore (Roger) sent a villain flying through the clock face in the film *Moonraker*.

After lengthy restoration, the tower reopened in 2007. The tour reveals the workings of the clock, which dates from 1753 and was a remake of the original of 1499. Until 1998 the clock was wound manually by a *temperatore* who lived in the tower. Amid controversy the last incumbent was replaced by an electrical mechanism. The tour concludes on the roof of the tower with a fine view over piazza San Marco, the basilica and the palace.

La Zecca

*San Marco 7, piazzetta San Marco. Vaporetto San Marco Vallaresso or San Zaccaria. **Map** p82 L11.*

The Mint, designed by Sansovino, was completed by 1547. It coined Venice's gold ducats – later referred to as *zecchini*, whence comes the English word 'sequins'. It is more impregnable in appearance than the neighbouring Biblioteca Marciana (*see p91*), though the façade had to accommodate large windows on the piano nobile (for relief from the heat) and open arches on the ground floor, where the procurators of St Mark's operated a number of cheese shops. It now houses most of the contents of the civic library.

Restaurants

♥ Gran Caffè Quadri €€€€

*San Marco 120, piazza San Marco (041 522 2105, www.alajmo.it/grancaffe-quadri). Vaporetto San Marco Vallaresso or San Zaccaria. **Café** 9am-midnight daily. **ABC Bistrot** noon-3pm, 7-10.30pm daily. **Restaurant** 12.30-2.30pm, 7.30-10.30pm Tue-Sun. **Map** p82 L11* ❶ *Modern Venetian*

Marcel Proust used to bring his maman to eat in this Venetian classic that has been operating since 1638, and you can still imagine the couple in the plush red upper dining room with its spectacular view across St Mark's square. But the food – the exquisite, sometimes surprising creations of star chef Massimiliano Alajmo – might surprise them

Gran Caffè Quadri

(as might the bill). Since the advent of the Alajmos (brother Raffaele runs the house) in 2011, everything here is recherché, from the extraordinary coffee specially toasted for the café at *piazza* level, through the club sandwiches and deceptively simple pasta plates served (at slightly lower prices than the restaurant) in the ABC Bistrot, to the marvels cooked up (prawn and curried clam cappuccino, wild duck risotto with truffle and foie gras drops, seabass with olive, caper and chicory pesto) for what is arguably the city's finest eating experience, recognised with a Michelin star in 2017. There are taster menus at €170, €235 and €300. Originally called Il Rimedio, the Gran Caffè takes its name from Giorgio Quadri, who was among the first to bring Turkish-style coffee to Venice when he took the place over in the late 18th century. Stendhal, Wagner and Balzac were habitués. In the evening, a palm court orchestra competes out in the square with the one at Florian's (*see p98*) opposite, and romantics pay small fortunes to sip cocktails under the stars.

Cafés, bars & gelaterie

▶ *See also p97 Gran Caffè Quadri.*

♥ Caffè Florian

San Marco 56, piazza San Marco (041 520 5641, www.caffeflorian.com). Vaporetto San Marco Vallaresso. **Open** *9am-midnight daily.* **Map** *p82 L11* ❷

Florian sweeps you back to 18th-century Venice with its mirrored, stuccoed and frescoed interior. Founded in 1720 as Venezia Trionfante, Florian's present appearance dates from an 1859 remodelling. Rousseau, Goethe and Byron hung out here – the last in sympathy with those loyal Venetians who boycotted the Quadri (*see p97*) across the square, where Austrian officers used to meet. These days, having a drink at Florian is more bank statement than political statement,

especially if you sit at one of the outside tables, where not even a humble *caffè* costs less than €10.

Shops & services

♥ Bevilacqua

San Marco 337B, ponte della Canonica (041 528 7581, www.bevilacquatessuti.com). Vaporetto San Zaccaria. **Open** *10am-7pm Mon-Sat; 10am-5pm Sun.* **Map** *p82 H12* ❹ *Fabric*

This diminutive shop offers exquisite examples of hand- and machine-woven silk brocades, damasks and velvets. *See p53* **Material Makers. Other location** San Marco 2520, campo Santa Maria del Giglio (041 241 0662).

Studium

San Marco 337C, calle Canonica (041 522 2382, www.libreriastudium.eu). Vaporetto San Zaccaria. **Open** *9am-7.30pm Mon-Sat; 9.30am-6pm Sun.* **Map** *p82 M10* ❷⓪ *Books & music*

This shop stocks a wide selection of works on Venice, as well as travel books and novels in English. Its true speciality is revealed as you step into the back room, which is filled with theology studies, icons and prayer books.

PIAZZA SAN MARCO TO THE RIALTO

▶ *Vaporetto Rialto, San Marco Vallaresso or San Zaccaria.*

Piazza San Marco is linked to the Rialto by the busiest, richest and narrowest of shopping streets: the **Mercerie**. The name is plural, since it's divided into five parts: the Merceria dell'Orologio; di San Zulian (on which stands the church of the same name, *see p99*); del Capitello; di San Salvador (with its church of the same name, *see p99*) and del 2 Aprile.

Mercerie means 'haberdashers', but we know from John Evelyn's 1645 account of 'one of the most delicious streets in the world' that in among the textile emporia were shops selling perfumes and medicines too. Most of the big-name fashion designers are to be found here now. The **ponte dei Baretteri** (Hatmakers' Bridge), in the middle of the Mercerie, is a record holder in Venice: six roads lead directly off the bridge.

The Mercerie emerge near **campo San Bartolomeo**, the square at the foot of the Rialto, with the statue of playwright Carlo Goldoni looking amusedly down at the milling crowds.

Sights & museums

San Salvador

San Marco, campo San Salvador (041 523 6717, www.chiesasansalvador.it). Vaporetto Rialto. **Open** *8.30am-7.30pm daily.* **Map** *p82 K9.*

If you can't make it to Florence on this trip, come to San Salvador instead. Begun by Giorgio Spavento in 1506, it was continued by Tullio Lombardo and completed by Sansovino in 1534. But even though the geometrical sense of space and the use of soft-toned greys and whites exude Tuscan elegance, the key to the church's structure is in fact a combination of three domed Greek crosses, which look back to the Byzantine tradition of St Mark's. The church contains two great Titians, the *Annunciation* at the end of the right-hand aisle (with the signature '*Tizianus fecit, fecit*' – 'Titian made this, made this'; the repetition was either intended to emphasise the wonder of the artist's creativity or is a simple mistake) and the *Transfiguration* on the high altar. Note the exquisite glass water jug in the lower right-hand corner of the former painting; the latter conceals a silver reredos, revealed at Christmas, Easter and 6 August (the feast of San Salvador).

There's also some splendid Veneto-Tuscan sculpture, including Sansovino's monument to Doge Francesco Venier, situated between the second and third altars on the right. At the end of the right transept is the tomb of Cristina Cornaro, the hapless Queen of Cyprus (died 1510), a pawn in a game of Mediterranean strategy that ended with her being forced into abdicating the island to Venetian rule. In the left aisle, the third altar belonged to the school of the Luganagheri (sausage makers), and has vibrant figures of San Rocco and San Sebastiano by Alessandro Vittoria, influenced by Michelangelo's *Slaves*. The sacristy (rarely accessible) contains delightful 16th-century frescoes of birds and leafage.

San Zulian

San Marco, mercerie San Zulian (041 523 5383). Vaporetto San Marco Vallaresso or San Zaccaria. **Open** *8am-7.30pm daily.* **Map** *p82 L10.*

The classical simplicity of Sansovino's façade (1553-55) for San Zulian is offset by a grand monument to Tommaso Rangone, a wealthy and far from self-effacing showman-scholar from Ravenna, whose fortune was made by a treatment for syphilis, and who wrote a book on how to live to 120 (he only made it to 80). He unilaterally declared his library to be one of the seven wonders of the world, and had himself prominently portrayed in all three of Tintoretto's paintings for the Scuola Grande di San Marco (now housed in the Gallerie dell' Accademia; *see p180).* The interior of San Zulian has a ceiling painting of The Apotheosis of St Julian by Palma il Giovane, and a Titianesque Assumption by the same painter on the second altar on the right, which also has good statues of St Catherine of Alexandria and Daniel by Alessandro Vittoria. The first altar on the right has a Pietà by Veronese.

▶ *Mass is said here in English at 11.30am on Sundays. Anglicans head across the Grand Canal to St George's (Dorsoduro 870, campo San Vio) for sung service at 10.30am on Sundays.*

TIM Italia Future Centre

San Marco 4826, campo San Salvador (041 947 770, www.telecomfuturecentre.it). Vaporetto Rialto. **Open** *During exhibitions 10am-6pm Tue-Sun.* **Admission** *free.* **Map** *p82 K9.*

The 16th-century cloisters of the monastery of San Salvador underwent a thorough restoration in the 1980s to provide a showcase for the latest offerings of the building's owner, Telecom Italia. The cloisters now host occasional exhibitions and conferences. If it happens to be open for an event, be certain not to miss the splendid refectory with its 16th-century frescoed ceiling.

Cafés, bars & gelaterie

There's a great bar and restaurant in the T Fondaco dei Tedeschi (*see p101).*

Bacarando in Corte dell'Orso

San Marco 5495, calle dell'Orso (041 5238280). Vaporetto Rialto. **Open** *11am-2am daily (closes earlier in winter).* **Map** *p82 K8* ❶

Completely hidden away from the busy Rialto tourist trail, this lively cave of a place offers respite to anyone caught out by the city's early closing times. The glass case next to the bar is piled high with cicheti, which cater to vegetarians as well as meat- and fish-lovers and can easily serve as a stand-in for a more formal meal.

Caffetteria Doria

San Marco 4665, calle dei Fabbri (329 351 7367 mobile). Vaporetto Rialto. **Open** *6am-8.30pm Mon-Sat; 1-8.30pm Sun.* **No cards.** **Map** *p82 K10* ❸

Take a page out of the locals' book and squeeze into this popular, standing-room-only bar for a delicious cup of coffee, mid-afternoon snack or one of the best spritz in town. Service is always friendly and welcoming. Knowledgeable owners Andrea and Riccardo stock a huge selection of wine and spirits.

♥ Rosa Salva

San Marco 950, calle Fiubera (041 521 0544, www.rosasalva.it). Vaporetto Rialto or San Marco Vallaresso. **Open** *8am-8pm Mon-Sat.* **No cards.** *Map p82 K10* ⑧

This long-established family-owned café and *pasticciere* makes one of the smoothest *cappuccini* in town, and some very delicious cakes to go with it. If it's ice-cream you fancy, all the flavours are made on the premises. There's a good lunch spread, with interesting sandwiches and filled rolls, as well as pastas and simple salads. The candied fruit in intriguing jars and piles of sugared rose buds and violet leaves are delightful. **Other location** Castello 6778, campo Santi Giovanni e Paolo (041 522 7949).

Shops & services

Araba Fenice

San Marco 1822, Frezzeria (041 522 0664). Vaporetto Giglio or San Marco Vallaresso. **Open** *9.30am-7.30pm Mon-Sat.* **Map** *p82 J11* ❷ *Fashion/accessories*

A classic yet original line of women's clothing made exclusively for this boutique, plus jewellery in ebony and mother-of-pearl.

Daniela Ghezzo Segalin Venezia

San Marco 4365, calle dei Fuseri (041 522 2115, www.danielaghezzo.it). Vaporetto Rialto or San Marco Vallaresso. **Open** *10am-1pm, 3-7pm Mon-Fri; 10am-1pm Sat.* **Map** *p82 J10* ❾ *Accessories*

The shoemaking tradition that was established by 'the Cobbler of Venice', Rolando Segalin, continues through his talented former apprentice Daniela Ghezzo. Check out the footwear in the window, including an extraordinary pair of gondola shoes. A pair of Ghezzo's creations will set you back anything between €650 and €1,800. Repairs are done as well.

Diesel

San Marco 5315-6, salizada Pio X (041 241 1937, www.diesel.com). Vaporetto Rialto. **Open** *10am-7.30pm Mon-Sat; 11am-7pm Sun.* **Map** *p82 K8* ❿ *Fashion*

This well-known Veneto-based company's kooky, club-wise, lifestyle-based styles have invaded Europe and North America; its hipper-than-hip store is a landmark on the Venetian shopping scene.

♥ L'O.FT

San Marco 4773, calle dell'Ovo (041 522 5263, www.otticofabbricatore.com). Vaporetto Rialto. **Open** *9am-12.30pm, 3.30-7.30pm Mon-Sat; 11am-7pm Sun.* **Map** *p82 J9* ⓯ *Accessories*

Also known as L'Ottico Fabbricatore, this ultra-modern shop specialises in designer eyewear – the kind you won't find anywhere else, with extraordinary frames in anything from buffalo horn to titanium. Pop in for a pair of sunglasses, or bring along your prescription and treat yourself to glasses the likes of which chain-store opticians can only dream of. The boutique also sells gossamer-like cashmere and sensual silk apparel, plus a selection of luxurious bags in materials ranging from calfskin to ostrich.

Paropàmiso

San Marco 1701, Frezzeria (041 522 7120). Vaporetto San Marco Vallaresso or Rialto. **Open** *10.30am-7.30pm Mon-Sat; 11am-7pm Sun.* **Map** *p82 K11* ⓱ *Accessories/homewares*

An overwhelming mix of beads in minerals, glass, coral and metal makes this wholesale emporium a true delight. As well as Venetian wares, Paropàmiso has imports from Africa and the Far East. You can buy ready-made jewellery or put together your own: clasps and materials for stringing are also available. There's a selection of other ethnic goods here too, including fabrics, rugs, masks and small items of furniture.

Pot-Pourrì

San Marco 1810, ramo dei Fuseri (041 241 0990, www.potpourri.it). Vaporetto San Marco Vallaresso. **Open** *3.30-7.30pm Mon; 10am-1.30pm, 3.30-7.30pm Tue-Sat; 11am-7pm Sun.* **Map** *p82 J11* ⓲ *Fashion/homewares*

Walking into this shop is like stepping into an elegant friend's bedroom. Clothes are draped over armchairs or hang from wardrobe doors, while charming knick-knacks cover the dressing table. This faux-boudoir houses designers such as Cristina Effe and Marzi and also stocks homewares.

Rizzo Regali

San Marco 4739, calle dei Fabbri (041 522 5811). Vaporetto Rialto. **Open** *9am-8pm Mon-Sat.* **Map** *p82 K9* ⓳ *Food & drink*

This old-fashioned shop sells traditional cakes, sweets and chocolates. For *pesce d'aprile* (April Fool's Day), you can buy bags of foil-wrapped chocolate goldfish. If you can't find the *torrone* (nougat) you're looking for here, then it doesn't exist.

❤ T Fondaco dei Tedeschi

San Marco, calle del Fontego dei Tedeschi (041 314 2000), Vaporetto Rialto. **Open** *10am-8pm daily.* **Map** *p82 K8* ❷❶ *Mall*

Venetians struggle to recognise this glitzy tax-free shopping mall as the gloomy if rather monumental building that served as their main post office until a few years ago. A radical makeover, courtesy of architects Rem Koolhaas and Jamie Fobert, has transformed what was the 16th-century headquarters of German traders into a sparkling (almost blindingly so) luxury haven for anyone with deep pockets and a taste for designer labels. The **AMO** café/restaurant (run by super-chef Massimiliano Alajmo) serves meals in the courtyard, but, for those not wishing to splash out, an *aperitivo* in the bar itself, beautifully decked out in onyx by Philippe Starck, is a worthy alternative. Make sure to head up to the roof terrace, which offers a stunning view of the Grand Canal.

FROM THE RIALTO TO THE ACCADEMIA BRIDGE

▶ *Vaporetto Accademia, Rialto, San Samuele or Sant'Angelo.*

The route from the Rialto to the Accademia passes through a series of ever-larger squares. From cosily cramped campo San Bartolomeo, the well-marked path leads to campo San Luca, then **campo Manin** with its 19th-century statue of Daniele Manin, leader of the 1848 uprising against the Austrians (*see p265*). An alley to the left of this campo will lead you to the **Scala del Bòvolo** (*see p102*), a striking Renaissance spiral staircase. Back on the main drag, the calle della Mandola leads to broad **campo Sant'Angelo** with its dramatic view of the leaning tower of **Santo Stefano** (*see p102*); off calle della Mandola to the right is the Gothic **Palazzo Fortuny** (*see below*), once home to the Spanish fashion designer Mariano Fortuny.

Just before the **Accademia bridge** (*see p103*), **campo Santo Stefano** is second in size only to piazza San Marco in the *sestiere*. The tables of several bars scarcely encroach on the space where children play on their bikes or kick balls around the statue of Risorgimento ideologue Nicolò Tommaseo. (Poor Tommaseo is known locally as *il cagalibri*, 'the bookshitter', for reasons which become clear when the statue is viewed from the rear.) At the Accademia bridge end of the square is the 18th-century church of **San Vidal** (*see p102*).

On the Grand Canal to the west of campo Santo Stefano is **campo San Samuele**, with

a deconsecrated 11th-century church and the massive **Palazzo Grassi** exhibition centre (*see p101*). Leading north-west from the campo, **calle delle Botteghe** is a hotch-potch of fascinating shops. Nearby, in **calle Malipiero**, the 18th-century love machine, Giacomo Casanova, was born (though in which house exactly is not known). The neighbourhood is full of Casanova associations, including the site of the theatre where his mother performed (corte Teatro).

Sights & museums

Palazzo Fortuny

San Marco 3958, campo San Beneto (041 520 0995, http://fortuny.visitmuve.it/). Vaporetto Sant'Angelo. **Open** *during exhibitions 10am-6pm.* **Admission** *€12, €10 reductions (with exhibition).* **No cards.** **Map** *p82 H10.*

This charming 15th-century *palazzo*, which belonged to Spanish fashion designer Mariano Fortuny (1871-1949), should not be missed on the occasions when it opens for temporary exhibitions. These are often photographic, photography being one of Fortuny's interests, alongside theatrical set design, cloth dyes and some elegant silk dresses. Also on display are some of Fortuny's paintings of Middle Eastern views.

Palazzo Grassi

San Marco 3231, campo San Samuele (041 240 1308, www.palazzograssi.it). Vaporetto San Samuele. **Open** *during exhibitions 10am-7pm Mon, Wed-Sun.* **Admission** *€15 (€18 Palazzo Grassi & Punta della Dogana; see p185); €10 (€15 both) reductions.* **Map** *p82 F11.*

This superbly – though boringly – regular 18th-century *palazzo* on the Grand Canal was bought in 2005 by French billionaire

Palazzo Fortuny

businessman François-Henri Pinault. Pinault brought in Japanese superstar-architect Tadao Ando for an expensive overhaul, which increased the exhibition space by 2,000sq m (21,000sq ft). Most of the *palazzo*'s shows centre on Pinault's own massive contemporary art collection. Next door at no.3260, the Teatrino Grassi – another Ando makeover – shows art videos and hosts events.

▶ *François-Henri Pinault's mega-gallery in the Punta della Dogana is even more impressive; see p185.*

▶ *François-Henri Pinault's mega-gallery in the Punta della Dogana is even more impressive; see p185.*

Santo Stefano

San Marco, campo Santo Stefano (041 275 0462, www.chorusvenezia.org). Vaporetto Accademia or San Samuele. **Open** *10.30am-4.30pm Mon-Sat.* **Admission** *€3 (or Chorus; see p65).* **Map** *p82 G11.*

Santo Stefano is an Augustinian church, built in the 14th century and altered in the 15th. The façade has a magnificent portal in the florid Gothic style. The large interior, with its splendid ship's-keel roof, is a multicoloured treat, with different marbles used for the columns, capitals, altars and intarsia, and diamond-patterned walls. On the floor is a huge plaque to Doge Morosini (best known for blowing up the Parthenon) and a more modest one to composer Giovanni Gabrieli. On the interior façade to the left of the door is a Renaissance monument by Pietro Lombardo and his sons, decorated with skulls and festoons. In the sacristy are two tenebrous late works by Tintoretto, *The Washing of the Feet* and *The Agony in the Garden* (*The Last Supper* is by the great man's assistants), and three imaginative works by Gaspare Diziani (*Adoration of the Magi, Flight into Egypt, Massacre of the Innocents*).

San Vidal

San Marco, campo San Vidal (041 277 0561, 522 5061). Vaporetto Accademia. **Open** *9am-5.30pm daily.* **Map** *p82 G12.*

This early 18th-century church, with a façade derived from Palladio, was for years used as an art gallery. It has now been restored and hosts concerts. Over the high altar is a splendid Carpaccio painting (1514) of St Vitalis riding what appears to be one of the bronze horses of San Marco. The third altar on the right has a painting by Piazzetta, *Archangel Raphael and Saints Anthony and Louis.*

▶ *Classical music concerts by the Interpreti Veneziani are held here most days, beginning at 8.30pm. For information, see p249.*

Scala Contarini del Bòvolo & Sala del Tintoretto

Palazzo Contarini del Bòvolo, San Marco 4299, corte dei Risi (041 309 6605, www. scalacontarinidelbovolo.com). Vaporetto Rialto. **Open** *10am-1.30pm, 2-6pm daily. Last admission 30mins before closing.* **Admission** *€7.* **Map** *p82 J10.*

Follow the signs for the Scala del Bòvolo from campo Manin and you will emerge in a narrow courtyard entirely dominated by this elegant Renaissance spiral staircase, built sometime around 1499 by Giovanni Candi (spiral staircases are *scale a chiocciola*, snail staircases, in Italian; *bòvolo* is Venetian dialect for snail). It was beautifully restored in 1986 and again more recently, and offers a stunning view from the summit. Halfway up, a small doorway opens on to the Sala del Tintoretto, which houses a handful of artworks from Venetian private collections. The standout piece, which gives the room its name, is Tintoretto's study for his far more grandiose *Paradise* in the Palazzo Ducale.

Cafés, bars & gelaterie

Fiore

San Marco 3461, calle de le Botteghe. **Open** *9am-10.30pm Mon, Wed-Sun.* **Map** *p82 G11* ❹

At *aperitivo* and lunch time, locals flock to this friendly *osteria* just off campo Santo Stefano to wet their whistles and stave off hunger by choosing from a wide selection of *cicheti*. Perch at the bar or rest your drink precariously on the ledge outside and sample the local specialities spilling over the counter – meatballs, *folpéti* (octopus) and celery, battered fish, fresh vegetables.

Marchini Time

San Marco 4598, campo San Luca (041 241 3087). Vaporetto Rialto. **Open** *7.30am-8.30pm Mon-Sat; 9am-8.30pm Sun.* **No cards.** **Map** *p82 J10* ❻

The Marchini pastry empire is the oldest in *La Serenissima*. This space lights up campo San Luca with its colourful windows displaying the latest cakes, cookies and chocolates. There's a dizzying array of *cornetti* to enjoy with your breakfast coffee – the raspberry jam-filled one is mouth-watering.

Shops & services

▶ *For details of the kiosk selling accessories in campo Santo Stefano, see also p192 Garden of Marvels.*

Alberto Bertoni – Libreria

San Marco 3637B, rio terà degli Assassini (041 522 9583, www.bertonilibri.com). Vaporetto

Sant'Angelo. **Open** *9am-1pm, 3-7.30pm Mon-Sat.* **Map** *p82 H11* ❶ *Books & music*

Just off calle de la Mandola (look for the display case marking the turn-off), this well-hidden cavern is home to art books, exhibition catalogues and the like, all with significant reductions on cover prices.

Arcobaleno

San Marco 3457, calle delle Botteghe (041 523 6818). Vaporetto Sant'Angelo. **Open** *9am-12.30pm, 4-7.30pm Mon-Fri; 9am-12.30pm Sat.* **No cards.** **Map** *p82 G11* ❸ *Artists' materials*

Arcobaleno stocks a vast assortment of artists' pigments. As well as art supplies, it carries all the basics in hardware, light bulbs and detergents.

Chiarastella Cattana

San Marco 3216, salizada San Samuele (041 522 4369, www.chiarastellacattana.com). Vaporetto San Samuele. **Open** *10am-1pm, 3-7pm Mon-Sat.* **Map** *p82 G11* ❼ *Homewares*

Chiarastella Cattana's elegantly stylish tablecovers, duvet and sheet covers, bathrobes and accessories are crafted from natural hand-loomed textiles in gorgeously muted colours with botanical motifs.

Ebrû

San Marco 3471, campo Santo Stefano (041 523 8830, www.albertovallese-ebru. com). Vaporetto Accademia or Sant'Angelo. **Open** *10am-1.30pm, 2.30-7pm Mon-Wed; 10am-1pm, 2.30-7pm Thur-Sat; 11am-6pm Sun.* **Map** *p82 G11* ⓫ *Accessories/stationery*

Beautiful, marbled handcrafted paper, scarves and ties. These are Venetian originals, whose imitators can be found in other shops around town.

L'Isola – Carlo Moretti

San Marco 2970, calle delle Botteghe (041 5233 1973, www.lisola.com). Vaporetto Sant'Angelo or San Samuele. **Open** *10.30am-7.30pm daily.* **Map** *p82 G11* ⓮ *Homewares*

This long-established family firm produces exquisitely coloured contemporary glasses, bowls, vases, light fixtures and much else. Each piece is hand-crafted, some are limited editions and many find their way into important glass collections. The showroom closes some Sundays in August and all Sundays from January to March.

Ottica Carraro Alessandro

San Marco 3706, calle della Mandola (041 520 4258, www.otticacarraro.it). Vaporetto

Venetian Dreams

Sant'Angelo. **Open** *9.30am-1pm, 3-7.30pm Mon-Sat.* **Map** *p82 H10* ⓰ *Accessories*

Get yourself some unique and funky eyewear – the frames are exclusively produced and guaranteed for life. Ottica Carraro Alessandro offers extraordinary quality at reasonable prices.

❤ Venetian Dreams

San Marco 3805, calle della Mandola (041 523 0292, www.marisaconvento.it), Vaporetto Sant'Angelo. **Open** *10.30am-6pm Wed-Sun.* **Map** *p82 H11* ㉓ *Beads*

A treasure trove glittering with jewellery, household items and other decorative pieces fashioned out of antique beads by owner Marisa Convento, who lovingly keeps alive the 19th-century craft of the *imperaresse* – women who sat on bridges and *fondamenta* painstakingly sorting and threading seed beads. Bead-threading classes and themed rambles can also be organised on request.

THE ACCADEMIA BRIDGE TO PIAZZA SAN MARCO

▶ *Vaporetto Accademia, Giglio or San Marco Vallaresso.*

The route from Santo Stefano back to piazza San Marco zigzags at first, passing through small squares, including **campo San Maurizio**, with its 19th-century church now transformed into the **Museo della Musica** (*see p104*), and campo Santa Maria del Giglio (aka **Santa Maria Zobenigo**; *see p104*). It winds past banks, hotels and top-dollar antique shops, to end in wide via XXII Marzo, with an intimidating view of the Baroque statuary of **San Moisè** (*see p104*). Off to the left as you make your way towards

San Marco is the opera house, **La Fenice** (*see p247*), and more streets of supersmart shops, in the **Frezzeria** district.

Press on and you will be ready for what is arguably the greatest view anywhere in the world: piazza San Marco from the west side.

Sights & museums
Museo della Musica
San Marco 2601, campo San Maurizio (041 241 1840, www.museodellamusica.com). Vaporetto Giglio. **Open** *9.30am-7.30pm daily.* **Admission** *free.* **Map** *p82 H12.*

This small private museum, in the former church of San Maurizio, is run by the Interpreti Veneziani concert group (*see p249*). Serving partly as a sales and promotion outlet, the museum contains an interesting collection of period instruments, but also presents an opportunity to appreciate the neoclassical interior of the church, designed by Giannantonio Selva, the architect of the Fenice theatre (*see p247*). The museum puts on concerts, mainly Vivaldi and other baroque favourites, at the church of San Vidal (*see p102*); tickets can be bought at the museum.

San Moisè
San Marco, campo San Moisè (041 528 5840). Vaporetto San Marco Vallaresso. **Open** *9.30am-12.30pm, 3-6.30pm daily.* **Map** *p82 K12.*

The Baroque façade of San Moisè has been lambasted by just about everybody as one of Venice's truly ugly pieces of architecture. Inside, an extravagant Baroque sculpture occupies the high altar, representing not only Moses receiving the stone tablets but also Mount Sinai itself. Near the entrance is the grave of John Law, author of the disastrous Mississippi Bubble scheme that almost sank the French central bank in 1720.

Santa Maria del Giglio
San Marco, campo Santa Maria Zobenigo (041 275 0462, www.chorusvenezia.org). Vaporetto Giglio. **Open** *10.30am-4.30pm Mon-Sat.* **Admission** *€3 (or Chorus; see p65).* **No cards.** **Map** *p82 H12.*

This church's façade totally lacks any Christian symbols (give or take a token angel or two). Built between 1678 and 1683, it's a huge exercise in defiant self-glorification by Admiral Antonio Barbaro, who was dismissed by Doge Francesco Morosini for incompetence in the War of Candia (Crete). On the plinths of the columns are relief plans of towns where he served; his own statue (in the centre) is flanked by representations of Honour, Virtue, Fame and Wisdom. The

interior is more devotional. You may not have heard of the painter Antonio Zanchi (1631-1722), but this is his church. Particularly interesting is *Abraham Teaching the Egyptians Astrology* in the sacristy, while the Cappella Molin has *Ulysses Recognised by his Dog* (an odd subject for a church). The chapel also contains a *Madonna and Child*, which is proudly but erroneously attributed to Rubens. Behind the altar there are two paintings of the Evangelists by Tintoretto, formerly organ doors.

Restaurants
Osteria San Marco €€€
San Marco 1610, Frezzeria (041 528 5242, www.osteriasanmarco.it). Vaporetto San Marco Vallaresso. **Open** *12.30-11pm Mon-Sat. Closed 2wks Jan.* **Map** *p82 K11* ❷ *Venetian*

This smart, modern *osteria* on a busy shopping street is a breath of fresh air in this touristy area. The guys behind the operation are serious about food and wine, and their attention to detail shows through both in the selection of bar snacks and wines by the glass, and in the sit-down menu, based on the freshest of local produce. Prices are high, but you're paying for the area as well as the quality. This is one of the few places in Venice where you can eat a proper meal throughout the day.

Cafés, bars & gelaterie
Harry's Bar
San Marco 1323, calle Vallaresso (041 528 5777, www.cipriani.com). Vaporetto San Marco Vallaresso. **Open** *10.30am-11pm daily.* **Map** *p82 K12* ❺

This historic watering hole, founded by Giuseppe Cipriani in 1931, has changed little since the days when Ernest Hemingway came here to work on his next hangover... except for the prices and the numbers of tourists. But despite the crush, a Bellini at the bar is as much a part of the Venetian experience as a gondola ride. At mealtimes, diners enjoy Venetian-themed international comfort food at steep prices (€140-plus for three courses). Stick with a Bellini, and don't even think of coming in here wearing shorts or ordering a spritz.

L'Ombra del Leone
Ca' Giustinian, San Marco 1364, calle del Ridotto (041 241 3519). Vaporetto San Marco Vallaresso. **Open** *Mar-Oct 9am-10pm daily. Nov-Feb 9am-10pm Mon-Sat.* **Map** *p82 K12* ❼

Ponte dell' Accademia

Located inside the Grand Canal-side Ca' Giustinian, the headquarters of the Biennale (*see p121*), this sleek modern café-restaurant offers a superb panorama from its terrace on the water as well as good (and reasonably affordable) light lunches and a hopping evening *aperitivo* scene, especially in the warmer months. If you're travelling with little ones, check out the play space (*see below* In the know).

Shops & services

Bugno Art Gallery
San Marco 1996D, campo San Fantin (041 523 1305, www.bugnoartgallery.it). Vaporetto San Marco Vallaresso. **Open** *4-7.30pm Mon, Sun; 10.30am-7.30pm Tue-Sat.* **Map** *p82 J11* ❺ *Gallery*

Large windows overlooking the Fenice opera house reveal a space devoted to artists working in all types of media. Well-known local artists are also included in the gallery's collection. So packed is the exhibition calendar that shows often spill over into a smaller exhibition space nearby.

Caterina Tognon
San Marco 2158, Palazzo Treves, corte Barozzi (041 520 1566, www.caterinatognon. com). Vaporetto San Marco Vallaresso. **Open** *10am-7pm Tue-Sat.* **Map** *p82 J12* ❻ *Gallery*

Following the success of her first gallery, which she opened in Bergamo in 1992, renowned curator Caterina Tognon created this Venetian showcase for contemporary art in glass in 1998. Various shows take place each year by emerging and renowned artists.

Cristina Linassi
San Marco 2434, ponte delle Ostreghe (041 522 8107, www.cristinalinassi.it). Vaporetto Giglio. **Open** *10am-7.30pm Mon-Sat; 10.30am-6.30pm Sun.* **Map** *p82 H12* ❽ *Homewares*

This boutique sells gorgeous hand-embroidered nightgowns, towels and sheets made in its own workshop. The catalogue has designs for made-to-order items.

Galerie Bordas
San Marco 1994B, calle dietro la Chiesa (041 522 4812, www.galerie-bordas.com). Vaporetto San Marco Vallaresso. **Open** *11am-1pm, 4-7pm Tue-Sat.* **Map** *p82 J11* ⓭ *Gallery*

The only gallery dealing in serious graphics by internationally renowned masters. The space is small but the collection of artists' books held here is huge.

Trois
San Marco 2666, campo San Maurizio (041 522 2905). Vaporetto Giglio. **Open** *4-7.30pm Mon; 10am-1pm, 4-7pm Tue-Sat.* **No cards.** **Map** *p82 H12* ㉒ *Fabric*

This is one of the best places in *La Serenissima* to buy original Fortuny fabrics – and at considerable savings on the prices you'd find in the UK and the US (though this still doesn't make them particularly cheap). Made-to-order beadwork, masks and accessories are also available.

Venetia Studium
San Marco 2425, calle delle Ostreghe (041 523 6953, www.venetiastudium.com). Vaporetto Giglio. **Open** *10am-7.30pm Mon-Sat; 11am-6pm Sun.* **Map** *p82 K8* ㉔ *Accessories/homewares*

Venetia Studium is the sole authorised manufacturer of the distinctive Fortuny lamps. It also stocks splendid silk pillows, scarves, handbags and other accessories in a marvellous range of colours. They're certainly not cheap, but they do make perfect gifts. **Other location** San Marco, Torre dell'Orologio (041 522 6791).

> **In the know**
> **Kids' space**
>
> The ground floor of Ca'Giustinian is a bright place for young children to play and parents to recover from the rigours of sightseeing. There are toys, books and nappy-changing facilities - and it's all completely free.

Castello

Castello is not only Venice's largest *sestiere*. It's also the most remarkably varied, stretching from the bustle and splendour in the north-west around Santa Maria Formosa and Santi Giovanni e Paolo, to the homely, washing-festooned stretches around and beyond wide via Garibaldi.

To this mix add the immense Arsenale complex – Venice's former shipbuilding centre and great military powerhouse, currently awaiting a comprehensive development project – plus the giardini della Biennale, where the world's contemporary art and architecture aficionados flock for extraordinary shows through the summer, a slew of remarkable churches, a football pitch whose days may be numbered and some seriously good restaurants. Castello really is a Venice unto itself.

♥ Don't miss

1 La Biennale *p121*
Prestigious showcase of international art and architecture.

2 Santi Giovanni e Paolo *p111*
Monuments and masterpieces.

3 Arsenale *p118*
Any chance to enter this fascinating complex should be seized.

4 Museo della Fondazione Querini Stampalia *p112*
Superb art collection, urbane café.

5 Scuola di San Giorgio degli Schiavoni *p123*
Enchanting works by Carpaccio.

6 San Francesco della Vigna *p112*
Palladio and Bellini in a deserted corner of the city.

DEO VTRIVSQ TEMPLI AEDIFICATORI AC REPARAT

AC
CEDE
AD
HOC

NE
DESERAS
SPI
RITVALE

NON SINE
IVGI
EXTERI
ORI

San Francesco della Vigna

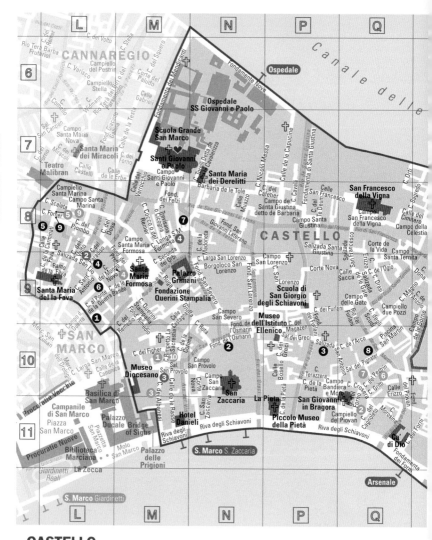

CASTELLO

Restaurants

1. L'Aciugheta
2. Al Covo
3. Alla Basilica
4. Alle Testiere
5. Al Portego
6. Corte Sconta
7. Il CoVino
8. Dai Tosi Piccoli
9. Osteria di Santa Marina
10. Il Ridotto

Cafés, bars & gelaterie

1. Angiò
2. Boutique del Gelato
3. Da Bonifacio
4. La Mascareta
5. Pasticceria Melita
6. El Refolo
7. Serra dei Giardini
8. Vincent Bar

Shops & services

1. I Tre Mercanti
2. Anticlea Antiquariato
2. Banco Lotto N° 10
4. Filippi Editore Venezia
5. Giovanna Zanella
6. Kalimala
7. Papier Mâché
8. Vino e... Vini
9. VizioVirtù

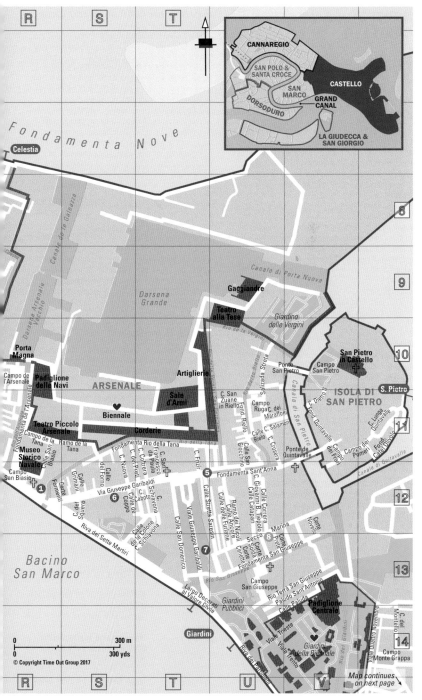

CANNAREGIO

SAN POLO &
SANTA CROCE

SAN
MARCO

DORSODURO

GRAND
CANAL

CASTELLO

LA GIUDECCA &
SAN GIORGIO

Fondamenta Nove

Celestia

Canale de le Galazze

Canale di Porta Nuova

Darsena
Grande

Gaggiandre

Teatro
alla Tese

Giardino
delle Vergini

Rio de la Vergini

Darsena Arsenale Vecchio

Porta
Magna

Campo de
l'Arsenale

Padiglione
delle Navi

ARSENALE

Artiglierie

Salizada Streta

Ponte
San Pietro

Campo
San Pietro

San Pietro
in Castello

ISOLA DI
SAN PIETRO

S. Pietro

Sale
d'Armi

C. San
Zuane
in Riello

Fond. Riello

Calle San
Riello

Calle C. Salamon

Calle San
Gioccholo

C. del
Marafoni

C. Dieno

Canale di San Pietro

C. Crosera

C. Lunga
Quintavalle

C. Lunga
Quintavalle

Teatro Piccolo
Arsenale

Biennale

Corderie

Fondamenta de l'Arsenale

Campo de la
Tana

Ramo de la
Tana

Museo
Storico
Navale

Campo
San Biasio

Fondamenta Rio della Tana

Calle San
Biasio

Corte
Grimani

Calle
Jeppi

Corte
Formenti

Calle
del Forno

Via Giuseppe Garibaldi

C.
Cabotto

C. Nuova

C. dei Prati

C. Cottera

Calle de
Coppo

Calle Schiavona

Calle de
le Colone

C. Schiavona

C. Sant'
Francesco
da Paula

Calle Stretta Sarasin

Calle San Domenico

Viale Giuseppe Garibaldi

C. Friziri

Ponte de
Quintavalle

Fond. Quintavalle

Fond.
Calle Chiodolo

C. Chiodolo

Canale di Quintavalle

Campo dei
Pomeri

Campo del
Frari

Fondamenta Sant'Anna

Ramo dei Nigoli

Calle del Forno

Calle delle Furlane

C. Giovanni J. Tiepolo

Calle Correra

Calle Catapati

Rio San Giuseppe

Secco
Marina

Corte
Solda

Corte
Zentili

Fondamenta San Giuseppe

Corte
Novella

Riva dei Sette Martiri

Bacino
San Marco

Largo Decorati
al Valore Civile

Giardini
Pubblici

Campo
San Giuseppe

Rio Terà San Giuseppe
Calle Paludo Sant'Antonio

Calle Paluda

Padiglione
Centrale

C. del
Montello

Campo
Monte Grappa

Giardini

Viale Trieste

Viale Trento

Giardini
della Biennale

Riva dei Partigiani

Rio della Tana

Rio San Giuseppe

Map continues
on next page

0   300 m
0   300 yds
© Copyright Time Out Group 2017

R   S   T   U   V

8

9

10

11

12

13

14

1

6

5

7

8

NORTHERN & WESTERN CASTELLO

▶ *Vaporetto Bacini, Celestia, Fondamente Nove, Ospedale, Rialto or San Zaccaria.*

The canal dividing the **Doge's Palace** (*see p92*) from the prison marks the end of the *sestiere* of San Marco. This means that the **Museo Diocesano di Arte Sacra** (*see p112*) and stately **San Zaccaria** (*see p114*), although closely associated with San Marco, actually belong to Castello. But the heart of northern and western Castello lies inland: **campo Santa Maria Formosa** (literally, 'Shapely St Mary'; *see p114*), a large, bustling, irregular-shaped square on the road to just about everywhere.

This square has all you could possibly need: a fine church, a market, a couple of bars and an undertaker. Nearby is the museum-cum-library of the **Fondazione Querini Stampalia** (*see p106*). Buzzing with locals and tourists, the campo is surrounded by *palazzi* that range in style from the very grand to the very homely. It is, in effect, Castello in miniature.

You'll have to trek west from here, to hard up against the border with the *sestiere* of San Marco, to visit the church of **Santa Maria della Fava** (*see p114*).

Southward from Santa Maria Formosa runs the busy shopping street of **ruga Giuffa**, named after either a community of Armenian merchants from Julfa, or a band of thugs – *gagiuffos* in 13th-century dialect – who used to terrorise the area. The first turn to the left off this street leads to the grandiose 16th-century **Palazzo Grimani** (*see p112*).

For more grandeur, head north to **campo Santi Giovanni e Paolo**. The Gothic red brick of the **Dominican church** (*see p111*) is beautifully set off by the glistening marble on the trompe l'oeil façade of the **Scuola Grande di San Marco** (*see p123*) – now housing the civic hospital, but with a series of magnificent rooms of the historic *scuola* open to the public – and the bronze of the equestrian **monument** to **Bartolomeo Colleoni** (*see p110*) gazing contemptuously down.

It's a short walk through narrow *calli* from Santi Giovanni e Paolo to the **fondamenta Nove**, where the northern lagoon comes into view. The cemetery island of **San Michele** (*see p202*) is always in sight, acting as a grim memento mori for patients in the hospital.

Eastwards from Santi Giovanni e Paolo, a road called barbaria delle Tole (the meaning of the name is shrouded in mystery: *tole* – *tavole* in Italian – are planks; *barbaria*, on the other hand, could refer to the wild appearance of the area, the presence of numerous barbers' shops, the barbaric behaviour of local carpenters, or the fact that the planks were destined mainly for the Barbary Coast) passes the Baroque church of **Santa Maria dei Derelitti** (*see p114*) by Baldassare Longhena, with its teetering façade adorned with leering faces. The church now belongs to an old people's home, which contains an exquisite 18th-century music room. Barbaria delle Tole leads into one of the least touristy areas of the city. Here, beyond the old gasworks, is austere **San Francesco della Vigna** (*see p112*).

Sights & museums

Monument to Bartolomeo Colleoni
Castello, campo Santi Giovanni e Paolo. Vaporetto Ospedale or Fondamente Nove. **Map** *p108 M7.*

Bartolomeo Colleoni was a famous *condottiere* (mercenary soldier) who left a legacy to the Republic on the condition that a statue be erected to him in front of St Mark's. Not wishing to clutter up St Mark's square with the statue, but loath to miss out on the money, Venice's wily rulers in 1479 gave him a space in front of the Scuola di San Marco. Geddit? To make up for this flagrant deception, the Republic did Colleoni proud, commissioning the Florentine artist Andrea Verrocchio to create this fine equestrian statue. On Verrocchio's death it was completed, together with the pedestal, wsby Alessandro Leopardi (1488-96). It is

---

❤ **Time to eat & drink**

Coffee the Venetian way
Da Bonifacio *p116*

Feast on some of Venice's best cicheti
Al Portego *p115*

Hidden seafood gem
Alle Testiere *p115*

Simple, local pizza
Dai Tosi Piccoli *p124*

❤ **Time to shop**

A cornucopia of chocolate delights
VizioVirtù *p117*

Hand-made masks with contemporary themes
Papier Mâché *p117*

High fashion behind bars
Banco Lotto N°10 *p125*

💜 Santi Giovanni e Paolo (San Zanipolo)

Castello, campo Santi Giovanni e Paolo (041 523 5913, www.basilicasantigiovanniepaolo. it). Vaporetto Ospedale or Fondamente Nove. **Open** *9am-6pm Mon-Sat; noon-6pm Sun.* **Admission** *€2.50, €1.25 reductions. No cards.* **Map** *p108 M7.*

Santi Giovanni e Paolo was founded by the Dominican order in 1246 but not finished until 1430. Between 1248 and 1778, 25 doges were buried here. The vast interior – 101 metres (331 feet) long – is a single spatial unit; the monks' choir was removed in the 17th century, leaving nothing to impede the view. Santi Giovanni e Paolo is packed with monuments to Venetian heroes as well as doges.

The entrance wall is dedicated to a series of funerary tributes to the Mocenigo family. The grandest – a masterpiece by Pietro, Tullio and Antonio Lombardo – belongs to Pietro Mocenigo, who died in 1476: the doge stands on his own sarcophagus, supported by three warriors representing the three ages of man. The religious reference above – the three Marys at the sepulchre – seems almost an afterthought.

The second altar on the right features an early polyptych by Giovanni Bellini (1465)

in its original frame. Continuing down the right side of the church, the huge Baroque mausoleum by Andrea Tirali (1708) has two Valier doges and a *dogaressa* taking a bow before a marble curtain. Tirali also designed the Chapel of St Dominic, notable for its splendid ceiling painting by Giovani Battista Piazzetta of *St Dominic in Glory* (c1727). The right transept has a painting of *St Antonine Distributing Alms* (1542) by Lorenzo Lotto. Above are splendid stained-glass windows, to designs by such Renaissance artists as Bartolomeo Vivarini and Cima da Conegliano (1470-1520).

On the right side of the chancel, with its Baroque high altar, is the Gothic tomb of Michele Morosini; opposite is the tomb of Doge Andrea Vendramin, by the Lombardo family.

The rosary chapel, off the left transept, was gutted by fire in 1867, just after two masterpieces by Titian and Bellini had been placed here for safe keeping. It now contains paintings and furnishings from suppressed churches. The ceiling paintings, *The Annunciation*, *Assumption* and *Adoration of the Shepherds*, are by Paolo Veronese. There is another Veronese, *Adoration* to the left of the door.

not a portrait, but a stylised representation of military pride and might. Colleoni's coat of arms (on the pedestal) includes three fig-like objects, a reference to his name, which in Italian sounds very similar to *coglioni* – testicles, of which this soldier was said to possess three.

❤ Museo della Fondazione Querini Stampalia

Castello 5252, campo Santa Maria Formosa (041 271 1411, www.querinistampalia.it). Vaporetto Rialto. **Open** *Museum 10am-8pm Tue-Sun.* **Admission** *€10; €8 reductions.* **Map** *p108 M9.*

This Renaissance *palazzo* and its art collection were bequeathed to Venice by Giovanni Querini, a 19th-century scientist, man of letters and silk producer from one of the city's most ancient families. Querini specified in his will that a library should be created here that would open 'particularly in the evenings for the convenience of scholars', and that the foundation should promote 'evening assemblies of scholars and scientists'. Today, the Querini Stampalia still exudes something of its founder's spirit: the first-floor library is a great place to study.

The ground floor and gardens, redesigned in the 1960s by Carlo Scarpa, offer one of Venice's few successful examples of modern architecture (*see p273* Scarpa in Venice). On the second floor, the gallery contains some important paintings, including Palma il Vecchio's portraits of Francesco and Paola Querini (for whom the palace was built in the 16th century), as well as a marvellous *Presentation in the Temple* by Giovanni Bellini, and a striking *Judith and Holofernes* by Vincenzo Catena. It also has a fascinating series of minor works, such as Gabriele Bella's 67 paintings of Venetian festivals, and a selection of Pietro Longhi's scenes of bourgeois life in 18th-century Venice. On the top floor is a gallery designed by Mario Botta, which hosts exhibitions of contemporary art. For library hours, *see p302*.

Museo Diocesano di Arte Sacra

Castello 4312, ponte della Canonica (041 522 9166, www.veneziaubt.org). Vaporetto San Zaccaria. **Open** *10am-6pm Tue-Sun.* **Admission** *€5, €2.50 reductions.* **No cards**. **Map** *p108 M10.*

This museum is situated in the ex-monastery of Sant'Apollonia, whose Romanesque cloisters are unique in Venice (you're meant to have a ticket to view the cloisters but staff will probably let you take a peek). The museum contains a number of works of art and clerical artefacts (reliquaries, chalices, missals, crucifixes) from suppressed churches and monasteries. The *quadreria* is notable

for two energetic paintings by Luca Giordano (*Christ and the Money-Lenders, Massacre of the Innocents*) and for three recently acquired works by Venice's great colourist Tintoretto. From the church of San Donato there is a fine altarpiece by Paolo Veneziano, *San Donato e Devoti*, with the saint in relief, in gilded and painted wood.

Palazzo Grimani

Castello 4858, ramo Grimani (041 241 1507, www.polomusealeveneto.beniculturali.it/musei/museo-di-palazzo-grimani). Vaporetto San Zaccaria. **Open** *10am-7pm Tue-Sun.* **Admission** *€5, €2.50 reductions (see also p65 Grimani & Ca' D'Oro).* **No cards**. **Map** *p108 M9.*

Inaugurated in December 2008 after a restoration process lasting 27 years, this magnificent *palazzo* in a tiny street off the ruga Giuffa has an original nucleus built by Antonio Grimani, doge of Venice, in the 1520s. However, it is most closely associated with his nephew Giovanni Grimani, cardinal and collector of antiquities. He enlarged and extended the palace, imposing a style of Roman classicism that is especially noticeable in the courtyard, and calling artists from central Italy, including Francesco Salviati and Federico Zuccari, to decorate it. The *palazzo* was conceived as a grand showcase for his fine collection of antiquities. Its fame was such that it was one of the buildings that Henry III of France insisted on seeing during his visit to Venice in 1574. Film buffs may remember the palace as the setting for the final gory scenes of Nicholas Roeg's film, *Don't Look Now*.

A grand staircase, modelled on the Scala d'Oro of the Doge's palace, leads up to the piano nobile. Highlights of the tour are the Michelangelo-esque Sala della Tribuna, with its multicoloured marbles, where the most important pieces of statuary were once exhibited (a Ganymede being borne off by Jupiter hangs from the ceiling as an example), and the Sala ai Fogliami, the ceiling of which is decorated with foliage and birds painted with scrupulous naturalistic accuracy.

▶ *Cardinal Grimani's collection of antiquities is now mostly in the Museo Archeologico; see p91.*

❤ San Francesco della Vigna

Castello, campo San Francesco della Vigna (041 520 6102). Vaporetto Celestia. **Open** *8am-12.30pm, 3-6pm daily.* **Map** *p108 Q8.*

San Francesco may be off the beaten track, but the long trek over to the down-at-heel area beyond the gasworks is worth it. In 1534, Jacopo Sansovino was asked by his friend

Well-heads Through the Ages

A once-practical architecture that still adds beauty to many a campo

It's estimated that the number of well-heads in Venice is now around 2,500 – a dramatic drop from the 6,782 counted by city authorities in 1858. The ground level in squares with wells at their centre is often raised, to keep salt water out during high tide. The paving is angled towards drains, where rain water would disappear, sink through filtering systems, and then find its way into cisterns beneath the well-heads. In 1882-84, pipes were laid to bring fresh water to the lagoon city from the mainland. With no practical purpose, monumental well-heads became just one more thing that poor Venetians could flog off to wealthy foreigners.

The most ancient
Corte Correr (between San Zaccaria and Santa Maria Formosa): a square well-head

dating from the ninth or tenth century; the sculpted rosettes are 15th century.

Byzantine
Corte del Remer (near San Giovanni Crisostomo): elegant arches in red Verona marble.

Gothic
Corte Veniera (off campo Santi Giovanni e Paolo): a fine specimen with ogival arches.
Ca' d'Oro (*see p130*): an elaborately carved late-Gothic well in the courtyard.

Renaissance
Campo Santi Giovanni e Paolo: an elegant well-head with festoon-draped putti.
Campo San Zaccaria, campo San Giovanni Crisostomo, campo della Maddalena: inspired by Corinthian capitals, these have delicate carvings of foliage.
Campo Angelo Raffaele: cylindrical, with charming carvings of Tobias and the guardian angel.

Mannerist and Baroque
Campo dei Frari: a large cylindrical well with a swelling waist.
Campo San Marcuola: a lavish well with lion heads and scrolled shields amid ornate curlicues.

19th century
Campo San Polo: this octagonal well-head is the largest in the city.

Doge Andrea Gritti to design this church for the Observant Franciscan order. The Tuscan architect opted for a deliberately simple style to match the monastic rule of its inhabitants. The façade (1568-72) was a later addition by Andrea Palladio; it is the first example of his system of superimposed temple fronts.

The dignified, solemn interior consists of a single broad nave with side chapels. The Cappella Giustiniani on the left of the chancel holds a marvellous cycle of bas-reliefs by Pietro Lombardo and school, moved here from an earlier church on the same site. In the nave, the fourth chapel on the right has a *Resurrection* attributed to Paolo Veronese. In the right transept is a fruity, flowery *Madonna and Child Enthroned* (c1450), a signed work by the Greek artist Antonio da Negroponte. From the left transept, a door leads into the Cappella Santa, which contains a *Madonna and Saints* (1507) by Giovanni Bellini (perhaps assisted by Girolamo da Santacroce). From here, it is possible to

make a detour and visit two of the church's peaceful Renaissance cloisters.

Back in the church, the fifth chapel on the left is home to Paolo Veronese's first Venetian commission, the stunning *Holy Family with Saints John the Baptist, Anthony the Abbot and Catherine* (c1551). The third chapel has trompe l'œil frescoes in chiaroscuro by GB Tiepolo (1743, recently restored). The second chapel has three powerful statues of saints Roch,

> **In the know**
> **Giulia Lama**
>
> Giulia Lama, whose painting in **Santa Maria Formosa** (*see p114*) is one of only a few by women displayed in the city, has been described as a pupil of Giovani Battista Piazzetta. But Piazzetta's only known portrait from life (in the Thyssen-Bornemisza collection in Madrid) is of none other than Giulia Lama: its tenderness suggests she was more than a pupil.

Anthony the Abbot and Sebastian (1565) by Alessandro Vittoria.

Santa Maria dei Derelitti
(Ospedaletto)

Castello 6691, barbaria delle Tole (041 271 9012, www.scalacontarinidelbovolo.com/it/sala-della-musica/). Vaporetto Fondamente Nove. **Open** *Church 3.30-6.30pm Thur-Sun. Music room by appt.* **Admission** *(incl guided tour) €2.* **No cards.** **Map** *p108 N8.*

The church was built in 1575 within the complex of the Ospedaletto, a hospice for the poor and aged. There is still an old people's home here. Between 1668 and 1674 Baldassare Longhena gave the church its staggering façade, complete with bulging telamons (architectural supports in the shape of male figures) and leering faces. The interior contains interesting 18th-century paintings, including one of Giambattista Tiepolo's earliest works, *The Sacrifice of Isaac* (fourth painting over the arch on the right). The hospice contains an elegant music room with charming frescoes by Jacopo Guarana (1776), depicting girl musicians performing for Apollo; the scene is stolen by a dog in the foreground being tempted with a doughnut. There is also a spiral staircase, apparently unsupported, designed by Sardi and completed by Longhena.

Santa Maria della Fava

Castello, campo della Fava (041 522 4601). Vaporetto Rialto. **Open** *9.30-11.30am, 4.30-7pm Mon-Sat; 4.30-7pm Sun.* **Map** *p108 L9.*

St Mary of the Bean – the name is said to refer to a popular bean cake produced by a bakery that stood nearby – is on one of the quieter routes between the Rialto and San Marco. This 18th-century church is worth visiting for two paintings by the city's greatest artists of that period, which neatly illustrate their contrasting temperaments. Tiepolo's *Education of the Virgin* (first altar on the right) is an early work, painted when he was still under the influence of Giovanni Battista Piazzetta; but the bright colours

---

In the know
Nuns behaving badly

Attached to the church of **San Zaccaria** (see *right*) was a convent where aristocrats with more titles than cash dumped female offspring to avoid having to rake together a dowry. The nuns were not best known for their piety. While the tales of rampant licentiousness may have been exaggerated, a painting in **Ca' Rezzonico** (see *p175*) shows that such convents were more worldly salon than place of contemplation.

---

and touchingly human relationships of the figures are nonetheless in contrast with the sombre browns and reds of the latter's *Virgin and Child with St Philip Neri* (second altar on the left). In Piazzetta's more earnest painting, which still bears traces of Counter-Reformation gravity, the lily, bishop's mitre and cardinals' hats show the worldly honours rejected by the saint.

Santa Maria Formosa

Castello, campo Santa Maria Formosa (041 275 0462, www.chorusvenezia.org). Vaporetto San Zaccaria or Rialto. **Open** *10.30am-4.30pm Mon-Sat.* **Admission** *€3 (or Chorus; see p65).* **No cards.** **Map** *p108 M9.*

In the pre-Freudian seventh century, St Magnus, Bishop of Oderzo, had a vision in which the Virgin appeared as a buxom (*formosa*) matron, and a church was built in this bustling square to commemorate the fact. The present church was designed by Mauro Codussi in 1492 and has something fittingly bulgy about it. Codussi retained the Greek cross plan of the original in his Renaissance design. It has two façades, one on the canal (1542), the other on the campo (1604). The Baroque campanile has a grotesque mask, now recognised as a portrait of a victim of the disfiguring Von Recklinghausen's disease.

The first chapel in the right aisle has a triptych painted by Bartolomeo Vivarini, *Madonna of the Misericordia* (1473), which includes a realistic *Birth of the Virgin*. The altar in the right transept was the chapel of the Scuola dei Bombardieri, with an altarpiece of St Barbara, patron saint of gunners (a heaven-sent lightning bolt saved Barbara's life when it struck her father as he prepared to kill her) by Palma il Vecchio. Half-hidden by the elaborate high altar is one of the few works on show in Venice by a female artist: an 18th-century *Allegory of the Foundation of the Church, with Venice, St Magnus and St Maria Formosa* by Giulia Lama.

San Zaccaria

Castello, campo San Zaccaria (041 522 1257). Vaporetto San Zaccaria. **Open** *10am-noon, 4-6pm Mon-Sat; 4-6pm Sun.* **Map** *p108 N10.*

Founded in the ninth century, this church has always had close ties with the Doge's Palace. Eight Venetian rulers were buried in the first church on the site, one was killed outside and another died while seeking sanctuary inside. The body of St Zacharias, the father of John the Baptist, was brought to Venice in the ninth century; it still lies under the second altar on the right.

The current church was begun in 1444 but took decades to complete, making it a curious combination of Gothic and

Renaissance. The interior is built on a Gothic plan – the apse, with its ambulatory and radiating cluster of tall-windowed chapels, is unique in Venice – but the architectural decoration is predominantly Renaissance. The façade is a happy mixture of the two styles.

Inside, every inch is covered with paintings, though of varying quality. Giovanni Bellini's magnificent *Madonna and Four Saints* (1505), on the second altar on the left, leaps out of the confusion. In the right aisle is the entrance to the Chapel of St Athanasius (admission €1), which contains carved 15th-century wooden stalls and *The Birth of St John the Baptist*, an early work by Tintoretto, and a striking *Flight into Egypt* by Giandomenico Tiepolo. The adjoining Chapel of St Tarasius was the apse of an earlier church that occupied this site; it has three altarpieces (1443) by Antonio Vivarini and Giovanni d'Alemagna – stiff, iconic works in elaborate Gothic frames.

The frescoed saints in the fan vault are by the Florentine artist Andrea del Castagno. Though painted a year before the altarpieces, they have a realistic vitality that is wholly Renaissance in spirit. In front of the altar are remains of the mosaic floor from the early Romanesque church; the tenth-century crypt below is usually flooded.

Scuola Grande di San Marco
Castello, campo Santi Giovanni e Paolo (041 529 4323, www.scuolagrandesanmarco.it). Vaporetto Ospedale or Fondamente Nove. **Open** *9.30am-5.30pm Tue-Sun.* **Admission** *free.* **Map** *p108 M7.*

Once home to one of the six *scuole grandi* – the confraternities of Venice (*see p164* Scuole Stories) – this is now occupied mainly by the city hospital. But late in 2013 some of the finest of the *scuola* rooms were opened to the public, beautifully restored.

The *scuola*'s façade by Pietro Lombardo and Giovanni Buora (1487-90) was completed by Mauro Codussi (1495). It features magnificent trompe l'oeil panels by Tullio and Antonio Lombardo representing two episodes from the life of St Mark and his faithful lion. Over the doorway is a lunette of *St Mark with the Brethren of the School* attributed to Bartolomeo Bon.

Inside, the immense column-punctuated entrance to the *scuola* is also the entrance to the hospital: surely one of the grandest hospital entrances in the world. At the top of a staircase designed by Mauro Codussi, the chapter house has a magnificent gilded coffered ceiling. Cases here contain ancient manuscripts pertaining to medical practice, and historical records of the Venetian hospital. On the walls are excellent reproductions of works done for the *scuola*

but carried off over the centuries: Palma il Giovane's *Christ in Glory with St Mark* hangs over the altar, and around the walls are four magnificent scenes from the life of St Mark by the Tintoretto clan. The Sala dell'Albergo, which contains the hospital's ancient library, is dominated by a reproduction of *St Mark Preaching in Alessandria* by Giovanni and Gentile Bellini. Originals of some of the *scuola*'s art works can be seen in the Accademia gallery (*see p180*).

Restaurants

▶ *See also p116* **I Tre Mercanti.**

Alla Basilica €
Castello 4255, calle degli Albanesi (041 522 0524, www.allabasilicavenezia.it). Vaporetto San Zaccaria. **Meals served** *noon-3pm Tue-Sun.* **Map** *p108 M10* ❸ *Traditional Italian*

Run by the diocese of Venice, Alla Basilica has all the charm of a company canteen, and the solid home cooking will win no prizes. But at a fixed price of €16 for a full meal (wine is extra), it's a cheap way to fill an empty space, and it's brilliantly central, located (as the name implies) right behind St Mark's basilica. Groups can eat here in the evenings too if they book ahead.

❤ Alle Testiere €€€
Castello 5801, calle del Mondo Novo (041 522 7220, www.osterialletestiere.it). Vaporetto Rialto. **Meals served** *noon-2pm, 7-10.30pm Tue-Sat. Closed late Dec-mid Jan & late July-Aug.* **Map** *p108 L9* ❹ *Seafood*

This tiny restaurant is today one of the hottest culinary tickets in Venice. There are so few seats that staff do two sittings each evening; booking for the later one (at 9pm) will ensure a more relaxed meal. Bruno, the chef, offers creative variations on Venetian seafood; *caparossoli* (local clams) sautéed in ginger and John Dory fillet sprinkled with aromatic herbs in citrus sauce are two mouth-watering examples. Sommelier Luca guides diners around a small but well-chosen wine list. The desserts, too, are spectacular.

❤ Al Portego €€
Castello 6015, calle Malvasia (041 522 9038). Vaporetto Rialto. **Open** *11.30am-3pm, 5.30-10pm daily.* **No cards. Map** *p108 L8* ❺ *Bacaro*

With its wooden decor and happy drinkers in the *calle* outside, this rustic *osteria* is every inch the traditional Venetian *bacaro*. Alongside a big barrel of wine, the bar is loaded down with a selection of *cicheti*, from meatballs and stuffed squid to *nervetti* (Milanese salad) stewed with onions. In a second room, simple pasta dishes and soups and *secondi*, such as *fegato alla veneziana* (liver), are served up for early lunch and dinner. A glass and a plateful of *cicheti* at the bar should cost around €10-€15, sitting down more than double that.

Osteria di Santa Marina €€€
Castello 5911, campo Santa Marina (041 528 5239, www.osteriadisantamarina.com). Vaporetto Rialto. Meals served 7.30-9.30pm Mon; 12.30-2.30pm, 7.30-9.30pm Tue-Sat. Closed 2wks Jan. Map p108 L8 ❾ *Modern Venetian*

This upmarket *osteria* in pretty campo Santa Marina has the kind of professional service and standards that are too often lacking in Venice, and the ambience and the high level of the seafood-oriented cuisine justify the price tag. Raw fish features strongly among the antipasti; *primi* give local tradition a creative twist in dishes such as the turbot- and mussel-filled ravioli in celery sauce. The joy of this place is in the detail: the bread is all home-made; a taster course turns up just when you were about to ask what happened to the *branzino* (sea bass). Book ahead.

Cafés, bars & gelaterie

Boutique del Gelato
Castello 5727, salizzada San Lio (041 522 3283). Vaporetto Rialto. Open Feb-May, Oct, Nov 10am-8.30pm daily. June-Sept 10am-11.30pm daily. Closed Dec-Jan. No cards. Map p108 L9 ❷

Be prepared to be patient at this tiny outlet on busy salizzada San Lio because there's always a huge crowd waiting to be served. The choice of flavours is limited but the quality is high. And though the staff at peak times are not always charming, it's worth the wait.

♥ Da Bonifacio
Castello 4237, calle degli Albanesi (041 522 7507). Vaporetto San Zaccaria. Open 6.30am-7.30pm Mon-Wed, Fri; 7.30am-7.30pm Sat, Sun. No cards. Map p108 M10 ❸

In a narrow *calle* behind the Danieli Hotel, this is a firm favourite with Venetians, whom you'll find outside the entrance in great numbers, waiting to squeeze inside for a coffee, drink and something from the cake cabinet. As well as a tempting array of snacks and traditional cakes such as *mammalucchi* (deep-fried batter cakes with candied fruit), Da Bonifacio is famous for its creative *fritelle* (fried dough balls, with wild berry, chocolate, almond or apple fillings), which appear in January and remain through Carnevale.

La Mascareta
Castello 5183, calle lunga Santa Maria Formosa (041 523 0744, www.ostemaurolorenzon.it). Open 7pm-2am daily. Map p108 M8 ❹

Genial, bow-tied Mauro Lorenzon keeps hundreds of wines – including some rare vintages – in his cellars, serving them up by the bottle or glass along with plates of cheeses, seafood, cold meats or *crostini*. His current kick is natural unfiltered wine – but you might prefer to insist on the more traditional stuff. At mealtimes, the pressure will be on to sit down and eat a proper meal, but though the food here is good, it's not exceptional and prices are high: it's better to stick with the drink and the personality-led Lorenzon experience.

Shops & services

I Tre Mercanti
Castello 5364, campo de la Guerra (041 522 2901, www.itremercanti.it). Vaporetto Rialto. Open 11am-7.30pm daily. Map p108 L9 ❶ *Food & drink*

There's an interesting selection here of seriously good Italian food and wine, much of it from local producers but some from further afield. Stock includes excellent olive oils, preserved vegetables, pastas and rice – none of them cheap but all of them chosen with an eye to quality. At a street-side window, passersby can pick up sandwiches and rolls: a choice of locally made breads with 30-odd fillings. And there are gourmet variations on tiramisu to go as well. (A couple of perching-tables inside mean you can consume on the premises if you prefer.)

Anticlea Antiquariato
Castello 4719A, calle San Provolo (041 528 6946). Vaporetto San Zaccaria. Open 10.30am-1.30pm, 2-6pm Mon-Sat. Map p108 N10 ❷ *Antiques*

Packed with curious antique treasures, as well as an outstanding selection of Venetian glass beads.

VizioVirtù

Filippi Editore Venezia

Castello 5284, calle Casseleria (041 523 6916, www.libreriaeditricefilippi.com). Vaporetto San Zaccaria. **Open** *9am-12.30pm, 3-7.30pm Mon-Sat.* **Map** *p108 L9* ❹ *Books & music*

Venice's longest-running publishing house has over 400 titles on Venetian history and folklore – all limited editions in Italian. The beautiful tomes can also be ordered online.

Giovanna Zanella

Castello 5641, calle Carminati (041 523 5500, www.giovannazanella.it). Vaporetto Rialto. **Open** *9.30am-1pm, 3-7pm Mon-Sat.* **Map** *p108 L8* ❺ *Shoes & accessories*

Venetian designer-cobbler Giovanna Zanella creates a fantastic line of handmade shoes in an extraordinary variety of styles and colours. A pair of shoes costs €450 to €1,000. There are bags and other accessories too.

Kalimala

Castello 5387, salizada San Lio (041 528 3596, www.kalimala.it). Vaporetto Rialto. **Open** *9.30am-7.30pm Mon-Sat, 10.30am-7.30pm Sun.* **Map** *p108 L9* ❻ *Shoes & accessories*

Unlike Giovanna Zanella (*see left*) and Daniela Ghezzo (*see p100*), Kalimala is a Venetian cobbler whose shoes are stylish without being quirky, and the prices are less idiosyncratic too (from about €80 upwards). Handmade in beautiful Tuscan leather, in a wonderful range of colours, Kalimala's range covers boots, loafers and sandals, plus bags and tablet holders.

❤ Papier Mâché

Castello 5174B, calle lunga Santa Maria Formosa (041 522 9995, www.papiermache. it). Vaporetto Rialto. **Open** *9am-7.30pm Mon-Sat; 10am-7pm Sun.* **Map** *p108 M8* ❼ *Gifts & souvenirs*

This workshop uses traditional techniques to create contemporary masks inspired by the works of Klimt, Kandinsky, Tiepolo and Carpaccio. It stocks ceramics and painted mirrors too.

❤ VizioVirtù

Castello 5988, calle Forneri (041 275 0149, www.viziovirtu.com). Vaporetto Rialto. **Open** *10am-7.30pm daily.* **Map** *p108 L8* ❾ *Food & drink*

VizioVirtù serves up plenty of gluttonous pleasures. Here, you can witness chocolate being made while nibbling on a spicy praline or sipping an iced chocolate. This cornucopia of cocoa has unusual delights such as blocks of chocolate Parmesan, and cocoa tagliatelle (the chef recommends teaming it with game sauces).

SOUTHERN & EASTERN CASTELLO

▶ *Vaporetto Arsenale, Giardini, San Pietro, San Zaccaria or Sant'Elena.*

The low-rise, clustered buildings of working-class eastern Castello housed the employees of the **Arsenale** (*see p118*) – Venice's docklands. Also here were Venice's foreign communities, as local churches testify: there's **San Giorgio dei Greci** (Greeks; *see p122*), with its adjoining **Museo dell'Istituto Ellenico** (*see p119*) icon museum; and there's also the **Scuola di San Giorgio degli Schiavoni** (Slavs; *see p123*), with its captivating cycle of paintings by Vittorio Carpaccio. The great promenade along the lagoon – the riva degli Schiavoni – was named after the same community.

Inland from the *riva* is the quaint Gothic church of **San Giovanni in Bragora** (*see p123*) in the square of the same name. Antonio Vivaldi was born on this campo on 4 March 1678, though it's not known in which house. Further back in the warren of streets is the church of **Sant'Antonin** – undoubtedly the only church in Venice in which an elephant has been shot. The unfortunate animal escaped from a circus on the *riva* in 1819 and took refuge in the church, only to be finished off by gunners summoned from the Arsenale.

Back on the riva degli Schiavoni is the church of **La Pietà** (*see p120*), where Vivaldi was choir master. In calle della Pietà, alongside the church, is the **Piccolo Museo della Pietà** (*see p120*), dedicated to the Pietà (a foundling home) and the composer.

Head on eastwards past the **Ca' di Dio**, once a hostel for pilgrims setting out for the Holy Land and now an old people's home, and the *forni pubblici* (public bakeries), where the biscuit (*bis-cotto*, literally 'twice-cooked') – that favourite, scurvy-encouraging staple of ancient mariners – was reputedly invented.

Crossing the bridge over the rio dell'Arsenale, you can see the grand Renaissance entrance to the **Arsenale** shipyard (*see p118*). Once a hive of empire-building industry, it's now an expanse of empty warehouses and docks, though parts have been beautifully restored and are used for Biennale-related events (*see p121*).

Just beyond the rio dell'Arsenale, the model-packed **Museo Storico Navale** (*see p119*) lovingly charts Venice's shipbuilding history. A little further on, the wide and lively **via Garibaldi** forks off to the left. This road, like the nearby *giardini pubblici* (public gardens), is a legacy of French occupation in the early 19th century. Via

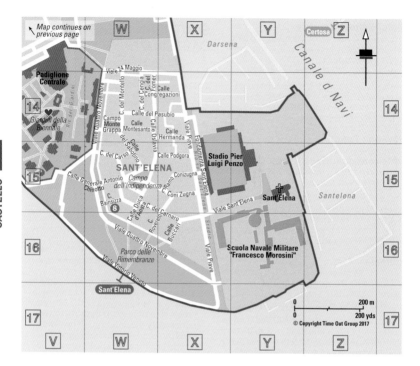

Garibaldi leads eventually to the island of **San Pietro**, where the former cathedral (*see p123*) stands among modest, washing-garlanded houses.

Back on the lagoon, the riva degli Schiavoni changes its name after the rio dell'Arsenale to become the **riva dei Sette Martiri**, named after seven partisans executed here in 1944 (a striking statue located by the Giardini vaporetto stop recalls the event). Just beyond here, the shady **Giardini Pubblici** occupy the place where four suppressed convents once stood. A Renaissance archway from one has been reconstructed in a corner of the gardens. In another corner lies the entrance to the **Giardini della Biennale** (*see p121*); the international pavilions, ranging in style from the seedy to the pompous, used to remain locked up except for those few weeks every two years when a major contemporary art bonanza would be set up; other more recently created events mean the pavilions now get more frequent airings.

The *riva* ends in the sedately residential district of **Sant'Elena**. This, in Venetian terms, is a 'modern' district. In 1872 work began to fill in the *barene* (marshes) that lay between the edge of the city and the ancient island of Sant'Elena, with its charming Gothic church (*see p122*). Also tucked away

here is Venice's football stadium – though fans are hoping for a new mainland ground sometime in the not-too-distant future (*see p122* Stadium Controversy).

Sights & museums

♥ Arsenale

Castello, campo dell'Arsenale (www.comune. venezia.it/content/arsenale-di-venezia). Vaporetto Arsenale. **Map** *p108.*

The word *arsenale* derives from the Arabic *dar sina'a*, meaning 'house of industry': the industry, and efficiency, of Venice's Arsenale was legendary: the *arsenalotti* could assemble a galley in just a few hours. Shipbuilding activities began here in the 12th century; at the height of the city's power, 16,000 men were employed. Production expanded until the 16th century, when Venice entered its slow but inexorable economic decline.

Porta Magna, the imposing land gateway by Antonio Gambello (1460) in campo dell'Arsenale, is the first example of Renaissance classical architecture to appear in Venice, although the capitals of the columns are 11th-century Veneto-Byzantine. The winged lion gazing down from above holds a book without the traditional words *Pax tibi Marce* (Peace to you, Mark) –

Arsenale

unsuitable in this military context. Outside the gate, four lions keep guard. Those immediately flanking the terrace were looted from Athens in 1687; the larger one stood at the entrance to the port of Piraeus and bears runic inscriptions on its side, hacked there in the 11th century by Norse mercenary soldiers in Byzantine service. The third lion, whose head is clearly less ancient than its body, came from Delos and was placed here to commemorate the recapture of Corfu in 1716.

Shipbuilding activity ceased in 1917, after which the complex remained largely unused navy property until 2013 when much of it returned to town council hands... not that they're entirely sure what to do with it now. It is destined, authorities say, to become a 'scientific and cultural hub'. Exhibitions and performances will continue to be held in some of the cavernous spaces within its walls: the **Artiglierie** and the grandiose **Gaggiandre**, dockyards designed by Sansovino. In campo della Tana, on the other side of the rio dell'Arsenale, is the entrance to the **Corderia** (rope factory), an extraordinary building 316 metres (1,038 feet) long. This vast space is used to house large swathes of the Biennale (*see p121*). In May the **Mare Maggio** sea-, boat- and travel-themed festival (www. maremaggio.it) opens up much of the Arsenale to the curious.

Museo dell'Istituto Ellenico

Castello 3412, ponte dei Greci (041 522 6581, www.istitutoellenico.org). Vaporetto San Zaccaria. Open 9am-5pm daily. Admission €4; €2 reductions. No cards. Map p108 P9.

The adjacent church of San Giorgio dei Greci was a focal point for the Greek community, which was swollen by refugees after the Turkish capture of Constantinople in 1453. There have been a Greek church, college and school at this location since the end of the 15th century. The oldest piece in the museum's collection is the 14th-century altar cross behind the ticket desk. The icons on display mainly follow the dictates of the Cretan school, with no descent into naturalism, though some of the 17th- and 18th-century pieces make jarring and often kitsch compromises with Western art. The best pieces are those that are resolute in their hieratic (traditional-style Greek) flatness, such as *Christ in Glory among the Apostles* and the Great Deesis from the first half of the 14th century. St George is a popular subject: there is one splendid painting of him dating from the late 15th century. Also on display are priestly robes and other Greek-rite paraphernalia.

▶ *For information on the church itself, see p122.*

Museo Storico Navale

Castello 2148, campo San Biagio (041 244 1399, www.visitmuve.it/it/musei/museo-storico-navale-di-venezia/). Vaporetto Arsenale. Closed at time of writing. Padiglione delle Navi: Castello 2162, rio della Tana. Open 8.45am-5pm daily. Admission €5. Map p108 R10 & R12.

This museum dedicated to ships and shipbuilding continues an old tradition:

under the Republic, the models created for shipbuilders in the final design stages were kept in the Arsenale. Some of the models on display are from that collection. The museum was undergoing repairs as this guide went to press, but anyone yearning for a bit of naval exposure can visit the nearby **Padiglione delle Navi** ('ships pavilion'), a huge warehouse (worth a visit in its own right) housing a motley assortment of vessels from different eras.

The ground floor of the museum itself has warships, cannons, explosive speedboats and dodgy-looking manned torpedoes, plus a display of ships through the ages. On the walls are relief models in wood and papier mâché, dating from the 16th to the 18th century, of Venetian fortresses and possessions.

On the first floor are ornamental trimmings and naval instruments, plus a series of impressive models of Venetian ships. Here, too, is a richly gilded model of the Bucintoro, the doges' state barge. The second floor has uniforms, more up-to-date sextants and astrolabes, and models of modern Italian navy vessels. On the third floor there are models of Chinese, Japanese and Korean junks, cruise ships and liners, and a series of fascinating naïve votive paintings, giving thanks for shipwrecks averted or survived.

A room at the back has a display of gondolas, including a 19th-century example with a cabin, and the last privately owned covered gondola in Venice, which belonged to the larger-than-life art collector and bon vivant Peggy Guggenheim.

Piccolo Museo della Pietà 'Antonio Vivaldi'

*Castello 3701, calle della Pietà (041 522 2171, www.pietavenezia.org). Vaporetto Arsenale or San Zaccaria. **Open** by appt only. **Admission** €3. **No cards**. Map p108 P11.*

This museum chronicles the activities of the Ospedale della Pietà, the orphanage where Antonio Vivaldi was violin teacher and choir master. Numerous documents recount such details as the rules for admission of children and the rations of food allotted them; the 'Daughters of the Choir' received more generous portions of food and wine. There is also a selection of period instruments.

La Pietà (Santa Maria della Visitazione)

*Castello, riva degli Schiavoni (041 522 2171, www.pietavenezia.org). Vaporetto San Zaccaria. **Open** 10am-6pm. **Admission** €3. Map p108 P11.*

By the girls' orphanage of the same name, the church of La Pietà was famous for its music. Antonio Vivaldi, violin and choir master here

❤ La Biennale

Information 041 521 8711, www.labiennale.org. **Date** *May/June-Nov.*

Officially known as l'Esposizione internazionale d'arte della Biennale di Venezia, Venice's Biennale was responsible for putting the city on the map of international contemporary art back in 1895. Since then this massive exhibition has been 'invading' Venice throughout the summer of every odd year.

It was the first (its closest rival Sao Paolo didn't start until 1951), and to this day it remains one of the few to include national exhibits as part of a wider-ranging collective event.

In 1980, Biennale organisers decided to fill in even years with an architecture equivalent – a far lower-profile event to start off with but now as extravagant, sprawling and (almost as) well-attended as its arty sister.

From the start, the Biennale spread over the leafy **Giardini del Biennale** park in eastern Castello, where some 30 small national pavilions cluster around the far larger central pavilion – previously Italy's Biennale home but now renovated and called the **Palazzo delle Esposizioni**, housing the Biennale archive and part of the themed event.

Much more of the curated section of the Biennale now straggles into the glorious spaces of Venice's **Arsenale** (*see p118*), where each year an internationally renowned artist, architect, critic or expert selects exhibits around a theme of his or her choosing. And all over town, shows mounted by nations with no foothold in the Giardini and no space in the Arsenale occupy *palazzi*, galleries, gardens and other settings, opening up rarely glimpsed spaces to a curious public in a three-month art jamboree.

Unusually for Italy, the Biennale has a US-style financial model mixing sponsorship, public funds and income generated by ticket sales and merchandising. With money from sources other than the public purse, this organisation enjoys an autonomy from political manoeuvring envied by many.

Installation by Thu Van Tran at the 57th Biennale

Stadium Controversy

Plans to replace a decrepit but distinctive ground

As you round the easternmost point of Venice proper, a strange sight comes into view. The dark, square bell tower (a 1950s reconstruction of a 16th-century structure) of the church of Sant'Elena peers down at banks of arc lights and what looks like a pile of rusting scaffolding. This is the **Stadio Pierluigi Penzo**, home to Venezia FC. And yes, when it comes down to it... it's a pile of scaffolding.

Under the leadership of manager Filippo Inzaghi, of Milan fame, the club has regained some of its luck. Since its one glorious season in Serie A (in 1998/9), its grip on the higher rungs of Italian football had slipped, but at the time of writing, in 2017, it had just achieved early promotion into Serie B. The stadium, however – which can only be reached on foot or by boat – is now in urgent need of renewal.

If the Stadio Penzo seems picturesquely, forlornly Venetian to those few intrepid visitors who make it this far (Japanese fans arrived by the dozen for matches in Venezia's Serie A season when Hidetosha Nakata was on loan to the lagoon side) it is merely an inconvenience for jaded mainlanders who would rather drive their cars up to the stadium entrance.

The blueprint for a state-of-the-art, eco-friendly, 30,000-seater Green Venice Arena was fully drawn up by former owner Jurij Korablin several years ago. But attempts to agree with local authorities on construction of the grounds in Tessera, near Venice airport, had run up against a solid wall of local politicking. New president Joe Tacopina has had more luck in pitching his design to the current administration (mayor Luigi Brugnaro once sat on the board), and construction on the new complex is expected to start in 2019.

Until such time as the new ground is ready, fans will continue to board the dedicated vaporetti and chug across the lagoon to Sant'Elena for home matches. To join them, you must purchase tickets in advance: online on the team's website (www.veneziafc.club) or in person in authorised retail points (see website). Note that tickets are personal: you must present a valid ID document for each match-goer when purchasing (or fill in ID details when buying online). Take the same ID with you to the stadium: the details on your ticket will be checked against your document as you enter.

Stadio Pierluigi Penzo

---

from 1703 until 1740, wrote some of his finest music for his young charges. The present building, by Giorgio Massari, was begun in 1745, four years after Vivaldi's death. Music inspired its architecture: the interior, reached through a vestibule resembling a foyer, has the oval shape of a concert hall. The ceiling has a *Coronation of the Virgin* (1755) by Giambattista Tiepolo.

▶ *For concerts held in the church, see p250.*

Sant'Elena

Castello 3, Servi di Maria, campo Chiesa Sant' Elena (041 520 5144). Vaporetto Sant'Elena. **Open** *5-7pm Mon-Sat.* **Map** *p118 Y15.*

The red-brick Gothic church of Sant'Elena contains no great works of art (the church was deconsecrated in 1807, turned into an iron foundry, and not opened again until 1928) but its austere Gothic nakedness is a relief after all that Venetian ornament. In the chapel to the right of the entrance lies the body of St Helen, the irascible mother of the Emperor Constantine and finder of the True Cross. (Curiously enough, her body is also to be found in the Aracoeli church in Rome.) To the left are the charming cloisters and rose garden tended by the three monks left in the monastery.

San Giorgio dei Greci

Castello, fondamenta dei Greci (041 522 6581, www.istitutoellenico.org). Vaporetto San Zaccaria. **Open** *9am-12.30pm, 2.30-4.30pm Mon, Wed-Sat.* **Map** *p108 P10.*

By the time the church of San Giorgio was begun in 1539, the Greeks were well established in Venice and held a major stake in the city's scholarly printing presses. Designed by Sante Lombardo, the church's interior is fully Orthodox in layout, with its women's gallery, and high altar behind the iconostasis. A heady smell of incense lends the church an Eastern mystique, enhanced by dark-bearded priests in flowing robes. The campanile is decidedly lopsided. Next to the church are the Scuola di San Nicolò (now the **Museo dell'Istituto Ellenico**) and the Collegio Flangini (now seat of the Istituto Ellenico di Studi Bizantini e post-Bizantini), both by Baldassare Longhena.

▶ *For information about the museum, see p119.*

San Giovanni in Bragora

Castello, campo Bandiera e Moro (041 520 5906). Open 9am-noon, 3.30-5pm Mon-Sat. Map p108 Q11.

San Giovanni in Bragora (the meaning of *bragora* is obscure) is an intimate Gothic structure. The church where composer Antonio Vivaldi was baptised (a copy of the entry in the register is on show), San Giovanni also contains some very fine paintings. Above the high altar is the recently restored *Baptism of Christ* (1492-95) by Cima da Conegliano, with a landscape recalling the countryside around the painter's home town of Conegliano. A smaller Cima, on the right of the sacristy door, shows *Constantine Holding the Cross and St Helen* (1502). On the same wall, just before the second altar, is a triptych by Bartolomeo Vivarini, *Madonna and Child and Two Saints*, dated 1478. The church also contains three paintings by his nephew Alvise Vivarini, one of them a splendidly heroic *Resurrection* (1498); the figure of Christ in this picture is based on a statue of Apollo in the Museo Archeologico (*see p91*).

San Pietro in Castello

Castello, campo San Pietro (041 275 0462, www.chorusvenezia.org). Vaporetto San Pietro. Open 10.30am-4pm Mon, 10.30am-4.30pm Tue-Sat. Admission €3 (or Chorus; see p65). No cards. Map p108 V10.

Until 1807, San Pietro in Castello was the cathedral of Venice, and its remote position testifies to the determination of the Venetian government to keep the clerical authorities far from the centre of temporal power. There has probably been a church here since the seventh century, but the present building was constructed in 1557 to a design by Palladio.

The body of the first patriarch of Venice, San Lorenzo Giustiniani, is preserved in an urn elaborately supported by angels above the high altar, a magnificent piece of Baroque theatricality designed by Baldassare Longhena (1649). In the right-hand aisle is the so-called 'St Peter's Throne', a delicately carved marble work from Antioch containing a Muslim funerary stele and verses from

the Koran. The Baroque Vendramin Chapel in the left transept was again designed by Longhena, and contains a *Virgin and Child* by the prolific Neapolitan Luca Giordano. Outside the entrance to the chapel is a late work by Paolo Veronese, *Saints John the Evangelist, Peter and Paul.*

♥ Scuola di San Giorgio degli Schiavoni

Castello 3259A, calle dei Furlani (041 522 8828). Vaporetto Arsenale or San Zaccaria. Open 2.45-6pm Mon; 9.15am-1pm, 2.45-6pm Tue-Sat; 9.15am-1pm Sun. Admission €5; €3 reductions. No cards. Map p108 P9.

The *schiavoni* were Venice's Slav inhabitants, who had become so numerous and influential by the end of the 15th century that they could afford to build this *scuola* (or meeting house) by the side of their church, San Giovanni di Malta. The *scuola* houses one of Vittore Carpaccio's two great Venetian picture cycles. In 1502, eight years after completing his St Ursula cycle (now in the Accademia, *see p180*), Carpaccio was commissioned to paint a series of canvases illustrating the lives of the Dalmatian saints George, Tryphone and Jerome. In the tradition of the early Renaissance *istoria* (narrative painting cycle), there is a wealth of incidental detail, such as the decomposing virgins in *St George and the Dragon*, or the little dog in the painting of *St Augustine in his Study* (receiving the news of the death of St Jerome in a vision) – with its paraphernalia of humanism (astrolabe, shells, sheet music, archaeological fragments).

It's worth venturing upstairs to see what the meeting hall of a working *scuola* looks like. San Giorgio degli Schiavoni still provides scholarships, distributes charity and acts as a focal point for the Slav community. Opening hours are notoriously changeable.

Restaurants

Al Covo €€

Castello 3968, campiello della Pescaria (041 522 3812, www.ristorantealcovo.com). Vaporetto Arsenale. Meals served 12.45-2pm, 7.30-10pm Mon, Tue, Fri-Sun. Closed mid Dec-mid Jan & 2wks Aug. Map p108 Q11 ❷ *Seafood*

Though Al Covo is hidden in an alley behind the riva degli Schiavoni, it's very much on the international gourmet map. Its reputation is based on a dedication to serving the best seafood, including a sashimi of Adriatic fish and crustaceans, and *paccheri* pasta with pistachio pesto, mussels and aubergines. The restaurant's decor should make it ideal for a romantic dinner, but in fact it's more for foodies than lovers, and service can be prickly. Chef/owner Cesare Benelli's American wife Diane talks English speakers through the menu. Desserts are delicious.

Corte Sconta €€€
*Castello 3886, calle del Pestrin (041 522 7024, www.cortescontavenezia.it). Vaporetto Arsenale. **Meals served** 12.30-2.30pm, 7-10pm Tue-Sat. Closed Jan & mid July-mid Aug. **Map** p108 Q10* 6 *Seafood*

This trailblazing seafood restaurant is such a firm favourite on the well-informed tourist circuit that it's a good idea to book well in advance. The main act is a procession of seafood antipasti. The pasta is home-made and the warm *zabaione* dessert is a delight. Decor is of the modern Bohemian *trattoria* variety, the ambience loud and friendly. In summer, try to secure one of the tables in the pretty, vine-covered courtyard.

Il CoVino €€
*Castello 3829, calle del Pestrin (041 241 2705, www.covinovenezia.com). Vaporetto Arsenale. **Meals served** 12.30-2.30pm, 9-10.30pm Mon, Tue, Fri-Sun. **Map** p108 Q10* 7 *Modern Venetian*

In one corner of the tiny room, Dmitri juggles pots and pans in his open-to-view kitchen, while affable Andrea mans the very few tables. The inventive dishes (meat, fish, no pasta) on the ever-changing menu are market-fresh and very tasty. But the fact that diners are obliged to pay a set price of €36, even if they don't want all three included courses, will put some off; with wine and extras, none of which comes free, the bill is unlikely to be much less than €50 a head. There's an interesting wine list, of mainly natural unfiltered wines.

❤ Dai Tosi Piccoli €
*Castello 738, secco Marina (041 523 7102, www.trattoriadaitosi.com). Vaporetto Giardini. **Meals served** noon-2pm Mon, Tue, Thur; noon-2pm, 7-9.30pm Fri-Sun. Closed 2wks Aug. **Map** p108 U13* 8 *Pizzeria*

In one of Venice's most working-class areas, this *pizzeria* is a big hit with locals. Beware of another restaurant of the same name on the street: this place (at no.738) is better. The cuisine is humble but filling, the pizzas are tasty, and you can round the meal off nicely with a killer *sgropin* (a post-prandial refresher made with lemon sorbet, vodka and prosecco). In summer, angle for one of the garden tables.

Il Ridotto €€€€
*Castello 4509, campo Santi Filippo e Giacomo (041 520 8280, www.ilridotto.com). Vaporetto San Zaccaria. **Meals served** noon-2pm,*

7-11pm Mon, Tue, Fri-Sun; 7-10pm Thur. **Map** p108 M10 10 *Modern Venetian*

Gianni Bonaccorsi's restaurant is a natural stop-over for upcoming chefs passing through the lagoon city. Though expertise flows in both directions, Gianni's policy of using the freshest and best of local ingredients in unfussy ways to produce something remarkably sophisticated is adhered to with memorable results. The five-course taster menu (€70) gives the best scope for experiencing Il Ridotto's range, which might include octopus on a broad bean purée with turnip tops, a superb *caciucco* fish soup or seabass served on a bed of creamed celeriac. The place – two narrow rooms – is tiny, the decor is ultra-simple and the service is warmly professional. There's a good lunch deal, at €28 for a selection of *cicheti* plus a fish or meat main. Be sure to book: gourmets whether local or visiting know that this is one of the city's best foody attractions.

▶ *Across the campo (no.4357), Gianni's trattoria L'Aciugheta serves decent pizzas and good cicheto snacks, and has an interesting selection of wines.*

Cafés, bars & gelaterie
See also p160 Majer.

Angiò
*Castello 2142, ponte della Veneta Marina (041 277 8555). Vaporetto Arsenale. **Open** 7am-9pm Mon, Wed-Sun. **Map** p108 R12* 1

Angiò is the finest stopping point along one of Venice's most tourist-trafficked spots – the lagoon-front riva degli Schiavoni. Tables stretch towards the water's edge, with a stunning view across to San Giorgio Maggiore; ultra-friendly staff serve up pints of Guinness, freshly made sandwiches and interesting selections of cheese and wine. Closing time is pushed back to midnight or later in summer months, when music events are held on Saturday evenings.

Pasticceria Melita
*Castello 1000-4, fondamenta Sant'Anna (no phone). Vaporetto Giardini or San Pietro. **Open** 8am-2pm, 3.30-8.30pm Tue-Sun. **No cards**. **Map** p108 T12* 5

The welcome in this family café-bakery is not always sunny, but the quality of the pastries behind the old-fashioned bar counter will compensate. There's no sitting down for a languorous coffee and cake session: it's a stand-up or takeaway only kind of place, but it's a favourite with locals and with zoned-in visitors to Biennale (*see p121*) events at the nearby Arsenale.

El Refolo

Castello 1580, via Garibaldi (no phone).
Vaporetto Giardini. **Open** *During Biennale*
10.30am-midnight Tue-Sun. Rest of year
5.30pm-12.30am Tue-Sun **No cards.** *Map*
p108 S12 ⑥

If you want to settle at one of the high stools
on the pavement outside this tiny bar, be
prepared to wait. Because friendly El Refolo,
with its well-priced wine (from €2.50 a glass),
interesting and ever-changing selection of
filled rolls and excellent salami and/or cheese
platters is everybody's favourite, especially
when the area throngs with Biennale-goers
(*see p121*). Over summer weekends, owner
Massimiliano doesn't pull down the shutters
until very late indeed.

Serra dei Giardini

Castello 1254, viale Garibaldi/
giardini pubblici (041 296 0360, www.
serradeigiardini.org). Vaporetto Giardini.
Open *10am-8pm Tue- Sun. Map p108 T13* ⑦

This gorgeous greenhouse has stood inside
the Giardini pubblici since 1894, when its
purpose was to provide winter shelter for the
exotic plants brought out in summer to grace
the national pavilions in the neighbouring
Biennale gardens. Restored and run by a
local cooperative, it now houses a plant shop,
spaces for children's activities, parties and
exhibitions, and a café/tea shop with garden
tables when the weather permits. The setting
is charming, and the coffee, juices and light
meals on offer are good. The idyll can be
slightly marred by less-than-charming staff.

Vincent Bar

Sant'Elena, viale IV novembre 36 (041
520 4493). Vaporetto Sant'Elena. **Open**
7am-10pm Tue-Sun. **No cards.** *Map p118*
W15 ⑧

Sant'Elena is surely the only place in Venice
you'll find more residents, trees and grassy
expanses than tourists and churches. Grab a
seat – and a drink – outside this bar and join
the locals gazing lazily across the lagoon at
passing boats or keeping a watchful eye on
their *bambini* as they play in the park. The
big mixed salads served at lunch make a great
light meal, and there are huge helpings of
competently prepared pasta dishes too. Ice-
cream is made on the premises.

Shops & services

♥ Banco Lotto N°10

Castello 3478B, salizada Sant'Antonin (041
522 1439, www.ilcerchiovenezia.it). Vaporetto
Arsenale. **Open** *3.30-7.30pm Mon; 10am-1pm,*
3.30-7.30pm Tue-Sat. **Map** *p108 N10* ②
Fashion/accessories

The quirky dresses, bags and accessories sold
in this little outlet all hail from the workshops
of Venice's women's prison on the Giudecca
island. Many of the designs are one-offs, and
there's a strong vintage flavour, and some
interesting recycling goes on too. *See p192*
Gardens of Marvels.

Vino e... Vini

Castello 3566, salizada Pignater (041 521
0184). Vaporetto Arsenale. **Open** *9am-1pm,*
5-8pm Mon-Sat. **Map** *p108 Q10* ⑧ *Food &*
drink

Vino e... Vini stocks a wide-ranging selection
of major Italian wines, as well as French,
Spanish, Californian and even Lebanese
vintages.

Running in Venice

Giving the city the runaround

Venice's bridges and narrow alleys make it
a difficult holiday venue for those that need
to pound pavements to get their daily fix of
oxygen. But choose your time (best hour for
'*footing*' is early morning) and your location,
and you'll find that there are others who
share your passion for running. Popular
spots include the *fondamenta* by the Giardini
vaporetto stop, further east under the shady
pineta (pine forest) of Sant'Elena and the
wider pavements on the Zattere.

For something more competitive, the
Venice Marathon (*see p233*) takes place in
October. The starting line is at the Villa Pisani
at Strà; the race passes along the **Brenta
Canal**, over the bridge to Venice, then by a
specially erected pontoon over the lagoon to
the finishing line on the riva degli Schiavoni.
The less competitive **Su e Zo per i Ponti** (*see
p230*) takes place in March.

Venice Marathon

Cannaregio

The train trip across the lagoon from Mestre on the mainland towards the northern shores of Cannaregio is already a romantic idyll, but step out of Santa Lucia station and be prepared to be dazzled: you're greeted not by a dingy car park or snarling flurry of taxis but by the glorious sight of the Grand Canal itself. What comes next, if you walk to the centre, is altogether less grand: a jostling array of souvenir stalls, grotty bars and downmarket hotels on busy lista di Spagna, Cannaregio's main thoroughfare. Concealed beyond, however, is a blissfully calm area of long canalside walks and the occasional, mostly undemanding, church. The only big surprise of the area comes in the Ghetto, where what remains of a thriving Jewish community creates a sudden burst of activity amid the quiet of this second-largest *sestiere*.

❤ Don't miss

1 The Ghetto *p137*
The original and (now) the most picturesque.

2 Madonna dell'Orto *p140*
Where the Tintoretto clan let rip.

3 Santa Maria dei Miracoli *p134*
A miracle of multicoloured marble.

4 I Gesuiti *p140*
Over-the-top marble decoration and a Titian.

Santa Maria dei Miracoli

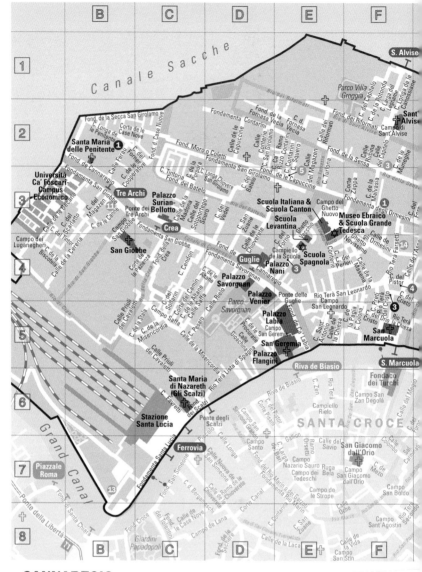

CANNAREGIO

Restaurants

1. Algiubagiò
2. Alla Frasca
3. Anice Stellato
4. Antica Adelaide
5. Bea Vita
6. Boccadoro
7. La Bottega ai Promessi Sposi
8. Ca' D'Oro (Alla Vedova)
9. La Cantina
10. Da Alberto
11. Dalla Marisa
12. Da Rioba
13. F30
14. Orient Experience
15. Trattoria Storica
16. Vini da Gigio

Cafés, bars & gelaterie

1. Al Timon
2. Bar Puppa
3. Panificio Volpe Davide
4. Pasticceria Nobile
5. Santo Bevitore
6. El Sbarlefo
7. Vino Vero

Shops & services

1. Cibele
2. Gianni Basso Stampatore
3. Mori & Bozzi
4. Nicolao Atelier
5. Testolini
6. Vittorio Costantini

FROM THE STATION TO THE RIALTO

▶ *Vaporetto Ca' d'Oro, Ferrovia, Guglie, Rialto or San Marcuola.*

Heading away from the **station** towards the Rialto, the tourist-tack-filled *lista* leads to the large **campo San Geremia**, overlooked by the church of the same name (containing the shrivelled body of St Lucy) and **Palazzo Labia**, currently occupied by the RAI (Italian state television). The *palazzo* contains frescoes by Tiepolo, visible by appointment (041 781 111, direzione. veneto@rai.it).

Once over the **Cannaregio Canal** (*see p132*) – by way of **ponte delle Guglie**, a grandiose bridge with obelisks – the route assumes more character, taking in lively street markets with Venetians going about their daily business. Off to the right, in a square giving on to the Grand Canal, is the church of **San Marcuola** (*see p133*), with an unfinished façade. A bit further on, the more picturesque church of **La Maddalena**, inspired by the Pantheon in Rome, stands in the small campo della Maddalena adorned with a large assortment of fantastic chimney pots.

Beyond this, wide strada Nova begins. Off to the left is the church of **San Marziale** (*see p133*), with whimsical ceiling paintings; on the strada Nova itself stands the church of **Santa Fosca**, another mainly 18th-century creation. In front of the church stands a statue of Paolo Sarpi, who helped Venice resist a Papal interdict in the 17th century and faced an assassination attempt as a result. Further along, down a *calle* to the right is the entrance to the **Ca' d'Oro** (*see below*), Venice's most splendid Gothic *palazzo*.

The strada Nova ends by the church of **Santi Apostoli** (*see p134*); beyond here, the route to the Rialto soon becomes narrow and crooked, passing the church of **San Giovanni Crisostomo** (*see p133*) and the adjacent courtyard of the **corte Seconda del Milion**, where Marco Polo was born in 1256. Some of the Veneto-Byzantine-style houses in the courtyard date from that time.

It was to this courtyard that we imagine Marco Polo returning with his father and uncle in 1295, after 24 years travelling the Far East. As the story goes, the three men turned up in the old Polo home dressed in shabby Tartar costume. Nobody recognised them until they threw back their hoods. Then, to general amazement, Marco slit open the lining of their rough clothes and out poured a glittering shower of diamonds and precious stones. The name of the courtyard derives from the title of his own account of his adventures.

There's a plaque commemorating Marco Polo on the rear of the **Teatro Malibran** (*see p248*), formerly the **Teatro di San Giovanni Crisostomo**, one of Venice's earliest theatres. Just to the north-east is the miniature marvel of **Santa Maria dei Miracoli** (*see p134*).

Sights & museums

Ca' d'Oro (Galleria Franchetti)
Cannaregio 3932, calle Ca' d'Oro (041 520 0345, www.cadoro.org). Vaporetto Ca' d'Oro. **Open** *8.15am-2pm Mon; 8.15am-7.15pm Tue-Sat; 9am-7pm Sun.* **Admission** *€13; €6.50 reductions; price varies during special exhibitions.* **No cards.** *Map p128 J6.*

In its 15th-century heyday, the façade of this pretty townhouse on the Grand Canal must have looked a psychedelic treat: the colour scheme was light blue and burgundy, with 24-carat gold highlights. Though the colour

---

In the know
Death in Venice

The **corte Seconda del Milion** (see *above*) has a splendidly carved horseshoe arch. It was on the well-head in the centre of the *corte* that Dirk Bogarde collapsed in Visconti's *Death in Venice*, his hair dye and mascara trickling down his face in the rain.

♥ **Time to eat & drink**

Let your sweet tooth take over
Pasticceria Nobile *p136*

Venetian classics in a lively setting
Anice Stellato *p142*

Ludicrously picturesque seafood trattoria
Alla Frasca *p142*

Spritz and spices
Bar Puppa *p143*

♥ **Time to shop**

Shoes to die for
Mori e Bozzi *p136*

Venetian glass animals
Vittorio Costantini *p143*

The best Jewish pastries
Panificio Volpe Davide *p139*

has worn off, the Grand Canal frontage of Ca'
d'Oro – built for merchant Marin Contarini
between 1421 and 1431 – is still the most
elaborate example of the florid Venetian
Gothic style besides the Doge's Palace.

Inside, little of the original structure and
decor has survived. The pretty courtyard was
reconstructed with its original 15th-century
staircase and well-head a century ago
by Baron Franchetti; the mosaic floor is
a 19th-century imitation of the floors in
San Marco. The baron also assembled the
collection of paintings, sculptures and coins
that is exhibited inside.

The highlight of the collection is
Mantegna's *St Sebastian*, a powerful late
work; the Palladian frame contrasts oddly
with the saint's existential anguish. The
rest is good in parts, though not necessarily
the parts you would expect. A small medal
of Sultan Mohammed II by Gentile Bellini
(a souvenir of his years in Constantinople,
being restored at the time of writing) is
more impressive than the worse than faded
frescoes by Titian and Giorgione removed
from the Fondaco dei Tedeschi (*see p101*).
There are some good Renaissance bronzes
from deconsecrated churches, and small
but vigorous plaster models by Bernini
for the statues on the fountains in Rome's
piazza Navona.

Gli Scalzi

*Cannaregio, fondamenta degli Scalzi
(041 822 4006, www.centroscalzi.it, www.
giardinomistico.it). Vaporetto Ferrovia.* **Open**
7-11.50am, 4-7pm daily. **Map** *p128 C6.*

Officially Santa Maria di Nazareth, this
church is better known as Gli Scalzi after
the order of *Carmelitani scalzi* (Barefoot
Carmelites) to whom it belongs. They
bought the plot in 1645 and subsequently
commissioned Baldassare Longhena to
design the church. The fine façade (1672-80)
is the work of Giuseppe Sardi; it was paid for
by a newcomer to Venice's ruling patrician
class, Gerolamo Cavazza, determined to make
his mark on the landscape.

The interior is striking for its coloured
marble and massively elaborate baldachin
over the high altar. There are many fine
Baroque statues, including *St John of the
Cross* by Giovanni Marchiori in the first
chapel on the right and the anonymous
marble crucifix and wax effigy of Christ
in the chapel opposite. An Austrian shell
that plummeted through the roof in 1915
destroyed the church's greatest work of
art, Tiepolo's fresco, *The Transport of the
House of Loreto*, but spared some of the
artist's lesser frescoes, *Angels of the Passion*
and *Agony in the Garden*, in the first chapel

Ca d'Oro

Cannaregio Canal

Explore this impressive waterway

Apart from the Grand Canal and the Giudecca, there is only one waterway in the city that is dignified by the name of 'canal', and that is the **Cannaregio Canal**. Until the 19th century, when Austrian occupiers built the rail bridge across the canal (the road bridge came later, in 1932), this waterway was the main route into Venice from the mainland – and it provides a suitably impressive introduction, with wide *fondamente* on each side and several imposing *palazzi*. It's spanned by two stately bridges, the **ponte delle Guglie** (Bridge of the Obelisks, 1823), and the **ponte dei Tre Archi**, the only three-arch stone bridge in Venice, designed by Andrea Tirali in 1688. Heading towards the northern lagoon from the ponte delle Guglie on the right-hand *fondamenta*, you pass the *sottoportico* leading to the **Jewish Ghetto** (*see pp137-139*).

Beyond this stands the **Palazzo Nani** (no.1105), a fine Renaissance building dating from the 16th century. Some 200 metres (700 feet) further on is the **Palazzo Surian-Bellotto** (no.968); in the 18th century, this was the French Embassy, where Jean-Jacques Rousseau worked – reluctantly – as a secretary. Beyond, **Santa Maria delle Penitenti**, with its unfinished façade, was formerly a home for the city's fallen women.

On the left bank is the **Palazzo Priuli-Manfrin** (nos.342-343), another Tirali creation dating from 1735, in a neoclassical style of such severe plainness that it could almost prefigure 20th-century purist art.

The domineering 17th-century **Palazzo Savorgnan** (no.349) – now a school - has huge coats of arms and reliefs of helmets; the owners were descended from Federigo Savorgnan, who, in 1385, became the first non-Venetian to be admitted to Venice's patrician ruling clique. Behind it is the **Parco Savorgnan**, a charming public garden that is one of Venice's better-kept secrets. A little further on, the ponte della Crea spans a canal that was covered for centuries, only to be re-excavated in 1997.

After passing the ponte dei Tre Archi (with the Renaissance church of **San Giobbe**, *see p133*, off to the left), the *fondamenta* continues on to the ex-slaughterhouse, built in the 19th century by the Austrians. It has been taken over and revamped by Venice University's economics faculty.

Two fairly recent housing projects are easily reachable from the canal. From the left bank, calle delle due Corti leads to the **Area Saffa**, a complex built to designs by Vittorio Gregotti between 1981 and 1994; owing to the enclosed nature of the site and the use of high dividing walls, the overall effect is claustrophobic. More successful is the housing project of **sacca San Gerolamo**, at the end of the right bank, to designs by Franco Bortoluzzi (1987-90); the complex makes picturesque use of traditional elements, such as slabs of Istrian marble framing green-shuttered windows and large archways giving on to the lagoon.

on the left, and *St Theresa in Glory*, which hovers gracefully above a ham-fisted imitation of Bernini's sculpture, *Ecstasy of St Theresa*, in the second on the right. In the second chapel on the left lie the remains of the last doge of Venice, Lodovico Manin.

San Giobbe

*Campo San Giobbe (041 275 0462, www. chorusvenezia.org). Vaporetto Crea or Ponte Tre Archi. Closed for maintenance. **Admission** €3 (or Chorus; see p89). **Map** p128 B4.*

Job (Giobbe) has been given saint status by Venice, despite his Old Testament pedigree. The church named after him is out on a limb in the far west, beyond the Cannaregio canal, and was built to celebrate the visit in 1463 of St Bernardino of Siena, a high-profile Franciscan evangelist. The first Venetian creation of Pietro Lombardo, it introduced a new classical style, immediately visible in the doorway (three statues by Pietro Lombardo that once adorned it are now in the sacristy).

The interior of what was probably the first single-naved church in Venice is unashamedly Renaissance in style. Members of the Lombardo family are responsible for the carvings in the domed sanctuary, all around the triumphal arch separating the sanctuary from the nave, and on the tombstone of San Giobbe's founder, Cristoforo Moro, in the centre of the sanctuary floor. This doge's name has given rise to associations with Othello, the Moor of Venice; some have seen the mulberry symbol in his tombstone (*moro* can mean mulberry tree as well as Moor) as the origin of Desdemona's handkerchief, 'spotted with strawberries'.

Most of the church's treasures – altarpieces by Giovanni Bellini and Vittore Carpaccio – are now in the Accademia (*see p180*). An atmospheric *Nativity* by Gerolamo Savoldo remains, as does an *Annunciation with Saints Michael and Anthony* triptych by Antonio Vivarini in the sacristy. The Martini Chapel, the second on the left, is a little bit of Tuscany in Venice. Built for a family of silk-weavers from Lucca, it is attributed to the Florentine Bernardo Rossellino. The terracotta medallions of Christ and the Four Evangelists are by the Della Robbia studio – the only examples of its work in Venice.

San Giovanni Crisostomo

*Cannaregio, campo San Giovanni Crisostomo (041 523 5293, www.sancancianovenezia. it). Vaporetto Rialto. **Open** 7.15am-noon, 3-7.30pm daily. **Map** p128 K7.*

This small church by Mauro Codussi is dedicated to St John Chrysostomos, archbishop of Constantinople, and shows a Byzantine influence in its Greek-cross form.

It contains two great paintings. On the right-hand altar is *Saints Jerome, Christopher and Louis of Toulouse*, signed by Giovanni Bellini and dated 1513. This late work is one of his few Madonna-less altarpieces and shows the Old Master ready to experiment with the atmospheric colouring techniques of such younger artists as Giorgione. On the high altar hangs *Saints John the Baptist, Liberale, Mary Magdalene and Catherine* (c1509) by Sebastiano del Piombo, who trained under Bellini but was also influenced by Giorgione. (Novelist Henry James was deeply impressed by the figure of Mary Magdalene in Del Piombo's painting. She looked, he said, like a 'dangerous, but most valuable acquaintance'.) On the left-hand altar is *Coronation of the Virgin*, a fine relief (1500-02) by Tullio Lombardo.

San Marcuola

*Cannaregio, campo San Marcuola (041 713 872). Vaporetto San Marcuola. **Open** 10am-noon, Mon-Sat. **Map** p128 F5.*

There was no such person as St Marcuola; the name is a local mangling of the over-complicated *santi* Ermagora and Fortunato, two early martyrs. The church, designed by 18th-century architect Giorgio Massari, has been beautifully restored and its gleaming interior comes as a surprise after the unfinished brick façade. It contains some vigorous statues by Gianmaria Morlaiter and, in the chancel, a *Last Supper* (1547) by Tintoretto, his first treatment of the subject; the layout is uncharacteristically symmetrical but indications of the later Tintoretto can be seen in the restless movements of the disciples and the background figures. Opposite is a 17th-century copy of another Tintoretto (*Christ Washing the Feet of His Disciples*).

San Marziale

*Cannaregio, campo San Marziale (041 719 933). Vaporetto Ca' d'Oro or San Marcuola. **Open** 4-6pm Mon-Sat. **Map** p128 H4.*

The real joy of this church is its ceiling, with its four luminous paintings (1700-05) by the vivacious colourist Sebastiano Ricci. Two of them depict *God the Father with Angels* and *St Martial in Glory*; the other two recount the miraculous story of the wooden statue of the Madonna and Child that resides on the second altar on the left – apparently, it made its own way here by boat from Rimini. The high altar has an equally fantastic Baroque extravaganza: a massive marble group of Christ, the world and some angels looms over the altar while St Jerome and companions crouch awkwardly beneath.

♥ Santa Maria dei Miracoli

Cannaregio, campo Santa Maria dei Miracoli (041 275 0462, www.chorusvenezia.org). Vaporetto Fondamente Nove or Rialto. **Open** *10.30am-4.30pm Mon-Sat.* **Admission** *€3 (or Chorus; see p65). No cards.* **Map** *p128 L7.*

Arguably one of the most exquisite churches in the world, Santa Maria dei Miracoli was built in the 1480s to house a miraculous image of the Madonna, reputed to have revived a man who had spent half an hour underwater in the Giudecca Canal, and also to have cancelled all traces of a knife attack on a woman. The building is the work of the Lombardo family, early Renaissance masons who fused architecture, surface detail and sculpture into a unique whole.

Pietro Lombardo may have been a Lombard by birth but he soon got into the Venetian way of doing things, employing Byzantine spoils left over from work on St Mark's to create a work of art displaying an entirely Venetian sensitivity to texture and colour. There is an almost painterly approach to the use of multicoloured marble in the four sides of the church, each of which is of a slightly different shade. The sides have more pilasters than necessary, making the church appear longer than it really is.

Inside, the 50 painted ceiling panels by Pier Maria Pennacchi (1528) are almost impossible to distinguish without using binoculars. Instead, turn your attention to the church's true treasures: the delicate carvings by the Lombardos on the columns, steps and balustrade, with their exquisite, lifelike details.

Santi Apostoli

Cannaregio, campo Santi Apostoli (041 523 8297). Vaporetto Ca' d'Oro. **Open** *8.30am-noon, 5-7pm Mon-Sat; 4-7pm Sun.* **Map** *p128 K6.*

According to tradition, the 12 apostles appeared to the seventh-century Bishop of Oderzo, St Magnus, telling him to build a church where he saw 12 cranes together – a not uncommon sight when Venice was little more than a series of uninhabited islands poking out of marshes. Magnus followed orders, but the ancient church was rebuilt in the 17th century. Its campanile (1672), crowned by an onion dome added 50 years later, is a Venetian landmark.

The Cappella Corner, off the right side of the nave, is a century older than the rest of the structure. It was built by Mauro Codussi for the dispossessed Queen Caterina Cornaro of Cyprus; she was buried here in 1510 alongside her father and brother but subsequently removed to the church of San Salvador (*see p99*). On the altar is a splendidly theatrical *Communion of St Lucy* by Giambattista Tiepolo; the young saint,

Santa Maria dei Miracoli

whose gouged eyes are in a dish on the floor, is bathed in a heavenly light. The chapel to the right of the high altar has remnants of 14th-century frescoes while the one to the left has a dramatically stormy painting of *The Guardian Angel* by Francesco Maffei.

Restaurants

Antica Adelaide €€
Cannaregio 3728, calle larga Doge Priuli (041 523 2629, www.anticaadelaide.it). Vaporetto Ca d'Oro. **Open** *7am-midnight daily.* **Meals served** *noon-2.30pm, 7.30-10.30pm daily.* **Map** *p128 J4* ④ *Venetian*

This historic bar-*osteria* behind tack-filled strada Nova has dynamic restaurateur and wine buff Alvise Ceccato at the helm. Popular around *aperitivo* time, it has also made a splash on the culinary front, with its unusual menu of revisited traditional dishes from the Veneto – like *oca in onto* (goose in its own fat) or freshwater lagoon fish done *in saor* (in onions). There is a large selection of cheeses and cured meats, and a good pan-Italian wine list. Vegetarians are well catered for.

La Bottega ai Promessi Sposi €€
Cannaregio 4367, calle dell'Oca (041 241 2747). Vaporetto Ca d'Oro. **Meals served** *12-2.15pm Tue, Thur-Sun; 6.30-10.15pm Tue-Sun.* **No cards.** **Map** *p128 K6* ⑦ *Venetian*

This pared-back *osteria* has a wooden counter groaning with excellent *cicheti* and a good selection of wines by the glass, to be sampled at the bar or mingling with the standing, chatting crowds that form in the narrow alley outside. In the back rooms are a few tables where diners can sample simple dishes – mainly but not exclusively seafood – with some twists on local stalwarts, such as fried *schie* (tiny grey prawns) on rocket with balsamic vinegar.

Ca' D'Oro (Alla Vedova) €€
Cannaregio 3912, ramo Ca' d'Oro (041 528 5324). Vaporetto Ca' d'Oro. **Meals served** *11.30am-2.30pm, 6.30-10.30pm Mon-Wed, Fri, Sat; 6.30-11pm Sun. Closed Aug.* **No cards.** **Map** *p128 J6* ⑧ *Venetian*

Officially Ca' d'Oro, this place is known by locals as Alla Vedova – the Widow's Place. The widow has joined her *marito* (husband), but her family still runs the show. The traditional decor remains, though the warmth of the welcome can vary. Tourists head for the tables (it's best to book), where tasty pasta dishes (like spaghetti in cuttlefish ink) and *secondi* are served; locals stay at the bar snacking on classic *cicheti*, including the best *polpette* (meatballs) in Venice.

La Cantina €€
Cannaregio 3689, campo San Felice (041 522 8258). Vaporetto Ca' d'Oro. **Open** *11am-10pm Mon-Sat.* **Map** *p128 H6* ⑨ *Venetian*

The service here can verge on the plain rude. But the *aperitivo* snack offerings – including *crostini* made on the spot with whatever's in season – are so substantial that a quick drink can easily turn into a full meal. Seafood platters and the occasional hot dish are delicious, and the outside tables are the perfect place for watching the world bustle by. Around 30 wines are available by the glass.

F30 €€€
Cannaregio, Santa Lucia railway station (041 525 6154, www.f30.it). Vaporetto Ferrovia. **Open** *6.30am-12pm Mon, Tue, Thur, Sat, Sun; 6.30am-3am Wed, Fri.* **Meals served** *11am-10.30pm daily.* **Map** *p128 B7* ⑬ *Italian*

Part of the recent Santa Lucia station upgrade (*see p54* Station Shopping), this light-filled, modern café-restaurant has a view over, and tables on the pavement by, the Grand Canal – though not as you might imagine it. Vaporetti bustle beneath Calatrava's bridge over to the bus terminus at piazzale Roma as you eat excellent *tramezzini* (sandwich) or cakes perched at the bar, or put away a decent pizza, large mixed salad or classic pasta dish at restaurant tables inside or (weather permitting) out. Unlike the rest of the offerings in this global-label station complex, F30 is a one-off run by locals. With food served all day, this is a great spot if you're starving as you arrive or leave by train.

Orient Experience €€
Cannaregio 1847, rio Terà Farsetti (041 822 4337). Vaporetto San Marcuola. **Open** *11am-11.30pm Mon-Sat daily.* **Map** *p128 F4* ⑭ *Middle Eastern*

See review of other branch, p177.

Vini da Gigio €€
Cannaregio 3628, fondamenta San Felice (041 528 5140, www.vinidagigio.com). Vaporetto Ca' d'Oro. **Meals served** *noon-2.30pm, 7-10.30pm Wed-Sun. Closed 3wks Jan-Feb.* **Map** *p128 H5* ⑩ *Venetian*

Vini da Gigio is strong on Venetian antipasti, including raw seafood; there are also a number of good meat and game options, like seared cuts of breaded lamb or tuna in a sesame seed crust. As the name suggests, wine is another forte, with good international and by-the-glass selections. The only drawback in this highly recommended restaurant is the unhurried service. Book well ahead.

Venice Imagined

Deals, scheming and sex: the city in the 17th-century English psyche

The first years of the 17th century were very good – or perhaps very bad – for Venice on the London stage. Three runaway hits set in the lagoon city received rapturous welcomes between 1604 and 1606. The city, clearly, had made its mark on the English psyche.

Venice enters English literature care of William Shakespeare. The bard never actually set foot here, but nonetheless the city featured in *Othello* (first performed in 1604) and *The Merchant of Venice* (first performed in 1605) is a more fully realised place than, say, the Sicily of *Much Ado About Nothing*.

Clearly, Venice was already as powerful an icon as New York is today; the Rialto and gondolas could be mentioned as casually as Wall Street and yellow cabs. Shakespeare's Venice is very much a mercantile city, a place of deals, exchanges and bonds.

But it is also a place of licentiousness and scheming, where people aren't always what they seem. Desdemona, according to Iago, is a 'super-subtle Venetian'. Ben Jonson took the subterfuge to new depths in his *Volpone* (first performed in 1606) in which the wily manipulator of that name dupes grasping would-be heirs out of their own wealth in a show of nastiness that ends in the **Ospedale degli Incurabili** (see p182).

Cafés, bars & gelaterie

♥ Pasticceria Nobile

Cannaregio 1818, campiello de l'Anconeta (041 720 731, www.pasticcerianobile.it). Vaporetto San Marcuola. **Open** *6.40am-8.40pm daily.* **No cards.** **Map** *p128 F4* ❹

The bar at Boscolo's *pasticceria* is always packed; locals flock to enjoy an extra-strong *spritz al bitter* with one of the home-made *pizzette* (small pizza). There is also an excellent assortment of Venetian sweets: *frittelle* (fried dough balls) during Carnevale, as well as *zaleti* (polenta biscuits) and *pincia* (Veneto bread pudding, made with cornflour and raisins). Boscolo's range of chocolates in the form of interesting (and graphic) Kama Sutra positions has made this confectioner famous.

Santo Bevitore

Cannaregio 2393A, campo Santa Fosca (041 717 560, www.santobevitorepub.com). Vaporetto Ca' d'Oro or San Marcuola. **Open** *9.30am-1.30am Mon-Sat.* **No cards.** **Map** *p128 H4* ❺

This friendly pub-café on campo Santa Fosca, just off strada Nova, has consistently proved popular with both Venetian locals and visitors, who drop in to munch *cicheti* during the day or come to while away the evening over a craft beer.

El Sbarlefo

Cannaregio 4556C, salizada del Pistor (041 524 6650, www.elsbarlefo.it). Vaporetto Ca' d'Oro. **Open** *10am-11pm daily.* **Map** *p128 K6* ❻

Chic and sophisticated with great loungey background music, this update on the typical Venetian *bacaro* fills up around *aperitivo* time. By-the-glass wines range from the simple-but-good to some really excellent labels; the bar snacks offer a gourmet twist on Venetian traditions.

Shops & services

Cibele

Cannaregio 1823, campiello dell'Anconeta (041 524 2113). Vaporetto San Marcuola. **Open** *8.30am-1pm, 3.30-7.45pm Mon-Sat.* **Map** *p128 B2* ❶ *Food & drink/health & beauty*

A full range of natural health foods, cosmetics and medicines is on sale here. Staff will also prepare blends of herbal teas and remedies.

♥ Mori & Bozzi

Cannaregio 2367, rio terà Maddalena (041 715 261). Vaporetto San Marcuola. **Open** *9.30am-7.30pm daily. Closed Sun in July & Aug.* **Map** *p128 F4* ❸ *Shoes & accessories*

Women's shoes for the coolest of the cool: whatever the latest fad – pointy or square – it's here. There are enough trendy names and designer-inspired footwear to please the Carrie Bradshaw in us all. Also beautiful bags, clothes, hats and accessories of all kinds.

Testolini

Cannaregio 5587-88, Campiello Corner (041 522 9265, www.testolini.it). Vaporetto Rialto. **Open** *8.45am-7.15pm Mon-Sat.* **Map** *p128 K7* ❺ *Art & office supplies*

Testolini carries stationery, backpacks, briefcases, calendars and supplies for both art and office. The staff can be on the cool side but the choice is huge... by Venetian standards.

IL GHETTO

▶ *Vaporetto Guglie or San Marcuola.*

The word 'ghetto' (like 'arsenal' and 'ciao') is one that Venice has given to the world. It originally meant an iron foundry, a place where iron was *gettato* (cast). Until 1390, when the foundry was transferred to the Arsenale, casting was done on a small island in Cannaregio. In 1516, it was decided to confine the city's Jewish population to this island; here they remained until 1797.

Venetian treatment of the Jews was by no means as harsh as in many European countries, but neither was it a model of open-minded benevolence. The Republic's attitude was governed by practical considerations, and business was done with Jewish merchants at least as early as the tenth century. It was not until 1385, however, that Jewish moneylenders were given permission to reside in the city itself. Twelve years later, permission was revoked amid allegations of irregularities in their banking practices. For a century after that, residence in Venice was limited to two-week stretches. In 1509, when the Venetian mainland territories were overrun by foreign troops, great numbers of Jews took refuge in the city. The clergy seized the opportunity to stir up anti-Jewish feeling and demanded their expulsion. Venice's rulers, however, had begun to see the economic advantages of letting them stay, and in 1516 a compromise was reached. In a decision that was to mark the course of Jewish history in Europe, the refugees were given residence permits but confined to the Ghetto.

Restrictions were many and tough. Gates across the bridges to the island were closed an hour after sunset in summer (two hours after in winter), reopening at dawn. During the day, Jews had to wear distinctive badges or headgear. Most trades other than money-lending were barred to them. One exception was medicine, for which they were famous: Venetian practicality allowed Jewish doctors to leave the Ghetto at night for professional calls. Another was music: Jewish singers and fiddlers were hired for private parties.

The Ghetto became a stop on the tourist trail. In 1608, traveller Thomas Coryat came to gaze at the Jews – never having seen any in England – and marvelled at the 'sweet-featured persons' and the 'apparel, jewels, chains of gold' of the women.

The original inhabitants were mostly Ashkenazim from Germany; they were joined by Sephardim escaping persecution in Spain and Portugal and then, increasingly, by Levantine Jews from the Ottoman Empire. These latter proved key figures in trade between Venice and the East, particularly after Venice lost so many of her trading posts in the eastern Mediterranean. By the middle of the 16th century, the Levantine Jews, the richest community, were given permission to move from the Ghetto Nuovo to the confusingly named **Ghetto Vecchio** (the 'old Ghetto', the site of an earlier foundry); in 1633, they expanded into the **Ghetto Nuovissimo**. Nonetheless, the conditions here remained cramped (*see p138* Living in the Ghetto). Room was found for five magnificent synagogues, however. The German, Levantine and Spanish synagogues can all be visited as part of the **Museo Ebraico** tour (*see below*).

With the arrival of Napoleon in 1797, Jews gained full citizenship rights; many chose to remain in the Ghetto. In the deportations during the Nazi occupation of Italy in 1943, 202 Venetian Jews were sent to the death camps. The Jewish population of Venice and Mestre now stands at about 500 (see www.jvenice.org for information). Only around a dozen Jewish families still live in the Ghetto, but it remains the centre of spiritual, cultural and social life for the Jewish community. Orthodox religious services are held in the **Scuola Spagnola** in the summer and in the **Scuola Levantina** in winter. Most of the city, including the Ghetto, is an *eruv* – a defined area in which activities that are normally forbidden in public on the Sabbath are permitted.

CANNAREGIO

Jewish Ghetto

Living in the Ghetto

Creative solutions to cramped conditions

Today, pretty **campo del Ghetto Nuovo** gives little idea of the hardships suffered there through the centuries when it hosted the closed community of Jews. Note the houses on the southern and eastern sides of the campo: taller than any others in Venice, they bear witness to how the hopelessly cramped inhabitants, prevented from expanding horizontally, did so vertically. Similar upwards extensions on the other two sides of the square have since been demolished; in times past, however, the open space was hemmed in and towered over on all sides.

During the day, the *campo* would have buzzed with activity. Christians came to the Ghetto to visit not only the pawnbrokers and money-lenders but also the *strazzerie* (second-hand clothes sellers) and artisans. As successive waves of immigrants arrived, the Ghetto would have resounded with a babble of languages from around the Mediterranean, as well as the northern inflections of Polish and German.

At night, the gates were closed and guarded by armed boats that patrolled the canals circling the small island; the Jews themselves were forced to pay for this guard service.

The ground floors of the buildings around the campo were almost entirely devoted to commercial activities; everything else – residences, synagogues and schools – was located above. Ceilings were low and the staircases were narrow, to save space. For structural stability, the walls on the ground floor were reinforced and the interior structures made of wood. There are reports of floors collapsing under the feet of over-enthusiastic wedding parties.

Despite hardship and chronic overcrowding, these outwardly unassuming buildings manage to contain the splendid spaces of the synagogues. The **Scola Canton** and the **Scola Tedesca**, the earliest of the synagogues, are distinguished on the exterior only by the array of five windows and by the small wooden lantern in Scola Canton; inside, however, architects created room for impressive devotional spaces, with rich carvings and decorations (again, all in wood). Clearly, religion played an enormous part in the lives of the inhabitants.

It has been calculated that when the population was at its height (and before the Jews were allowed to spill over into the adjoining areas of the Ghetto Vecchio and Ghetto Novissimo), overcrowding was such that the inhabitants had to take it in turns to sleep.

Monument of the Holocaust in Campo del Ghetto Nuovo (Arbit Blatas, 1979)

Sights & museums

Museo Ebraico

Cannaregio 2902B, campo del Ghetto Nuovo (041 715 359, www.coopculture.it). *Vaporetto Guglie or San Marcuola*. **Open** *10am-5.30pm (7pm June-Sept) Mon-Fri, Sun. Guided tours (hourly) 10.30am-4.30pm Mon-Thur, Sun (5.30pm June-Sept); 10.30am-3.30pm Fri.* **Admission** *Museum only €8; €6 reductions. Museum & synagogues €12; €10 reductions.* **Map** *p128 E3.*

This well-run museum and cultural centre – founded in 1953 – has been spruced up in recent years, with a bookshop and a new section dedicated to the history and traditions of the various 'nations' that make up Venice's Jewish community, its relationship with the city after the 1797 opening of the Ghetto, some of its famous personages and the role of usury. In the older rooms there are ritual objects in silver – Torah finials, Purim and Pesach cases, menorahs – sacred vestments and hangings, and a series of marriage contracts. The museum is best visited as part of a guided tour. This takes in three synagogues – the Scuola Canton (Ashkenazi rite), the Scuola Italiana (Italian rite) and the Scuola Levantina (Sephardic rite). Tours of the Jewish cemetery on the Lido also set out from here.

Cafes, bars & gelaterie

♥ Panificio Volpe Davide

Cannaregio 1143, calle del Ghetto Vecchio (041 715 178). *Vaporetto Guglie*. **Open** *7am-7.30pm Mon-Sat, 8.30am-12.30am Sun.* **No cards.** **Map** *p128 E4* ❸

In the heart of the Ghetto, this bakery produces excellent breads, biscuits and cakes... all kosher, as its location implies.

NORTH & EAST

▶ *Vaporetto Orto, Fondamenta Nove or Sant'Alvise.*

If you're tired of the crowds, there's no better place for getting away from it all than the north-eastern areas of Cannaregio away from the canal. Built around three long parallel canals, it has no large animated squares and (with the exception of the Ghetto, *see p137*) no sudden surprises – just occasional views over the northern lagoon. At night, a lively scene unfolds around a handful of restaurants and bars along the Misericordia and Ormesin canals, with patrons spilling out onto the *fondamenta*, drinks in hand.

On the northernmost canal (the rio della Madonna dell'Orto) are the churches of the **Madonna dell'Orto** (*see p140*) and **Sant'Alvise** (*see p141*), as well as many fine *palazzi*. At the eastern end of the *fondamente* along this canal, **Palazzo Contarini dal Zaffo** was built for Gaspare Contarini, a 16th-century scholar, diplomat and cardinal. Behind, a large garden stretches down to the lagoon; in its far corner stands the **Casinò degli Spiriti** (best seen from fondamenta Nove). It was designed as a meeting place for the 'spirits' (wits) of the day, though the name and the lonely position of the construction have given rise to numerous ghost stories.

The Madonna dell'Orto area may have been the home of an Islamic merchant community in the 12th and 13th centuries, centring on the long-since-destroyed *Fondaco degli arabi* (a meeting place and storehouse). Opposite the church of **Santa Maria dell'Orto** is the 15th-century Palazzo Mastelli, also known as **Palazzo del Camello** because of its relief of a turbaned figure with a camel. The Arabic theme carries on across the bridge in **campo dei Mori** ('of the Moors'), named after the three turban-wearing stone figures set into the façade of a building here. The one with the iron nose dubbed 'Sior Antonio Rioba' was where disgruntled citizens or local wits would stick their rhyming complaints under cover of darkness; his name was used as a pseudonym for published satires. The three figures are believed to be the Mastelli brothers, owners of the adjacent *palazzo*, who came to Venice as merchants from the Greek Peloponnese (then known as Morea which offers another possible explanation of the campo's name).

To the south-east are the *vecchia* (old; 14th-century) and *nuova* (new; 16th-century) **Scuole della Misericordia**, the new one being a huge pile designed by Sansovino, its façade never completed. It has long been awaiting conversion into a cultural institute. Behind the *scuole*, the picturesque **campo dell'Abbazia**, overlooked by the Baroque façade of the **Abbazia della Misericordia** and the Gothic façade of the *scuola vecchia*, is one of the most peaceful retreats in Venice; on the façade of the latter you can still see the outlines of sculptures (now in London's Victoria & Albert Museum) by Gothic master Bartolomeo Bon. The building is used as an art-restoration workshop.

Behind the straight edge of the fondamenta Nove, eastern Cannaregio is more intriguingly closed in, with many narrow alleys (including the Venetian record holder, calle Varisco, which is 52 centimetres/20 inches wide at its narrowest point), charming courtyards and well-heads, but no major sights, with the exception of the spectacularly ornate church of **I Gesuiti** and the **Oratorio dei Crociferi**. Titian had a house here, with a garden extending to the lagoon; the courtyard where the house was located is raised to the dignity of a 'campo' and named after the artist.

Sights & museums

♥ I Gesuiti

Cannaregio, salizada dei Spechieri (041 523 1610). Vaporetto Fondamente Nove. **Open** *10am-noon, 4-6pm daily.* **Map** *p128 L4.*

The Jesuits were never very popular in Venice, and it wasn't until 1715 that they felt secure enough to build a church here. Even then they chose a comparatively remote plot on the edge of town. But once they made up their mind to go ahead, they went all out: local architect Domenico Rossi was given explicit instructions to dazzle. The result leaves no room for half measures: you love it or you hate it, and many people do the latter.

The exterior, with a façade by Gian Battista Fattoretto, is conventional enough; the interior is anything but. All that tassled, bunched, overpowering drapery is not the work of a rococo set designer gone berserk with luxurious brocades: it's plain old green and white marble. Bernini's altar in St Peter's in Rome was the model for the baldachin over the altar, by Fra Giuseppe Pozzo. The statues above the baldachin are by Giuseppe Torretti, as are the rococo archangels at the corners of the crossing. Titian's *Martyrdom of St Lawrence* (1558-59), over the first altar on the left side, came from an earlier church on this site, and was one of the first successful night scenes ever to be painted.

♥ Madonna dell'Orto

Cannaregio, campo Madonna dell'Orto (041 719 933, www.madonnadellorto.org). Vaporetto Orto. **Open** *10am-5pm Mon-Sat; noon-5pm Sun.* **Admission** *€2.50. No cards.* **Map** *p128 H2.*

The 'Tintoretto church' was originally dedicated to St Christopher (a magnificent statue of whom stands over the main door), the patron saint of the gondoliers (who ran the ferry service to the islands from a nearby jetty). However, a cult developed around a large, unfinished and supposedly miraculous statue of the Madonna and Child that stood in a nearby garden. In 1377, the sculpture was transferred into the church (it's now in the chapel of San Mauro), and the church's name was changed to the Madonna dell'Orto – of the Garden.

The church was rebuilt between 1399 and 1473, and a monastery was constructed alongside. The false gallery at the top of the beautiful Gothic façade is unique in Venice; the sculptures are all fine 15th-century works. But it is the numerous works by Tintoretto that have made the Madonna dell'Orto famous. Tradition has it that the artist began decorating the church as penance for insulting a doge: in fact, it took very little to persuade Tintoretto to get his palette out, and the urgent sincerity of his work here speaks for itself.

Two colossal paintings dominate the side walls of the chancel. On the left is *The Israelites at Mount Sinai*. Opposite is a gruesome *Last Judgement*. Tintoretto had no qualms about mixing religion and myth: note the classical figure of Charon ferrying the souls of the dead. His paintings in the apse include *St Peter's Vision of the Cross* and *The Beheading of St Paul* (or Christopher, according to some), both maelstroms of swirling angelic movement. On the wall of the right aisle is the *Presentation of the Virgin in the Temple*. The Contarini Chapel, off the left aisle, contains the artist's beautiful *St Agnes Reviving the Son of a*

Roman Prefect. It is the swooping angels in their dazzling blue vestments that steal the show. Tintoretto, his son Domenico and his artistically gifted daughter Marietta are buried in a chapel off the right aisle.

When the Tintorettos get too much for you, take a look at Cima da Conegliano's masterpiece *Saints John the Baptist, Mark, Jerome and Paul* (1494-95) over the first altar on the right. The saints stand under a ruined portico against a sharp, wintry light. There used to be a small *Madonna and Child* by Giovanni Bellini in the chapel opposite, but it was stolen in 1993. The second chapel on the left contains, on the left-hand wall, a painting by Titian of *The Archangel Raphael and Tobias* (and dog) that has been moved here from the church of San Marziale (*see p133*). In a room beneath the bell tower, a small treasury contains reliquaries and other precious objects.

Oratorio dei Crociferi
Cannaregio 4905, campo dei Gesuiti (041 271 9012, www.scalacontarinidelbovolo. com). Vaporetto Fondamente Nove. **Open** *by appt.* **Admission** *€9 (with Scala del Bovolo).* **Map** *p128 L5.*

Founded in the 13th century by Doge Renier Zeno, the oratory is a sort of primitive *scuola* (*see p164* Scuole Stories), with the familiar square central meeting hall but without the quasi-masonic ceremonial trappings. Palma il Giovane's colourful cycle of paintings shows Pope Anacletus instituting the order of the Crociferi (cross-bearers), and dwells on the pious life of Doge Pasquale Cicogna, who was a fervent supporter of the order.

Sant'Alvise
Cannaregio, campo Sant'Alvise (041 275 0462, www.chorusvenezia.org). Vaporetto Sant'Alvise. **Open** *10.30am-4pm Mon, 10.30am-4.30pm Tue-Sat.* **Admission** *€3 (or Chorus; see p65). No cards.* **Map** *p128 F2.*

A pleasingly simple Gothic building of the 14th century, Sant'Alvise's interior was remodelled in the 1600s with extravagant, if not wholly convincing, trompe l'oeil effects on the ceiling. On the inner façade is a *barco*, a hanging choir of the 15th century with elegant wrought-iron gratings. Beneath the *barco* are eight charmingly naïve biblical paintings in tempera, attributed to Lazzaro Bastiani. On the right wall of the church are two paintings by Tiepolo, *The Crowning with Thorns* and *The Flagellation*. A larger and livelier work by the same painter, *Road to Calvary*, hangs on the right wall of the chancel, with rather ill-suited circus pageantry.

Restaurants
Algiubagiò €€
Cannaregio 5039, Fondamenta Nove (041 523 6084, www.algiubagio.net). Vaporetto Fondamente Nove. **Open** *7am-midnight daily. Closed Jan.* **Meals served** *noon-3pm, 7-10.30pm Mon, Wed-Sun.* **Map** *p128 L5* ❶
European

Madonna dell'Orto

This busy spot has morphed from bar to full-on restaurant, now with a vast waterside terrace. The menu ranges from seafood, meat, salad and cheese antipasti, through pasta dishes such as tagliolini with duck and autumn greens, to Angus steak (the house speciality), prepared every which way. Vegetarians are well served, and there's a small but well-chosen wine list. Right by the Fondamente Nove vaporetto stop, this is the perfect place for a quick bite before heading out to the islands of the northern lagoon.

❤ Alla Frasca €€

Cannaregio 5176, campiello della Carità (041 241 2585). Vaporetto Fondamente Nove. **Meals served** *noon-2pm Tue, Thur-Sun, 7-10pm Tue-Sun.* **Map** *p128 L5* ❷ *Seafood*

Alla Frasca is a pleasant *trattoria* with a good seafood menu: the *zuppa di pesce* (fish soup) and spaghetti with lobster are particularly fine. With outside tables on a tiny square just south of fondamenta Nove, it is almost ridiculously picturesque.

❤ Anice Stellato €€

Cannaregio 3272, fondamenta della Sensa (041 720 744). Vaporetto Guglie or Sant'Alvise. **Meals served** *12.30-2pm, 7.30-10pm Wed-Sun.* **Map** *p128 F2* ❸ *Venetian*

The bar in this friendly *bacaro* fills up with *cichetari* (snacking locals) in the hour before lunch and evening meals. Tables take up two simply decorated rooms, and spill out on to the canalside walk in summer. What emerges from the kitchen are mostly Venetian classics such as *bigoli in salsa* (pasta with onion and anchovies or sardines), some given a novel twist.

Bea Vita €€

Cannaregio 3082, fondamenta delle Cappuccine (041 275 9347). Vaporetto Santa Marta or Tre Archi. **Meals served** *noon-2.30pm, 7.30-10.30pm Mon-Sat.* **Map** *p128 E3* ❺

On the long canal-side promenade just north of the Ghetto, Bea Vita attracts locals with its ample portions and decent prices. After a single antipasto you're likely to feel full – but it's worth pushing on through the creative menu. Desserts are mouth-watering. The small wine list includes a decent by-the-glass selection. There's a good €28 taster menu.

Boccadoro €€€

Cannaregio 5405A, campiello Widman (041 521 1021, www.boccadorovenezia.it). Vaporetto Fondamente Nove. **Meals served** *12.30-2.30pm, 7.30-9.30pm daily.* **Map** *p128 L6* ❻ *Fish & seafood*

The cuisine in this restaurant with pleasantly modern decor is very good, with a focus on fresh fish – such as tuna tartare or *cozze pepate* (peppery mussels). *Secondi* range from simple grilled fish to more adventurous seafood and vegetable pairings. In summer, there are tables outside on a small neighbourhood campo – a great play-space for bored kids.

Dalla Marisa €€

Cannaregio 652B, fondamenta San Giobbe (041 720 211). Vaporetto Crea or Tre Archi. **Meals served** *noon-2.30pm Mon, Tue, Sun; noon-2.30pm, 8-9.15pm Wed-Sat. Closed Aug.* **No cards. Map** *p128 B3* ⓫ *Venetian*

Signora Marisa is a culinary legend in Venice, with locals calling up days in advance to ask her to prepare ancient recipes such as *risotto con le secoe* (risotto made with a cut of beef from around the spine). Pasta dishes include the excellent *tagliatelle con sugo di masaro* (in duck sauce), while *secondi* range from tripe to roast stuffed pheasant. In summer, tables spill out from the tiny interior on to the *fondamenta*. Book well ahead – and remember, serving times are rigid: turn up late and you'll go hungry. There's a €15 lunch menu.

Da Alberto €€

Cannaregio 5401, calle Giacinto Gallina (041 523 8153, www.osteriadaalberto.it). Vaporetto Rialto. **Meals served** *noon-3pm, 6.30-10.30pm daily.* **Map** *p128 L7* ❿ *Venetian*

This *bacaro* with traditional decor, not far from campo Santi Giovanni e Paolo, has a well-stocked bar counter, at which you can stand and snack. Served on tables in the back, the wide-ranging, sit-down menu is rigidly Venetian, offering utterly traditional *granseola* (spider crab) and *seppie in umido* (stewed cuttlefish), plus seafood pastas and risottos. Book ahead if you want a table.

Da Rioba €€

Cannaregio 2553, fondamenta della Misericordia (041 524 4379, www.darioba. com). Vaporetto Orto. **Meals served** *12.30-2.30pm, 7.30-10.30pm Tue-Sun. Closed 3wks Jan & 3wks Aug.* **Map** *p128 H4* ⓬ *Venetian*

Taking its name from the iron-nosed stone figure of a turbaned merchant – known as Sior Rioba – set into a wall in nearby campo dei Mori, Da Rioba is a pleasant place for lunch on warm days, when tables are laid out along the canal. This nouveau-rustic *bacaro* attracts a predominantly Venetian clientele – always a good sign. The menu ranges from local standards like *schie con polenta* (shrimp polenta) to forays like red mullet fillets on a bed of artichokes with balsamic sauce.

Trattoria Storica €€
*Cannaregio 4858, salizada Sceriman (041 528 5266). Vaporetto Fondamenta Nove or Ca' D'Oro. **Meals served** 12.30-2.30pm, 7-10pm Mon-Sat. **Map** p128 L5* ⓰ *Venetian*

Located after the bridge that heads south out of campo dei Gesuiti, this family restaurant is simple, not generally overrun with tourists, and good value for hearty servings of good traditional Venetian fare. This is especially true at lunchtime, when there's a generous €15 set menu.

Cafés, bars & gelaterie
Al Timon
*Cannaregio 2754, fondamenta dei Ormesini (041 524 6066). Vaporetto Guglie. **Open** daily 6pm-1am. **Map** p128 F3* ❶

Often described as 'that place with the boat' – a vessel moored outside, which provides additional seating space in summer along a canal that is as peaceful in the daytime as it is lively at night – this buzzing *aperitivo* spot offers a tasty selection of *cicheti* and wines by the glass. Also on the menu are large slabs of meat with ample garnish, if you're looking for something more substantial; but be prepared for slow service if you sit down.

♥ Bar Puppa
*Cannareggio 4800, calle del Spezier (041 476 1454). Vaporetto Fondamenta Nove. **Open** 8am-11pm daily. **No cards**. **Map** p128 K5* ❷

Blink and you might miss this small bar on a narrow street well removed from the main drag. It's worth the detour: exceptionally friendly Bangladeshi host Masud makes a great classic spritz and a number of popular variations (try his *spritz bianco* with ginger and mint). The kitchen offers a selection of dishes (using fresh local ingredients with a non-Venetian twist – herbs and spices abound) at extremely reasonable prices, from seafood pasta to the chef's trademark hamburgers and vegetable samosas.

Vino Vero
*Cannaregio 2497, fondamenta della Misericordia (041 275 0044). Vaporetto Orto. **Open** 11am-midnight Tue-Sun, 6pm-midnight Mon. **Map** p128 H4* ❼

A buzzy wine bar specialising in natural wines and *cicheti*, which can be enjoyed in a picturesque setting along the Misericordia canal. You'll have to get there early to secure one of the tables on the *fondamenta* outside, as locals flock here after work.

Shops & services
Gianni Basso Stampatore
*Cannaregio 5306, calle del Fumo (041 521 4681). Vaporetto Fondamenta Nove. **Open** 9am-1pm, 2.30-6pm Mon-Sat. **Map** p128 L6* ❷ *Gifts & stationery*

Gianni Basso is an amiable character, who moves among his ancient printing presses, chatting about his latest jobs while pulling open drawer after drawer of superb printing blocks so that you can choose the perfect motif for your hand-printed business cards, ex libris or stationery. Around the walls are cards made for his many faithful clients: actors, writers, intellectuals – you'll recognise the names.

Nicolao Atelier
*Cannaregio 2590, fondamenta della Misericordia (041 520 7051, www.nicolao. com). Vaporetto Guglie. **Open** 9am-1pm, 2-6pm Mon-Fri. **Map** p128 G3* ❹ *Carnival costumes*

A very simple costume can be hired from €150 per day; the more elaborate ones can go up to as much as €300 a day. There is, however, a reduction for each additional day that you keep the costume thereafter. Costumes are also for sale and can be purchased online.

♥ Vittorio Costantini
*Cannaregio 5311, calle del Fumo (041 522 2265, www.vittoriocostantini.com). Vaporetto Fondamenta Nove. **Open** 9.30am-1pm, 2.30-5.30pm Mon-Fri. **Map** p128 L6* ❻ *Glass*

Vittorio is internationally renowned as one of the most original Venetian glass workers. His intricate animals, insects, fish and birds are instantly recognisable for their fine workmanship.

Lionfish created by Vittorio Costantini

San Polo & Santa Croce

Within the bulge created by the great bend in the Grand Canal lie the *sestieri* of San Polo and Santa Croce. Working out where one stops and the other begins is an arduous task. The area ranges from an eastern portion, tightly clustered around the Rialto Markets – which were the city's ancient heart and where, despite the invasion of stalls selling trashy tourist-trinkets, you can still feel its steady throb – to a quieter, more down-at-heel residential area in the far west, extending to the university zone by San Nicolò da Tolentino.

Between the two extremes are the large open space of campo San Polo, the great religious complex of I Frari and the *scuole* of San Rocco and San Giovanni Evangelista.

❤ Don't miss

1 I Frari *p162*
Artworks in a barn of a church.

2 Mercato di Rialto *p149*
Source of all that's good and fresh on Venetian plates.

3 Scuola Grande di San Rocco *p166*
Tintoretto lets rip in this temple to his genius.

4 Palazzo Mocenigo *p156*
The history of Venetian fashion explained.

5 Da Lele *p167*
A Venetian institution, and the cheapest *aperitivo* in Venice.

Scuola Grande di San Rocco

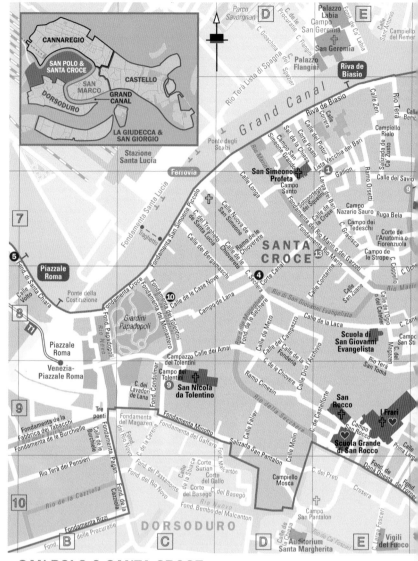

SAN POLO & SANTA CROCE

Restaurants

1. All'Amarone
2. Al Nono Risorto
3. Antiche Carampane
4. Bancogiro
5. Birraria La Corte
6. Da Fiore
7. Da Ignazio
8. Frary's
9. Il Refolo
10. Vecio Fritolin
11. La Zucca

Cafés, bars & gelaterie

1. Alaska Gelateria-Sorbetteria
2. Alla Ciurma
3. All'Arco
4. Al Mercà
5. Al Prosecco
6. Bar ai Nomboli
7. Caffè del Doge

Shops & services

❽ Caffè Dersut
❾ Da Lele
❿ Do Mori
⓫ Majer
⓬ Naranzaria
⓭ Pasticceria Rio Marin
⓮ Rizzardini

❶ Atelier Pietro Longhi
❷ Attombri
❸ Il Bottegon
❹ Ceramiche La Margherita
❺ Coop
❻ Drogheria Mascari
❼ Francis Model
❽ Gilberto Penzo

❾ Laberintho
❿ Mare di Carta
⓫ Monica Daniele
⓬ Piedàterre
⓭ Rialto Biocenter
⓮ Sabbie e Nebbie
⓯ Tragicomica
⓰ ZaZú

RIALTO MARKETS

▶ *Vaporetto Rialto or Rialto Mercato.*

Rialto, most experts agree, derives from *Rivoaltus* (high bank). It was on this point of higher ground at the mid-point along the Grand Canal that one of the earliest settlements was founded, in the fifth century. The district has been the commercial centre of the city since the market was placed here in 1097.

The present layout of the market zone is the result of a reconstruction project by Scarpagnino, undertaken after a devasting fire in 1514. The project made use of the existing foundations, so the present street plan probably reflects quite faithfully the earliest urban arrangement, with long, narrow parallel blocks running behind the grand *palazzi* along the riva del Vin, and smaller square blocks further inland for the market workers.

At the foot of the Rialto Bridge, where the tourist stalls are thick on the ground, stand (to the south) the **Palazzo dei Dieci Savi**, which housed the city's tax inspectors but is now used by the ancient but extant lagoon water authority, Il magistrato alle acque; and (to the north) the **Palazzo dei Camerlenghi**, which housed the city's finance department.

Beyond these, the small church of **San Giacomo di Rialto** (known affectionately as San Giacometto; *see p148*) is generally agreed to be the oldest of the city's churches.

On the other side of **campo San Giacomo** from the church, behind the fruit stalls, is a 16th-century statue of a kneeling figure supporting a staircase leading up to a small column of Egyptian granite, from which laws and sentences were pronounced. It was to this figure – the **Gobbo di Rialto** (the Hunchback of the Rialto, although you'll note that he is, in fact, merely crouching) – that naked malefactors clung in desperate and bloody relief, since the statue marked the end of the gauntlet they were condemned to run from piazza San Marco as an alternative to gaol.

Beyond the market extends a warren of medieval low-rent housing interspersed with proud *palazzi*. This area is traversed by two main pedestrian routes from the Rialto Bridge, one running south-west (*see p152*) more or less parallel to the Grand Canal, towards **campo San Polo**, and the other zigzagging north-westward (*see p155*) via a series of small squares towards **campo San Giacomo dell'Orio** (*see p157*) and the station.

Sights & museums

San Giacomo di Rialto
San Polo, campo San Giacomo (041 522 4745). Vaporetto Rialto or Rialto Mercato. **Open** *9.30am-noon, 4-5pm Mon-Sat.* **Map** *p146 J8.*

The traditional foundation date for this church is that of the city itself: 25 March 421. It has undergone several radical reconstructions since then, the last in 1601. Nonetheless, the original Greek-cross plan was always preserved, as were its minuscule dimensions. The interior has columns of ancient marble with 11th-century Corinthian capitals. One 16th-century guidebook to the city suggests that the domes of this church may have provided a model for those of St Mark's basilica (*see p86*).

In 1177, Pope Alexander III granted plenary indulgence to all those who visited the church on Maundy Thursday; among the eager visitors every year was the doge. The special role of this church in Venetian history was given official recognition after

Attombri

❤ Mercato di Rialto

West of the Rialto Bridge (*see p155*) and all around the church of San Giacometto (*see p148*) stretch the stalls of the Rialto market – the best place in Venice to buy seasonal fruit, veg and seafood. It's the heartbeat of this quintessentially mercantile city, where locals have been mingling and trading goods for almost a thousand years. The market specializes in food from the lagoon and its islands: delicacies such as *castraure* (the first tender artichoke buds), sweet green peas and white asparagus, or extraordinarily fresh seafood, including *moeche* (soft-shell crab), *schie* (tiny grey shrimp) and *sepe* (cuttlefish). Venetians and tourists converge in front of the fish stalls of the **Pescaria** from early morning, lured in by the sellers' colourful clamour and by sea monster-like offerings from the Venetian lagoon. (The more recognizable fish, such as sea bass and swordfish, tend to come from the Adriatic and Atlantic.) A historic plaque on the side of the neo-Gothic arcade lists the minimum size that each fish should measure in order to be sold. In recent years, this area has taken on a new lease of life as a centre of Venetian nightlife, with a number of bars opening under the porticos of the Renaissance **Fabbriche Vecchie** building (Scarpagnino, 1520-22), including some on **Campo Erbaria**. The name Erbaria denotes the fact that vegetables are sold here; there are other examples of such names in the streets and squares nearby (Naranzeria –

oranges; Casaria – cheese; Speziali – spices), while the narrower alleys mostly bear the names of ancient inns and taverns – some still in operation – such as 'the Monkey', 'the Two Swords', 'the Two Moors', 'the Ox' and 'the Bell'. Then, as now, market traders hated to be too far from liquid refreshment.

SAN POLO & SANTA CROCE

1532, when Pope Clement VII bestowed the patronage of the church on the doge, effectively annexing it to the Ducal Chapel of St Mark's. The church currently hosts an exhibition of ancient musical instruments, organised by Interpreti Veneziani (*see p249*).

Restaurants

▶ *See also* **All'Arco** *(p150)*, **Alla Ciurma** *(p150) and* **Naranzaria** *(p151).*

Bancogiro €€
San Polo 122, campo San Giacomo di Rialto (041 523 2061, www.osteriabancogiro.it). Vaporetto Rialto Mercato. **Meals served** *noon-11pm daily.* **Map** *p146 J8* ④ *Venetian*

The location of this updated *bacaro* is splendid: the main entrance gives on to the busy Rialto square of San Giacomo, while the back door leads to a prime bit of Grand Canal frontage, with (hotly contested) tables from which to soak in the view. Bancogiro dispenses excellent wines and *cicheti* to an appreciative crowd downstairs; upstairs, the restaurant has creative seafood dishes.

Cafés, bars & gelaterie

♥ Alla Ciurma
San Polo 406, calle Galeazza (041 523 9514). Vaporetto Rialto or Rialto Mercato. **Open** *8am-3pm, 5.30-9pm Mon-Sat.* **No cards.** **Map** *p146 J8* ②

Packed, loud and casually friendly, Alla Ciurma mixes market stallholders with locals and tourists in a happy confusion around a high counter packed with *cicheti* (snacks) of all kinds, including skewers of deep-fried

seafood and – their speciality – king prawns wrapped in bacon. Most people drop by for a glass of wine or a spritz (and alcohol is consumed throughout daylight hours here by stallholders whose day begins before dawn). There are a couple of tables to consume at, beneath the boat suspended from one wall: if you can bag a seat at lunch you can enjoy good salads and an excellent *baccalà mantecato* (creamed cod).

All'Arco
San Polo 436, calle Ochialera (041 520 5666). Vaporetto Rialto or Rialto Mercato. **Open** *8am-2.30pm Mon-Sat.* **No cards.** **Map** *p146 J8* ③

If you don't like crowds, you should steer clear of this hugely popular *bacaro*; throughout the day, friendly bar staff serve *ombre* (glasses of wine), stiffer stuff and wonderfully fresh *cicheti* to an enthusiastic clientele ranging from Rialto Market stallholders to bewildered tourists. At €1.50 a *cicheto*, you can put together a delicious meal for very little, but it won't be a comfortable one: it's standing room only here. If you can handle that, join the crowd.

♥ Al Mercà
San Polo 213, campo Cesare Battisti già Bella Vienna (347 100 2583 mobile). Vaporetto Rialto or Rialto Mercato. **Open** *9am-3pm, 6-9pm Mon-Sat; 6-9pm Sun.* **No cards.** **Map** *p146 J7* ④

Quite literally a hole in the wall, with standing room only in this campo in the market, Al Mercà (or Al Marcà, the spelling varies) has been serving Rialto marketgoers since 1918. Today's owners dispense the usual choice of wine, and a decent spritz,

Alla Ciurma

plus snacks – meatballs, artichoke hearts and mini-sandwiches, in addition to numerous options for panini toppings.

Do Mori

*San Polo 429, calle dei Do Mori (041 522 5401). Vaporetto Rialto, Rialto Mercato or San Silvestro. **Open** 8am-7.30pm Mon-Fri, 8am-5pm Sat. **No cards**. **Map** p146 J7*

Do Mori claims to be the oldest *bacaro* in Venice, dating back to 1462. Batteries of copper pans hang from the ceiling, and at peak times the narrow bar is a heaving mass of bodies lunging for the excellent mini-sandwiches and the selection of fine wines. Don't point to a label at random, as prices can sometimes be in the connoisseur bracket. You won't go far wrong if you stick to a glass of the classic *spento* – prosecco minus the bubbles.

Naranzaria

*San Polo 130, Erbaria (041 724 1035, www. naranzaria.it). Vaporetto Rialto or Rialto Mercato. **Open** 12.30-3pm, 7.30-10.30pm Mon-Sun. Closed 10 days Jan. **Map** p146 J8*

From a superb location – one side gives on to campo San Giacomo, the other on to the market and the Grand Canal – this nouveau-*bacaro* offers a selection of fine wines, many of them produced by co-owner Brandino Brandolini.These can be enjoyed on foot outside with the regulars or perched at a table if you're lucky, as you absorb the view. There's also a restaurant but you're best opting for liquid refreshment and moving on: prices are high and the vibe is not always friendly.

Shops & services

♥ Attombri

*San Polo 65, sottoportego degli Orafi (041 521 2524, www.attombri.com). Vaporetto Rialto or Rialto Mercato. **Open** 10am-1pm, 2.30-7pm Mon-Sat. **Map** p146 J8* ❷ *Jewellery*

Underneath the arches at the north-western foot of the Rialto, Stefano and Daniele Attombri peddle their sumptuous creations. Intricate, unique pieces combine metal-wire and antique Venetian glass beads, or blown glass cameos of their own designs. They also produce interior design pieces, including mirrors and lamps. **Other location** San Marco 1179, Frezzeria (041 241 1442).

♥ Drogheria Mascari

*San Polo 381, ruga degli Spezieri (041 522 9762). Vaporetto Rialto Mercato or San Silvestro. **Open** 8am-1pm, 4-7.30pm Mon-Sat. **No cards**. **Map** p146 J7* ❻ *Food & drink*

Dry-goods stores like Mascari are a rarity these days, which makes a visit to this old-fashioned emporium such as treat. It's overflowing with Venetian goodies (bigoli pasta, buranei biscuits) and with teas, coffees, herbs and spices from all over the world: a reminder that Venice was once a major centre of international trade.

Piedàterre

*San Polo 60, sottoportego degli Orafi (041 528 5513, www.piedaterre-venice.com). Vaporetto Rialto or Rialto Mercato. **Open** 10am-12.30pm, 2.30-7.30pm Mon-Sat. **Map** p146 J8* ❷ *Shoes*

Furlane (or *friulane*) are those traditional slipper-like shoes that you'll see on the feet of many gondoliers. In this little shop at the foot of the Rialto Bridge, brilliantly coloured bundles of them line the walls. The design is traditional, as is the use of recycled materials such as old tyres to make the soles. But the colours and textiles are eye-catchingly modern. There are shoes here for adults and children.

Drogheria Mascari

SOUTH-WEST FROM THE RIALTO

The route to campo San Polo traverses a series of busy shopping streets, passing the church of **San Giovanni Elemosinario** (*see p152*) and the deconsecrated church of **Sant'Aponal**, which has fine Gothic sculpture on its façade. To the south of this route, towards the Grand Canal, stands **San Silvestro** (*see p153*), with a good Tintoretto, while to the north is a fascinating network of quiet, little-visited alleys and courtyards.

Curiosities worth seeking out (take calle Bianca Cappello from campo Sant'Aponal) include **Palazzo Molin-Cappello**, birthplace of Bianca Cappello, who in 1563 was sentenced to death *in absentia* for eloping with a bank clerk but managed to right things between herself and the Most Serene Republic by later marrying Francesco de' Medici, Grand Duke of Tuscany. North-westwards from here is **campiello Albrizzi**, overlooked by **Palazzo Albrizzi**, with its sumptuous Baroque interior (unfortunately, it's closed to the public).

After the shadowy closeness of these *calli*, the open expanse of **campo San Polo** – home to the church (*see p152*) of the same name – comes as a sudden, sunlit surprise. This is the largest square on this side of the Grand Canal and, in the past, was used for popular occasions such as bull-baiting, religious ceremonies, parades and theatrical spectacles. Now the venue for an open-air film season in the summer and a skating rink in the winter, its main day-to-day function for much of the year is that of a vast children's playground.

The curving line of *palazzi* on the east side of the square is explained by the fact that these buildings once gave on to a canal, which was subsequently filled in. The two **palazzi Soranzo** (nos.2169 and 2170-71) are particularly attractive Gothic buildings, with marble facing and good capitals. In the north-west corner is a view of **Palazzo Corner** (the main façade is on rio di San Polo), a 16th-century design by Sanmicheli. Novelist Frederick Rolfe stayed here until his hosts read the manuscript of his work, *The Desire and Pursuit of the Whole* (1909), which contained vitriolic pen-portraits of their friends. They turned him out of the house, thus earning a place for themselves too in this grudge novel.

From the south-west of the square, salizada di San Polo leads to **Palazzo Centani**, the birthplace of Carlo Gondoli, the prolific Venetian playwright, which contains a small museum and library: the **Casa di Carlo Goldoni** (*see right*).

Sights & museums

Casa di Carlo Goldoni
*San Polo 2794, calle dei Nomboli (041 275 9325, www.visitmuve.it). Vaporetto San Tomà. **Open** 10am-5pm Mon, Tue, Thur-Sun. **Admission** €5; €3.50 reductions (see also p65 Museum passes). No cards. **Map** p146 F10.*

Officially the Casa di Goldoni e Biblioteca di Studi Teatrali (Goldoni's House and Library of Theatre Studies), this museum is really for specialists, though the attractive Gothic courtyard, with its carved well-head and staircase, is worth seeing. It is the birthplace of Venice's greatest writer, the playwright Carlo Goldoni. Over the course of his career, he transformed Italian theatre, moving it away from the clichés of the *commedia dell'arte* tradition and introducing a comedy based on realistic observation. On the first floor, there are reproductions of prints based on Goldoni's works and a few 18th-century paintings; however, the best item is a splendid 18th-century miniature theatre complete with puppets of *commedia dell'arte* figures. The library on the upper floor has theatrical texts and original manuscripts.

San Giovanni Elemosinario
*San Polo, ruga vecchia San Giovanni (041 275 0462, www.chorusvenezia.org). Vaporetto Rialto, Rialto Mercato or San Silvestro. **Open** 10.30am-1.15pm Mon-Sat. **Admission** €3 (or Chorus; see p65). No cards. **Map** p146 J8.*

This small Renaissance church – a Greek cross within a square – was founded in the ninth or tenth century but rebuilt after a fire in 1514, probably to a design by Scarpagnino. On the high altar is a painting by Titian of the titular saint, *St John the Alms Giver*. In the left aisle is a medieval fragment of sculptural relief (12th or 13th century) of the Nativity, which shows an ox and donkey reverently licking the face of the Christ child.

San Polo
*San Polo, campo San Polo (041 275 0462, www.chorusvenezia.org). Vaporetto San Silvestro or San Tomà. **Open** 10.30am-4.30pm Mon-Sat. **Admission** €3 (or Chorus; see p65). No cards. **Map** p146 G9.*

The church of San Polo (Venetian for Paolo, or Paul) faces away from the square, towards the canal, although later buildings have deprived it of its façade and water entrance. The campanile (1362) has two 12th-century lions at the base, one brooding over a snake and the other toying with a human head, which Venetians like to think of as that of Count Carmagnola, who was beheaded for treachery in 1402. The Gothic church was extensively altered in the 19th century, when a neoclassical look was imposed on it. Some of this was removed in 1930, but the interior remains a rather awkward hybrid.

Paintings include a *Last Supper* by Tintoretto, to the left of the entrance, and a Tiepolo: *The Virgin Appearing to St John of Nepomuk*. Giambattista Tiepolo's son, Giandomenico, is the author of a brilliant cycle of Stations of the Cross in the Oratory of the Crucifix (entrance is under the organ), freshly restored. He painted these, as well as the ceiling paintings, at the age of 20.

San Silvestro
San Polo, campo San Silvestro (041 523 8090). Vaporetto San Silvestro. **Open** *7am-11.30am Mon-Sat, 7am-noon Sun.* **Map** *p146 H9.*

The church of San Silvestro was rebuilt in the neo-classical style between 1837 and 1843. It contains a *Baptism of Christ* (c1580) by Tintoretto, located over the first altar on the right, with the river Jordan represented as a mountain brook. Opposite this is *St Thomas à Becket Enthroned* (1520) by Girolamo da Santacroce, with the saint in startling white robes against a mountain landscape; the other two saints are 19th-century additions. Off the right aisle (ask the sacristan to let you in) is the former School of the Wine Merchants; on the upper floor there's a chapel with 18th-century frescoes by Gaspare Diziani. Opposite the church is the house (no.1022) where the artist Giorgione died in 1510.

Restaurants

All'Amarone €€
San Polo 1131, calle del Luganegher (041 523 1184, www.allamarone.com). Vaporetto Rialto Mercato or San Silvestro. **Meals served** *10am-11pm Mon, Tue, Thur-Sun.* **Map** *p146 H9* ❶ *Italian*

This low-key wine bar-restaurant has a friendly feel and a very interesting wine list. Run by an Italo-French couple, Amarone offers all the usual Venetian bar snacks, plus an à la carte menu for sit-down meals of well-prepared and reasonably priced pan-Italian staples, and some good salads for a healthy light lunch. The wine list leans heavily towards the North-East but also includes vintages from elsewhere in Italy, and some kosher wines too. If anything grabs your fancy, they'll organise a vertical tasting just for you.

❤ Antiche Carampane €€€
San Polo 1911, rio terà delle Carampane (041 524 0165, www.antichecarampane.com). Vaporetto San Silvestro. **Meals served** *12.30-2.30pm, 7.30-11pm Tue-Sat. Closed Aug.* **Map** *p146 G8* ❸ *Seafood*

Fiendishly difficult to find, Antiche Carampane is a Venetian classic but be warned: there are a lot of tables packed into a very small space so don't expect privacy; and demand is so great that there are two evening sittings – at 7.30pm and 9.30pm – arrive later than you booked and your table will be given away. What eager diners pile in here for is fine (though not cheap) seafood that goes beyond the ubiquitous standards with recherché local specialities such as *spaghetti in cassopipa* (a spicy sauce of shellfish and crustaceans). Leave room for an unbeatable *fritto misto* (mixed seafood fry-up) and their delicious desserts. Inside is cosy; outside is better.

Birraria La Corte €€
San Polo 2168, campo San Polo (041 275 0570, www.birrarialacorte.it). Vaporetto San Silvestro or San Tomà. **Meals served** *noon-3pm, 6-10.30pm daily.* **Map** *p146 G8* ❺ *Pizzeria*

The outside tables of this huge, no-nonsense pizzeria are a great place to observe life in the campo – and a boon for parents with small children, who can chase pigeons while mum and dad tuck into a decent pizza. The restaurant occupies a former brewery, and beer still takes pride of place over wine. There's also a regular menu with decent pasta options and some good grilled-meat *secondi*.

Da Ignazio €€€
San Polo 2749, calle dei Saoneri (041 523 4852). Vaporetto San Tomà. **Meals served** *noon-3pm, 7-10pm Mon-Fri, Sun.* **Map** *p146 F9* ❼ *Venetian*

The big attraction of this tranquil, no-frills neighbourhood restaurant is its pretty, pergola-shaded courtyard. The cooking is safe, traditional Venetian: mixed seafood antipasti might be followed by a good rendition of *spaghetti con caparossoli* (spaghetti with a type of clam) or *risi e bisi* (risotto with peas), and grilled fish *secondi*.

Cafés, bars & gelaterie

Bar ai Nomboli
San Polo 2717C, rio terà dei Nomboli (041 523 0995). Vaporetto San Tomà. **Open** *7am-9pm Mon-Fri. Closed 3wks Aug.* **No cards.** **Map** *p146 F9* ❻

This bar, much loved by Venice's students, has expanded its already impressive repertoire of sandwich combinations to more than 100 sandwiches and almost 50 *tramezzini* (crustless, triangular white sandwiches): try the 'Serenissima' with tuna, peppers, peas and onions or perhaps the 'Appennino' with roast beef, broccoli and pecorino – or ask them to build your own creation with their fresh ingredients.

Caffè del Doge

San Polo 609, calle dei Cinque (041 522 7787, www.caffedeldoge.com). Vaporetto Rialto Mercato or San Silvestro. **Open** *7am-7pm daily.* **No cards**. **Map** *p146 J8* ❼

Italians scoff at the idea of drinking cappuccino after 11am, but rules like this go by the board at the Caffè del Doge, where any time is good for indulging in the richest, creamiest, most luscious cup of coffee in Venice. Two signature blends and a variety of single-origin coffees are available to consume or purchase. Don't overlook the pastries, and watch out for the speciality coffees.

Rizzardini

San Polo 1415, campiello dei Meloni (041 522 3835). Vaporetto San Silvestro. **Open** *7am-8pm Mon, Wed-Sun. Closed Aug.* **No cards**. **Map** *p146 G9* ⓵❹

An eye-catching *pasticceria* with pastries, cookies and snacks to go with your *caffè*, cappuccino or *aperitivo*. When owner Paolo is behind the bar, there's never a dull moment. It's especially good for traditional Venetian pastries, cookies, coffee, *frittelle* (fried pastry balls) during Carnevale... anything, if you can manoeuvre up to the counter and place your order.

Shops & services

❤ Atelier Pietro Longhi

San Polo 2608, rio terà dei Frari (041 714 478, www.pietrolonghi.com). Vaporetto San Tomà. **Open** *9.30am-3.30pm Mon-Fri.* **Map** *p146 F9* ❶ *Costumes*

This atelier makes exquisite period costumes and accessories for rent or purchase. Prices vary greatly, but renting something simple will cost about €160 for the first day, and less for subsequent days. The atelier also organises private events and stages historical re-enactments, details of which are on their site. They'll send costumes all over the world.

Atelier Pietro Longhi

Il Bottegon

San Polo 806, calle del Figher (041 522 3632). Vaporetto San Silvestro. **Open** *9am-12.30pm, 4-7.30pm Mon-Sat.* **Map** *p146 H7* ❸ *Homewares*

Il Bottegon is one of those everything-you-could-possibly-need shops: crammed into this tiny space are cosmetics and toiletries, pots, pans, rugs and general hardware. Can't find it, ask: they'll probably uncover it out.

Francis Model

San Polo 773A, ruga Rialto/ruga del Ravano (041 521 2889). Vaporetto Rialto Mercato or San Silvestro. **Open** *10am-7pm daily.* **Map** *p146 H8* ❼ *Accessories*

Beautifully coloured and crafted handbags, belts and briefcases are produced by hand in this tiny *bottega* by a father-and-son team.

Gilberto Penzo

San Polo 2681, calle II dei Saoneri (041 719 372, www.veniceboats.com). Vaporetto San Tomà. **Open** *8.30am-12.30pm, 3-6pm Mon-Sat.* **Map** *p146 F9* ❽ *Model boats*

Gilberto Penzo creates astonishingly detailed models of gondolas, *sandolos*, *topos* and vaporetti. Inexpensive kits are also on sale – if you would like to practise the fine art of shipbuilding yourself.

Sabbie e Nebbie

San Polo 2768A, calle dei Nomboli (041 719 073). Vaporetto San Tomà. **Open** *10am-12.30pm, 4-7.30pm Mon-Sat.* **Map** *p146 F9* ⓵❹ *Homewares*

A beautiful selection of Italian ceramic pieces are on display here, as well as refined Japanese works. The shop also sells handmade objects (such as lamps and candlesticks) by Italian designers.

Tragicomica

San Polo 2800, calle dei Nomboli (041 721 102, www.tragicomica.it). Vaporetto San Tomà. **Open** *10am-7pm daily.* **Map** *p146 F9* ⓵❺ *Masks*

A spellbinding collection of masks: mythological subjects, Harlequins, Columbines and Pantaloons, as well as 18th-century dandies and ladies.

ZaZú

San Polo 2750, calle dei Saoneri (041 715 426). Vaporetto San Tomà. **Open** *3.30-7.30pm Mon; 11am-1.30pm, 3.30-7.30pm Tue-Sat.* **Map** *p146 F9* ⓵❻ *Fashion/jewellery*

This brilliantly coloured store has clothing and jewels from the East that are very wearable in the West. There are handbags and other accessories as well.

NORTH-WEST FROM THE RIALTO

Yellow signs pointing to 'Ferrovia' mark the zigzagging north-western route from the Rialto, past the fish market, and on past **campo San Cassiano**. The uninspiring plain exterior of the church here (*see p157*) gives no clue as to its heavily decorated interior.

Across the rio di Ca' Pesaro is **campo Santa Maria Mater Domini** with its Renaissance church (*see p159*). Before entering the campo, stop on the bridge to admire the view of the curving Grand Canal-facing marble flank of **Ca' Pesaro**, the seat of the **Museo Orientale** and **Galleria d'Arte Moderna** (for both, *see right*). On the far side of the square, which contains a number of fine Byzantine and Gothic buildings, the yellow road sign indicates that the way to the station is to the left *and* to the right. Take your pick.

The quieter route to the right curls parallel to the Grand Canal. The road towards Ca' Pesaro passes **Palazzo Agnusdio**, a small 14th-century house with an ogival five-light window decorated with bas-reliefs of the Annunciation and symbols of the evangelists; the house used to belong to a family of sausage-makers, who were given patrician status in the 17th century.

Many of the most important sights face on to the Grand Canal (*see p74*), including the 18th-century church of **San Stae** (*see p158*) and the **Fondaco dei Turchi** (Warehouse of the Turks), home to the **Museo di Storia Naturale** (*see p156*).

On the wide road leading towards San Stae is **Palazzo Mocenigo** (*see p156*), with its collection of perfumes, textiles and costumes. Nearby is the quiet square of **San Zan Degolà** (**San Giovanni Decollato**), with a well-preserved 11th-century church (*see p158*). From here, a series of narrow roads leads past the church of **San Simeone Profeta** (*see p158*) to the foot of the Scalzi Bridge across the Grand Canal.

Leave campo Santa Maria Mater Domini by the route to the left, on the other hand, and you'll make your way past the near-legendary **Da Fiore** restaurant (*see p159*) to the house (no.2311) where Aldus Manutius set up the Aldine Press in 1490, and where the humanist Erasmus came to stay in 1508. To the right, by a building with a 14th-century relief of Faith and Justice above its doorway, the rio terà del Parrucchetta (reportedly named after a seller of animal fodder who used to wear a ridiculous wig, or *parrucca*) leads to the large leafy **campo San Giacomo dell'Orio** (*see p157*). The campo (which translates as

St James of the wolf, the laurel tree, the rio or the Orio family – take your pick) has a pleasantly downbeat feel, with its trees, bars and children. It's dominated by the church with its plump apses and stocky 13th-century campanile. The church has its back and sides to the square; the main entrance was directly from the water.

Sights & museums

Ca' Pesaro – Galleria Internazionale d'Arte Moderna

Santa Croce 2076, fondamenta Ca' Pesaro (041 524 0695, www.visitmuve.it). Vaporetto San Stae. Open 10am-6pm Tue-Sun. Admission (incl Museo Orientale) €14; €11.50 reductions; see also p65 Museum Passes. Map p146 H6.

This grandiose *palazzo* was built in the second half of the 17th century for the Pesaro family, to a project by Baldassare Longhena. When Longhena died in 1682, the family called in Gian Antonio Gaspari, who finished it in 1710. The interior of the *palazzo* still contains some of the original fresco and oil-painted decorations, although the family's great collection of Renaissance paintings was auctioned off in London by the last Pesaro before he died in 1830.

The *palazzo* passed through many hands until its last owner, Felicita Bevilacqua La Masa, bequeathed it to the city. Into it went the city's collection of modern art, gleaned from the Biennale (*see p121*). The museum now covers a century of mainly Italian art, from the mid 19th century to the 1950s. The stately ground floor is used for temporary shows. At the foot of the staircase stands Giacomo Manzù's tapering bronze statue, *Cardinal*.

The first rooms on the *piano nobile* contain atmospheric works by 19th-century painters and some striking sculptures by Medardo Rosso. In the central hall are works from the early Biennali (up to the 1930s), including pieces by Gustav Klimt and Vassily Kandinsky, alongside more conventional, vast-scale 'salon' paintings. Room 4 holds works by Giorgio Morandi, Joan Mirò and Giorgio De Chirico. After rooms devoted to international art from the 1940s and '50s, the collection finishes up with works by notable post-war Venetian experimentalists such as Armando Pizzinato, Giuseppe Santomaso and Emilio Vedova.

Ca' Pesaro – Museo Orientale

Santa Croce 2070, fondamenta Ca' Pesaro (041 524 1173, www.visitmuve.it). Vaporetto San Stae. Open 10am-6pm Tue-Sun. Admission (incl Galleria d'Arte Moderna) €14; €11,50 reductions; see also p65 Museum Passes. Map p146 H6.

Palazzo Mocenigo

If Japanese art and weaponry of the Edo period (1600-1868) are your thing, you'll love this eclectic collection, put together by Count Enrico di Borbone – a nephew of Louis XVIII – in the course of a round-the-world voyage between 1887 and 1890. After the count's death, the collection was sold off to an Austrian antique merchant; it bounced back to Venice after World War I as reparations.

The collection features parade armour, dolls, decorative saddles and case upon case of curved samurai swords forged by smiths who had to perform a ritual act of purification before putting their irons in the fire. There is also a dwarf-sized lady's gilded litter, and lacquered picnic cases that prove that the Japanese obsession with compactness indeed pre-dates the Sony Walkman.

Museo di Storia Naturale

Santa Croce 1730, salizada del Fondaco dei Turchi (041 275 0206, www.visitmuve.it). Vaporetto San Stae. **Open** *10am-5pm Tue-Fri, 10am-6pm Sat, Sun.* **Admission** *€8; €5.50 reductions; see also p65 Museum Pass.* **Map** *p146 F6.*

The Natural History Museum is housed in the Fondaco dei Turchi, a Venetian-Byzantine building leased to the Turks in the 17th century as a residence and warehouse. The Acquario delle Tegnue is devoted to the aquatic life of the northern Adriatic, and the Sala dei Dinosauri contains a state-of-the-art exhibition chronicling the Ligabue expedition

to Niger (1973), which unearthed a fossil of the previously unknown *Auronosaurus nigeriensis* and a giant crocodile. With vast storerooms holding some two million items from scientific collections put together over the centuries – as well as teams of restorers making sure that time doesn't take too much of a toll on their precious artefacts – this museum is a hive of scientific activity.

♥ Palazzo Mocenigo

Santa Croce 1992, salizada San Stae (041 721 798, www.visitmuve.it). Vaporetto San Stae. **Open** *10am-5pm Tue-Sun.* **Admission** *€8; €5.50 reductions (see also p77).* **No cards.** **Map** *p146 G6.*

Palazzo Mocenigo is a rather splendid showcase for life of the aristocracy in 18th-century Venice. Already extant in an earlier form by 1500, this predominantly 17th-century *palazzo* was the home of the Mocenigo family, which provided the Republic with seven doges; the paintings, friezes and frescoes by late 18th-century artists such as Jacopo Guarana and Gian Battista Canal glorify their achievements. A collection of period costumes – including an andrienne dress with bustles so horizontal you could rest a cup and saucer on them, antique lace and silk stockings, and a whalebone corset – are displayed among fine furniture and fittings, in rooms with walls now covered with exquisite Rubelli (*see p53* Material Makers) reproductions of the original fabrics. Added to the museum during the restoration is a fascinating section on perfumes and perfumery, with intriguing essences in lovely glass jars to explore and sniff.

San Cassiano

San Polo, campo San Cassiano (041 721 408). Vaporetto Rialto Mercato or San Stae. **Open** *9am-noon, 5-7pm Mon-Sat.* **Map** *p146 H7.*

This church has a singularly dull exterior and a heavily decorated interior, with a striking ceiling (which has been freshly restored) by the Tiepolesque painter Constantino Cedini.

The chancel contains three major Tintorettos: *Crucifixion*, *Resurrection* and *Descent into Limbo*. The *Crucifixion* is particularly interesting for its viewpoint. As Ruskin puts it, 'The horizon is so low, that the spectator must fancy himself lying full length on the grass, or rather among the brambles and luxuriant weeds, of which the foreground is entirely composed.' In the background, the soldiers' spears make a menacing forest against a dramatic stormy sky. Off the left aisle is a small chapel with coloured marbles and inlays of semi-precious stones.

On the wall opposite the altar is a painting by Antonio Balestra, which at first glance looks like a dying saint surrounded by *putti*. On closer inspection it transpires that the chubby children are, in fact, hacking the man to death: the painting represents *The Martyrdom of St Cassian*, a teacher who was murdered by his pupils with their pens. This, of course, makes him the patron saint of schoolteachers.

San Giacomo dell'Orio

Santa Croce, campo San Giacomo dell'Orio (041 275 0462, www.chorusvenezia. org). Vaporetto Riva di Biasio. **Open** *10.30am-4.30pm Mon-Sat.* **Admission** *€3 (or Chorus; see p65).* **No cards.** **Map** *p146 F7.*

The main entrance of San Giacomo dell'Orio faces the canal rather than the campo. The interior is a fascinating mix of architectural and decorative styles. Most of the columns have 12th- or 13th-century Veneto-Byzantine capitals; one has a sixth-century flowered capital and one is a solid piece of smooth verd-antique marble, perhaps from a Roman temple sacked during the Fourth Crusade. Note, too, the fine 14th-century ship's-keel roof. The Sacrestia Nuova, in the right transept, was built in 1903 on the site of the Scuola del Sacramento. This was the original home of the five gilded compartments on

San Giacomo dell'Orio

the ceiling with paintings by Veronese: an *Allegory of the Faith* surrounded by four Doctors of the Church. Among the paintings in the room is *St John the Baptist Preaching* by Francesco Bassano, which includes a portrait of Titian (in the red hat).

Behind the high altar is a *Madonna and Four Saints* by Lorenzo Lotto, one of his last Venetian paintings. There is a good work by Giovanni Bonconsiglio at the end of the left aisle, *St Lawrence, St Sebastian* and *St Roch*; St Roch's plague sore has an anatomical precision that is really rather unsettling. St Lawrence also has a chapel all to himself in the left transept, with a central altarpiece by Veronese and two fine early works by Palma il Giovane. As you leave, be sure to have a look at the curious painting to the left of the main door, a naïve 18th-century work by Gaetano Zompini, showing a propaganda miracle involving a Jewish scribe who attempted to profane the body of the Virgin on its way to the sepulchre.

San Giovanni Decollato (San Zan Degolà)

Santa Croce, campo San Giovanni Decollato (338 475 3739). Vaporetto Riva di Biasio. **Open** *10am-noon Mon-Sat.* **Map** *p146 F6.*

The church of Headless Saint John – or San Zan Degolà in Venetian dialect – is a good building to visit if you want relief from the usual Baroque excesses and ecclesiastic clutter. Restored and reopened in 1994, it preserves much of its original 11th-century appearance. The church's interior has Greek columns with Byzantine capitals supporting ogival arches, and an attractive ship's-keel roof. During the restoration, a splendidly heroic 14th-century fresco of St Michael the Archangel came to light in the right apse. The left apse has some of the earliest frescoes in Venice, Veneto-Byzantine works of the early 13th century. The church is used for Russian Orthodox services.

San Simeone Profeta

Santa Croce, campo San Simeone Profeta (041 718 921). Vaporetto Ferrovia. **Open** *9am-noon Mon-Sat.* **Map** *p146 D6.*

More usually known as San Simeone Grande, this small church of possibly tenth-century foundation underwent numerous alterations in the 18th century. The interior retains its ancient columns with Byzantine capitals. To the left of the entrance is Tintoretto's *Last Supper*, with the priest who commissioned the painting standing to one side, a spectral figure in glowing white robes. The other major work is the stark, powerful statue of a recumbent St Simeon, with an inscription dated 1317 attributing it to an otherwise unknown Marco Romano. The prophet has

a 'face full of quietness and majesty, though very ghastly,' as Ruskin puts it. Outside, beneath the portico flanking the church, is a fine 15th-century relief of a bishop praying.

San Stae

Santa Croce, campo San Stae (041 275 0462, www.chorusvenezia.org). Vaporetto San Stae. **Open** *1.45-4pm Mon; 1.45-4.30pm Tue-Sat.* **Admission** *€3 (or Chorus; see p65).* **No cards. Map** *p146 G6.*

Stae is the Venetian version of Eustachio or Eustace, a martyred saint who was converted to Christianity by the vision of a stag with a crucifix between its antlers. This church on the Grand Canal has a dramatic late-Baroque façade (1709) by Swiss-born architect Domenico Rossi. The form is essentially Palladian but enlivened by a number of vibrant sculptures, some apparently on the point of leaping straight out of the façade. Venice's last great blaze of artistic glory came in the 18th century, and the interior is a temple to this swansong. On the side walls of the chancel, all the leading painters operating in Venice in 1722 were asked to pick an apostle. The finest of these are: Tiepolo's *Martyrdom of St Bartholomew* and Sebastiano Ricci's *Liberation of St Peter*, perhaps his best work (both left wall, lower row); Pellegrini's *Martyrdom of St Andrew* and Piazzetta's *Martyrdom of St James*, a disturbingly realistic work showing the saint as a confused

old man in the hands of a loutish youth (both right wall, lower row).

Santa Maria Mater Domini
*Santa Croce, calle della Chiesa (041 721 408). Vaporetto San Stae. **Open** 10am-noon Mon-Sat. **Map** p146 G7.*

This church is set just off the campo of the same name. It was built in the first half of the 16th century to a commission by either Giovanni Buora or Maurizio Codussi. The façade is attributed to Jacopo Sansovino; the harmonious Renaissance interior alternates grey stone with white marble. The *Vision of St Christine*, on the second altar on the right, is by Vincenzo Catena, a spice merchant who painted in his spare time. St Christine was rescued by angels after being thrown into Lake Bolsena with a millstone tied around her neck; in the painting she adores the Risen Christ, while angels hold up the millstone for her. In the left transept hangs *The Invention of the Cross*, a youthful work by Tintoretto.

Restaurants

Al Nono Risorto €€
*Santa Croce 2338, sottoportico di Siora Bettina (041 524 1169, www.nonorisortovenezia.com). Vaporetto San Stae. **Meals served** noon-2.30pm, 6-11pm daily. **No cards**. **Map** p146 G7* ② *Pizzeria*

Vecio Fritolin

You don't come to this spit and sawdust *trattoria-pizzeria* for culinary excellence, but if you're looking for a pleasant courtyard in which to sit among noisy diners tucking into decent pizzas, then it might be for you. It also does traditional Venetian *trattoria* fare, at traditional Venetian *trattoria* prices.

♥ Da Fiore €€€€
*San Polo 2202, calle del Scaleter (041 721 308, www.dafiore.net). Vaporetto San Stae or San Tomà. **Meals served** 12.30-2.30pm, 7.30-10.30pm Tue-Sat. **Map** p146 G8* ⑥ *Venetian*

Michelin-starred Da Fiore is considered by many to be Venice's best restaurant. Host Maurizio Martin treats his guests with egalitarian courtesy, while his wife Mara concentrates on getting the food right. Raw fish and seafood is a key feature of the antipasti; *primi* are equally divided between pasta dishes and a series of faultless risottos. *Secondi* are all about bringing out the flavour of the fish without smothering it in sauce. It's a classic, rather than a superlative, dining experience; but that's Venice for you. There's a choice of €50 set lunch menus, and taster menus at €120 and €140 in the evening.

Il Refolo €€
*Santa Croce 1459, campiello del Piovan (041 524 0016). Vaporetto Riva di Biasio or San Stae. **Open** noon-4pm, 6-11pm daily. **Map** p146 F7* ⑨ *Italian*

Until spring 2014 this was the gourmet pizza offshoot of the Michelin-starred Da Fiore restaurant. Then the premises passed to Nardini, the grappa producer from Bassano. The location is certainly the most appealing feature of this venue, tucked in a corner of a lively campo beside a canal. While the outdoor seating makes it the perfect place for warm-weather days, the indoor space is tiny. Food ranges from oysters and tuna tartare, to gourmet pizzas, hearty lamb chops and beautifully arranged cheese platters. Prices, accordingly, tend to be higher than average. However, the quality of service and food is not always consistent.

Vecio Fritolin €€€
*Santa Croce 2262, calle della Regina (041 522 2881, www.veciofritolin.it). Vaporetto San Stae. **Meals served** 12.30-2.30pm, 7-10.30pm Mon, Thur-Sun; 7-10.30pm Wed. **Map** p146 G7* ⑩ *Modern Venetian*

Wooden beams, sturdy tables and the long bar at the back of the main dining room set the mood in this old-style *bacaro*. But the seasonally-changing menu is more creative than the decor might lead you to expect, with dishes such as cocoa tagliatelle with squid, or a main course of turbot in a crust of black rice with sautéed baby artichokes.

❤ La Zucca €€
Santa Croce 1762, ponte del Megio (041 524 1570, www.lazucca.it). Vaporetto San Stae. **Meals served** *12.30-2.30pm, 7-10.30pm Mon-Sat.* **Map** *p146 F6* ⓫ *Modern Italian*

One of Venice's first 'alternative' *trattorias* and still one of the best – not to mention one of the best value. By a pretty bridge, the vegetarian-friendly Pumpkin offers a break from all that seafood. The menu is equally divided between meat (ginger pork with pilau rice) and vegetables (pumpkin and seasoned ricotta quiche). Always book ahead, especially in summer for one of the few outside tables.

Cafés, bars & gelaterie

Alaska Gelateria-Sorbetteria
Santa Croce 1159, calle larga dei Bari (041 715 211). Vaporetto Riva de Biasio. **Open** *11am-9pm daily. Closed Dec-Jan.* **No cards.** **Map** *p146 E6* ❶

The jury is out about Alaska's gelato: some find the fruit flavours insufficiently creamy, others object to the fact that novelty flavours (celery anyone?) are hardly sweet. But to those who appreciate the eccentricities, Carlo Pistacchi's ice-cream is some of Venice's best. There are tried and true choices such as hazelnut, pistachio or yoghurt, or seasonally changing exotic flavours, such as artichoke, fennel, asparagus or ginger.

Al Prosecco
Santa Croce 1503, campo San Giacomo dell'Orio (041 524 0222, www.alprosecco. com). Vaporetto San Stae. **Open** *9am-8pm Mon-Sat.* **Map** *p146 F7* ❺

Prosecco – whether sparkling or still (aka *spento*) – is second only to spritz in terms of daily Venetian consumption, and (as the name suggests) this bar is a good place for consuming it. But you can also drop by here for morning coffee or a light lunch. The shaded outside tables are a fantastic vantage point for observing daily life in a lively campo, but the interior is just as convivial on cool days. Exceptional wines are served by the glass, accompanied by a first-rate choice of cheeses, cold meats, marinated fish and oysters. Closes around 8pm in winter.

Majer
Santa Croce 1658, campo San Giacomo dell'Orio (041 275 0267, www.majer.it). Vaporetto San Stae. **Open** *7am-9pm Mon-Sat; 8am-9pm Sun.* **Map** *p146 F7* ❶

Everywhere you look in Venice, a sleek new branch of this hyperactive café-store seems to be luring passersby in with the perfume of freshly made *cornetti* and loaves: there's another on this same campo at number 1630. Most of the outlets have tables at which to consume an excellent cappuccino with one of their delicious pastries. Most also serve light lunches and snacks throughout the day. But there's also wine, bread, cakes and their own-brand coffee to take away. **Other locations** Santa Croce 287A, fondamenta Pagan (041 722871); Santa Croce 1906, salizada Carminati (041 524 6762); San Polo 2307, campiello Sant'Agostin (041 710 862); Dorsoduro 3108D, rio terà Canal (041 528 9014); Castello 1591, via Garibaldi (041 241 3663); Cannaregio 1227, calle Ghetto Vecchio (041 524 6737).

Shops & services

▶ *See also above* **Majer**.

Laberintho
San Polo 2236, calle del Scaleter (041 710 017, www.laberintho.it). Vaporetto San Stae or San Tomà. **Open** *10.30am-1pm, 3-6.30pm Mon, Sat; 9.15am-1pm, 3-7.15pm Tue-Fri.* **Map** *p146 G9* ❾ *Jewellery*

The pair of goldsmiths who work in this tiny *bottega* produce startling retro and contemporary designs in gold, plus some (slightly less expensive lines) in silver. In addition to the one-of-a-kind rings, earrings and necklaces on display, the shop will produce made-to-order pieces.

Monica Daniele
San Polo 2235, calle Scaleter (041 524 6242, www.monicadaniele.com). Vaporetto San Silvestro or San Stae. **Open** *9am-12.30pm, 2.15-6pm Mon-Sat.* **Map** *p146 F7* ⓫ *Fashion*

Monica Daniele has single-handedly brought the *tabarro* – that sweeping cloak seen in many an 18th-century Venetian print – back into vogue: a heavy woollen one will cost €500 or more. But this odd little shop also has a range of hats, from panamas to stylish creations by the shop's owner.

Rialto Biocenter
San Polo 2264, calle della Regina (041 523 9515). Vaporetto Rialto Mercato or San Stae. **Open** *8.30am-8pm Mon-Sat.* **Map** *p146 E7* ⓭ *Food & drink*

A little bit of just about everything can be found in this health food shop, from wholemeal pasta, grains, honey and freshly baked breads to natural cosmetics and incense. Now in larger premises,it also offers a wide range of organic fruit and veg, dairy produce, lactose-free ice-cream and sulphite-free wine.

I FRARI & AROUND

In the southern portion of the two *sestieri* of San Polo and Santa Croce lies the great gothic bulk of **Santa Maria Gloriosa dei Frari** (aka **I Frari**; *see p162*), with its 70-metre (230-foot) campanile, matched by the Renaissance magnificence of the **scuola** and **church of San Rocco** (*see p166* and *p164*), both treasure troves for Tintoretto-lovers. These buildings contain perhaps the greatest concentration of influential works of art in the city outside piazza San Marco and the Accademia.

North of the Frari's convent – which houses Venice's historic archives (*see p165* In the Know) – is the **Scuola di San Giovanni Evangelista** (*see p165*), another one of the six *scuole grandi* (*see p164* Scuole Stories).

North of here runs rio Marin, a canal with *fondamente* on both sides, lined by some fine buildings; these include the late 16th-century **Palazzo Soranzo Capello** (no.770), with a small rear garden that figures in Henry James' *The Aspern Papers*;

and the 17th-century **Palazzo Gradenigo** (no.768), the garden of which was once large enough to host bullfights.

South-east of the Frari is the quiet square of **San Tomà**, with a church on one side and the **Scuola dei Calegheri** ('of the cobblers') opposite; the *scuola* (now a library) has a protective mantle-spreading Madonna over the door. Above it is a relief by Pietro Lombardo of *St Mark Healing the Cobbler Annanius*, who became bishop of Alexandria and subsequently the patron saint of shoemakers.

Heading west from **San Rocco**, the route ends up in a fairly bland area of 19th-century housing. At the edge of this stands the Baroque church of **San Nicolò da Tolentino** (*see p164*); the adjoining former monastery houses part of the Venice University Architecture Institute.

The rather forlorn **Giardino Papadopoli**, a small park with Grand Canal views, stands on the site of the church and convent of Santa Croce. The name survives as that of the *sestiere*, but the church is one of many suppressed by the French at the beginning

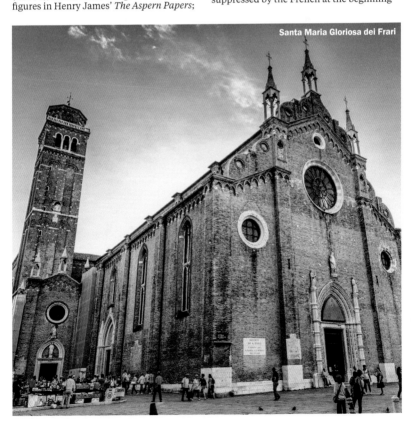
Santa Maria Gloriosa dei Frari

💜 I Frari

*San Polo, campo dei Frari (041 275 0462, www.chorusvenezia.org). Vaporetto San Tomà. **Open** 9am-6pm Mon-Sat; 1-6pm Sun. **Admission** €3 (or Chorus; see p65). **No cards. Map** p146 E9.*

A gloomy Gothic barn, the brick house of God known officially as Santa Maria Gloriosa dei Frari, is one of the city's most significant artistic storehouses. The Franciscans were granted the land in about 1250 and completed a first church in 1338. At this point they changed their minds and started work on a larger building, which was finally completed just over a century later. The church is 98m (320ft) long, 48m (158ft) wide at the transept and 28m (92ft) high – just slightly smaller than the Dominicans' Santi Giovanni e Paolo (*see p111*) – and has the second highest campanile in the city. And while the Frari may not have as many dead doges as its Dominican rival, it undoubtedly has the artistic edge. This is one church where the entrance fee is not a recent imposition: tourists have been paying to get into the Frari for over a century. At the entrance you are brought face to face with the long sweep of church with Titian's glorious *Assumption* above the high altar.

Right aisle

In the second bay, on the spot where Titian is believed to be buried (the only victim of the 1575-76 plague who was allowed a city burial), is a loud monument to the artist, commissioned nearly 300 years after his death by the Emperor of Austria. On the third altar is a finer memorial, Alessandro Vittoria's statue of St Jerome, generally believed to be a portrait of his painter friend.

Madonna and Child (Bellini, 1488)

Right transept

To the right of the sacristy door is the tomb of the Blessed Pacifico (a companion of St Francis), attributed to Nanni di Bartolo and Michele da Firenze (1437); the sarcophagus is surrounded by a splendidly carved canopy in the florid Gothic style. The door itself is framed by Lorenzo Bregno's tomb of Benedetto Pesaro, a Venetian general who died in Corfu. To the left of the door is the first equestrian statue in Venice, the monument to Paolo Savelli (d.1405). The third chapel on the right side of this transept has an altarpiece by Bartolomeo Vivarini, in its original frame, while the Florentine Chapel, next to the chancel, contains the only work by Donatello in the city: a striking wooden statue of a stark, emaciated St John the Baptist.

Sacristy

Commissioned by the Pesaro family, this contains one of Giovanni Bellini's greatest paintings: the *Madonna and Child with Saints Nicholas, Peter, Benedict and Mark* (1488), still in its original frame. 'It seems painted with molten gems, which have been clarified by time,' wrote Henry James, his eye, as ever, firmly on the prose structure, 'and it is as solemn as it is gorgeous and as simple as it is deep.' Also in the sacristy is a fine Renaissance tabernacle, possibly by Tullio Lombardo, for a reliquary holding Christ's blood.

Chancel

The high altar is dominated by Titian's *Assumption*, a work that seems to open the church up to the heavens. In the golden haze encircling God the Father, there may be a reminiscence of the mosaic tradition of Venice. The upward-soaring movement of the painting may owe something to the Gothic architecture of the building, but the drama and grandeur of the work essentially herald the Baroque.

On the right wall of the chancel is the monument to Francesco Foscari, the saddest doge of all. The story of his forced resignation and death from heartbreak (1547) after the exile of his son Jacopo is recounted in Byron's *The Two Foscari*, which was turned into a particularly gloomy opera by Verdi. The left wall hosts one of the finest Renaissance tombs in Venice, the monument to Doge Niccolò Tron, by Antonio Rizzo (1473). This is the first ducal tomb in which the subject is upright; he sports a magnificent bushy beard grown as a sign of perpetual mourning after the death of his favourite son.

Monks' choir

In the centre of the nave stands the choir, with wooden stalls carved by Marco Cozzi (1468), inlaid with superb intarsia decoration. The choir screen is a mixture of Gothic work by Bartolomeo Bon and Renaissance elements by the Lombardi family.

Left transept

In the third chapel, with an altarpiece by Bartolomeo Vivarini and Marco Basaiti, a slab on the floor marks the grave of composer Claudio Monteverdi. The Corner chapel, at the end, contains a mannered statue of St John the Baptist by Sansovino; this sensitively wistful figure could hardly be more different from Donatello's work of a century earlier.

Left aisle

Another magnificent Titian hangs to the right of the side door: the *Madonna di Ca' Pesaro*. This work was commissioned by Bishop Jacopo Pesaro in 1519 and celebrates victory in a naval expedition against the Turks, led by the bellicose cleric in 1502. The bishop is kneeling and waiting for St Peter to introduce him and his family to the Madonna. Behind, an armoured warrior bearing a banner has Turkish prisoners in tow. This work revolutionised altar paintings in Venice. It wasn't just that Titian dared to move the Virgin from the centre of the composition to one side, using the splendid banner as a counterbalance; the real innovation was the rich humanity of the whole work, from the beautifully portrayed family (with the boy turning to stare straight at us) to the Christ child, so naturally active and alive, twisting away from his mother (said to be a portrait of Titian's wife) to gaze curiously at the saints clustered around him. The timeless 'sacred conversation' of

Bellini's paintings here becomes animated, losing some of its sacredness but gaining in drama and realism.

The whole of the next bay, around the side door, is occupied by another piece of Pesaro propaganda – the mastodontic mausoleum of Doge Pesaro (d.1659), attributed to Longhena, with sculptures by Melchior Barthel of Dresden. Supporters of the Baroque have some difficulty defending this one, with its 'blackamoor' caryatids, bronze skeletons and posturing allegories.

The penultimate bay harbours a monument to Canova, carried out by his pupils in 1827, five years after his death, using a design of his own that was intended for the tomb of Titian. His body is buried in his native town of Possagno, but his heart is conserved in an urn inside the monument. The despondent winged lion has a distinct resemblance to the one in *The Wizard of Oz*.

Doge Pesaro Mausoleum

Scuole Stories

Venice's confraternities were part of a complicated social system

Scuole – a blend of art-treasure house and social institution – are uniquely Venetian establishments. Essentially, they were devotional lay brotherhoods, subject to the state rather than the church. In Venice's complicated system of social checks and balances (*see p96* Machinery of State), they gave citizens of wealth – but with no hope of ever entering the ruling elite – a place to feel they exerted some influence.

The earliest were founded in the 13th century; by the 15th century, there were six *scuole grandi* and as many as 400 minor *scuole*. The six *scuole grandi* had annually elected officers drawn from the 'citizen' class (sandwiched between the governing patriciate and the unenfranchised *popolani*). While members of the *scuole grandi* – such as the

Scuola Grande di San Rocco (*see p166*), the recently restored **Scuola Grande di San Marco** (*see p115*) and **Scuola Grande di San Giovanni Evangelista** (*see p165*) – were mainly drawn from the wealthier professional classes, the humbler *scuole piccole* were exclusively devotional groups, trade guilds or confraternities of foreign communities (such as the **Scuola di San Giorgio degli Schiavoni**; St George of the Slavs, *see p123*).

The wealthier confraternities devoted a great deal of time and expense to beautifying their meeting houses (the *scuole* themselves), sometimes hiring one major painter to decorate the whole building; this was the case with Tintoretto at San Rocco and Carpaccio at San Giorgio degli Schiavoni.

---

of the 19th century. All that remains of Santa Croce is a crenellated wall next to a hotel on the Grand Canal. The garden was much larger until the rio Novo was cut in 1932-33 to provide faster access from the new car park for the St Mark's area. The canal subsequently had to be closed to regular waterborne traffic, in the early 1990s, owing to subsidence in the adjacent buildings.

Beyond the garden there is little but the carbon-monoxide kingdom of piazzale Roma and the multi-storey car parks. One last curiosity is the complex of bridges across the rio Novo known as **Tre Ponti** (three bridges); there are, in fact, five interlocking bridges.

Sights & museums

San Nicolò da Tolentino

Santa Croce, campo dei Tolentini (041 710 806). Vaporetto Piazzale Roma. **Open** *8am-noon, 4-7pm Mon-Sun.* **Map** *p146 C9.*

This church (1591-95), usually known as I Tolentini, was designed by Vincenzo Scamozzi. Its unfinished façade has a massive Corinthian portico (1706-14) added by Andrea Tirali.

The interior is a riot of Baroque decoration, with lavish use of stucco and sprawling frescoes. The most interesting paintings – as so often in the 17th century – are by out-of-towners. On the wall outside the chancel to the left is *St Jerome Succoured by an Angel* by Flemish artist Johann Liss. Outside the chapel in the left transept is *The Charity of St Lawrence* by the Genoese Bernardo Strozzi, in which the magnificently hoary old beggar in the foreground upstages

the rather wimpish figure of the saint. In the chancel hangs an *Annunciation* by Neapolitan Luca Giordano; opposite is a splendidly theatrical monument to Francesco Morosini (a 17th-century patriarch of that name, not the doge) by Filippo Parodi (1678), with swirling angels drawing aside a marble curtain to reveal the patriarch lounging at ease on his tomb.

In 1780, the priests of this church handed over all their silverware to a certain 'Romano', who claimed to have a secret new method for cleaning silver and jewellery. He was never seen again.

San Rocco

San Polo, campo San Rocco (041 523 4864, www.scuolagrandesanrocco.org). Vaporetto San Tomà. **Open** *9.30am-5.30pm daily.* **Map** *p146 E9.*

If you have toured the school of San Rocco (*see p166*) and are in the mood for yet more Tintorettos (perhaps after a stiff drink or a lie down), look no further. Built in Venetian Renaissance style by Bartolomeo Bon from 1489 to 1508, but radically altered by Giovanni Scalfarotto in 1725, the church has paintings by Tintoretto, or his school, on either side of the entrance door, between the first and second altar on the right, and on either side of the chancel. Nearly all are connected with the life of St Roch; the best is probably *St Roch Cures the Plague Victims* (chancel, lower right). The altar paintings are all rather difficult to see; they're high up and not very well lit. Even if you could get a good view, you might not be much the wiser: even Ruskin, Tintoretto's greatest fan, was completely baffled as to their subject matter.

Scuola Grande di San Giovanni Evangelista

San Polo 2454, campiello della Scuola
(041 718 234, www.scuolasangiovanni.it).
Vaporetto San Tomà. **Open** *9am-2pm, 2.30-*
5.15pm daily. Closed during conferences.
Admission *€8; €6 reductions.* **No cards.**
Map *p146 E8.*

Used frequently during the day for
conferences and in the evening for concerts,
this *scuola* is open to the public at other
times: there's a list of visiting days on
the website.

The Scuola Grande di San Giovanni
Evangelista is one of the six *scuole grandi*
(*see p164* **Scuole Stories**); founded in 1261,
it is the most ancient of the still existing
scuole. Originally attached to the church
of Sant'Aponal, the *scuola* moved to its
present premises in 1340. It grew in size and
prestige, especially after the acquisition
(1396) of a fragment of the True Cross, an
event celebrated in a series of paintings now
housed inside the Gallerie dell'Accademia
(*see p180*). The *scuola* was closed at the Fall
of the Republic then refounded in 1929 with
the blessing of the Pope. Its building and its
contents now carefully restored, this is one
of Venice's most magnificent structures.

The *scuola* stands in a small courtyard,
at the entrance of which is a screen with
a superb eagle pediment carved by Pietro
Lombardo. The ground floor, with the large
Sala delle Colonne, mostly maintains its
medieval aspect, with fragments of medieval
carvings on the walls; it was used as a space
where members and pilgrims could gather.

The upper floor of the *scuola* is accessed
by a magnificent double staircase, a
masterpiece by the Renaissance architect
Mauro Codussi.

The decoration in the Sala Capitolare is
mainly 18th century. The floor is especially
fine, with its geometrical patterns of
multicoloured marbles that mirror the
arrangement of the ceiling paintings.
Giambattista Tiepolo was originally
commissioned to execute the ceiling-
paintings of the Apocalypse but left for
Madrid without fulfilling his obligations.
His son Giandomenico painted some of the
smaller scenes on the ceiling (*The Woman
Clothed with the Sun* and *The Four Angels
and the Four Evil Winds*); despite their size
they easily outshine the larger works at
the centre of the sequence. The walls are
hung with 17th- and 18th-century paintings
recounting the life of St John the Evangelist,
by Domenico Tintoretto and others.

Also decorated in the 18th century was
the Oratorio della Croce, where a tabernacle
holding the precious piece of cross is one
of the finest pieces of Venetian goldwork;
it is rarely on display. This room originally

In the know
Nothing thrown away

The monastery buildings of the *Frari* (see
p162) contain the State Archives, a
monument to Venetian reluctance ever to
throw anything away. In 300 rooms, about
15 million volumes and files are conserved,
starting from the year 883. Faced with such
a daunting wealth of detailed information –
from ambassadors' dispatches on foreign
courts to spies' reports on noblemen's non-
regulation cloaks – grown historians have
been reduced to quivering wrecks.

contained a cycle of paintings by Gentile
Bellini and Vittore Carpaccio, now in the
Accademia; these days it has to make do
with rather less inspired devotional works
by Francesco Maggiotto, set within dainty
stucco-work. Beyond this room is the Sala
dell'Albergo, which contains a series of
paintings by Palma il Giovane. The most
spirited of these is *St John's Vision of the
Four Horsemen*, recently restored.

The custodian will also open up the
church of San Giovanni Evangelista across
the courtyard, which has a Gothic apse
but is mainly 17th and 18th century in its
decoration.

Scuola Grande di San Giovanni Evangelista

💝 Scuola Grande di San Rocco

*San Polo 3054, campo San Rocco (041 523
4864, www.scuolagrandesanrocco.it).
Vaporetto San Tomà.* **Open** *9.30am-5.30pm
daily.* **Admission** *€10; €8 reductions.* **Map**
p146 E9.

The Archbrotherhood of St Roch was the
richest of the six *scuole grandi* (*see p164*
Scuole Stories) in 15th-century Venice. Its
members came from the top end of the
mercantile and professional classes. It was
dedicated to Venice's other patron saint, the
French plague protector and dog-lover St
Roch (also known as St Rock or San Rocco),
whose body was brought here in 1485. To
celebrate the feast day of St Roch (16 August),
admission to the *scuola* is free on that day.

The *scuola* operated out of rented
accommodation for many years, but at the
beginning of the 16th century a permanent
base was commissioned. The architecture,
by Bartolomeo Bon and Scarpagnino, is far
less impressive than the interior decoration,
which was entrusted to Tintoretto in 1564
after a competition in which he stole a march
on his main rivals – Salviati, Zuccari and
Veronese – by presenting a finished painting
rather than the required sketch.

In three intensive sessions spread out
over the following 23 years, Tintoretto went
on to make San Rocco his epic masterpiece.
Fans and doubters alike should start
here; the former will no doubt agree with
John Ruskin that paintings such as the
Crucifixion are 'beyond all analysis and
above all praise', while the latter may well
find their prejudices crumbling. True,
the devotional intensity of his works can
shade a touch too much into kitsch for the
21st-century soul; but his feel for narrative
structure remains timeless.

To follow the development of Tintoretto's
style, pick up the free explanatory leaflet
and the audio guide and begin in the smaller
upstairs hall – the Albergo. Here, filling up
the whole of the far wall, is the *Crucifixion*
(1565). More than anything it is the perfect
integration of main plot and sub-plots that
strikes the viewer; whereas most paintings
are short stories, this is a novel. Note that
some restoration work was underway as this
guide went to press.

Tintoretto began work on the larger
upstairs room in 1575, with Old Testament
stories on the ceiling and a Life of Christ
cycle around the walls, in which the artist
experimented relentlessly with form,

lighting and colour. Below the canvases is
a characterful series of late 17th-century
wooden carvings, including a caricature of
Tintoretto himself, just below and to the left
of his painting of *The Agony in the Garden*.

Finally, in the ground-floor hall – which
the artist decorated between 1583 and 1587,
when he was in his sixties – the paintings
reach a visionary pitch that has to do with
Tintoretto's audacious handling of light and
the impressionistic economy of his brush
strokes. The *Annunciation*, with its domestic
Mary surprised while sewing, and *Flight
into Egypt*, with its verdant landscape, are
among the painter's masterpieces.

Scuola Grande di San Rocco

Restaurants

Frary's €€
San Polo 2558, fondamenta dei Frari (041 720 050, www.frarys.it). Vaporetto San Tomà. **Meals served** *11.30am-3pm, 6-11pm Mon, Wed-Sun.* **Map** *p146 F9* ⑧ *Middle Eastern*

A friendly, reasonably-priced spot specialising in Arab cuisine, though there are some Greek and Kurdish dishes too, plus gluten-free options. Couscous comes with a variety of sauces: vegetarian, mutton, chicken or seafood. The *mansaf* (rice with chicken, almonds and yoghurt) is good.

Cafés, bars & gelaterie

Caffè Dersut
San Polo 3014, campo dei Frari (041 303 2159). Vaporetto Tomà. **Open** *6am-7pm Mon-Sat; 8am-1pm Sun.* **No cards.** **Map** *p146 G9* ⑧

Right by the side of I Frari (*see p162*) and no distance from the Scuola di San Rocco (*see p166*), this coffee bar is a great place to refuel after an excess of art. An outlet for the Treviso-based coffee roasters of the same name, the café serves excellent breakfast coffee and pastries, good fresh fruit juices and smoothies, plus sandwiches for a light lunch.

♥ Da Lele
Santa Croce 183, campo dei Tolentini (no phone). Vaporetto Piazzale Roma. **Open** *6am-8pm Mon-Fri; 6am-2pm Sat.* **No cards.** **Map** *p146 C9* ⑨

Gabriele's (Lele's) place is the first authentic *osteria* for those arriving in Venice – or the last for those leaving; look for the two barrels outside – and the crowds of people milling – and you've found this Venetian institution. It's so small in here, there isn't even room for a phone, but there are local wines from Piave, Lison and Valdobbiadene on offer, as well as rolls that are filled to order with meat and/or cheese. A basic but good glass of chardonnay costs just 60c, a mini-*panino* 90c (don't leave it too late if you're hungry or they'll run out of bread). Don't bother asking for coffee: no room for the machine.

Pasticceria Rio Marin
Santa Croce 784, rio Marin (041 718 523). Vaporetto Riva di Biasio. **Open** *6.30am-8pm Mon, Tue, Thur-Sun. Closed Aug.* **Map** *p146 E7* ⑬

Just a short hop across the Grand Canal from the train station, Bianca and Dario's delicious cakeshop is a rewarding stopover on arrival in (or departure from) Venice – or at any other time, for that matter. There's a world of choice here. Individual portions can be consumed

with a coffee or drink at one of the tables along the rio Marin. Alternatively, treats such as a wonderful creation with cream and fresh fruit can be purchased family-size to take away.

Shops & services

Ceramiche La Margherita
Santa Croce 659, corte Canal (393 210 0272, www.lamargheritavenezia.com). Vaporetto San Stae. **Open** *9.30am-1pm, 3.30-7pm Mon-Sat.* **Map** *p146 D8* ④ *Homewares*

A delightful collection of handpainted terracotta designed by the owner. Plates, bowls, teapots, ornaments and mugs are all available in a variety of colours and patterns.

Coop
Santa Croce 506A, piazzale Roma (041 296 0621). Vaporetto Piazzale Roma. **Open** *8.30am-9pm daily.* **Map** *p146 B7* ⑤ *Food & drink*

In a city where old-fashioned grocers and butchers are increasingly thin on the ground, the appearance of Coop and InCoop cornershops all over is a welcome development. Most (including branches listed below) are open Monday to Saturday. If you need to restock on Sunday, though, you'll need to make your way to piazzale Roma. This is good supermarket food at good prices (for Venice). This branch caters to tourists, with a handy salad bar, snacks and Venetian specialities conveniently lumped together. **Other locations** Castello 5890, calle Larga (041 522 9214); Santa Croce 1493, campo San Giacomo dell'Orio (041 275 0218); Giudecca 484, calle dell'Olio (041 241 3381).

♥ Mare di Carta
Santa Croce 222, fondamenta dei Tolentini (041 716 304, www.maredicarta.com). Vaporetto Piazzale Roma. **Open** *9am-1pm, 3.30-7.30pm Mon-Wed; 9am-7.30pm Thur-Fri; 9am-12.30pm, 3-7.30pm Sat.* **Map** *p146 C8* ⑩ *Books*

A small but well-stocked bookshop specialising in all things nautical: naval history, fishing techniques, water sports and pretty much anything aquatic.

Dorsoduro

Cradling the southern flank of Venice proper, Dorsoduro – literally 'hard back' – stretches from its smart, artsy eastern district of elegant *palazzi* and quiet *campielli* to the little-visited docks and university area in the *sestiere*'s far western reaches. The concentration of art – from the very contemporary at the Punta della Dogana to the modern at the Peggy Guggenheim Collection to the grand masters at the Gallerie dell'Accademia – is outstanding. But there are fine churches here too, including the magnificent Santa Maria della Salute, a Venetian icon in its pre-eminent position at the entrance to the Grand Canal. In between the geographical and social extremes comes the wholly democratic and buzzing campo Santa Margherita, around which much of the city's nightlife action takes place.

❤ **Don't miss**

1 Gallerie dell'Accademia *p180*
One of the world's great art collections.

2 Punta della Dogana *p185*
Contemporary art to complement the magnificent views.

3 Galleria Palazzo Cini *p186*
A tiny treasure trove of understated gems.

4 Peggy Guggenheim Collection *p183*
Great modern art in a pleasant *palazzo*.

5 Santa Maria della Salute *p182*
A Venice icon, dramatic outside, restful inside.

Santa Maria della Salute

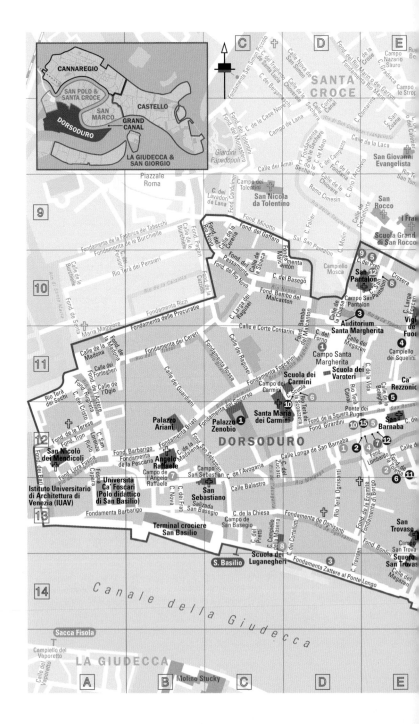

DORSODURO

Restaurants

1. Africa Experience
2. Ai Artisti
3. Ai Gondolieri
4. La Bitta
5. Oniga
6. Orient Experience
7. Pane, Vino e San Daniele
8. Riviera

Cafés, bars & gelaterie

1. Caffé Rosso
2. Cantinone (già Schiavi)
3. El Chioschetto
4. Corner Pub
5. Estro Vino e Cucina
6. Gelateria Lo Squero
7. Grom
8. Impronta Café
9. Malvasia all'Adriatico Mar
10. Osteria ai Pugni
11. Osteria al Squero
12. Tonolo

Shops & services

1. 3856 di Elvira Rubelli
2. Annelie
3. Arras
4. Cafoscarina 2
5. Ca' Macana
6. Canestrelli
7. Cornici Trevisanello
8. Le Forcole di Saverio Pastor
9. Genninger Studio
10. Libreria Marco Polo
11. Libreria Toletta
12. Madera
13. Marina & Susanna Sent
14. Il Pavone
15. Signor Blum

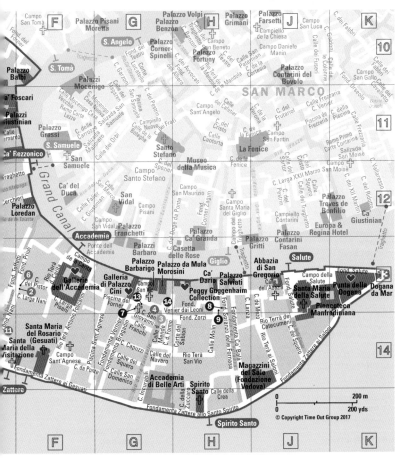

WEST

▶ *Vaporetto Santa Marta, San Basilio or Zattere.*

This was one of the first areas in the lagoon to be settled. One seventh-century church here is called **San Nicolò dei Mendicoli** (*see p173*) – 'of the beggars' – a hint that the locals have never been in the top income bracket. The church gave its name to the *nicolotti*, a faction of fishermen and salt-pan workers from the west of the city, who were the sworn rivals of the *castellani* workers from the east (*see also p174*). The *nicolotti* enjoyed a certain form of local autonomy under a figure known as the *gastaldo*, who, after his election, would be received with honours by the doge.

The area is still noticeably less sleek than the centre, although fishing was superseded as a source of employment by the port long ago, and subsequently by the Santa Marta cotton mill – now stunningly converted into the **Istituto Universitario di Architettura di Venezia (IUAV)**. Massive redevelopment schemes were talked about for much of this downbeat district, with plans to revitalise it in a vast 'university meets London Docklands' style project, to a design by the late Catalan architect Enric Miralles. The plans included an auditorium, a conference hall, a restaurant and a huge centralised university library, thus providing Venice's universities with something approaching a genuine campus. After various legal disputes, these ambitious schemes fell through and the two universities of Venice fell back on a more modest development plan, converting some of the ex-warehouses into classrooms and lecture halls; these constitute the **Polo didattico di San Basilio**, which was inaugurated in March 2008.

Moving eastwards, the atmosphere remains unpretentious around the churches of **Angelo Raffaele** (*see below*) and **San Sebastiano** (*see p173*), the latter with its splendid decoration by Paolo Veronese. Northwards from here, on the rio di Santa Margherita, are some grander *palazzi*, including **Palazzo Ariani**, with Gothic tracery that is almost oriental in its intricacy, and, further up, the grand **Palazzo Zenobio**, now an Armenian school and institute, containing Tiepolesque frescoes and giving on to an elaborate garden where plays are sometimes performed in the summer.

On the southern shore, the final and widest stretch of the **Zattere** promenade (*see p180*) passes several notable *palazzi*, including the 17th-century façade of the **Scuola dei Luganegheri** (sausage-makers' school), with a statue of the sausage-makers' protector, St Anthony Abbot, whose symbol was a hog.

Sights & museums

Angelo Raffaele
Dorsoduro, campo Angelo Raffaele (041 522 8548). Vaporetto San Basilio. **Open** *10am-noon, 3-5.30pm Mon-Sat; 9am-noon Sun.* **Map** *p170 B12.*

Tradition has it that this church was founded by St Magnus in the eighth century, but the present free-standing building – one of only two churches in the city that you can walk around – dates from the 17th century. The ceiling has a lively fresco by Gaspare Diziani of *St Michael Driving out Lucifer*, with Lucifer apparently tumbling out of the heavy stucco frame into the church. There are matching *Last Suppers* on either side of the organ (by Bonifacio de' Pitati on the left, and a follower of Titian on the right).

But the real jewels of the church are on the organ loft, where five compartments, painted by Giovanni Antonio Guardi (or

In the know
Loggia out front

Only two churches in Venice have loggias out front, and both are very old indeed. One is **San Nicolò dei Mendicoli** (see p173) and the other is **San Giacomo di Rialto** (see p148).

💙 **Time to eat & drink**

Creative luxury in a spectacular setting
Riviera *p174*

Cheap and cheerful ethnic fare
Orient Experience *p177*

A spritz with a twist
Malvasia all'Ariatico Mar *p178*

Edgy gourmet wine bar
Estro Vino e Cucina *p178*

Enjoy an ombra by a picturesque canal
Cantinone (già Schiavi) *p186*

💙 **Time to shop**

Beautifully embroidered homewares
Annelie *p179*

Be puzzled by Venice
Signor Blum *p179*

Quirky independent bookshop
Libreria Marco Polo *p179*

perhaps his brother Francesco), recount the story of *Tobias and the Angel* (1750-53). They are works of dazzling luminosity, quite unlike anything else done in Venice at the time. The paintings and the story they recount play a significant role in Sally Vickers' novel *Miss Garnet's Angel* (2000).

San Nicolò dei Mendicoli

Dorsoduro, campo San Nicolò (041 275 0382). Vaporetto San Basilio or Santa Marta. **Open** *10am-noon, 3-5.30pm Mon-Sat; 9am-noon Sun.* **Map** *p170 A12.*

San Nicolò is one of the few Venetian churches to have maintained its 13th-century Veneto-Byzantine structure, despite numerous refurbishments over the years. When the church underwent a thorough restoration in the 1970s, traces of the original foundations were uncovered, confirming the church's seventh-century origins. The 15th-century loggia at the front is one of only two extant examples of a once-common architectural feature; it originally served as a shelter for the homeless.

The interior contains a marvellous mishmash of architectural and decorative styles that creates an effect of cluttered charm. The structure is that of a 12th-century basilica, with two colonnades of stocky columns topped by 14th-century capitals. Above are gilded 16th-century statues of the Apostles. The paintings are mainly 17th century. There are also some fine wooden sculptures, including a large statue of San Nicolò made in the 15th century in the workshop of sculptor Bartolomeo Bon. In the small campo outside the church is a column with a diminutive winged lion.

San Sebastiano

Dorsoduro, fondamenta di San Sebastiano (041 275 0642, www.chorusvenezia.org). Vaporetto San Basilio. **Open** *10.30am-3.45pm Mon; 10.30am-4.15pm Tue-Sat.* **Admission** *€3 (or Chorus; see p65). No cards.* **Map** *p170 C13.*

This contains perhaps the most brilliantly colourful church interior in Venice, and it's all the work of one man: Paolo Veronese. His first commission was for the sacristy (*see p174*). From then on, there was no stopping him: between 1556 and 1565 he completed three large ceiling paintings for the nave of the church, frescoes along the upper parts of the walls, organ shutters, huge narrative canvases for the chancel, and the painting on the high altar.

In July 2008, restoration work began on the ceiling paintings. They depict scenes from the life of Esther (*Esther Taken to Ahasuerus, Esther Crowned Queen by Ahasuerus* and *The Triumph of Mordecai*).

In the know
Don't Look Now

Film buffs should recognise the church of **San Nicolò dei Mendicoli** (*see p173*) from Nicolas Roeg's Venice movie *Don't Look Now*. Other locations used include **Palazzo Grimani** (*see p112*), where the gruesome final scene was shot.

Esther was considered a forerunner of the Virgin, interceding for Jews in the same way that the Virgin interceded for Christians – or (more pertinently) for Venice. These works are full of sumptuous pageantry: no painter gets more splendidly shimmering effects out of clothing, which is probably why Veronese's nude St Sebastians are the least striking figures in the compositions.

The enormous canvases on the side walls of the chancel depict, on the right, *The Martyrdom of St Sebastian* and, on the left, *St Sebastian Encouraging St Mark and St Marcellan*. Other paintings in the church include *St Nicholas*, a late painting by Titian, in the first altar on the right. Paolo Veronese and his brother Benedetto are buried here.

Fondamenta Zattere

DORSODURO

The sacristy (10am-5pm Sat, 1-5pm Sun) contains ceiling paintings of the *Coronation of the Virgin* and the four panels of *The Evangelists*, which are among Veronese's earliest works in Venice (1555). Around the walls are works by Bonifacio de' Pitati and others. Restoration work on the frescoes and structure of the church will continue for some years.

Restaurants

Pane, Vino e San Daniele €€

Dorsoduro 1722, campo dell'Angelo Raffaele (041 523 7456). Vaporetto San Basilio. **Meals served** noon-2.30pm, 7-10.15pm daily; closed Wed in winter. **Map** p170 B12 **❼** Modern Italian

This nouvelle-*osteria* belongs to a chain specialising in the wine and ham of the Friuli region, but the place has a character of its own, determined partly by its high proportion of university patrons, and partly by the fact that the Friulian imprint is varied by dishes reflecting the chef's Sardinian roots, including *coniglio al mirto* (rabbit baked with myrtle). It functions as a bar all day (9am-11pm daily) – handy if you just want a drink in the pretty square.

❤ Riviera €€€€

Dorsoduro 1473, fondamenta Zattere Ponte Longo (041 522 7621). Vaporetto San Basilio or Zattere. **Meals served** 12.30-3pm, 7-10.30pm Mon-Tue, Fri-Sun. **Map** p170 C13 **❽** Seafood

Riviera is rarely less than an experience. The setting is spectacular to start with: in warm weather tables on the *fondamenta* afford views across the splendid Giudecca Canal, to San Giorgio Maggiore and the Redentore. The service is friendly, as the ever-present owner – former musician GP Cremonini – makes your enjoyment his business. What's on the plate – mainly but not solely seafood-based dishes – is creative, excellent... and pricey: this is a place for special occasions.

In the know
Barnabotti

In the final years of the Venetian Republic, penniless patricians used to end up in **San Barnaba** (see p175), where apartments were provided by the state for their use. The *barnabotti*, as they were known, could make a few *zecchini* (gold coins) by peddling their votes in the *maggior consiglio* (Great Council); otherwise they hung around in their tattered silk, muttering (after 1789) subversive comments about Liberty, Fraternity and Equality.

NORTH & CENTRE

▶ *Vaporetto Accademia, Ca' Rezzonico, San Basilio or Zattere.*

A long, irregular-shaped campo with churches at both ends, **campo Santa Margherita** buzzes day and night, with shoppers at the morning market (Monday to Saturday), hurrying students and scavenging pigeons during the day, and hordes of Venice's twentysomethings thronging bars at night.

There are several ancient *palazzi* around the square, with Byzantine and Gothic features. Isolated in the middle is the **Scuola dei Varoteri**, the School of the Tanners. At the north end is the former church of **Santa Margherita**, long used as a cinema and now beautifully restored as a conference hall for the university; the interior (sneak in the back for a quick gawp if there's anything going on) is so theatrical, it's difficult to imagine how it was ever used for religious purposes. St Margaret's dragon features on the campanile, and the sculpted saint also stands triumphant on the beast between the windows of a house at the north end of the square. A miraculous escape from the dragon's guts for some reason makes her the patron saint of pregnant women. At the other end of the square are the **scuola** and **church of the Carmini** (for both, *see p176*).

North out of Santa Margherita is **campo San Pantalon**. Its church (*see p176*) has an extraordinary Hollywood-rococo interior. If you walk out of the church towards the canal, an alley to the left will take you into little **campiello d'Angaran**, where there is a carved roundel of a Byzantine emperor, which possibly dates from the tenth century. Returning to the campo, you'll see a slab in the wall by the canal, which indicates the minimum lengths allowed for the sale of various types of fish. The narrow streets behind San Pantalon have seen several popular new *bacari* spring up in recent years, making it a fashionable but secluded *aperitivo* haunt for those in the know.

Leaving campo Santa Margherita by the southern end, on the other hand, you reach the picturesque rio di San Barnaba. At the eastern end of the *fondamenta* is the entrance to **Ca' Rezzonico** (*see p175*), designed by Longhena and now the museum of 18th-century Venice.

The middle bridge of the three that cross the canal is **ponte dei Pugni**; white marble footprints indicate that this was one of the bridges where punch-ups were held between the rival factions of the *nicolotti*, from the western quarters of the city, and the *castellani*, from the east. These violent brawls were tolerated by the authorities, who saw them as a chance for the working classes to let off steam in a way that was not disruptive to the state. They were banned, however, in 1705, after a particularly bloody fray.

Across the bridge is **campo San Barnaba**. The church of **San Barnaba** (often used for contemporary art shows) has a picturesque 14th-century campanile; the campo is a fine place for sitting outside a bar and watching the world go by. Katharine Hepburn fell into the canal flanking the campo in the film *Summertime*, causing permanent damage to her eyesight. In *Indiana Jones and the Last Crusade*, on the other hand, Harrison Ford entered the church (a library in the film) and, after contending with most of Venice's rat population, emerged from a manhole on to the pavement outside.

From the campo, the busy route towards the **Accademia** (*see p180*) passes alongside the **rio della Toletta** (where a small plank or *tola – tavola* in Italian – once served as a bridge) towards **rio San Trovaso**. This handsome canal has twin *fondamente* lined by fine Gothic and Renaissance palaces housing secondary schools and university buildings. On the campo of the same name is the church of **San Trovaso** (*see p176*), with two identical façades, one on to the canal and one on to its own campo. Backing on to the campo is a picturesque *squero*, one of the few remaining yards where gondolas are made.

Sights & museums

Ca' Rezzonico
(Museo del Settecento Veneziano)
Dorsoduro 3136, fondamenta Rezzonico (041 241 0100, www.visitmuve.it). Vaporetto Ca' Rezzonico. **Open** *10am-6pm Mon, Wed-Sun.* **Admission** *€10; €7.50 reductions (see also p65 Museum Passes).* **Map** *p170 E11.*

The Museum of 18th-century Venice is a gleaming (if somewhat chilly) showcase for the art of the Republic's twilight years. For most visitors, the paintings on display here will appear less impressive than the *palazzo* itself, an imposing Grand Canal affair designed by Baldassare Longhena for the Bon family in 1667. Bon ambitions exceeded Bon means, and the unfinished palace was sold on to the Rezzonico family – rich Genoese bankers who bought their way into Venice's nobility. The Rezzonicos' bid for stardom was crowned in 1758 by two events: the election of Carlo Rezzonico as Pope Clement XIII, and the marriage of Ludovico Rezzonico into one of Venice's oldest noble families, the Savorgnan.

Giambattista Tiepolo was called upon to celebrate the marriage on the ceiling of the Sala del Trono; he replied with a composition so playful it's easy to forget that it's all about purchasing rank and power. Giovanni Battista Crosato's over-the-top ceiling frescoes in the ballroom have aged less well but, together with the Murano chandeliers and intricately carved furniture by Andrea Brustolon, they provide an accurate record of the lifestyles of the rich and famous.

There are historical canvases by Giovanni Battista Piazzetta and Antonio Diziani, plus other gems. Detached frescoes of *pulcinellas* by Giandomenico Tiepolo capture the leisured melancholy of the moneyed classes as *La Serenissima* went into terminal decline. Originally painted for the Tiepolo family villa, they were moved here in 1936 and recently restored. There are some good genre paintings by Pietro Longhi, and a series of pastel portraits by Rosalba Carriera, a female 'prodigy' who was kept busy by English travellers eager to bring back a souvenir of their Grand Tour. On the third floor is the Egidio Martini gallery, a collection of mainly Venetian works, and a reconstruction of an 18th-century pharmacy, with fine majolica vases.

A staircase at the far end of the entrance hall leads to the 'Mezzanino Browning', where the poet Robert Browning died in 1889. This contains the Mestrovich Collection of Veneto paintings, donated to the city by Ferruccio Mestrovich as a sign of gratitude for the hospitality afforded to his family after they had been expelled from Dalmatia in 1945.

Campo Santa Margherita

San Pantalon

*Dorsoduro, campo San Pantalon (041
523 5893). Vaporetto San Tomà. **Open**
10am-noon, 1-3pm Mon-Sat. **Map** p170 E10.*

The dedicatee of this church is St Pantaleon,
a court physician to Emperor Galerius, who
was arrested, tortured and finally beheaded
during Diocletian's persecution of the
Christians in the late third century. The
saint's story is depicted inside the church in
an extraordinary ceiling painting – a huge
illusionist work, painted on 40 canvases, by
the Cecil B De Mille of the 17th century, Gian
Antonio Fumiani. It took him 24 years to
complete the task (1680-1704), and at the end
of it all he fell with choreographic grace from
the scaffolding to his death. Veronese depicts
the saint in less melodramatic fashion in the
second chapel on the right, in what is possibly
his last work, *St Pantaleon Healing a Child*.

To the left of the chancel is the Chapel
of the Holy Nail. The nail in question,
supposedly from the Crucifixion, is
preserved in a small but richly decorated
Gothic altar. On the right wall is a fine
Coronation of the Virgin by Antonio Vivarini
and Giovanni d'Alemagna.

San Trovaso

*Dorsoduro, campo San Trovaso (041 522
2133). Vaporetto Zattere. **Open** 2.30-5.30pm
Mon-Sat. **Map** p170 E13.*

This church overlooking a quiet campo has
two almost identical façades, both modelled
on the sub-Palladian church of Le Zitelle (*see
p192*) on the Giudecca. The story goes that
San Trovaso was built on the very border of
the two areas of the city belonging to the rival
factions of the *nicolotti* and *castellani*; in the
event of a wedding between members of the
two factions, each party was able to make its
own sweeping entrance and exit. There was
no actual saint called Trovaso: the name is a
Venetian telescoping of martyrs San Protasio
and San Gervasio.

There are five works by the Tintoretto
family in the church; three are probably
by the son, Domenico, including the two
on either side of the high altar, which are
rich in detail but poor in focus. In the left
transept is a smaller-than-usual version of
one of Tintoretto's favourite subjects, *The
Last Supper*; the tavern setting is strikingly
realistic.

In the chapel to the left of the high altar
is *The Temptations of St Anthony the Abbot*,
with enough vices to tempt a saint – note
the harlot with 'flames playing around her
loins', as John Ruskin so coyly put it. On the
side wall is a painting in the international
Gothic style by Michele Giambono, *St
Chrisogonus on Horseback* (c1450); the saint
is a boyish figure on a gold background, with

a shyly hesitant expression and a gorgeously
fluttering cloak and banner. In the Clary
chapel (right transept) are Renaissance
marble reliefs (c1470) showing angels
playing musical instruments or holding
instruments of the Passion, attributed
only to the conveniently named 'Master of
San Trovaso'.

Santa Maria dei Carmini

*Dorsoduro, campo dei Carmini (041 522
6553). Vaporetto Ca' Rezzonico or San
Basilio. **Open** 7am-noon, 2.30-7pm Mon-Sat;
8am-noon, 5-7pm Sun. **Map** p170 C11.*

The church officially called Santa Maria del
Carmelo has a tall campanile topped by a
statue of the Virgin. It is richly decorated
inside, with 17th-century gilt wooden statues
over the arcades of the nave and, above, a
series of Baroque paintings illustrating the
history of the Carmelite order. The best
paintings in the church are a *Nativity* by
Cima da Conegliano, on the second altar on
the right, and *St Nicholas of Bari* by Lorenzo
Lotto, opposite; the latter has a dreamy
landscape containing tiny figures of St
George and the dragon. To the right of the
Lotto painting is a Veronese *Holy Family*,
moved here from the church of San Barnaba.
In the chapel to the right of the high altar is
a graceful bronze relief of *The Lamentation
over the Dead Christ*, including portraits of
Federico da Montefeltro and Battista Sforza,
by the Sienese sculptor, painter, inventor,
military architect and all-round Renaissance
man Francesco di Giorgio.

Scuola dei Carmini

*Dorsoduro 2617, campo dei Carmini (041
528 9420, www.scuolagrandecarmini.it).
Vaporetto Ca' Rezzonico or San Basilio.
Open 11am-5pm daily. **Admission** €5; €4
reductions. **No cards. Map** p170 C11.*

Begun in 1670 to plans by Baldassare
Longhena, the building housing this *scuola*
(*see p115* Scuole Stories) run by the Carmelite
order was spared the Napoleonic lootings
that dispersed the fittings of most other
scuole. So we have a good idea of what an
early 18th-century Venetian confraternity
HQ must have looked like, from the elaborate
Sante Piatti altarpiece to the staircase with its
excrescence of gilded cherubs.

In the main hall of the first floor is one
of the most impressive of Giambattista
Tiepolo's Venetian ceilings: the airy panels
were painted from 1740 to 1743. Don't even
try to unravel the story – a celestial donation
that supposedly took place in Cambridge,
when Simon Stock received the scapular
(the badge of the Carmelite order) from the
Virgin. What counts, as always with Tiepolo,
is the audacity of his off-centre composition.

If the atmosphere were not so ultra-refined, there would be something disturbing in the Virgin's sneer of cold contempt and those swirling clouds. The central painting fell from the woodworm-ridden ceiling in August 2000 but has been beautifully restored. In the two adjoining rooms are wooden sculptures by Giacomo Piazzetta and a dramatic *Judith and Holofernes* by his more gifted son Giovanni Battista Piazzetta.

Restaurants

Africa Experience €€
Dorsoduro 2722, calle lunga San Barnaba (041 476 7865, www.africaexperience.eu). Vaporetto Ca' Rezzonico. **Open** *noon-3pm, 7-11pm daily.* **Map** *p170 D12* ❶ *African*

This sister venture to the successful Orient Experience (*see right*) uses food and decor to tell the story of the long journey undertaken by its staff of refugees and asylum seekers, and by countless migrants following similar routes. The colourful interiors, warm – if at times a little chaotic – service and wide selection of African-inspired dishes at reasonable prices, from Ethiopian bread and spiced vegetables to beef stew, are enough to make you forget your Venetian surroundings.

Ai Artisti €€
Dorsoduro 1169A, fondamenta della Toletta (041 523 8944, www.enotecaartisti.com). Vaporetto Accademia or Ca' Rezzonico. **Meals served** *12.45-2.30pm, 7-11pm Mon-Sat. Closed 3wks Dec-Jan.* **Map** *p170 E12* ❷ *Italian*

This tiny *trattoria* expands out on to the pretty canal-side walk in the warmer months, which is good because the demand is overwhelming: you are advised to book. In the kitchen, Francesca prepares everything from scratch, from a menu that changes day by day depending on what's good in the market. On Monday, meat dominates because the boats don't go out on Sunday; other days, you might find delicious prawn-stuffed squid, or a fillet of john dory lightly pan-fried with artichokes. If prices seem to be on the high-ish side, bear in mind that main courses have vegetables included (unusual in Italy).

La Bitta €€
Dorsoduro 2753A, calle lunga San Barnaba (041 523 0531). Vaporetto Ca' Rezzonico. **Meals served** *6.30-10.30pm Mon-Sat.* **Map** *p170 E12* ❹ *Italian*

La Bitta, a warm and rustic *osteria* with a small courtyard, stands out by having virtually no fish on the menu. Dishes like *straccetti di pollo ai finferli* (chicken strips with chanterelle mushrooms) or *oca in umido*

(stewed goose) make a welcome change. There's also a good selection of cheeses, served with honey or chutney, and intelligent by-the-glass wine options.

Oniga €€
Dorsoduro 2852, campo San Barnaba (041 522 4410, www.oniga.it). Vaporetto Ca' Rezzonico. **Meals served** *noon-3pm, 7-11pm daily. Closed 3wks Jan.* **Map** *p170 E12* ❺ *Modern Venetian*

With tables outside on campo San Barnaba, Oniga has a friendly, local feel. The menu is adventurous Venetian and changes frequently but the pasta is consistently excellent. Fish and meat figure among the *secondi*: the pork chop with potatoes and figs is good. Marino is a wine expert, and will guide you through the select list.

❤ Orient Experience €€
Dorsoduro 2920, campo Santa Margherita (041520 0217). Vaporetto Ca' Rezzonico. **Open** *11am-11.30pm daily.* **Map** *p170 D11* ❻ *Middle Eastern*

A welcome break from Venice-as-usual for both the palate and the wallet. This fast-expanding ethnic joint, which today counts a takeaway and restaurant in Santa Margherita and a second sit-down branch in Cannaregio (*see p135*), offers up a choice of dishes from the Middle East and Central Asia (falafel, rice recipes from Syria and Iran, spicy vegetable and meat sides) that channel the culinary heritage of its genial founders and staff.

Cafés, bars & gelaterie

Caffè Rosso
Dorsoduro 2963, campo Santa Margherita (041 528 7998, www.cafferosso.it). Vaporetto Ca' Rezzonico. **Open** *7am-1am Mon-Sat.* **No cards.** **Map** *p170 D11* ❶

Laid back and eclectic, the campo's oldest bar says 'Caffè' over the door, but it's universally known as 'Caffè Rosso' — perhaps for the decor, or for the political leanings of its boho-chic clientele. It attracts a mixed crowd of all ages who spill out from its single room to sip a spritz in the campo or to choose from the impressive wine list.

El Chioschetto
Dorsoduro 1406A, fondamenta delle Zattere (348 396 8466 mobile). Vaporetto Zattere. **Open** *Mar-Nov 8.30am-2am daily. Dec-Feb weather permitting.* **No cards.** **Map** *p170 D14* ❸

A much-loved spot not only for scrumptious panini and nibbles, but also for the tranquillity of sitting outside along the Giudecca Canal with a glass of wine and a sweeping view from industrial Marghera to Palladian San Giorgio Maggiore. There is no inside seating. From April to September there's live blues and jazz out on the *fondamenta* on Wednesday and Sunday evenings (6-9pm).

❤ Estro Vino e Cucina

Dorsoduro 3778, calle Crosera (041 476 4914, www.estrovenezia.com), Vaporetto San Tomà. **Open** *noon-2.30pm, 7-10.30pm Wed-Mon.* **Map** *p170 E10* ❺

This bustling *bacaro*, founded in 2014 by two brothers from Murano, offers up a refreshing blend of traditional and contemporary Venetian styles, and is fast becoming a favourite with young gourmands. Perch at the high wooden tables (crafted from lagoon marker-posts) by the bar and sample a selection of tasty snacks and quality wines from small Italian producers, or stay for a sit-down meal that gives a novel, unorthodox take on local recipes.

Grom

Dorsoduro 2761, campo San Barnaba (041 241 3531, www.grom.it). Vaporetto Ca' Rezzonico. **Open** *11am-9pm Mon-Fri, Sun; 11am-10pm Sat.* **Map** *p170 E12* ❼

Founded in Turin and now spreading as far afield as New York, the Grom *gelato* empire has also begun to colonise Venice, serving their trademark ice-cream with high-quality ingredients such as *Sfusato* lemons from Amalfi, *tonda gentile* hazelnuts from Lombardy, and pistachios from Bronte in Sicily. Note that prices are higher than at most other *gelaterie* in town. **Other locations** Cannaregio 3844, Strada Nova (041 260 2349); Stazione FS Santa Lucia (041 244 0120).

Impronta Café

Dorsoduro 3815, crosera San Pantalon (041 275 0386, www.improntacafevenice.com). Vaporetto San Tomà. **Open** *7am-noon Mon-Fri; 8am-1am Sat.* **Map** *p170 E10* ❽

Modern and minimalist, Impronta is an all-day operation, serving excellent coffee and *cornetti* at breakfast time to nightcaps into the wee hours. It's normally packed to the gills – especially with students during term time. The restaurant food (served 11am-midnight) is good and reasonably priced, and there's a list of 150-odd wines with which to wash it down. But you might prefer just to turn up for an *aperitivo* and experience the vibe in this buzzing part of town.

❤ Malvasia all'Adriatico Mar

Dorsoduro 3771, calle Crosera (041 476 4322), Vaporetto San Tomà. **Open** *10am-10pm Tue-Sun, 5-10pm Mon.* **Map** *p170 D10* ❾

For a different take on the spritz, as well as a good selection of wines, duck into this friendly, nautically themed watering hole, which has rejected 'industrial' brands Aperol and Campari in favour of Rosso and Rabarbaro (rhubarb) Nardini, from the historic distillery in Bassano. A door opposite the bar opens onto a small jetty providing cool and picturesque relief in warmer months, if you're lucky enough to bag a spot.

Osteria ai Pugni

Dorsoduro 2836, fondamenta Gherardini (346 960 7785 mobile, www.osteriaaipugni. com). Vaporetto Ca' Rezzonico. **Open** *8am-12.30am Mon-Sat, 11am-11pm Sun.* **No cards.** **Map** *p170 D12* ❿

There's always a warm welcome at this friendly bar at the foot of the Pugni Bridge, where locals and students pile in from breakfast time until late at night for time-appropriate beverages and snacks. As the day wears on, a selection of good sandwiches and *cicheti* appears on the counter. There's a sister establishment on neighbouring campo San Barnaba; called **Ai Artisti** (Dorsoduro 2771; open 7am-9pm Mon-Fri; 8am-late Sat; 9am-late Sun), it is similarly friendly but not to be confused with the nearby restaurant of the same name.

Tonolo

Dorsoduro 3764, calle San Pantalon (041 523 7209). Vaporetto San Tomà. **Open** *7.45am-8pm Tue-Sat; 7.45am-1pm Sun. Closed Aug.* **No cards.** **Map** *p170 E10* ⑫

This Venice institution has been operating in the same spot since 1953. The coffee is exceptional. On Sundays, the place fills up with locals buying sweet offerings to take to lunch – don't be shy about asserting your rights or you may never get served. All the delectable pastries come in miniature sizes to make sampling a little bit easier.

Shops & services

3856 di Elvira Rubelli

Dorsoduro 3749, calle San Pantalon (041 720 595). Vaporetto San Tomà. **Open** *11am-6pm Mon; 10am-1pm, 2.30-7pm Tue-Sat; 11am-6pm Sun.* **Map** *p170 C12* ❶ *Fashion/ accessories*

This boutique is particularly popular with fashion-conscious students. Jewellery, scarves and bags sit alongside clothes and shoes. Quality is high, and there is a huge range of fabric colours to choose from.

♥ Annelie

Dorsoduro 2748, calle lunga San Barnaba (041 520 3277). Vaporetto Ca' Rezzonico. **Open** *9.30am-12.30pm, 4-7pm Mon-Sat.* **Map** *p170 E12* ❷ *Homewares/children's*

A delightful shop run by a delightful lady who has a beautiful selection of sheets, tablecloths, curtains, shirts and baby clothes, either fully embroidered or with lace detailing. Antique lace is also stocked.

Arras

Dorsoduro 3235, campiello Squellini (041 522 6460, arrastessuti.wordpress.com). Vaporetto Ca' Rezzonico. **Open** *9am-1pm Mon; 9am-1.30pm, 2-6.30pm Tue-Fri.* **Map** *p170 D10* ❸ *Accessories*

In this venture involving disabled people, a variety of handwoven fabrics are created in a vast range of gorgeous colours and textures. These unique textiles are then worked into bags, clothing and scarves. Customised designs can be ordered. Arras also has ceramics and homewares... and it produces brilliantly coloured robes for priests, too.

Cafoscarina 2

Dorsoduro 3259, campiello degli Squellini (041 240 4802, www.cafoscarina.it). Vaporetto Ca' Rezzonico or San Tomà. **Open** *10am-7pm Mon-Fri; 10am-1pm Sat.* **Map** *p170 E11* ❹ *Books & music*

This is the official bookstore of the Università Ca' Foscari, selling mostly scholarly texts on a wide variety of topics. On the other side of the *campiello* is **Cafoscarina 3** (Dorsoduro 3224, 041 240 4803), which stocks a good selection of books in English.

Ca' Macana

Dorsoduro 3172, calle delle Botteghe (041 520 3229, www.camacana.com). Vaporetto Ca' Rezzonico. **Open** *10am-7.30pm daily.* **Map** *p170 E11* ❺ *Carnival masks*

This workshop packed with traditional papier-mâché masks from the commedia dell'arte theatre tradition makes all its own products, unlike so many of the carbon-copy shops that plague the city. This is where Stanley Kubrick came to stock up when making *Eyes Wide Shut*. Explanations of the mask-making process, as well as courses, are given by the artist in residence. **Other locations** Dorsoduro 1169, fondamenta della Toletta (041 522 9749); Dorsoduro 3215, calle del Capeler.

Canestrelli

Dorsoduro 1173, calle della Toletta (041 277 0617, www.venicemirrors.com). Vaporetto Accademia. **Open** *11am-1.30pm, 3.30-7.30pm Mon-Sat.* **Map** *p170 E12* ❻ *Mirrors*

Designer-producer Stefano Coluccio specialises in beautifully framed convex mirrors.

♥ Libreria Marco Polo

Dorsoduro 2899, rio Terà Canal (041 822 4843, www.libreriamarcopolo.com). Vaporetto Ca' Rezzonico. **Open** *10am-10pm Mon-Sat; 11am-8pm Sun.* **Map** *p170 D11* ❿ *Books & music*

Claudio Moretti's quirky bookshop is a labour of love. Selling books for adults and children from independent publishers in Italian, English and other languages, it moved to the area a few years ago and has benefited from the resulting influx of culture-hungry locals and university students. There are book presentations, meetings with writers and events of all kinds.

Libreria Toletta

Dorsoduro 1214, calle Toletta (041 523 2034, www.latoletta.com). Vaporetto Accademia or Ca' Rezzonico. **Open** *9am-7.30pm Mon-Sat; 3-7pm Sun.* **Map** *p170 E12* ⓫ *Books & music*

Toletta offers 20-40% off the usual retail prices. Italian classics, art, cookery, children's books and history (mostly in Italian) all feature, along with a vast assortment of dictionaries and reference books.

Madera

Dorsoduro 2762, campo San Barnaba (041 522 4181, www.maderavenezia.it). Vaporetto Ca' Rezzonico. **Open** *10am-1pm, 3.30-7.30pm Tue-Sat.* **Map** *p170 E12* ⓬ *Homewares/accessories*

Fusing minimalist design with traditional techniques, the young architect and craftswoman behind Madera creates unique objects in wood. She also sells exceptional lamps, ceramics, jewellery and textiles by other craftspeople, many of them Venice-based. Some of the homeware is now just down the road in calle Lunga San Barnaba (2729).

♥ Signor Blum

Dorsoduro 2840, campo San Barnaba (041 522 6367, www.signorblum.com). Vaporetto Ca' Rezzonico. **Open** *9.45am-1.30pm, 2.45-7.15pm daily.* **Map** *p170 E12* ⓯ *Jigsaw puzzles*

Mr Blum's colourful handmade wooden puzzles of Venetian *palazzi*, gondolas and animals make great gifts for children and adults alike. **Other locations** Castello 5786B, calle del Mondo Nuovo (041 523 3056); Cannaregio 1370, rio terà San Leonardo (041 719 695).

▶ *Vaporetto Accademia, Salute or Zattere.*

The eastern reaches of Dorsoduro, from the rio di San Trovaso, past the **Accademia** (*see right*) and the **Salute** to the **Punta della Dogana**, is an area of elegant, artsy prosperity, home to artists, writers and wealthy foreigners. Ezra Pound spent his last years in a small house near the Zattere promenade; Peggy Guggenheim hosted her collection of modern artists in her truncated *palazzo* on the Grand Canal (now the **Peggy Guggenheim Collection**; *see p183*); artists use the vast spaces of the old warehouses on the Zattere as studios. On Sunday mornings, **campo San Vio** is some corner of a foreign land, as British expats home in on the Anglican church of **St George**. Overlooking the campo, the **Galleria Palazzo Cini** (*see p186*) houses a charming collection of Ferrarese and Tuscan art.

It is a district of quiet canals and cosy *campielli*, perhaps the most picturesque being **campiello Barbaro**, behind pretty, lopsided **Ca' Dario** (rumoured, due to sudden deaths of owners over the centuries, to be cursed). But all that money has certainly driven out the locals: nowhere in Venice are you further from a simple *alimentari* (grocery store).

The colossal magnificence of Longhena's church of **Santa Maria della Salute** (*see p182*) brings the residential area to an end. Beyond is the **Punta della Dogana**, a triangle of land that served as Venice's maritime customs post (**Dogana da Mar**). Debate about redeploying this empty space raged for years: in the end, the contract for redevelopment went to French magnate Francois Pinault. With the **Punta Della Dogana gallery** (*see p185*) open, it is once again possible to stroll around the *punta*, with its spectacular view across the water towards St Mark's.

South from punta della Dogana, the mile-long stretch of **Le Zattere**, Venice's finest promenade after the riva degli Schiavoni, leads westwards along the Giudecca Canal. It is named after the *zattere* (rafts) that used to moor here, bringing wood and other materials across from the mainland. The paved quayside was created by decree in 1519. It now provides a favourite strolling

❤ Gallerie dell'Accademia

*Dorsoduro 1050, campo Carità (041 520 0345, www.gallerieaccademia.org). Vaporetto Accademia. **Open** 8.15am-2pm Mon; 8.15am-7.15pm Tue-Sun. **Admission** €12; €6 reductions; under-18s free; price varies for special exhibitions. Audio guide €6. **Map** p170 F13.*

The Accademia is the essential one-stop shop for Venetian painting, and one of the world's greatest art treasure houses. It was Napoleon who made the collection possible: first, by suppressing hundreds of churches, convents and religious guilds, confiscating their artworks for the greater good of the state; and second, by moving the city's Accademia di Belle Arti art school here, with the mandate both to train students and to act as a gallery and storeroom for all the evicted artworks, which were originally displayed as models for pupils to aspire to. The art school moved to a new site on the nearby Zattere in 2004, leaving the freed-up space for a long-awaited gallery extension that opened in 2015. The Accademia galleries now incorporate parts of the church and Scuola della Carità (the oldest of the Venetian *scuole*, founded in the 13th century) and the 12th-century monastery of the Lateran Canons, which was remodelled by Andrea Palladio. (His superb oval staircase is now on view.) Note that the arrangement of art in the galleries may alter as restoration work continues.

The collection is arranged roughly chronologically, with the exception of the 15th- and 16th-century works in rooms 19-24 at the end. It opens with 14th- and 15th-century devotional works by Paolo Veneziano and others – stiff figures against gold backdrops in the Byzantine tradition. This room was the main hall of the *scuola grande*: note the original ceiling of gilded cherubim. Rooms 2 and 3 have devotional paintings and altarpieces by Carpaccio, Cima da Conegliano and Giovanni Bellini (a fine *Enthroned Madonna with Six Saints*).

In Room 4 are works by Bellini and Giorgione's *Old Woman*, while room 5 exhibits works from the museum's archives. In Room 6, two of the greats of 16th-century Venetian painting – Tintoretto and Veronese – are first encountered. But the battle of the giants gets under way in earnest in Room 10, where they are joined by Titian. Tintoretto's ghostly chiaroscuro *Transport of the Body*

In the know
As the wind blows...

The tower of the Dogana da Mar is crowned by two statues of Atlas holding a golden globe on their shoulders. The goddess of Fortune stands on one leg on the top, spinning in the wind.

Christ in the House of Levi (Paolo Veronese, 1573)

of St Mark vies for attention with Titian's moving *Pietà* – his last painting – and Veronese's huge *Christ in the House of Levi*.

Room 11 covers two centuries, with canvases by Tintoretto (the exquisite *Madonna dei Camerlenghi*), Bernardo Strozzi and Tiepolo. The series of rooms beyond brings the plot up to the 18th century, with all the old favourites: Canaletto, Guardi, Longhi and soft-focus, bewigged portraits by female superstar Rosalba Carriera.

Rooms 19 and 20 take us back to the 15th century; the latter has the rich *Miracle of the Relic of the Cross* cycle, a collaborative effort by Gentile Bellini, Carpaccio and others, which is packed with telling social details; there's even a black gondolier in Carpaccio's *Miracle of the Cross at the Rialto*.

An even more satisfying cycle has Room 21 to itself (closed for restoration during 2017). Carpaccio's *Life of St Ursula* (1490-95) tells the story of the legendary Breton princess who embarked on a pilgrimage to Rome with her betrothed so that he could be baptised into the true faith. All went swimmingly until Ursula and all the 11,000 virgins accompanying her were massacred by the Huns in Cologne (the initial 'M' – for martyr – used in one account of the affair caused the multiplication of the number

In the know
By any other name…

Paolo Veronese's vast *Christ in the House of Levi* in the Accademia gallery was painted as a *Last Supper*. In 1573, the Inquisition took offence at a *Last Supper* in which figures of 'buffoons, drunkards, Germans, dwarves' supposedly insulted church decorum, and threatened Veronese with heresy charges. The artist – with admirable chutzpah – simply changed its name.

of accompanying maidens from 11 to 11,000, M being the Roman numeral for 1,000). More than the ropey legend, it's the architecture, the ships and the pageantry in these meticulous paintings that grab the attention. Perhaps most striking, amid all the closely thronged, action-packed scenes, is the rapt stillness and solitude of *The Dream of St Ursula*.

Room 23 is the former church of Santa Maria della Carità: here are Giorgione's *The Tempest*, devotional works by Vivarini, the Bellinis and others. Room 24 – the Albergo room (or secretariat) of the former *scuola* – contains the only work in the whole gallery that is in its original site: Titian's magnificent *Presentation of the Virgin*.

181

ground, punctuated by some spectacularly situated (if somewhat shadeless) benches for a picnic.

The eastern end is usually quiet, with the occasional flurry of activity around the rowing clubs now occupying the 14th-century salt warehouses, one of which now hosts the **Fondazione Vedova** gallery (*see below*).

Westward from these are the church of **Spirito Santo** and the long 16th-century façade of the grimly named **Ospedale degli Incurabili** (the main incurable disease of the time was syphilis). In Ben Jonson's play *Volpone*, the title character's property is confiscated and he himself sent to this hospital at the end of the play. Today the hospital building houses the **Accademia di Belle Arti** (the school of fine arts that was evicted from the Accademia).

The liveliest part of the Zattere is around the churches of **I Gesuati** (*see below*) and **Santa Maria della Visitazione** (*see p184*). Venetians flock here at weekends and on warm evenings to savour ice-cream or sip drinks at canalside tables.

Sights & museums

Fondazione Vedova

Dorsoduro 50, fondamenta zattere ai Saloni (041 522 6626, www.fondazionevedova. org). Vaporetto Salute or Zattere. **Open** *10.30am-6pm Mon, Wed-Sun.* **Admission** *€8; €6 reductions.* **Map** *p170 J14.*

A selection of works by Venetian artist Emilio Vedova (1919-2006) is now housed in a stunning new gallery, designed by Renzo Piano, in the Magazzini del Sale (salt warehouses). Immense canvasses by this leading member of the European avant-garde are suspended from moving brackets in what curators describe as a 'dynamic' exhibition.

I Gesuati

Dorsoduro, fondamenta Zattere ai Gesuati (041 275 0642, www.chorusvenezia.org). Vaporetto Zattere. **Open** *10.30am-4.30pm Mon-Sat.* **Admission** *€3 (or Chorus; see p65). No cards.* **Map** *p170 F14.*

This church is officially Santa Maria del Rosario, but it is always known as the Gesuati, after the minor religious order that owned the previous church here. The order merged with the Dominicans – the present owners – in 1668. I Gesuati is a great piece of teamwork by a trio of remarkable rococo artists: architect Giorgio Massari, painter Giambattista Tiepolo and sculptor Giovanni Morlaiter.

The façade deliberately reflects the Palladian church of the Redentore opposite, but the splendidly posturing statues give it that typically 18th-century touch

of histrionic flamboyance. Plenty more theatrical sculpture is to be found inside the church, all by Morlaiter. Above is a magnificent ceiling by Tiepolo, with three frescoes on Dominican themes. These works reintroduced frescoes to Venetian art after two centuries of canvas ceiling paintings. The central panel shows St Dominic passing on to a crowd of supplicants the rosary he has just received from the cloud-enthroned Madonna. Tiepolo also painted the surrounding grisailles, which, at first sight, look like stucco reliefs.

There is another brightly coloured Tiepolo on the first altar on the right, *The Virgin and Child with Saints Rosa, Catherine and Agnes*. Tiepolo here plays with optical effects, allowing St Rosa's habit to tumble out of the frame. In his painting of three Dominican saints on the third altar on the right, Giovanni Battista Piazzetta makes use of a narrower and more sober range of colours, going for a more sculptural effect.

♥ Santa Maria della Salute

Dorsoduro, campo della Salute (041 274 3928, www.basilicasalute.it). Vaporetto Salute. **Open** *9.30am-noon, 3-5.30pm daily.* **Admission** *Church free. Sacristy €4.* **No cards.** **Map** *p170 J13.*

This magnificent Baroque church, queening it over the entrance of the Grand Canal, is almost as recognisable an image of Venice as St Mark's or the Rialto Bridge. It was built between 1631 and 1681 in thanksgiving for the end of Venice's last bout of plague, which had wiped out at least a third of the population in 1630. The church is dedicated to the Madonna, as protector of the city. Every year on 21st November (*see p233*), a processions from San Marco makes it way across a specially erected pontoon bridge to the church.

The terms of the competition won by 26-year-old architect Baldassare Longhena presented a serious challenge, which beat some of the best architects of the day. The church was to be colossal but inexpensive; the whole structure was to be visually clear on entrance, with an unimpeded view of the high altar, the ambulatory and side altars coming into sight only as one approached the chancel; the light was to be evenly distributed; and the whole building should *creare una bella figura* – show itself off to good effect.

Longhena succeeded brilliantly in satisfying all of these requisites – particularly the last and most Venetian of them. The church takes superb advantage of its dominant position and pays homage to both the Byzantine form of San Marco across the Grand Canal and the classical

💙 Peggy Guggenheim Collection

Dorsoduro 701, fondamenta Venier dei Leoni (041 240 5411, www.guggenheim-venice.it). Vaporetto Accademia or Salute. **Open** *10am-6pm Mon, Wed-Sun.* **Admission** *€15; €9-€13 reductions.* **Map** *p170 H13.*

This remarkable establishment, tucked behind a high wall off a quiet street (but with a Grand Canal frontage), is the third most visited museum in the city. It was founded by one of Venice's most colourful expat residents, Peggy Guggenheim.

She turned up in the lagoon city in 1949 looking for a home for her already sizeable art collection. A short-sighted curator at the Tate Gallery in London had described her growing pile of surrealist and modernist works as 'non-art'. Venice, still struggling to win back the tourists after World War II, was less finicky, and Peggy found a perfect, eccentric base in Palazzo Venier dei Leoni, a truncated 18th-century Grand Canal *palazzo*.

There are big European names in her art collection, including Picasso, Duchamp, Brancusi, Giacometti and Max Ernst, plus a few Americans such as Calder and Jackson Pollock. Highlights include the beautifully enigmatic *Empire of Light* by Magritte and Giacometti's disturbing *Woman with Her Throat Cut*. The flamboyant *Attirement of the Bride*, by Peggy's husband, Max Ernst, often turns up as a Carnevale costume. But perhaps the most startling exhibit of all is the rider of Marino Marini's *Angel of the City* out on the Grand Canal terrace, who thrusts his manhood towards passing vaporetti. (Never the shrinking wallflower, Peggy took delight in unscrewing the member and pressing it on young men she fancied.) The gallery has a pleasant garden and café.

In the know
Another Venetian eccentric

Peggy Guggenheim wasn't the first eccentric female to occupy **Palazzo Venier dei Leoni**, which now houses the Peggy Guggenheim Collection; from 1910 to 1924 the building was the home of the Marchesa Luisa Casati, who liked to parade through piazza San Marco with a pair of cheetahs on diamond-studded leashes.

form of Palladio's Redentore, across the Giudecca Canal.

The architect said he chose the circular shape with the reverent aim of offering a crown to the Madonna. She stands on the lantern above the cupola as described in the Book of Revelations: 'Clothed in the sun, and the moon under her feet, and upon her head a crown of twelve stars.' Beneath her, on the great scroll-brackets around the cupola, stand statues of the Apostles – the 12 stars in her crown. This Marian symbolism continues inside the church, where in the centre of the mosaic floor, amid a circle of roses, is an inscription, *Unde origo inde salus* (from the origin comes salvation) – a reference to the legendary birth of Venice under the Virgin's protection.

Longhena's intention was for the visitor to approach the high altar ceremoniously through the main door, with the six side altars only coming into view upon reaching the very centre of the church, where they appear framed theatrically in their separate archways. However, the main door is rarely open and often the central area of the church is roped off, so you have no choice but to walk round the ambulatory and visit the chapels separately.

Dome of Santa Maria della Salute

The three on the right have paintings by Luca Giordano, a prolific Neapolitan painter who brought a little southern brio into the art of the city at a time (the mid 17th century) when most painting had become limply derivative.

On the opposite side is a clumsily restored *Pentecost*, by Titian, transferred here from the island monastery of Santo Spirito (demolished in 1656). The high altar has a splendidly dynamic sculptural group by Giusto Le Corte, the artist responsible (with assistants) for most of the statues inside and outside the church. This group represents *Venice Kneeling before the Virgin and Child*, while the plague, in the shape of a hideous old hag, scurries off to the right, prodded by a tough-looking *putto*. In the midst of all this marble hubbub is a serene Byzantine icon of the *Madonna and Child*, brought from Crete in 1669 by Francesco Morosini, the Venetian commander later responsible for blowing up the Parthenon.

Sacristy

The best paintings are in the sacristy (open from 10am). Tintoretto's *Marriage at Cana* (1551) was described by Ruskin as 'perhaps the most perfect example which human art has produced of the utmost possible force and sharpness of shadow united with richness of local colour'. He also points out how difficult it is to spot the bride and groom in the painting.

On the altar is a very early Titian of *Saints Mark, Sebastian, Roch, Cosmas and Damian*, saints who were all invoked for protection against the plague; the painting was done during the outbreak of 1509-14. Three later works by Titian (c1540-49) hang on the ceiling, violent Old Testament scenes also brought here from the church of Santo Spirito: *The Sacrifice of Abraham, David Killing Goliath* and *Cain and Abel*. These works established the conventions for all subsequent ceiling paintings in Venice: Titian decided not to go for the worm's-eye view adopted by Mantegna and Correggio, which sacrificed clarity for surprise, and instead chose an oblique viewpoint, as if observing the action from the bottom of a hill. More Old Testament turbulence can be seen in Salviati's *Saul Hurling a Spear at David* and Palma il Giovane's *Samson and Jonah*, in which the whale is represented mainly by a vast lolling rubbery tongue.

Santa Maria della Visitazione

Dorsoduro, fondamenta Zattere ai Gesuati (041 522 4077). Vaporetto Zattere. **Open** *8am-noon, 3-6pm daily.* **Map** *p170 F14.*

Confusingly, this has the same name as the Vivaldi church on the riva degli Schiavoni – though the latter is usually known as La Pietà (*see p120*). Santa Maria della Visitazione is now the chapel of the Istituto Don Orione,

💙 Punta della Dogana

*Dorsoduro 2, campo della Salute (041 200 1057, www.palazzograssi.it). Vaporetto Salute. **Open** 10am-7pm Mon, Wed-Sun. **Admission** €18; €15 reductions (Punta & Palazzo Grassi; see p101). **Map** p170 K13.*

Due to its strategic location between San Marco, the Grand Canal and the Giudecca Canal, the Punta della Dogana served as Venice's customs post from the 15th century. The triangular complex of warehouses, with the distinctive Customs House tower at its tip, was completed in the late 17th century and remained in use until the 1980s. The buildings were left empty until 2007 when French tycoon Francois Pinault beat the Peggy Guggenheim Collection (*see p183*) in a bid to turn them into a contemporary art gallery – much to the annoyance of many Venetians who felt that Pinault's outpost at Palazzo Grassi (*see p101*) was more than enough. Inaugurated in June 2009 after a remarkable makeover by Japanese archistar Tadao Ando, the Punta della Dogana gallery masterfully mixes contemporary architectural elements, such as concrete floors, reinforced steel and glass fixtures, with the original stuccoes, exposed brick walls and wooden beams of the 17th-century buildings. The gallery shows revolving themed exhibitions based around Pinault's own immense art collection and has confirmed Venice's key place on Europe's contemporary art circuit. In 2017 it hosted a major solo show by Damien Hirst.

The Fate of a Banished Man (Damien Hirst) at Punta della Dogana, 2017

DORSODURO

which has taken over the vast complex of the monastery of the Gesuati next door.

Designed by Tullio Lombardo or Mauro Codussi and built in 1423, the church has an attractive early Renaissance façade. It was suppressed (that rascal Napoleon again) at the beginning of the 19th century and stripped of all its works of art with the exception of the original coffered ceiling,

an unexpected delight containing 58 compartments with portraits of saints and prophets by an Umbrian painter of Luca Signorelli's school, one of the few examples of central Italian art in Venice. To the right of the façade is a lion's mouth for secret denunciations: the ones posted here went to the *Magistrati della sanità*, who dealt with matters of public health.

💙 Galleria Palazzo Cini

Dorsoduro 864, piscina del Forner (041 2710217, www.palazzocini.it). Vaporetto Accademia. **Open** *Apr-Nov 11am-7pm Mon, Wed-Sun. Closed Dec-Mar.* **Admission** *€10; €8 reductions.* **Map** *p170 G13.*

Portrait of Two Friends (Jacopo Pontormo, c1522)

This lovely house-turned-museum showcases a stunning private collection of Ferrarese and Tuscan art, assembled by industrialist Vittorio Cini. Cini is better known for his restoration of the monastic complex on the island of San Giorgio Maggiore (*see p195*) as a cultural foundation, but this smaller project is well worth a visit.

A core collection of paintings, sculptures, porcelain and glass work gathered in the 1940s and '50s was supplemented in 1989 and, again, in 2015 by pieces of Ferrarese art. Among the pieces on display are a few gems, including a collection of Tuscan primitives, the unfinished Pontormo double *Portrait of Two Friends* (on the first floor) and Dosso Dossi's *Allegorical Scene* (on the second), a vivacious character study from the D'Este Palace in Ferrara. There are also some delicate late-medieval ivories and a rare 14th-century wedding chest decorated with chivalric scenes.

As you explore, take time to appreciate the oval spiral staircase and the dining room, designed by architect Tommaso Buzzi.

Restaurants

▶ *See also right* **Osteria al Squero.**

Ai Gondolieri €€€€

Dorsoduro 366, fondamenta Ospedaletto (041 528 6396, www.aigondolieri.com). Vaporetto Accademia or Salute. **Meals served** *noon-3pm, 7-11.15pm daily.* **Map** *p170 G14* ❸

Modern Italian

If you're looking to splash out, Ai Gondolieri offers a creative menu that belies its ultra-traditional decor and service. It's also, unusually for Venice, fish-free. Rooted in the culinary traditions of north-east Italy, dishes include a warm salad of venison with blueberries, *panzerotti* (pasta parcels) filled with Jerusalem artichokes in Montasio cheese sauce, and pork fillet in pear sauce with wild fennel. Enquire about the price before tasting truffle delights in autumn.

Cafés, bars & gelaterie

💙 Cantinone (già Schiavi)

Dorsoduro 992, fondamenta Nani (041 523 0034). Vaporetto Accademia or Zattere. **Open** *8am-8pm Mon-Sat.* **Map** *p170 F13* ❷

Two generations of the Gastaldi family work in the Cantinone (also, confusingly, known as Il Bottegon) filling glasses, carting cases of wine, and preparing huge panini with mortadella or more delicate *crostini* with, for example, creamed pistachio or cream cheese with fish roe. Give yourself ample opportunity to select from the day's offerings by arriving before the crowds pour in at 1pm. When the bar itself is full, you'll be in good company on the bridge outside – an apt setting for the Venetian ritual of spritz and prosecco consumption.

Corner Pub

Dorsoduro 684, calle della Chiesa (349 457 6739 mobile). Vaporetto Accademia or Salute. **Open** *8am-midnight Mon, Wed-Sun.* **Map** *p170 G13* ❹

With an Irish-pub feel that belies its distinctly Venetian setting, this small bar close to the Guggenheim is a handy place to refuel after a full modern art immersion. When the weather allows, patrons spill out onto the street and the pretty bridge behind, to consume their spritz and sandwich al fresco.

Gelateria Lo Squero

Dorsoduro 989-990, fondamenta Nani (347 269 7921 mobile). Vaporetto Accademia or Zattere. **Open** *10am-8pm daily.* **No cards.** **Map** *p170 F13* ❻

Simone Sambo makes some of the finest ice-cream in Venice. He's hard-pressed to pinpoint a favourite flavour, but can happily rattle off those in his current repertoire – which always depends on the freshest ingredients available. His mousse series (blueberry, strawberry, chocolate and hazelnut, among others) is so light and creamy, it's served in a waffle cone so it doesn't fly away.

Osteria al Squero

Dorsoduro 944, fondamenta Nani (335 600 7513 mobile). Vaporetto Zattere or Accademia. **Open** *11am-9.30pm Mon, Tue, Thur-Sun.* **No cards.** **Map** *p170 E14* ⓫

This simple, friendly *bacaro*, located opposite one of Venice's very few remaining gondola building/repairing yards (*squero*), looks as if it has been here since time immemorial, but that's an illusion. The former teachers who run the place, however, have perfectly captured the spirit of the traditional Venetian drinking den, adding only some truly gourmet *cicheti* at very reasonable prices: many customers turn up for a single glass of wine, and end up making a full meal out of a plate of these delicious titbits. There are no tables, just benches and perching places; on fine days, much of the clientele will be standing out on the *fondamenta*, gazing across at the *squero*.

Shops & services

Cornici Trevisanello

Dorsoduro 662, fondamenta Bragadin (041 520 7779). Vaporetto Accademia. **Open** *9am-1pm, 3-7pm Mon-Fri; 9am-1pm Sat.* **Map** *p170 G13* ❼ *Frames*

This workshop is home to a father, son and daughter team that makes beautiful gilded frames, many with pearl, mirror and glass

inlay. Custom orders and shipping are not a problem.

Le Forcole di Saverio Pastor

Dorsoduro 341, fondamenta Soranzo de la Fornace (041 522 5699, www.forcole.com). Vaporetto Salute. **Open** *8am-6pm Mon-Fri.* **Map** *p170 H13* ❽ *Oar-makers/gifts*

This is the place to come when you need a new *forcola* (walnut-wood rests) or pair of oars for your favourite gondola. Saverio Pastor is one of only three recognised *marangon* (oar-makers) in Venice; he specialises in making the elaborate *forcole* that are the symbols of the gondolier's trade. There are also bookmarks, postcards and some books (in English) on Venetian boatworks.

Genninger Studio

Dorsoduro 364, campiello Barbaro (041 522 5565, www.genningerstudio.com). Vaporetto Accademia or Salute. **Open** *10am-12.30pm, 3-6.30pm daily.* **Map** *p170 H13* ❾ *Accessories/homewares*

After years in a studio with a Grand Canal frontage, designer Leslie Ann Genninger has moved her brilliantly coloured creations to pretty campiello Barbaro: her flame-worked and blown beads, custom jewellery, knick-knacks, lighting and mirrors offer a contemporary take on Venetian luxury and decadence.

Marina & Susanna Sent

Dorsoduro 669 & 681, campo san Vio (041 520 8136, www.marinaesusannasent.com). Vaporetto Accademia. **Open** *10am-6pm daily.* **Map** *p170 G13* ⓭ *Accessories*

Some of Venice's finest contemporary glass jewellery is created by the Sent sisters. There's also a good selection of the work of the contemporary design house Arcade. **Other locations** San Marco 2090, ponte San Mosie (041 520 4014); Murano, fondamenta Serenella 20 (041 527 4665).

Il Pavone

Dorsoduro 721, fondamenta Venier dei Leoni (041 523 4517). Vaporetto Accademia. **Open** *9.30am-1.30pm, 2.30-6.30pm daily.* **Map** *p170 G13* ⓮ *Gifts & stationery*

This is a place to seek out for handmade paper with floral motifs in a variety of colours. Il Pavone also stocks boxes, picture frames and other objects, all decorated in the same style.

La Giudecca & San Giorgio

Once a place of flourishing monasteries and lush gardens, the gondola-shaped island of La Giudecca, just across the water from the south of Venice proper, might appear run-down today. Its nature changed in the 19th century when city authorities began converting abandoned religious houses into factories and prisons. The factories have almost all closed down, but the prisons remain in use. The Giudecca now has a reputation as one of the poorer areas in the city, but it manages to attract more than its fair share of celebrities, and locals in the know come here for its community spirit and alternative arty scene.

With its splendid Palladian church facing the Doge's Palace across the lagoon, the island of San Giorgio is an immediately recognisable Venetian icon.

❤ **Don't miss**

1 San Giorgio Maggiore *p195*
The view from the bell tower is unique.

2 Fortuny Tessuti Artistici *p194*
An Aladdin's cave of fabulous fabrics.

3 Fondazione Giorgio Cini *p194*
Don't miss the amazing maze in the grounds.

Elaborate carving in the sacristy of the church of San Giorgio Maggiore

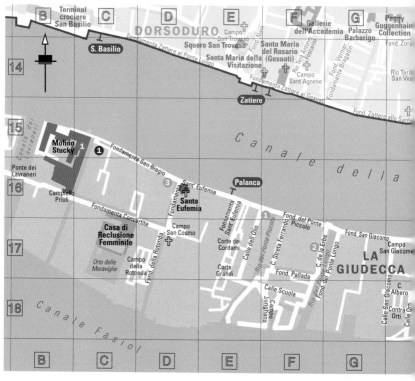

LA GIUDECCA & SAN GIORGIO

Restaurants

1. Alla Palanca
2. Altanella
3. Harry's Dolci

Cafés, bars & gelaterie

1. Skyline Bar

Shops & services

1. Fortuny Tessuti Artistici

♥ **Time to eat & drink**

Aperitivo with a view
Skyline bar *p193*

Fab food with a view
Alla Palanca *p193*

Family cooking off the beaten track
Altanella *p193*

♥ **Time to shop**

Fabrics galore
Fortuny Tessuti *p194*

Growing behind bars
Women's prison weekly market *p192*

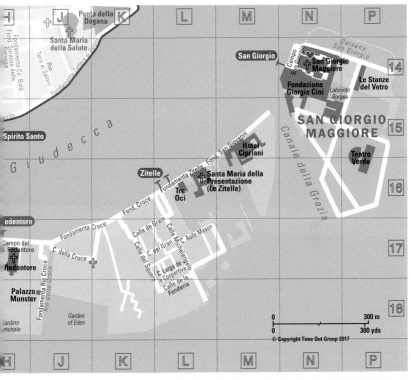

San Giorgio Maggiore

LA GIUDECCA

The Giudecca was once known as 'Spinalonga', from an imagined resemblance to a fish-skeleton (*spina* means fish bone). Some claim that the present name derives from an early community of Jews, and others to the fact that the island was a place of exile for troublesome nobles who had been *giudicati*: 'judged'. The exile was sometimes self-chosen, however, as people used the islands as a place of rural retreat. Michelangelo, when exiled from Florence in 1529, chose to mope here; three centuries later, during his steamy and highly public love affair with George Sand, Alfred de Musset wrote in praise of the flowery meadows of 'la Zuecca'.

The Giudecca's industrial heritage is in the process of being shaken up: some of the factories remain abandoned, contributing to the run-down appearance of the south side of the Giudecca, but a few have been converted into new residential complexes. The greatest transformation has been that of the **Molino Stucky**, the vast turreted and crenellated Teutonic mass at the western end of the Giudecca. The largest building in the lagoon, it was built as a flour mill in 1896 and continued to function until 1955. After decades of rat-ridden abandonment, it now hosts the **Hilton Hotel** with its conference centre, rooftop **Skyline Bar** (*see p193*), swimming pool and private flats.

The *palazzi* along the northern *fondamenta* enjoy a splendid view of Venice and attract well-heeled outsiders (Elton John and Giorgio Armani, for example) in search of picturesque holiday homes. Apart from the Hilton, there are a number of other major hotels, including the swanky **Cipriani** (*see p291*), at the eastern end. The island's disused warehouses are popular as studios for artists.

The main sights of the Giudecca are all on this northern *fondamenta*: **Santa Eufemia** (*see p193*), the Palladian church of **Le Zitelle** ('the spinsters': the convent ran a hospice for poor girls who were trained as lace-makers), which is nearly always closed, and the 16th-century church known as **Il Redentore** (*see p193*), as well as several fine *palazzi*.

Near Le Zitelle is the neo-Gothic **Casa De Maria**, with its three large inverted-shield windows. The Bolognese painter Mario De Maria built it for himself from 1910 to 1913. It's now home to **Tre Oci** (www.treoci.org), a space hosting regular photography exhibitions. It is the only private *palazzo* to have the same patterned brickwork as the Doge's Palace.

On the fondamenta Rio della Croce (no.149, close to Il Redentore) stands the **Palazzo Munster**, a former infirmary for English sailors. The vitriolic Anglo-Catholic writer Frederick Rolfe received the last sacraments here in 1911, after slagging the hospital off in his novel *The Desire and Pursuit of the Whole*. (He then lived for two more vituperative years.)

Garden of Marvels

Behind prison walls, female inmates grow organic vegetables

Before it became an industrial hub in the late 19th century, the Giudecca was Venice's garden island, home to secluded *palazzi* and monasteries, each with its extensive *orto* (vegetable garden) producing fruit and vegetables. In one (very) out-of-the-way corner of this little-visited island, a group of women continues this tradition. Behind the high walls of a 13th-century former convent on the fondamenta delle Convertite, the inmates of the **Casa di Reclusione Femminile** (women's prison) grow organic vegetables in a 6,400-square-metre (1.6-acre) plot. To sample the produce of the *Orto delle Meraviglie* – the 'Garden of Marvels', as the vegetable garden is known – turn up outside the prison walls on a Thursday morning. Throughout the year, whatever this lovingly tended, chemical-free oasis yields goes on sale to the public. Produce from the garden also makes its way into the prison's cosmetics lab, where gloriously perfumed toiletries with the label *Veneziana Coloniali e Spezie* are made for some of the city's swishest hotels.

But the activities of the 80-odd inmates don't stop there. The prison's leather workshop produces a contemporary line of bags, wallets and other accessories in leather and recycled PVC, on sale at a tiny green kiosk in campo Santo Stefano (open 10am-8pm Mon-Sat), which also sells hand-printed T-shirts, hoodies and bags made in the silk-screen workshop. When not producing costumes for La Fenice (*see p247*), the tailors' shop turns out reproduction historical clothing (for sale and hire), as well as a very smart contemporary line of women's clothes, bags and accessories, available at **Banco Lotto No.10** (Castello 3478, salizada Sant'Antonin), near the church of San Giovanni in Bragora.

For further information, check the websites www.rioteradeipensieri.org and www.ilcerchiovenezia.it.

Opposite is another expat landmark, the so-called **Garden of Eden**, pleasure ground of Frederic Eden, a disabled Englishman who, like Byron, discovered that Venice was the perfect city for those with disabilities – particularly if they could afford their own gondola and steam launch. After a period in which it belonged to the ex-Queen of Yugoslavia, the garden passed into the hands of the Austrian artist Friedensreich Hundertwasser. Since his death in 2000, it has belonged to a foundation in his name, which has, reportedly, allowed the garden to remain verdant but totally unkempt.

Sights & museums

Il Redentore

Giudecca, campo del Redentore (041 275 0462, www.chorusvenezia.org). Vaporetto Redentore. **Open** *10.30am-4pm Mon; 10.30am-4.30pm Tue-Sat.* **Admission** *€3 (or Chorus; see p65). No cards.* **Map** *p190 H17.*

Venice's first great plague church was commissioned to celebrate deliverance from the bout of 1575-77. An especially conspicuous site was chosen, one that could be approached in ceremonial fashion. The ceremony continues today, on the third Sunday of July, when a bridge of boats is built across the canal. Palladio designed an eye-catching building whose prominent dome appears to rise directly behind the Greek-temple façade, giving the illusion that the church is centrally planned, as was traditional with sanctuaries and votive temples outside Venice. A broad flight of steps leads to the entrance.

The solemn, harmonious interior, with a single nave lit by large 'thermal' windows, testifies to Palladio's study of Roman baths. But the Capuchin monks, the austere order to whom the building was entrusted, were not pleased by its grandeur; Palladio attempted to mollify them by designing their choir stalls in a plain style. The best paintings are in the sacristy, which is rarely open; they include a *Virgin and Child* by Alvise Vivarini and a *Baptism* by Veronese.

Santa Eufemia

Giudecca, fondamenta Santa Eufemia (041 522 5848). Vaporetto Palanca. **Open** *usually closed to the public.* **Map** *p190 D16.*

This church has a 16th-century Doric portico along its flank. The interior owes its charm to its mix of styles. The nave and aisles are mostly 11th century, with Veneto-Byzantine columns and capitals, while the decoration consists mainly of 18th-century stucco and paintings. Over the first altar on the right is *St Roch and an Angel* by Bartolomeo Vivarini (1480).

Restaurants

♥ Alla Palanca €€

Giudecca 448, fondamenta del Ponte Piccolo (041 528 7719). Vaporetto Palanca. **Meals served** *noon-2.30pm Mon-Sat.* **No cards.** **Map** *p190 F16* ❶ *Italian*

One of the cheapest meals-with-a-view in Venice is on offer at this hugely friendly bar-*trattoria* on the Giudecca quay. It's a lunch-only place: the rest of the day (7am-9pm) it operates as a bar. Sit at a quayside table and order from a good-value menu that includes some surprisingly gourmet options: tagliatelle with prawns and *funghi porcini*, or tuna steaks in balsamic and sesame. Finish up with a delicious chocolate mousse with candied fruit.

♥ Altanella €€

Giudecca 268, calle delle Erbe (041 522 7780). Vaporetto Palanca or Redentore. **Meals served** *noon-2.30pm, 7-10.30pm Wed-Sun.* **Map** *p190 F17* ❷ *Venetian*

The leafy canal-side terrace of this family-run *trattoria* on the Giudecca (blissfully far from the tourist trail) is one of the best places for an al fresco meal in the city. The menu is typically Venetian, including traditional dishes such as *schie* (lagoon prawns) with polenta and gnocchi with cuttlefish, and the service is friendly and professional.

Harry's Dolci €€€

Giudecca 773, fondamenta San Biagio (041 522 4844, www.cipriani.com). Vaporetto Sant' Eufemia. **Open** *10.30am-4pm Mon; 10.30am-11pm Wed-Sun. Closed Nov-Mar.* **Meals served** *noon-3pm, 7-10.30pm Mon, Wed-Sun.* **Map** *p190 D16* ❸ *Italian*

Arrigo Cipriani's second Venetian stronghold (after Harry's Bar; *see p104*), this open-air restaurant is a fair-weather-only venue. The cuisine is supposedly more summery than *chez* Harry, but in practice many dishes are identical (cuttlefish with polenta, for instance, or Piemontese ravioli). Outside of mealtimes, you can order just a coffee and one of the delectable pastries made on the premises. Come prepared for mosquitoes.

Cafés, bars & gelaterie

▶ See also above **Alla Palanca**.

♥ Skyline Bar

Molino Stucky Hilton Hotel, Giudecca 810, campo San Biagio (041 272 3310, www.skylinebarvenice.com). Vaporetto Palanca. **Open** *5pm-1am Tue-Sun.* **Map** *p190 C15* ❶

It's a hike across to the Hilton Hotel in the former Molino Stucky flour mill (*see p192*)

– and the bar is an expensive extravagance – but sit out on the rooftop terrace and survey Venice beneath you, beyond the grand sweep of the Giudecca Canal, and you may well feel that it's all worth it. Meals and light snacks are served but forget the expensive food and just savour the view, with a drink in hand.

Shops & services

♥ Fortuny Tessuti Artistici

Giudecca 805, fondamenta San Biagio (393 825 7651 mobile, www.fortuny.com). Vaporetto Palanca. Open Apr-Oct 10am-1pm, 2-6pm Mon-Sat. Nov-Mar 10am-1pm, 2-6pm Mon-Fri. Map p190 C15 ❶ Fabric

This wonderful factory showroom space glows with the exquisite colours and patterns of original Fortuny prints. At €427 a metre, you may not be tempted to buy, but it's worth the trip just to see it. The marvellous garden inside the factory can be visited by appointment. Check the Fortuny blog (through the website) for occasional clearance sales and cut-price discontinued lines. *See also p53* Shopping.

SAN GIORGIO MAGGIORE

The island of **San Giorgio**, facing St Mark's across the lagoon, realised its true potential under set designer extraordinaire Andrea Palladio, whose church of **San Giorgio Maggiore** (*see p195*) is one of Venice's most recognisable landmarks. Known originally as the Isola dei Cipressi (Cypress Island), it soon became an important Benedictine monastery and centre of learning – a tradition that is carried on today by the **Fondazione Giorgio Cini** (*see below*), which operates a research centre and craft school on the island.

Sights & museums

♥ Fondazione Giorgio Cini: Benedictine Monastery & Le Stanze del Vetro

041 271 0229, www.cini.it. Vaporetto San Giorgio. Monastery Guided tours every hour Sat, Sun; by appt only Mon-Fri (call 338 683 4601 mobile). Apr-Sept 10am-5pm Sat, Sun. Oct-Mar 10am-4pm Sat, Sun. Le Stanze del Vetro 10am-7pm Mon, Tue, Thur-Sun during exhibitions. Admission Monastery €10; €8 reductions. Le Stanze del Vetro free. No cards. Map p190 N14.

There has been a Benedictine monastery here since 982, when Doge Tribuno Memmo donated the island to the order. The

monastery continued to benefit from ducal donations, acquiring large tracts of land both in and around Venice and abroad. After the church acquired the remains of St Stephen (1109), it was visited yearly by the doge on 26 December, the feast day of the saint. The city authorities often used the island as a luxury hotel for particularly prestigious visitors, such as Cosimo de' Medici in 1433. Cosimo had a magnificent library built here; it was destroyed in 1614, to make way for a more elaborate affair by Longhena.

In 1800, the island hosted the conclave of cardinals that elected Pope Pius VII, after they had been expelled from Rome by Napoleon. In 1806, the French got their own back, supressing the monastery and sending its chief artistic treasure – Veronese's *Marriage Feast at Cana* – off to the Louvre, where it still hangs. For the rest of the century, the monastery did ignominious service as a barracks and ammunition store. In 1951, industrialist Vittorio Cini bought the island to set up a foundation in memory of his son, Giorgio, killed in a plane crash in 1949.

The Fondazione Giorgio Cini uses the monastery buildings for its activities, including artistic and musical research (it holds a collection of Vivaldi manuscripts, plus illuminated manuscripts), and a naval college. A portion of the complex is given back to the Benedictines; there are currently a handful of monks in the monastery. The foundation is now open to the public at weekends for guided tours (in Italian, English, French and German). There are two beautiful cloisters – one by Giovanni Buora (1516-40), the other by Palladio (1579) – an elegant library and staircase by Longhena (1641-53), and a magnificent refectory (where Veronese's painting once hung) by Palladio (1561). The tour also includes the splendid garden, including the **Labirinto Borges**, a maze by the late British designer Randoll Coate, behind the monastery.

Beyond the monastery complex, **Le Stanze del Vetro** (www.lestanzedelvetro. org) is an exhibition space that hosts excellent shows of Venetian glass.

Labirinto Borges

❤ San Giorgio Maggiore

041 522 7827, www.abbaziasangiorgio.it.
Vaporetto San Giorgio. **Open** *Apr-Oct 9am-*
7pm daily. Nov-Mar 8.30am-6pm daily.
Admission *Church free. Campanile €6; €4*
reductions. No cards. **Map** *p190 N14.*

This unique spot cried out for a masterpiece.
Palladio provided it. This was his first
complete solo church; it demonstrates how
confident he was in his techniques and
objectives. With no hint of influence from
the city's Byzantine tradition, Palladio here
develops the system of superimposed temple
fronts with which he had experimented in
the façade of San Francesco della Vigna (*see
p112*). The interior maintains the same
relations between the orders as the outside,
with composite half-columns supporting
the gallery and lower Corinthian pilasters
supporting the arches. The effect is of
luminosity and harmony, decoration being
confined to the altars. Palladio believed that
white was the colour most pleasing to God,
a credo that happily matched the demand
from the Council of Trent for greater
lucidity in church services.

There are several good works of art.
Over the first altar is an *Adoration of the
Shepherds* by Jacopo Bassano, with startling
lighting effects. The altar to the right of the
high altar has a *Madonna and Child with
Nine Saints* by Sebastiano Ricci.

On the side walls of the chancel hang
two vast compositions by Tintoretto, a
Last Supper and the *Gathering of Manna*,
painted in the last years of his life. The
perspective of each work makes it clear
that they were intended to be viewed from
the altar rails. Tintoretto combines almost
surreal visionary effects (angels swirling
out from a lamp's eddying smoke) with
touches of superb domestic realism (a cat
prying into a basket, a woman stooping over
her laundry). Tintoretto's last painting, a
moving *Entombment*, hangs in the Cappella
dei Morti (open for 11am Mass on Sundays
in winter only). It's possible that Tintoretto
included himself among the mourners: he
has been identified as the bearded man
gazing intensely at Christ's face.

In the left transept is a painting by Jacopo
and Domenico Tintoretto of the *Martyrdom
of St Stephen*, placed above the altar
containing the saint's remains (brought
from Constantinople in 1109).

From the left transept, follow the signs
to the campanile. Just in front of the ticket
office stands the huge statue of an angel
that crowned the bell tower until it was
struck by lightning in 1993. To the left of
the statue, a corridor gives access to the lift
that takes you up to the bell tower. The view
from the top of the tower is extraordinary:
the best possible panorama across Venice
itself and the lagoon.

San Giorgio Maggiore

Together (Jaume Plensa, 2014)

Lido & Lagoon

Venice lies more or less in the middle of a saltwater lagoon, separated from the open sea by two slender sand barriers – the Lido and Pellestrina. It is, on the whole, another world out here, inhabited by fishermen and rowers and flocks of lazy water birds. In high season, much-visited islands such as Murano and Burano can seem only marginally less crowded than St Mark's or the Rialto. But even at the busiest times, the views from the vaporetto of the lagoon's empty reaches are enough to soothe the most frayed of nerves. Other islands, such as Sant'Erasmo, are always bucolically tranquil and almost entirely tourist-free.

❤ Don't miss

1 Torcello *p212*
The first settlement on the lagoon.

2 Murano *p202*
For all your glassy needs.

3 Burano *p208*
Picturesque beyond belief, come for the colours, stay for the lace.

4 San Michele *p202*
An idyllic final resting place for centuries of Venetians.

5 San Pietro Martire *p205*
Impressive works by Giovanni Bellini and Tintoretto.

Murano glass

THE LIDO & SOUTHERN LAGOON

The **Lido** is the northernmost of the two strips of land that separate the lagoon from the open sea. It is no longer the 'bare strand/ Of hillocks heaped from ever-shifting sand' that Shelley described in *Julian and Maddalo*, nor is it the playground for wealthy aesthetes that fans of *Death in Venice* might come in fruitless search of. These days, Venice-by-the-sea is a placidly residential suburb, where pale young boys in sailor suits are in very short supply – an escape from the strangeness of Venice to a normality of supermarkets and cars. Things perk up in summer when buses are full of city sunbathers and tourists staying in the Lido's overspill hotels. However, the days of all-night partying and gambling are long gone. In 2001, the Lido Casinò closed. Now the only moment when the place stirs to anything like its former vivacity is at the beginning of September when the film festival (*see p236* Venice Film Festival) rolls into town for two weeks, with its bandwagon of stars, directors, PR people and sleep-deprived, caffeine-driven journalists.

The Lido has few tourist sights as such. Only the church of **San Nicolò** on the riviera San Nicolò – founded in 1044 – can claim any great antiquity. It was here that the doge would come on Ascension Day after marrying Venice to the sea in the ceremony known as *lo sposalizio del mare* (*see p230* Festa e Regata della Sensa). Inside is the tomb of Nicola Giustiniani, a Benedictine monk who was forced to leave holy orders in 1172 to assure the future of his illustrious family, of which he was the sole heir. He married the doge's daughter, had lots of kids, then went back to being a monk. After his death he was beatified for his spirit of self-sacrifice.

Fans of art nouveau and deco have plenty to look at on the Lido. On the Gran Viale there are two gems: the tiled façade of the **Hungaria Hotel** (no.28), formerly the Ausonia Palace, with its Beardsley-esque nymphs; and **Villa Monplaisir** at no.14, an art deco design from 1906. There are other smaller-scale examples in and around via Lepanto. For full-blown turn-of-the-century exotica, though, it's hard to beat the **Hotel Excelsior** on lungomare Marconi, a neo-Moorish party-piece, complete with minaret.

The bus ride south along the lagoon-side promenade of the Lido is uneventful but passes some submerged history. The old town of **Malamocco**, near the south end of the island, was engulfed by a tidal wave in 1107; it had been a flourishing port controlled by Padua. The new town, built further inland, never really amounted to much; today, its sights consist of a few picturesque streets and a pretty bridge.

Offshore from Malamocco is the tiny island of **Poveglia**, once inhabited by 200 families, descendants of the servants of Pietro Tradonico, a ninth-century doge murdered by his rivals. His servants barricaded themselves inside the Palazzo

---

In the know
Getting there & around

The main Lido–Santa Maria Elisabetta **vaporetto** stop (often just called 'Lido') is served by frequent boats from Venice and the mainland. The San Nicolò stop, to the north, is served by the no.17 car ferry from Tronchetto. Vaporetto 20 serves San Servolo and San Lazzaro before terminating at Lido Casino.

Bus routes: the A heads south from the main vaporetto stop through Malamocco and Alberoni to the very tip of the Lido. The B covers some of the same route, going south from the main vaporetto stop as far as Malamocco; in the other direction, the B cuts across the centre of the island and does the sea coast route northwards as far as the beach at San Nicolò. The V does a shorter route, cutting across the island from Santa Maria Elisabetta then trundling south past the seafront hotels and beaches. Buses 11 and N, with small variations, provide an epic ride, southwards from the vaporetto stop to the tip of the Lido, right on to the Pellestrina ferry, then along that sandbank-island to the ferry stop for Chioggia (*see p201*).

Cycling is a good way of getting around the pancake-flat Lido; for bike hire, see *p298*.

❤ **Time to eat & drink**

Lido's high-end seafood heaven
La Favorita *p201*

A cosy gem on Murano
La Perla ai Bisatei *p206*

Traditional cooking with a view
Busa alla Torre *p206*

Luxury dining in the lagoon
Venissa *p210*

❤ **Time to shop**

Glass old and new
Davide Penso *p207*, Marina e Susanna Sent *p207*, Seguso Viro *p207*

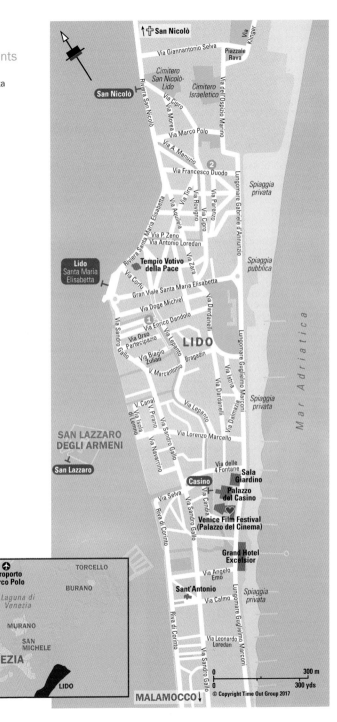

LIDO

Restaurants

1. Al Mercà
2. La Favorita

San Nicolò

Via Giannantonio Selva

Piazzale Rava

Via Klinger

Cimitero San Nicolò-Lido

Cimitero Israeletico

San Nicolò

Riviera San Nicolò

Via Cipro

Via Morea

Via Marco Polo

Via A. Manuzio

Via Francesco Duodo

Via dell'Ospizio Marino

Spiaggia privata

Lungomare Gabriele d'Annunzio

Via Parenzo

Via Cipro

Via Rovigno

Via Trieste

Via Aquileia

Riviera Santa Maria Elisabetta

Via P. Zeno

Via Antonio Loredan

Via Zara

Spiaggia pubblica

Tempio Votivo della Pace

Lido Santa Maria Elisabetta

Via Corfù

Gran Viale Santa Maria Elisabetta

Via Doge Michiel

Via Dardanelli

Via Enrico Dandolo

Via Sandro Gallo

Via Orso Partecipazio

Via Lepanto

Via Biagio Zulian

Bragadin

LIDO

Lungomare Guglielmo Marconi

Via Istria

Via Dardanelli

V. Marcantonio

Mar Adriatica

V. Canal V. Pisano

Via Isola di Lemno

Via Sandro Gallo

Via Navarrino

Via Lepanto

Via Dardanelli

Via Querini

Spiaggia privata

Via Lorenzo Marcello

SAN LAZZARO DEGLI ARMENI

San Lazzaro

Via delle 4 Fontane

Sala Giardino

Casino

Via Selva

Via Candia

Via Sandro Gallo

Palazzo del Casino

Riva di Corinto

Venice Film Festival (Palazzo del Cinema)

Grand Hotel Excelsior

Via Angelo Emo

Sant'Antonio

Via Calmo

Lungomare Guglielmo Marconi

Spiaggia privata

Riva di Corinto

Via Leonardo Loredan

Via Sandro Gallo

0   300 m
0   300 yds

MALAMOCCO

© Copyright Time Out Group 2017

LIDO & LAGOON

Aeroporto Marco Polo

TORCELLO

Laguna di Venezia

BURANO

MURANO

SAN MICHELE

VENEZIA

LIDO

Ducale and only agreed to leave when safe conduct to this new home was promised.

The southern part of the lagoon – between Venice, the Lido and the mainland – has 14 small islands, a few of which are still inhabited, though most are out of bounds to tourists. **La Grazia** was for years a quarantine hospital but the structure has now been closed. The huge **San Clemente**, originally a lunatic asylum and later a home for abandoned cats, was more recently a plush hotel that had closed down at the time of writing.

The islands of **San Servolo** and **San Lazzaro**, however, are served by vaporetto 20, and both are well worth visiting.

San Servolo

From the 18th century until 1978, San Servolo was Venice's mental hospital (in his poem *Julian and Maddalo*, Shelley describes a visit that he paid there with Byron); it is now home to **Venice International University** (*see p305*). In 2006, the **Museo del Manicomio di San Servolo** (San Servolo Asylum Museum; 041 524 0119, museomanicomio.servizimetropolitani.ve.it) was inaugurated. The museum is open for programmed visits only; call or see the website for details. It reveals the different ways in which mental illnesses have been treated over the years; there are not only examples of the more or less brutal methods of restraint (chains, straitjackets, handcuffs)

but also early examples of such treatments as hydro-massage and electrotherapy. The tour ends in the reconstructed 18th-century pharmacy, which relied partly on medicines obtained from some of the exotic plants grown on the island. After the tour, it is possible to visit the island's extensive and charming gardens.

San Lazzaro degli Armeni

A further five minutes on the no.20 will take you to the island of **San Lazzaro degli Armeni**. There are tours (041 526 0104) of the island every afternoon for visitors from the mid-afternoon tour (times vary seasonally) from San Zaccaria. The cost is €6 (no cards).

Individual visitors can join a guided tour every day at 15.25pm (ACTV line 20 leaves San Zaccaria at 15.10pm). Groups of more than 25 people can book visits at different times.

A black-cloaked Armenian priest meets the boat and takes visitors on a detailed tour of the **Monastero Mechitarista**. The tiny island is a global point of reference for Armenia's Catholic minority, visited and supported by Armenians from Italy and abroad. Near the entrance stand the printing presses that helped to distribute Armenian literature all over the world for 200 years. They are now silent, with the monastery's retro line in dictionaries and liturgical texts farmed out to a modern press.

Originally a leper colony, in 1717 the island was presented by the doge to an Armenian abbot called Mekhitar, who was on the run from the Turkish invasion of the Peloponnese. There had been an Armenian community in Venice since the 11th century, centring on the tiny Santa Croce degli Armeni church, just around the corner from piazza San Marco, but the construction of this church and monastery made Venice a world centre of Armenian culture. The monastery was the only one in Venice to be spared the Napoleonic axe: the emperor had a soft spot for Armenians and claimed this was an academic rather than a religious institute.

The tour takes in both the cloisters and the church, rebuilt after a fire in 1883. The museum and the modern library contain 40,000 priceless books and manuscripts, and a bizarre collection of gifts donated over the years by visiting Armenians that range from Burmese prayer books to an Egyptian mummy.

The island's most famous student was Lord Byron, who used to take a break from his more earthly pleasures in Venice and row over three times a week to learn Armenian (as he found that his 'mind

San Lazzaro degli Armeni

Chioggia

Discover beaches and churches south of Venice

A small town of Roman origin at the southern end of the lagoon, the fishing port of Chioggia spreads over a rectangular island split down the middle by the **Canal Vena**; to the east is the long arm of the beach resort of Sottomarina. From piazzetta Vigo, the long, wide corso del Popolo extends the whole length of the island, parallel to the canal.

The only sight not on the corso is the church of **San Domenico** (via Canali 4), on its very own island at the end of the street that begins across a balustraded bridge from piazzetta Vigo, where the ferry ties up. A barn-like, 18th-century reconstruction, it houses Vittore Carpaccio's last recorded work, a gracefully poised St Paul (after the second altar on the right; 1520). Other works of note are a huge wooden crucifix – possibly a German work of the 14th century – and a Rubens-like Tintoretto. More charming is the collection of naïve ex-voto paintings placed by grateful fishermen in a side chapel.

Halfway down the corso is the **Granaio**, the former municipal granary, built in 1322 but heavily restored in the 19th century; it now hosts the bustling fish market (8am-noon Tue-Sun).

Just beyond the Granaio is little piazza XX Settembre. Here stands the church of the **Santissima Trinità**, a small, elegant 18th-century building, which has been restored and converted into a museum. Some interesting paintings have been moved here since the restoration, but more interesting than the

church itself is the grandiose Oratorio dei Battuti, which begins just behind the high altar. This large space, built for a philanthropic confraternity of laymen devoted to the Madonna (and originally to flagellation), was decorated with a cycle of ceiling paintings by a number of the major names of 17th-century Mannerist painting in Venice. Particularly fine is the *Resurrection* by Alvise del Friso.

Near the end of the corso, two churches stand side by side on the right. The smaller one is **San Martino** (via Sottomarina 1468, 041 400 054), a Venetian Gothic jewel built in 1393. Next door, the huge 17th-century **Duomo** (rione Duomo 77, www.cattedralechioggia.it) was built to a design by Baldassare Longhena after a fire destroyed the original tenth-century church. Inside the Duomo, the chapel to the left of the chancel contains a series of grisly 18th-century paintings depicting the torturously prolonged martyrdom of the two patron saints of Chioggia, Felix and Fortunatus (Happy and Lucky).

The **Torre di Santa Maria** marks the end of the old town; just beyond, in campo Marconi, is the deconsecrated church of San Francesco, which has been turned into the **Museo Civico della Laguna Sud** (www.chioggia.org/museochioggia/en). The museum provides a good introduction to aspects of lagoon life. There's a small gallery with an attractive triptych by Ercole del Fiore (1436), *Justice between Saints Felix and Fortunatus*.

---

wanted something craggy to break upon') with the monks. He helped the monks to publish an Armenian-English grammar, although by his own confession he never got beyond the basics of the language. You can buy a completed version of this, plus a number of period maps and an illustrated children's Armenian grammar, in the shop just inside the monastery gate.

Restaurants

Al Mercà €€
*Via Enrico Dandolo 17A (041 243 1663). Vaporetto Lido. **Meals served** noon-2.30pm, 6.30-9.30pm daily. **Map** p199* ❶ *Seafood*

A success from the word go, Al Mercà is the Lido's coolest dining hangout with a lively *aperitivo* scene in the evening before eating begins. Charming hosts serve excellent mixed seafood antipasti, fishy pasta dishes

and grilled fish to contented diners out on the portico of the former produce market. Best to book.

❤ La Favorita €€€
*Via Francesco Duodo 33 (041 526 1626). Vaporetto Lido. **Meals served** 7.30-10.30pm Tue; 12.30-2.30pm, 7.30-10.30pm Wed-Sun. Closed Jan. **Map** p199* ❷ *Venetian*

With a lovely vine-shaded pergola for summer dining, this is an old-fashioned and reassuring sort of place that does textbook Venetian seafood classics like *spaghetti ai caparossoli* or *scampi in saor* (sweet-and-sour sauce), plus a few more audacious dishes such as pumpkin gnocchi with scorpion fish and radicchio. Service is professional, and the wine list has a fine selection of bottles from the north-east.

TOWARDS MURANO

♥ San Michele

▶ *Vaporetto Cimitero*

Halfway between Venice and Murano, this is the island where tourists begin their lagoon visit. For many Venetians, however, it's the last stop: **San Michele** is the city's cemetery (open Apr-Sept 7.30am-6pm daily; Oct-Mar 7.30am-4.30pm daily). Early in the morning, vaporetti are packed with locals coming over to lay flowers. This is not a morbid spot, though: it is an elegant city of the dead, with more than one famous resident.

These days San Michele is more a temporary parking lot than a final resting place: the island reached saturation point long ago, and even after paying through the nose for a plot, families know that after a suitable period – generally around ten years – the bones of their loved ones will be dug up and transferred to an ossuary elsewhere.

An orderly red-brick wall runs around the whole of the island, with a line of tall cypress trees rising high behind it – the inspiration for Böcklin's famously lugubrious painting *Island of the Dead*. The island was originally a Franciscan monastery, but during the Napoleonic period the grounds that used to extend behind the church were seconded for burials in an effort to stop unhygienic Venetians from digging graves in the campi around parish churches.

Before visiting the cemetery, take a look at the recently restored church of **San Michele in Isola** (open 7.30am-12.15pm, 3-4pm daily); turn left after entering the cemetery and pass through the fine cloisters. The view of the façade is particularly striking. Designed by Mauro Codussi in the 1460s, this white building of Istrian stone was Venice's first Renaissance church.

In a booth to the left of the entrance by the vaporetto stop, staff hand out maps, which are indispensable for celebrity hunts. In the Greek and Russian Orthodox section of the cemetery are the elaborate tomb of Sergei Pavlovich Diaghilev, who introduced the Ballets Russes to Europe, and a simpler monument to the composer Igor Stravinsky and his wife. The Protestant (*Evangelico*) section has a selection of ships' captains and passengers who ended their days in *La Serenissima*, plus the simple graves of Ezra Pound and Joseph Brodsky.

There's a rather sad children's section and a corner dedicated to the city's gondoliers, their tombs decorated with carvings and statues of gondolas. Visit the cemetery on the *Festa dei morti* – All Souls' Day, 2 November – and the vaporetto is free, but seriously packed.

♥ Murano

▶ *Vaporetto Colonna, Da Mula, Faro, Museo, Navagero or Venier (multiple lines)*

After San Michele, the vaporetto continues to **Murano**, one of the larger and more populous islands. In the 16th and 17th centuries, when it was a world centre of glass production and a decadent resort for

San Michele

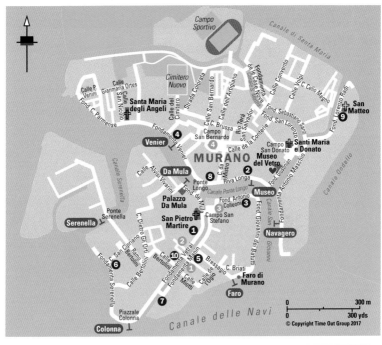

MURANO

Restaurants

1. Acquastanca
2. B-Restaurant alla Vecchia Pescheria
3. Busa alla Torre
4. La Perla ai Bisatei

Shops & services

1. Berengo Fine Arts
2. Davide Penso
3. Galliano Ferro
4. Luigi Camozzo
5. Manin 56
6. Marina e Susanna Sent
7. Murano Collezioni
8. Rossana e Rossana
9. Seguso Viro
10. Venini

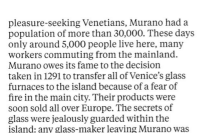

pleasure-seeking Venetians, Murano had a population of more than 30,000. These days only around 5,000 people live here, many workers commuting from the mainland. Murano owes its fame to the decision taken in 1291 to transfer all of Venice's glass furnaces to the island because of a fear of fire in the main city. Their products were soon sold all over Europe. The secrets of glass were jealously guarded within the island: any glass-maker leaving Murano was

proclaimed a traitor. Even today, there is no official glass school: the delicate skills of blowing and flamework are only learned by apprenticeship to one of the glass masters. At first sight, Murano looks close to being ruined by glass tourism. Dozens of 'guides' swoop on visitors as they pile off the ferry, to whisk them off on tours of furnaces. Even if you head off on your own, you'll find yourself on fondamenta dei Vetrai, a snipers' alley of shops selling glass knick-knacks, most of

❤ Murano glass

Murano has been the capital of glass since 1291. In that year, Venice's rulers banished all glass furnaces to this island to avert the kind of conflagrations that would regularly devastate swathes of what was then a largely wooden city. Over the following centuries, the island refined its particular craft. Its vases, chandeliers, mirrors and drinking vessels were shipped all over the world by Venice's great merchant fleet.

Nowadays, the assault of glass-blowing hustlers coupled with shop windows packed with glass objects of dubious taste, and even more dubious origin, make it hard to see the island's speciality as a noble art. But behind the tack, Murano remains a special place where centuries of glass-making techniques are still jealously preserved.

Murano glass is divided into medium to large furnace-made pieces (blown glass, sculpture and lamps) and smaller pieces (beads and animals) fashioned from sticks of coloured glass in the heat of a gas jet. Once made, these objects may be engraved or patterned with silver, and multi-piece objects need assembling – all of which keeps much of Murano's population employed.

But unless you have your wits about you, you may never get beyond shops and warehouses packed with glass shipped from the Far East. Most hotel porters and concierges in Venice have agreements of some kind with these emporia: don't expect disinterested advice on where to go. Tourist-trade Murano outlets with 'authentic' furnaces being used by 'authentic' glass-blowers rarely sell the articles you'll see produced, whatever the salesmen tell you. Glass shops range from the excellent to the downright rip-off: labels proclaiming 'vetro di Murano' mean very little ('vetro artistico di Murano' is meant to offer a firmer guarantee, though some top producers refuse to bow to this, believing that their reputation is all the guarantee needed).

So, how do you go about making sure you get the real thing? Real Murano glass is fiendishly expensive. There's no such thing as a real €30 vase, or a genuine €5 wine glass... at those prices you can be sure you're taking home something 'authentically' Chinese. If you want genuine without paying much for it, you'll have to resort to the odd glass bead. Moreover, the best workshops don't allow tourists in to gawp, though sometimes you can peer through an open front gate. And, occasionally, they'll invite

you in if you really intend to purchase. If you're after a true Murano glass experience, just be brave: ring that doorbell and see if they'll humour you and allow you a peek.

In the outlets listed in our Murano Shops & services section (see p207) you'll find fine examples of the real thing. More great glass can be found at **L'Isola – Carlo Moretti** (see p103), **Caterina Tognon** (see p105) and **Vittorio Costantini** (see p143).

Traditional glass-blowing

Seguso Viro p207

which are made far from Murano. But there *are* some serious glass-makers on the island and even the tackiest showroom usually has one or two gems.

There's more to Murano, however, than glass. At the far end of fondamenta dei Vetrai is the nondescript façade of the 14th-century parish church of **San Pietro Martire** (*see p205*), which holds important works of art, including Bellini's impressive altarpiece triptych.

Beyond the church, Murano's Canal Grande is spanned by an unattractive, 19th-century iron bridge. Before crossing, it is worth looking at the Gothic **Palazzo Da Mula**, just to the left of the bridge; this splendid 15th-century building has been recently restored and transformed into council offices. In the morning you can stroll through its courtyard, which contains a monumental carved Byzantine arch from an earlier (12th- or 13th-century) building.

On the other side of the bridge, a right turn takes you along riva Longa; 200 metres further along, it veers sharply to the left, becoming fondamenta Giustinian. The 17th-century **Palazzo Giustinian**, situated far from the tacky chandeliers and fluorescent clowns, is the **Museo del Vetro** (*see below*), the best place to learn about the history of glass. Just beyond this is Murano's greatest architectural treasure: the 12th-century basilica of **Santi Maria e Donato** (*see p205*), with its apse towards the canal.

Return to the bridge and walk to the end of fondamenta Sebastiano Venier. The church of **Santa Maria degli Angeli** backs on to the convent where Casanova conducted one of his most torrid affairs, with a libertine nun named Maria Morosoni.

Sights & museums
Museo del Vetro
Fondamenta Giustinian 8 (041 527 4718, museovetro.visitmuve.it). Vaporetto Museo. **Open** *Nov-Mar 10am-5pm, Apr-Oct 10am-6pm daily.* **Admission** *€12; €9.50 reductions (see also p306 Tourist information).* **Map** *p203.*

Housed in beautiful Palazzo Giustinian, built in the late 17th century for the bishop of Torcello, the museum has a huge collection of Murano glass. As well as the famed chandeliers, which were first produced in the 18th century, there are ruby-red beakers, opaque lamps and delicate Venetian *perle* – glass beads that were used in trade and commerce all over the world from the time of Marco Polo. One of the earliest pieces is the 15th-century Barovier marriage cup, decorated with portraits of the bride

and groom. In one room is a collection of 17th-century oil lamps in the shapes of animals, some of which are uncannily Disney-like. On the ground floor is a good collection of Roman glassware from near Zara on the Istrian peninsula.

♥ San Pietro Martire
Fondamenta dei Vetrai (041 739 704). Vaporetto Colonna or Faro. **Open** *9am-6pm Mon-Fri; 1-6pm Sat; 8am-5pm Sun.* **Map** *p203.*

Behind its unspectacular façade, the church of San Pietro Martire conceals an important work by Giovanni Bellini, backed by a marvellous landscape: *The Virgin and Child Enthroned with St Mark, St Augustine and Doge Agostino Barbarigo*. There is also a Tintoretto *Baptism*, two works by Veronese and his assistants (mainly the latter) and an ornate altarpiece (*Deposition*) by Salviati, which is lit up by the early morning sun. The sacristy (offering of €1.50) contains remarkable wood-carvings from the 17th century and a small museum of reliquaries and other ornaments.

Santi Maria e Donato
Campo San Donato (041 739 056). Vaporetto Museo. **Open** *7.45am-noon, 3.45-7pm Mon-Sat, 3.45-7pm Sun.* **Map** *p203.*

Although altered by over-enthusiastic 19th-century restorers, the exterior of this church is a classic of the Veneto-Byzantine style, with an ornate blind portico on the rear of the apse. Inside is a richly coloured mosaic floor, laid down in 1140 (at the same time as the floor of the basilica di San Marco), with floral and animal motifs. Above, a Byzantine apse mosaic of the Virgin looms out of the darkness surrounded by a field of gold.

Restaurants
Acquastanca €€
Fondamenta Manin 48 (041 319 5125, www. acquastanca.it). Vaporetto Faro. **Meals served** *noon-3.30pm, 7-10.30pm Mon, Fri; noon-3.30pm Tue-Thur, Sat.* **Bar open** *9am-11pm Mon, Fri; 9am-8pm Tue-Thur, Sat.* **Map** *p203* ❶ *Traditional Venetian*

In a former bakery, this restaurant is helmed by two local ladies and frequented more by their fellow islanders than by visitors. It's an all-day kind of place, where you can drop by for a cappuccino, a bar snack or a whole meal. In the kitchen, Caterina updates fishy Venetian classics, while out front Giovanna uses skills picked up over many years as events manager at Harry's Bar (*see p104*), to create an atmosphere far more understated than at that brash watering hole.

Battling the Sea

Protecting a much-loved natural environment

For Venetians, the greatest threat has always been the open sea, and efforts have been devoted over the centuries to strengthening the natural defences offered by Pellestrina and the Lido. In the 18th century, the *murazzi* were created: an impressive barrier of stone and marble blocks all the way down both islands.

Nowadays, the threat is seen as coming from the three *bocche di porto* (the lagoon's openings to the sea) between the Lido and Cavallino, between the Lido and Pellestrina and between Pellestrina and Chioggia. Works to create the highly controversial mobile dyke system known as MOSE – which when fully operational should protect the lagoon from tides of up to three metres – have experienced a series of delays (*see p33*).

There are 34 islands on the saltwater lagoon, most of them uninhabited, containing only crumbling masonry, and home to seagulls and lazy lizards. The lagoon itself covers some 520 square kilometres (200 square miles) – the world's biggest wetland. This wild, fragile environment is where Venetians take refuge from the tourist hordes, escaping by boat for picnics on deserted islands, or fishing for bass and bream. Others set off to dig up clams at low tide (most without the requisite licence), or organise hunting expeditions for duck, using the makeshift hides known as *botte* ('barrels', which is what they were originally, sunk into the floor of the lagoon). Many just head out after work, at sunset, to row.

The islands of the lagoon

B-Restaurant alla Vecchia Pescheria €€

*Murano, campiello Pescheria 4 (041 527 957). Vaporetto Faro. **Meals served** noon-3pm Mon, Tue; noon-3.30pm, 6-9pm Thur-Sun. Closed 3 wks Dec. **Map** p203* ❷ *Seafood*

A sideline for the glass-making Berengo dynasty, this *trattoria* in Murano's old fish market is chic and stylish inside, with tables beneath big green umbrellas outside on a pretty square in fine weather. The welcome is friendly, and some very good, rather creative seafood cooking is served up at reasonable prices (for Venice). The crew that runs the place is young and lively; large groups can be catered for; and children are very welcome in this family-run eaterie where the campo outside sometimes resembles a kiddies' playground. The hours given above refer to meal times; but B-Restaurant opens early in the morning for breakfast, and is a fine place for a pre-dinner *aperitivo* too.

❤ Busa alla Torre €€

*Murano, campo Santo Stefano 3 (041 739 662). Vaporetto Faro. **Meals served** noon-3.30pm daily. **Map** p203* ❸ *Seafood*

In summer, tables spill out into a pretty square opposite the church of San Pietro Martire. The service is deft and professional. The cuisine is reliable, no-frills seafood cooking, with good *primi* that might include ravioli filled with *branzino* (bream) in a spider-crab sauce, or tagliatelle with *canoce* (mantis shrimps). Note the lunch-only opening.

❤ La Perla ai Bisatei €€

*Murano, campo San Bernardo 1 (041 739 528). Vaporetto Museo or Venier. **Meals served** noon-2.30pm Mon, Tue, Thur-Sun. **No cards**. **Map** p203* ❹ *Traditional Venetian*

Davide Penso

La Perla is a rare gem in Venice: spit-and-sawdust, local, family-run, unreconstructed, with great mainly fishy dishes at sub-Venetian prices and an atmosphere that makes anyone who wanders this far into the heart of Murano feel like they've stumbled across a roomful of old friends. The traditional Venetian fare – both seafood and meat – is well prepared, served in generous helpings and very fresh.

Shops & services

Berengo Fine Arts
Fondamenta dei Vetrai 109A (041 739 453, www.berengo.com). Vaporetto Colonna or Faro. Open 9am-5.30pm daily. Map p203 ❶ Glass

Adriano Berengo commissions various international artists to design brilliantly coloured sculptures – in glass, of course.

♥ Davide Penso
riva Longa 48 (041 527 4634, www.davidepenso.com). Vaporetto Museo. Open 9.30am-6pm daily. Map p203 ❷ Glass jewellery

Davide Penso makes and shows exquisite glass jewellery. His own creations are all one-off or limited edition pieces with designs drawn from nature: zebra-striped, mother-of-pearl or crocodile- skinned. The shop sometimes closes from 1.30 to 2.30pm.

Galliano Ferro
Fondamenta Colleoni 6 (041 739 477, www.gallianoferro.it). Vaporetto Faro. Open by appointment. No cards. Map p203 ❸ Glass

Inspired by 18th-century classics of design, Ferro's rich, vibrant and intricate works in glass are some of Murano's most sought-after pieces. There are early 20th-century and Islamic art-inspired designs available too.

Luigi Camozzo
Fondamenta Venier 3 (041 736 875, www.luigicamozzo.com). Vaporetto Venier. Open 10am-6pm Mon-Fri; by appointment Sat, Sun. Map p203 ❹ Glass

It would be over-simplifying things to describe Luigi Camozzo as a glass-engraver. Using a variety of different tools, he carves, sculpts and inscribes wonderfully soft, natural bas-reliefs into glass. Drop by and you may even catch him in action.

Manin 56
Fondamenta Manin 56 (041 527 5392). Vaporetto Faro. Open 10am-6pm daily. Closed Jan. Map p203 ❺ Glass

Manin 56 sells modern (though slightly staid) lines in glassware, and vases from prestigious houses such as Salviati and Vivarini.

♥ Marina e Susanna Sent
Fondamenta Serenella 20 (041 527 4665, www.marinaesusannasent.com). Vaporetto Colonna. Open 10am-5pm Mon-Fri. Map p203 ❻ Jewellery

In the Sent sisters' recently expanded Murano workshop, you'll find clean, modern jewellery in glass, in interesting counterpoise to innovative jewellery in other materials, including wood, coral, paper and rubber.
Other locations San Marco 2090, ponte San Moise (041 520 4014); Dorsoduro 669 & 681, campo San Vio (041 520 8136).

Murano Collezioni
Fondamenta Manin 1C (041 736 272, www.muranocollezioni.com). Vaporetto Colonna. Open 10.30am-5.30pm Mon-Sat. Closed 2wks Jan. Map p203 ❼ Glass

This shop sells pieces by some of the lagoon's most-respected producers, including Carlo Moretti, Barovier e Toso, and Venini. Room to move about and good lighting will help you make your choice.

Rossana e Rossana
Riva Longa 11 (041 527 4076, www.ro-e-ro.com). Vaporetto Museo. Open 10am-6pm daily. Map p203 ❽ Glass

The place to come for traditional Venetian glass, from filigree pieces to Veronese vases and elegant goblets that are based on models that were popular in the early years of the last century – all produced by master glass-maker Davide Fuin.

♥ Seguso Viro
Fondamenta Venier 29 (041 527 4255, www.segusoviro.com). Vaporetto Museo or Venier. Open 11am-4pm Mon-Sat. Map p203 ❾ Glass

Giampaolo Seguso comes from a long line of Venetian glass-makers. His modern blown glass pieces are enhanced by experiments working around Murano traditions.

Venini
Fondamenta Vetrai 47 (041 273 7204, www.venini.com). Vaporetto Colonna. Open 9.30am-5.30pm Mon-Sat. Map p203 ❿ Glass

Venini was the biggest name in Murano glass for much of the 20th century, and remains in the forefront of the industry. Classic designs are joined by more innovative pieces, including a selection designed by major international glass artists. **Other location** San Marco 314, piazzetta dei Leoncini (041 522 4045).

❤ BURANO & AROUND

▶ *Vaporetto Burano or Mazzorbo (12, N).*

Mazzorbo, the long island next to Burano, is a haven of peace, rarely visited by tourists. It is worth getting off here just for the sake of the quiet walk along the canal and then across the long wooden bridge that connects Mazzorbo to Burano. The view from the bridge across the lagoon to Venice is stunning, and there's always a chance you'll have it to yourself.

Mazzorbo was settled around the tenth century. When it became clear that Venice itself had got the upper hand, most of the population simply dismantled their houses brick by brick, transported them by boat to Venice, and rebuilt them there. Today Mazzorbo is a lazy place of small farms, with a pleasant walk to the 14th-century Gothic church of **Santa Caterina** (opening times vary), whose wonky tower still has its original bell dating from 1318 – one of the oldest in Europe. Winston Churchill, a keen amateur painter, set up his easel here more than once after World War II. Facing Burano is an area of attractive, modern, low-cost housing, in shades of lilac, grey and green, designed by the architect Giancarlo De Carlo.

You could almost believe that they invented the adjective 'picturesque' to describe **Burano**. Together with its lace, its multicoloured houses make it a magnet for tourists armed with cameras. The locals are traditionally either fishermen or lace-makers, though there are fewer and fewer of the latter, despite the best efforts of the island's **Scuola di Merletti** (Lace School, now also home to the **Museo del Merletti**; *see p210*).

The street leading from the main quay throbs with souvenir shops selling lace, lace and more lace – much of it machine-made in Asia. But Burano is big enough for the visitor to meander through its quiet backstreets and avoid a lace overload. It was in Burano that Carnevale (*see p231*) was revived in the 1970s; the modest celebrations here are still far more authentically joyful than the antics of masked tourists cramming piazza San Marco.

Fishermen have lived on Burano since the seventh century. According to local lore they painted their houses different colours so that they could recognise them when fishing out on the lagoon – though in fact only a tiny proportion of the island's houses can actually be seen from the lagoon. Whatever the reason, the *buranelli* still go to great efforts to decorate their houses, and

Burano

Mud Houses

The challenges of building on a lagoon

If you absolutely must build a city on a squishy base of a hundred-odd marshy islets in an inhospitable lagoon, it's clear you're going to have to think about foundations. Especially if, in time, you want this city to grow into more than a collection of wooden huts on stilts, to become a flourishing trade empire, acquiring some stunning marble-clad churches and palazzi in the process.

Beneath the Venetian lagoon is a layer of compacted clay called caranto, the remains of the ancient Venetian plain that subsided aeons ago. On top of this firm base are silt deposits that vary in depth – from very shallow by the mainland to many metres deep out by the Adriatic.

As the builders of this most unlikely of cities were soon to realise, nothing of any size would stay vertical unless it was standing firmly on the caranto. So great trunks of larch and oak trees were driven down through the mud, to bear the weight of what would then be built above. Lack of oxygen in the clay saved the wood from decomposition, turning the stakes as hard as rock. As you walk through Venice's calli, you are, in effect, striding over a petrified forest.

The solution is a good one, but it's certainly not perfect. As the sea level inexorably rises and the caranto level subsides – at an estimated one millimetre per year – there's no way that the trunks can be stretched to keep the floor above water.

And occasionally the wood rots, especially if the piles are shaken – with the risk of oxygen sneaking in – by passing motorised water traffic. At which point, those wooden piles will need to be replaced, at a substantial cost – and it's no fun having a forest dragged through your living room floor either.

There are photos of uncovered wooden piles on www.venicebackstage.org.

Pile Drivers (Giovanni Grevembroch 1780)

social life centres on the *fondamente* where the men repair nets or tend to their boats moored in the canal below, while their wives – at least in theory – make lace.

Lace was first produced in Burano in the 15th century, originally by nuns, but the trade was quickly picked up by fishermen's wives and daughters. So skillful were the local lace-makers that in the 17th century many were paid handsomely to work in the Alengon lace ateliers in Normandy. Today, most work is done on commission, though interested parties will have to get to know one of the lace-makers in person, as the co-operative that used to represent the old ladies closed down in 1995.

The busy main square of Burano is named after the island's most famous son, Baldassare Galuppi, a 17th-century composer who collaborated with Carlo Goldoni on a number of operas and who was the subject of a poem by Robert Browning. The square is a good place for sipping a glass of prosecco. Across from the lace museum is the church of **San Martino** (open 8am-noon, 3-7pm daily), containing an early Tiepolo *Crucifixion* and, in the chapel to the right of the chancel, three small paintings by the 15th-century painter Giovanni Mansueti; the *Flight into Egypt* presents the Holy Family amid an imaginative menagerie of beasts and birds. From behind the church of San Martino, there is a view across the lagoon to the idyllic monastery island of **San Franceso del Deserto** (*see p210*). There's a lively morning fish market (Tue-Sat) on the **fondamenta della Pescheria**.

Sights & museums

Convento di San Francesco del Deserto

041 528 6863, www.sanfrancescodeldeserto. it. Open 9-11am, 3-5pm Tue-Sun. Admission by donation.

The island, with its 4,000 cypress trees, is inhabited by a small community of Franciscan monks. Getting there can be quite a challenge. If you take the water taxi from Burano, expect to pay at least €60 for the return ride. Individuals or smaller groups should call the Laguna Fla boat hire service (347 992 2959), which charges €10 per person return (no cards).

The other-worldly monk who shepherds visitors around will tell the story (only in Italian) of how the island was St Francis's first stop in Europe on his journey back from the Holy Land in 1220. He planted his stick, it grew into a pine and birds flew in to sing for him; there are certainly plenty of them in evidence in the cypress-packed gardens today. The medieval monastery – all warm stone and cloistered calm – is about as far as you can get from the worldly bustle of the Rialto.

Museo del Merletti

Piazza B Galuppi 187, Burano (041 730 034, museomerletto.visitmuve.it). Vaporetto 9, 12, N. Open 10am-6pm Tue-Sun. Admission €5; €3.50 reductions; see also p306 Tourist information. No cards.

Following a major revamp, the Lace School's rooms with painted wooden beams are looking resplendent. In a chronological layout, the display covers elaborate examples of lace-work from the 17th century onwards. There are fans, collars and parasols, and some of the paper pattern-sheets that lace-makers use. Some of Burano's remaining lace-makers can regularly be found at work here, displaying their handicraft to visitors.

Restaurants

Alla Maddalena €€

Mazzorbo 7B (041 730 151, www. trattoriamaddalena.com). Vaporetto Mazzorbo. Meals served noon-3pm, 7-9pm Mon-Wed, Fri-Sun. Traditional Venetian

Opposite the jetty on the island of Mazzorbo is this trattoria, which serves good lagoon cuisine. During the hunting season, wild duck is sourced directly from local hunters; the rest of the year, seafood dominates. Book ahead for Sunday lunch in summer, when the waterside tables and those in the quiet garden behind fill up. Service, though professional, is not always cheerful.

♥ Venissa €€€€

Mazzorbo, fondamenta Santa Caterina 3 (041 527 2281, www.venissa.it). Vaporetto Mazzorbo. Restaurant (Apr-Sept) noon-2.30pm, 7-9.30pm Mon, Tue- Sun. Osteria noon-10.30pm Mon, Tue-Sun. Modern Venetian

Inside a lovely high-walled vineyard, with views across to Burano's brightly coloured houses and a hotel attached, Venissa serves ambitious fare inspired by super-fresh produce, much of which comes from the nets of local fishermen and the on-site vegetable garden. The 2017 season saw the arrival of much-fêted young chef Francesco Brutto, who describes his creations as avant-garde. The main restaurant in the garden is a summer affair (open from April; bring mosquito repellent). Prices are high but you can avoid surprises at bill-paying time by opting for taster menus from €120 to €200. In the canalside HQ, Venissa's Osteria is open year-round. The menu here is slightly simpler and (very) slightly less demanding on the wallet. The Venissa initiative is the brainchild of prosecco producers Bisol, who have brought back to life the well-nigh-forgotten Dorona grape here.

SANT'ERASMO & AROUND

▶ *Vaporetto Capannone, Chiesa or Punta Vela (13, N); Forte Massimiliano (18).*

The largest island in the northern lagoon, Sant'Erasmo is a well-kept secret, with a tiny population that contents itself with growing most of the vegetables eaten in *La Serenissima* (on Rialto market stalls, the sign 'San Rasmo' is a mark of quality). Venetians refer to the islanders of Sant'Erasmo as *i matti* ('the crazies') because of their shallow gene pool – everybody seems to be called Vignotto or Zanella. There are cars on this island, but as they are only used to drive the few miles from house to boat and back, few are in top-notch condition, a state of affairs favoured by the fact that the island does not have a single policeman. It also lacks a doctor, pharmacy and high school, but there is a supermarket and a tiny primary school. There are also some restaurants, and a fishermen's bar-*trattoria* – **Ai Tedeschi** (041 244 4139, open 9am-11pm daily in summer) – hidden away on a small sandy beach by the **Forte Massimiliano**. The latter is a moat-surrounded 19th-century Austrian fort that has been restored. Before restoration it was used by a local farmer to store his tools. Nowadays it opens to the public on summer afternoons (11am-6pm Sat, Sun) and some weekend mornings too. Occasionally it hosts exhibitions.

The main attraction of the island lies in the beautiful country landscapes and lovely walks past traditional Veneto farmhouses, through vineyards and fields of artichokes and asparagus – a breath of fresh air after all the urban crowding of Venice. For those wanting to get around more swiftly, bicycles can be hired from the guesthouse **Lato Azzurro** (041 523 0642; €5 for the first two hours, then €1 per hour after; no cards). It's a ten-minute walk southwards from the vaporetto stop Capannone.

By the main vaporetto stop (**Chiesa**) is the 20th-century church (on the site of an earlier one founded before 1000; opening hours vary); it's technically named **Santi Erme and Erasmo**, but it's widely known as simply '**Chiesa**'. Over the entrance door is a gruesome painting, attributed to Domenico Tintoretto, of the martyrdom of St Erasmus, who had his intestines wound out of his body on a windlass. The resemblance of a windlass to a capstan resulted in St Erasmus becoming the patron saint of sailors.

If you're around on the first Sunday in October, don't miss the **Festa del Mosto**, held to inaugurate the first pressing of new wine. This is perhaps the only chance you'll ever get to witness – or even participate in – *a gara del bisato*: a game in which an eel is dropped into a tub of water blackened by squid ink. Contestants have to plunge their heads into the tub and attempt to catch the eel with their teeth.

Lazzaretto Nuovo & Vignole

▶ *Vaporetto 13 (request stop).*

Opposite Sant'Erasmo's Capannone vaporetto stop is the tiny island of **Lazzaretto Nuovo**. In the 15th century, the island was fortified as a customs depot and military prison; during the 1576 plague outbreak it became a quarantine centre. The island is now home to a research centre for the archaeologists of the Archeo Club di Venezia, who are excavating its ancient remains, including a church that may date back to the sixth century. Guided tours at 9.45am and 4.30pm (041 244 4011, www.lazzarettonuovo.com) are available from April to October on Saturday and Sunday. A donation is expected.

On the smaller island of **Vignole** (also served by the 13 vaporetto, on request), there is a medieval chapel dedicated to St Erosia.

Sant'Erasmo

❤ Torcello

▶ *Vaporetto Torcello (9, N).*

This sprawling, marshy island is where the history of Venice began. Torcello today is a picturesquely unkempt place with a resident population of about 15 (plus infinitely more mosquitoes). It's difficult to believe that in the 14th century more than 20,000 people lived here. It was the first settlement in the lagoon, founded in the fifth century by the citizens of the Roman town of Altino on the mainland. Successive waves of emigration from Altino were sparked off by barbarian invasions, first by Attila and his Huns, and, in the seventh century, by the Lombards. But Torcello's dominance of the lagoon did not last: Venice itself was found to be more salubrious (malaria was rife on Torcello) and more easily defendable. Even the bishop of Torcello chose to live on Murano, in the palace that now houses the glass museum (*see p205*). But past decline is present charm, and rural Torcello is a great antidote to the pedestrian traffic jams around San Marco.

From the ferry jetty, the cathedral **campanile** of Santa Maria Assunta can already be made out; to get there, simply follow the path along the main canal through the island. Halfway along the canal is the **ponte del Diavolo** (one of only two bridges in the lagoon without a

parapet), where there is an *osteria* called **Al Ponte del Diavolo** (041 730 401, closed dinner, all Mon and Dec-Jan, average €40) that caters mainly to tourists and local wedding/baptism/communion parties. For the classic Torcello restaurant, head to **Locanda Cipriani** (piazza Santa Fosca 29, 041 730 150, locandacipriani.com, Mar-Dec noon-3pm Wed-Mon, also 7-9pm Fri, Sat by appt, €€€€), which was one of Ernest Hemingway's haunts. The setting, just off Torcello's pretty square, is idyllic, with tables spread over a large vine-shaded terrace. And although there is nothing remotely adventurous about the cuisine, it's good in an old-fashioned way.

Torcello's main square has some desultory souvenir stalls, the small but interesting **Museo di Torcello** (*see right*), with archaeological finds from around the lagoon, a battered stone seat known arbitrarily as Attila's throne, and two extraordinary churches.

The 11th-century church of **Santa Fosca** (open 10am-6pm Mon-Sat, 9am-6pm Sun, free) looks somewhat like a miniature version of Istanbul's Santa Sophia, more Byzantine than European with its Greek-cross plan and external colonnade; its bare interior allows the perfect geometry of the space to come to the fore. Next door is the imposing cathedral of **Santa Maria**

Santa Fosca

Assunta (041 730 119, Nov-Feb 10am-5pm daily, Mar-Oct 10.30am-6pm daily, €5, €4 reductions). Dating from 639, the basilica of Santa Maria Assunta is the oldest building on the lagoon. The interior has an elaborate 11th-century mosaic floor, but the main draws are the vivid mosaics on the ceiling vault and walls, which range in date from the ninth century to the end of the 12th. The apse has a simple but stunning mosaic of a *Madonna and Child* on a plain gold background, while the other end of the cathedral is dominated by a huge mosaic of the *Last Judgement*. The theological rigour and narrative complexity of this huge composition suggest comparisons with the *Divine Comedy*, which Dante was writing at about the same time; however the anonymous mosaicists of Torcello were even more concerned than him with striking fear into the hearts of their audience. It's worth picking up an audioguide (€2) for a very good explanation of the church's history and artistic treasures.

Once you've explored inside, climb the campanile. The view of the lagoon from the top was memorably described by Ruskin: 'Far as the eye can reach, a waste of wild sea moor, of a lurid ashen grey.' And he concluded with the elegiac words: 'Mother and daughter, you behold them both in their widowhood, Torcello and Venice.'

The small but interesting **Museo di Torcello** (Palazzo del Consiglio, 041 730 761, Nov-Feb 10am-4pm, Mar-Oct 10.30am-5.30pm Tue-Sun, €3 or €8 with Santa Maria Assunta) has a worthwhile collection of sculptures and archaeological finds from the cathedral and elsewhere. Among the exhibits are late 12th-century fragments of mosaic from the apse of Santa Maria Assunta, and two of the *bocche di leone* (lions' mouths) where citizens with grudges could post their denunciations. Upstairs don't miss the exquisite carved ivory statuette of an embracing couple dating from the beginning of the 15th century.

Santa Maria Assunta

Last Judgement

Day Trips

Venice offers so much but it's not, of course, the only worthwhile destination in the Veneto region. Across the lagoon, on terra firma, are three other cities vying for your attention. Padua has a magnificent fresco cycle by Giotto; Verona stages opera in a Roman arena, while Vicenza boasts masterpieces by the architectural maestro, Palladio. These cities are easily accessible by road or rail as a day trip from Venice, but, if you've time to spare, they also repay more leisurely exploration in their own right.

❤ Don't miss

1 Cappella degli Scrovegni, Padua *p216*
Giotto's magnificent fresco cycle dominates the interior.

2 Basilica di Sant'Antonio, Padua *p217*
Saintly relics and artistic treasures.

3 Arena, Verona *p218*
A spectacular setting for summer operas.

4 Piazza delle Erbe, Verona *p218*
The heart of the city since Roman times; best viewed from the Torre dei Lamberti.

5 Basilica Palladiana, Vicenza *p224*
The great architect's take on urban restyling.

6 Teatro Olimpico, Vicenza *p225*
Experience concerts and drama in a Palladian theatre.

7 Villa Foscari la Malcontenta *p223*
A classic villa on the Brenta canal.

Piazza delle Erbe, Verona

PADUA

Agricultural communities lived in the Padua area from around 1200 BC, but it was the Romans who transformed this fertile spot into the thriving town of Patavium. Little survived the attacks of Attila and his Huns in 452. After becoming an independent republic in 1164, the city's political and cultural influence peaked under the Carrara family (1338-1405). Venice (1405-1797), Austria, Napoleon and again Austria had their turns ruling until 1866 when the Austrians were banished, and Padua and the Veneto were annexed to the united Kingdom of Italy.

If you only see one sight here, make it the dazzling **Cappella degli Scrovegni** (Scrovegni Chapel, piazza Eremitani 8, www.cappelladegliscrovegni.it), Giotto's masterpiece. Booking is obligatory. This externally unassuming building was commissioned in 1303 by Enrico Scrovegni who is pictured inside, dressed in violet – the colour of penitence – offering the chapel to Mary in the *Last Judgement* fresco at the far end. The sculptures on the altar, *Two Angels* and *The Virgin and Child*, are by Giovanni Pisano. But it's Giotto's magnificent fresco cycle that utterly dominates the interior. Painted c1304-13, it tells the story of mankind's salvation through the lives of the Virgin and Christ. The story of Christ unfolds in the middle and lower rows, with the middle of the

right-hand wall dominated by the scene of Judas's kiss.

The high dado at the base of the walls is decorated with fine grisaille paintings of the seven Virtues and seven Deadly Sins. Particularly striking are the figures of Envy blinded by her own serpentine tongue and Prudence equipped with pen and mirror. In the huge *Last Judgement*, covering the west wall of the chapel, suffering souls are tortured by demonic beasts. The chapel is part of the **Complesso Eremitani**, which encompasses the **Pinacoteca** (picture gallery), **Museo Archeologico** and **Museum of Applied Arts** in Palazzo Zuckerman.

Nearby, the 13th-century church of **Gli Eremitani** (piazza Eremitani 9) has frescoes by Mantegna, begun in 1448 when he was just 17 years old. Bizarrely, this church housed the original tomb of the very Protestant Prince Frederick William of Orange, who died here in 1799. It was removed to Delft, Holland in 1896, but a bronze copy of the marble *Pietà* (1806-08) by Antonio Canova that adorns the tomb can still be seen in the vestibule opposite the chapel.

In the city centre, **Gran Caffè Pedrocchi** (via VIII Febbraio 15, entrance from piazzetta Pedrocchi, www.caffepedrocchi. it) opened to the public in 1831. This café (it still functions as such) was designed by Venetian architect Giuseppe Jappelli. The upper floor contains a condensed tour of Western culture: the Etruscan, Greek, Roman, Renaissance, Moorish and Egyptian

Cappella degli Scrovegni

Saint Anthony of Padua

rooms, all lavishly decorated, surround the ballroom, or Sala Grande.

At Padua's heart are three main *piazze*: piazza della Frutta, piazza delle Erbe and piazza dei Signori. To the south of the latter, in piazza Duomo, lies the underwhelming **Duomo** (cathedral), and its splendid 12th-century baptistry, frescoed from floor to ceiling by the 14th-century Florentine Giusto de Menabuoi.

Between piazza del Duomo and via VIII Febbraio is the tranquil old **Ghetto**, now a beautifully renovated pedestrian zone with shops and bars lining the cobbled streets. Further south, the **Prato della Valle** claims to be the largest public square in Italy, its elliptical shape reflecting that of the Roman amphitheatre which once stood on the site.

A stone's throw away is the **Basilica di Sant'Antonio** (piazza del Santo, www. basilicadelsanto.org), known locally as 'Il Santo'. Work on the church began soon after St Anthony's death (1231) and canonisation (1232), although the main structure remained unfinished until around 1350, when his body was moved to its present tomb in the Cappella dell'Arca. This chapel also contains some of the basilica's great artistic treasures: a series of marble bas-reliefs of scenes from the life of the saint by Jacopo Sansovino, Tullio Lombardo and Giovanni Minello. On the high altar are Donatello's bronze panels and crucifix (1444-45); behind the altar is his stone bas-relief of the Deposition and other bronzes, including a bull and a lion representing the evangelists St Mark and St Luke. At the back

of the apse is the florid Cappella del Tesoro, to which Anthony's 'miraculous' relics were transferred in 1745 for safe-keeping. Here you can inspect the reliquary containing the saint's tongue.

In the *piazza* in front of the church stands the great Renaissance masterpiece, Donatello's monument to the famous *condottiere* (mercenary soldier) Erasmo da Narni (d.1443), aka Gattamelata, who is buried inside the basilica. Commissioned by the *condottiere's* family in 1453 and cast the same year, it was the first full-size equestrian bronze to be made since antiquity.

Nearby is the wonderful **Orto Botanico** (via Orto Botanico 15, www.ortobotanicopd. it), the world's oldest university botanical garden, which is home to 7,000 plant species.

In the know
Padua essentials

Trains from Venice to Padua leave several times each hour, take anything between 26 to 50 minutes and cost from €4.50 to €18 depending on the type of service. For intensive sightseeing, a **Padovacard** (www. turismopadova.it/en; €16 for 48 hours; €21 for 72 hours) covers transport in the city and entrance to major sights, including the Scrovegni Chapel (*see p216*), though a time slot for your visit must be booked in advance.

VERONA

Verona is perhaps best known as the home town of star-crossed lovers Romeo and Juliet, but the attraction today known as Juliet's House pales in comparison with the other glories that Verona has to offer. Verona more than makes up for Venice's lack of Roman remains: its amphitheatre – the Arena – hosts a world-famous opera season in the summer months.

After being colonised by the Romans in 89 BC, Verona became a frequent prize of conquest. By the 12th century, however, it had become an independent city-state, reaching its zenith in the 13th and 14th centuries, when the Della Scala (or Scaligero) dynasty (hence the ladder in local coats-of-arms – *scala* in Italian means 'ladder') brought a period of peace to a city that had long been racked by Montague and Capulet-style family feuding. The dynasty fell in 1387 and was replaced by Milan's Viscontis, superseded in turn by the Venetian Republic. Only in 1866 did Verona rid itself of foreign rulers, when it joined the newly united Kingdom of Italy.

Dominating the entrance to the old town in piazza Brà is the magnificent **Roman Arena** (www.arena.it), capacious enough to seat the city's population of over 20,000 when it was constructed in around AD30. The 44 tiers of stone seats inside the 139-metre by 110-metre (456-foot by 361-foot) amphitheatre are virtually intact, as is the columned foyer. An earthquake in 1117 destroyed most of the Arena's outer ring (the remaining four arches are known as the 'ala' – wing). Originally the site of gladiatorial games, it was used by post-Roman inhabitants as a shelter during fifth- and sixth-century Barbarian invasions. Later, it served as a law court and site of the occasional execution. It functioned as a theatre in the 17th and 18th centuries and became a football stadium in the early 20th century. It now provides a spectacular setting for summer operas (*see p221* Opera in the Arena).

North-east from piazza Brà, via Mazzini takes you to the adjoining squares of piazza delle Erbe and piazza dei Signori. Once the site of the Roman forum, **piazza delle Erbe** today is home to a morning market. The basin of the fountain (1368) in the square is Roman, as is the body of the statue known as the Madonna Verona that stands above it. The tall houses at the square's southern end marked the edge of the Jewish ghetto.

A detour south-east out of the piazza along via Cappello leads to **Casa di Giulietta** (via Cappello 23, casadigiulietta.comune. verona.it; *see p218*), which was certainly never occupied by any Capulets. Nearby **San Fermo Maggiore** (stradone San Fermo, www.chieseverona.it) is Romanesque downstairs, whereas the upper church, towering and full of light, is Gothic. Among the important frescoes is an *Annunciation* by Antonio Pisanello, to the left of the main entrance.

Linking piazze delle Erbe and dei Signori is the 12th-century Palazzo della Ragione, home to the **Achille Forti Gallery of Modern Art** on the first floor (cortile Mercato Vecchio, www. palazzodellaragioneverona.it). From one of the eight elegant arches in piazza dei Signori – **Arco della Costa** – hangs a whale bone. According to local legend, it will fall if an adult virgin ever passes beneath it. A gateway on the piazza dei Signori side of the *palazzo* leads into the **Mercato Vecchio** courtyard, with its huge Romanesque arches and magnificent outdoor Renaissance staircase. The *palazzo* is dominated by the 83-metre (272-foot) **Torre dei Lamberti** (1462). From the next courtyard on the right you can descend into the archaeological site of the **Scavi Scaligeri** (Corte del Tribunale, piazza Viviani, scaviscaligeri.comune. verona.it), where photographic exhibitions are also held. The excavations give a feel

San Fermo Maggiore

Ponte Scaligero

Romeo & Juliet

Sorting the fact from the fiction in Verona

Disentangling myth and history is difficult in Verona. The Montagues and Capulets may have been real enough, but young Juliet Capulet was not – as locals suggest – laid to rest in the Roman sarcophagus in the former convent of **San Francesco al Corso** (via del Pontiere 35), where Mme de Stael and Lord Byron, amongst others, went into Romantic raptures (and which Charles Dickens, more prosaically, described as 'a sort of drinking trough'). And the Capulets never lived in what's now known as the **Casa di Giulietta** (Juliet's house, *see p218*).

This doesn't stop starry-eyed visitors heading there in droves. Generations of visitors have crowded the courtyard of this pretty 13th-century *palazzo*, gazing enraptured at a balcony cunningly tacked on to the first floor in the 1920s, leaving their entwined signatures on graffiti-covered walls and having a furtive rub of the shiny right breast of a 20th-century bronze of Shakespeare's best-loved heroine.

For the record, **Romeo's house** – which at least may have actually belonged to the Montague family – is at Arche Scaligere 4.

Casa di Giulietta

DAY TRIPS

for the city's historical layering, as you move between Roman mosaics and roads, interspersed at random with medieval and Lombard remains.

At the eastern exit from piazza dei Signori are the **Della Scala family tombs** (via Santa Maria in Chiavica, www.turismoverona. eu). Dating from 1277 to the end of the 14th century, the lavish tombs (carved by the most sought-after stonemasons of the era) give a good idea of the family's sense of its own importance. Note the family's odd taste in first names. The monument to Cangrande (Big Dog, d.1329), above the doorway to the church of Santa Maria Antica, shows the valiant duke smiling in the face of death, guarded by crowned dogs (this is a copy, *see*

p220). Poking out from above the fence are the spire-topped final resting places of Cansignorio (Lord Dog, d.1375) and Mastino II (Mastiff the Second, d.1351). Among the less flamboyant tombs is that of Mastino I (d.1277), founder of the doggy dynasty.

Moving northwards, the peaceful, narrow streets are a captivating labyrinth dotted with medieval and Renaissance *palazzi*. The imposing church of **Sant'Anastasia** (piazza Sant'Anastasia, www.chieseverona.it) is best visited early in the morning, when sunlight streams in to illuminate Antonio Pisanello's glorious fresco (1433-38) of St George girding himself to set off in pursuit of the dragon that has been pestering the lovely princess of Trebizond.

Close by, **ponte Pietra** is Verona's oldest bridge: the two stone arches on the left bank of the river are Roman and date from before 50 BC. The other three brick arches date from between 1200 and 1500. Across the bridge are some of Verona's most beautiful churches, including **San Giorgio in Braida** (piazzetta San Giorgio 1, 045 834 0232), a domed Renaissance church, probably designed by Veronese military architect Michele Sanmicheli between 1536 and 1543, containing a *Baptism of Christ* by Tintoretto above the entrance door, a moving *Martyrdom of St George* by Paolo Veronese and a beautiful, serene *Madonna and Child with Saints Zeno and Lawrence* by local dark horse Girolamo dai Libri.

There's also **Santa Maria in Organo** (piazzetta Santa Maria in Organo, 045 591 440), a Renaissance church with arguably the most beautiful choir stalls in Italy. A humble monk, Fra Giovanni da Verona (d.1520), worked for 25 years cutting and assembling these infinitely complex wooden images of animals, birds, landscapes, cityscapes, religious scenes and musical and scientific instruments in dozens of intricate intarsia panels.

Also beyond the bridge is the **Museo Archeologico** (regaste Redentore 2, www.turismoverona.eu) with a collection of local remains and a spectacular view; the remains of the first-century BC **Teatro Romano** are in the same complex.

Head south-east from the bridge along regaste Redentore and its continuations for the pretty **Giardino Giusti** (via Giardino Giusti 2), a statue-packed garden with tall cypresses laid out in 1580. Back towards the river is the church of **San Tomaso Cantuariense** (piazza San Tomaso 1), where

Mozart, aged 13, played the organ on his visit to the city, birthplace of his future arch-rival, Salieri.

Corso Porta Borsari, Roman Verona's busy main street, leads out of the north end of piazza delle Erbe towards the Porta Borsari, the best-preserved of the city's Roman gates, and the medieval fortress of **Castelvecchio** (Corso Castelvecchio 2, museodicastelvecchio.comune.verona.it), now a museum and exhibition venue, with interiors beautifully redesigned in the 1960s by Venetian architect Carlo Scarpa. The museum contains important works by Mantegna, Giovanni Bellini, Veronese, Tintoretto and Canaletto, plus a magnificent collection of 13th- and 14th-century Veronese religious statuary. Arms and jewellery complete the collection.

Outside the centre, to the west of piazza Brà, is the basilica of **San Zeno Maggiore** (piazza San Zeno 2, www.chieseverona.it). One of the most spectacularly ornate Romanesque churches in northern Italy, it was built between 1123 and 1138 to house the tomb of San Zeno, an African who became Verona's first bishop in 362 and is now the city's patron saint. The façade, with its great rose window, is covered with magnificent 12th-century marble sculpture. Scenes from the Old Testament and the life of Christ mingle with hunting and jousting scenes. The great bronze doors have 48 panels showing scenes from the Bible and from the life of San Zeno, plus a few that experts have been hard-pressed to pin down, including a woman suckling two crocodiles. The panels on the left-hand door date from about 1030 and came from an earlier church.

Inside the lofty church (note the magnificent ceiling built in 1386), a staircase

Teatro Romano

Opera in the Arena

Music to your ears

Verona's **Arena** (*see p218*) seems particularly suited to grand productions of tragic magnitude – but any of the operas that are performed at this 2,000-year-old amphitheatre every night from June to September will certainly be pure magic.

The atmosphere is charged with excitement as music lovers start squeezing on to the (unnumbered) stone terraces a good two hours before the performance begins. All bring or rent a cushion, as a night perched on a piece of ancient marble can seem long and painful, whatever is happening on stage. Occupants of the more expensive *poltronissime*, the red-cushioned stalls seats, can saunter in just before the show commences.

A hush falls over the 15,000-strong audience as the overture is played to the flickering of *mocoleti*, the candles traditionally lit all around the amphitheatre for the prelude. Hours of magical music with natural acoustics and the stunning setting make a night in the world's largest open-air opera house a matchless experience.

Fondazione Arena di Verona

Via Dietro l'Anfiteatro 6B (045 800 5151, www. arena.it). Performances June-Aug 9pm Tue-Sun. Tickets from €22.

Arena di Verona

DAY TRIPS

descends into the crypt, which contains the tomb of San Zeno. A magnificent triptych – known as the *Pala di Mantegna* (1457-59) after its author Andrea Mantegna, dominates the altar. A huge, early 12th-century marble statue of the African bishop having a grand old chuckle is found in a niche to the left of the apse. His black face, with its distinctly African features, is unique in Italian religious statuary. When he wasn't converting Veronese souls to Christianity, he is said to have spent his time fishing in the River Adige, seated on a rock.

To the right of the church is a massive bell tower, 72 metres (236 feet) high, begun in 1045. To the left is a lower tower, which is all that remains of the Benedictine monastery that once stood on the site.

In the know
Verona essentials

Frequent **trains** from Venice to Verona take between one hour ten minutes, and two hours 15 minutes, and cost from €8.85 to €27 depending on the type of service. The **Verona Card** (€18 for 24 hours, €22 for 48 hours, www.turismoverona.eu, purchasable in all participating venues) gives admission to most of the city's major sites, including Juliet's house and the Arena.

VICENZA

Vicenza was a Roman settlement, and the city's ancient layout is still virtually intact. It became an important Lombard and Frankish centre, but was destroyed by Magyar ravagers in 899, only to flourish again later in the Middle Ages. In 1404, Vicenza came under the rule of Venice, and a veritable building boom began.

Bridling under the Venetian yoke, Vicenza's leading families proclaimed their superiority by commissioning sumptuous townhouses and country villas. But Venetian nobles were also encouraged to develop country estates in order to strengthen the Republic's grip on the surrounding territory. It was into this cauldron of Renaissance one-upmanship that Andrea Palladio (*see p270* Andrea Palladio) fell in the 1540s. The mark he left here would influence architecture the world over for centuries to come.

Now a major hub of the north-eastern economic miracle, Vicenza oozes wealth. The city is home to Italy's precious-metalworking industry, and the VicenzaOro trade fair (www.vicenzaoro.com) takes place here several times a year. The city's two main claims to fame – Palladio and gold – come together along the streets of the *centro*, where shop windows in ground floors of glorious Palladian *palazzi* glisten with world-class jewels, exorbitant trinkets and designer togs.

Despite its Roman origins, Vicenza's character is very much medieval and Renaissance. Just outside the town walls, to the west of the centre, is the statue-dotted **Giardino Salvi**. This pleasant public park houses Palladio's Loggia Valmarana, a Doric-style temple spanning the waters of a canal. Nearby is a Baroque loggia by Baldassare Longhena.

Inside the walls, piazza del Castello takes its name from a castle built in 1337-38; the tower in the corner of the *piazza* is all that remains of the castle. The *piazza* is home to the odd-looking **Palazzo Porto Breganze**, a tall awkward fragment in the southern corner, designed by Palladio but never finished.

Palladio had a hand in five of the grandiose *palazzi* lining corso Palladio. The first of note, on the left-hand side as you exit the *piazza*, is the magnificent **Palazzo Thiene Bonin Longare**, begun in 1562. At no.45 is **Palazzo Capra**, almost certainly designed by the young Palladio between 1540 and 1545.

A quick turn right into contrà Battisti (streets in Vicenza's centre are called '*contrà*' instead of '*via*') leads to the **Duomo** (piazza Duomo 8), a mainly 12th-century structure. The Gothic pink marble façade is attributed to Domenico da Venezia (1467); the banal brick interior contains an important polyptych by Lorenzo Veneziano, dated 1366.

Palladian Basilica

Palladio and His Villas

Seek out these architectural masterpieces

Andrea di Pietro della Gondola was born in Padua in 1508, but it was in Vicenza, where he was apprenticed to a stonecarver at the age of 13, that he really made his mark. Here, a chance meeting in the 1530s with Count Giangiorgio Trissino, the wealthy leader of a group of Humanist intellectuals dedicated to reviving classical culture, led to his new life as an architect, and a new name, 'Palladio', given to him by Trissino.

The countryside around Vicenza where Palladio built his masterpieces – his domestic villas – once compared favourably with the Tuscan hills. Ugly light industry and sprawling retail have put paid to that. But many of the visitable *ville* are saved by the fact that they have their own parks and gardens to act as a buffer. You'll need transport (it is possible to reach most by public transport, but it will be a hassle) and some rose-tinted spectacles so as not to notice the blighted landscape. Persevere: it's worth it.

What follows is a selection of Palladio's villas which are open to the public.

Villa Barbaro a Maser
Via Cornuda 7, Maser (0423 923 004, www. villadimaser.it).

Built between 1550 and 1557, this is an out-and-out exercise in rural utopianism. The two fanciful arcaded wings flanking the main porticoed building are actually *barchesse*, or farmhouse wings; while the mirror-image, sundial-adorned chapel fronts on either end are, in fact, dovecotes. Behind these is a nymphaeum – a semicircular pool surrounded by statues. Inside, the light, airy rooms house sumptuous trompe l'œil frescoes by Paolo Veronese.

Villa Emo
Via Stazione 5, Fanzolo di Vedelago (0423 476 334, www.villaemo.org).

Villa Emo contains joyous frescoes by Giambattista Zelotti, one of the major fresco artists of the late Italian Renaissance.

Villa Foscari La Malcontenta
Via dei Turisti 9, Malcontenta di Mira (041 520 3966, www.lamalcontenta.com).

Designed in 1554, this most acclaimed creation of Andrea Palladio is known as 'La Malcontenta' – perhaps because an unhappy (*malcontenta*) female member of the Foscari family was housed there in isolation. With its double staircase and elegant Greek temple façade, the Villa Foscari has been the inspiration for thousands of buildings throughout Europe and America. It can be reached by boat along the Brenta canal from Venice; see the website for details.

Villa Godi Valmarana ora Malinverni
Via Palladio 44, Lugo di Vicenza (0445 860 561, www.villagodi.com).

Commissioned by Pietro Godi and built in 1542, this was Palladio's first independent job and remains one of his most radically pared-back designs.

Villa Poiana
Via Castello 43, Poiana Maggiore (0444 898 554, 041 220 1297, www.villapoiana.it).

This villa demonstrates Palladio's skill as an architect of smaller dwellings. Completed around 1550, its façade is dominated by a Serlian arch (a central arched opening flanked by two rectangular ones) topped by circular indents.

Villa Saraceno
Via Finale 8, Finale di Agugliaro (0444 891 371, www.landmarktrust.org.uk).

The lovely Villa Saraceno (1550) is now the property of Britain's Landmark Trust. It was built for a gentleman farmer, and has an attic-granary lit by large grilled windows to keep the wheat ventilated. The villa is available as self-catering accommodation (see the website for details) but can be visited on Wednesday afternoons.

Villa Foscari La Malcontenta

Opposite the Duomo is the entrance to the incredibly preserved **Criptoportico Romano** (piazza Duomo), the only surviving remnant of Roman Vicetia and all that remains of a large, first-century *domus* (Roman townhouse). The 90 metres (295 feet) of vaulted tunnels formed part of the foundations supporting a walled internal garden. Opening times are irregular.

Back on corso Palladio, **Palazzo Pojana** (1564-66) at no.92 consists of two separate buildings that were cunningly joined together by Palladio.

In the vast and elegant piazza dei Signori, south of the *corso*, is the 82-metre (269-foot) **Torre di Piazza** clocktower, which dates from the 12th century. The Gothic **Palazzo della Ragione** (piazza dei Signori, www.museicivicivicenza.it), seat of city government, is known to all as the **Basilica Palladiana**. When the *palazzo*'s original loggia collapsed in 1496, city fathers canvassed the leading architects of the day; luckily for Palladio, who was only 17 at the time, they dithered for 20 years before accepting the audacious solution he proposed in 1546. Palladio's double-tiered loggia encases the original Gothic *palazzo* in a unifying Renaissance shell. The basilica is now used as an exhibition space and opens only for shows. Opposite is a fragment of Palladio's **Loggia del Capitanato**, built to celebrate Venice's victory over the Turks in the Battle of Lepanto in 1571.

Coming off corso Palladio to the north of piazza Signori is contrà Porti, a real *palazzo* feast. The clannish Porto family all built their houses in one street. At no.11 is the Palazzo Barbaran Da Porto, designed by Palladio (1569-71). It is home to the **Museo**

Palladiano (www.palladiomuseum.org), which offers an intelligently curated look at Palladio's works, techniques and times, and hosts temporary exhibitions on architectural themes. **Palazzo Iseppo Da Porto**, at no.21, is one of Palladio's earliest creations; its interior is decorated with frescoes by Tiepolo (not open to the public).

At the end of the street, across the Bacchiglione river, contrà San Marco is a wide street lined with fine 16th- and 17th-century *palazzi*, including **Palazzo Da Schio**, an elegant townhouse designed by Palladio in the 1560s.

On contrà Santa Corona – further north off the *corso* – **Gallerie di Palazzo Leoni Montanari** (no.25, www.gallerieditalia.com/it/vicenza/) hosts a collection of works by the 18th-century Venetian genre painter Pietro Longhi, plus several other Venetian scenes, including an interesting Canaletto. There's also an extraordinary collection of ancient Russian icons.

On the corner of this street and the *corso*, the magnificent Gothic brick church of **Santa Corona** was completed in 1270 to house a thorn from Christ's crown and is Palladio's final resting place. It contains an *Adoration of the Magi* (1573) by Paolo Veronese in the third chapel on the right. In the crypt is the Valmarana Chapel, designed by Palladio. The beautifully elaborate high altar (1670) by Francesco Antonio Corberelli is a masterpiece of intricate marble inlay. The church's highlight, however, in the fifth chapel on the left of the nave, is a beautiful 1502 *Baptism of Christ* by Giovanni Bellini.

The main street ends in piazza Matteotti, where two of Vicenza's real artistic treats await. Palazzo Chiericati (1550), one of

Teatro Olimpico

Villa Rotonda

Palladio's finest townhouses, is now the city's art gallery, the **Museo Civico** (www. museicivicivicenza.it). It holds a fascinating collection of works by local painters. The highlight is a 1489 Cima da Conegliano alterpiece, *Madonna Enthroned with Child between Saints James and Jerome*. There are also works by Van Dyck, Tintoretto, Veronese and Tiepolo, and a *Crucifixion* by the Flemish master Hans Memling.

Also on piazza Matteotti is Palladio's final masterpiece, the remarkable **Teatro Olimpico** (www.museicivicivicenza.it). Designed in 1579-80, just a few months before the architect's death, it was the first permanent indoor theatre to be built in Europe since the fall of the Roman Empire. His son, Silla, and his star pupil, Vincenzo Scamozzi, took over, and the two took considerable liberties with the original blueprint. The decorative flamboyance of the wood and stucco interior contrasts notably with the modest entrance and severe external walls.

Based on ancient theatres, it has 13 semicircular wooden steps, crowned by Corinthian columns holding up an elaborate balustrade topped with elegant 'antique' sculpted figures. The permanent stage set, designed by Scamozzi, with its seven trompe l'œil street scenes, represents the city of Thebes in Sophocles' *Oedipus Rex*, which was the theatre's first performance, on 3 March 1585. The elaborately frescoed antechambers to the theatre were also designed by Scamozzi and were used for meetings and smaller concerts. A chiaroscuro fresco in the entrance hall depicts a delegation of Japanese noblemen who visited Vicenza in 1585. A season of classical dramas in autumn usually includes a staging of *Oedipus Rex* (in Italian), while concerts take place in May and June – see www.teatrolimpicovicenza.it for performance details.

Perched on one of the hilltops that surround Vicenza to the south is the Santuario di Monte Berico church (viale X Giugno 87, www.monteberico.it), a breathtakingly beautiful spot with fantastic views. An attractive loggia leads up viale X Giugno to the church. It's a 20-minute walk beneath a shady 18th-century loggia from the centre.

To the south-east of the centre, at the end of viale Risorgimento, Palladio's **Arco della Scalette** arch stands at the foot of 192 steps leading to **Villa Valmarana 'Ai Nani'** (via dei Nani 8, www.villavalmarana. com), with a remarkable series of frescoes by Giambattista Tiepolo and his son Giandomenico (1757) and statues of dwarves (*nani*, 1785) lining the wall to the right of the main villa. The walk from the centre to the villa takes about 30 minutes.

Further along the same path is the Villa Capra Valmarana, better known as **Villa Rotonda** (via della Rotonda 45, www. villalarotonda.it). One of the most famous buildings in Western architecture, La Rotonda – designed by Palladio between 1567 and 1570, but not completed until 1606 – was not strictly speaking a villa at all, but a pleasure pavilion for a retired cleric. It was the first house to be given a dome, a form previously associated with churches. Opening hours for the interior are short, but it's worth seeing the grandiose exterior and the garden.

In the know
Vicenza essentials

Trains from Venice to Vicenza are frequent, take between 45 and 75 minutes, and cost from €6.10 to €20 depending on the type of service. The seven-day **Vicenza Museum Card** (€15, €12 reductions) allows entry into the Teatro Olimpico and several churches and museums, and can be purchased in the sights where it is valid.

DAY TRIPS

Experience

Orchestra di Padova e del Veneto perform at the
61st International Festival of Contemporary Music, Teatro alle Tese

Events

The Venetian year

Venice has never shied away from merry-making: saints' days, military victories, even the arrival in town of a foreign diplomat – they were all good excuses for a party. The arrival of Napoleon's troops in 1797 ended this state of affairs. By that time, Venice's celebrations had become frantic and excessive, the tawdry death throes of a city in terminal decline. It wasn't until well into the 20th century that the city's traditional revelries began to be resuscitated – this time by officials with an eye firmly on tourist revenue. The most famous example is Carnevale, dusted off in 1979 and now a tourist draw so immense that new spaces for events are being opened up. The Regata Storica, too, is something of a historical pastiche, though in this case one that dates from 1899 when it was hoped it would lend the Biennale a little Venetian colour. Despite the tourist focus of Venice's big events, the locals haven't lost the knack of enjoying themselves; residents enter enthusiastically into these revamped shindigs – especially if they take place on the water.

Carnevale, piazza San Marco

Spring

♥ Carnevale
Date 2wks before Shrove Tues.

See p231 Carnevale.

Su e Zo per i Ponti
041 590 4717, www.suezo.it. Date Sun in Mar or Apr.

Literally 'Up and Down the Bridges', this event is inspired by the traditional *bacarada* (bar crawl). It's an orienteering event in which you are given a map and a list of checkpoints to tick off. Old hands take their time checking out the *bacari* along the way. Individuals can register at the starting line in piazza San Marco on the morning of the event. Costumes, music and dancing liven up the route.

Benedizione del Fuoco
Basilica di San Marco, San Marco. Vaporetto San Marco Vallaresso or San Zaccaria. Date Easter Sat.

At around 8.30pm on Easter Saturday, all the lights are turned off inside St Mark's Basilica (*see p86*) and a fire is lit in the narthex (entrance porch) for the solemn Easter vigil ceremony. Communion is celebrated and the four elements are blessed: earth is represented by the faithful masses, fire by the large altar candle, water at the baptismal font and air by the surrounding environment.

Festa di San Marco
Bacino di San Marco. Vaporetto San Marco Vallaresso or San Zaccaria. Date 25 Apr.

The feast day of Venice's patron saint is a surprisingly low-key affair. In the morning, there is a solemn Mass in the basilica, followed by a gondola regatta between the island of Sant'Elena (*see p118*) and the Punta della Dogana (*see p185*) at the entrance to the Grand Canal. The day is also known as *La Festa del Bocolo* ('bud'): red rosebuds are given to wives and lovers.

Festa e Regata della Sensa
San Nicolò del Lido & Bacino di San Marco (www.sensavenezia.it). Date Weekend following Ascension Day (5th Thur after Easter).

In the days of the Venetian Republic, the doge would board the glorious state barge, the Bucintoro, and be rowed out to the island of Sant'Andrea. Once there, he would throw a gold ring overboard, to symbolise *lo sposalizio del mare* – Venice's marriage with the sea. Today, the mayor does the honours; the Bucintoro looks like a glorified fruit boat, and the ring is a laurel wreath. The ceremony is now performed at San Nicolò, on the Lido (*see p198*), and is followed by a regatta. If it rains, local lore says it'll tip down for the next 40 days.

▶ *There's a model of the Bucintoro in the Museo Storico Navale; see p156.*

Summer

♥ Vogalonga
041 521 0544, www.vogalonga.com. Date Sun in late May/early Jun.

See p71 Rowing regattas.

♥ Biennale d'Arte Contemporanea & Architettura
Ca' Giustinian, San Marco 1364A, calle Ridotto. Vaporetto San Marco Vallaresso (041 521 8711, www.labiennale.org). Date May-Nov (Architecture in 2018, 2020, etc; Art in 2019, 2021, etc).

See p121 La Biennale.

Venezia Jazz Festival
Information: via Corriva 10, Cavasagra di Vedelago (366 270 0299 mobile, www.venetojazz.com). Box office at venues before performances. Date Jun-July.

This annual event draws serious jazz-heads for great music in fantastic venues around Venice and in the Veneto.

♥ Best events

La Biennale *p121*
International cultural showcase.

Carnevale *p231*
Fabulous masks and costumes.

Festa del Redentore *p232*
Boats and fireworks.

Regata Storica *p71*
Pomp and pageantry on the Grand Canal.

Venice Film Festival *p236*
Film stars and film fans descend on the Lido.

Vogalonga *p71*
Messing about in boats.

In the know
Do more

For a full list of events, see www.comune.venezia.it, or download the free Venezia Unica app.

EVENTS

💜 Carnevale

EVENTS

*www.carnevale.venezia.it. **Date** 2 weeks before Shrove Tues.*

Venice's pre-Lenten Carnevale had existed since the Middle Ages, but it came into its own in the 18th century. As the Venetian Republic slipped into terminal decline, the city's pagan side began to emerge. Carnevale became an outlet for all that had been prohibited for centuries by the strong and sober arm of the doge. Elaborate structures would be set up in piazza San Marco as stages for acrobats, tumblers, wrestlers and other performers. Masks served not only as an escape from the drabness of everyday life but to conceal the wearer's identity – a useful ploy for nuns on the run or slumming patricians.

The Napoleonic invasion in 1797 brought an end to the fun and games, and Carnevale was not resuscitated until the late 1970s. When it was reintroduced, it was with money-earning in mind: the city authorities and hoteliers' association saw the potential, and today the heavily subsidised celebrations draw revellers from all over the world.

But if Carnevale fills Venetian hotels and coffers, it also gives the locals a chance for fun and games. The party starts two weekends before *martedì grasso* (Shrove Tuesday). Visitors flock to piazza San Marco, where professional poseurs in ornate costumes occupy prime spots and wait for the world's press photographers to immortalise them. Since 2014, organisers have sought to relieve the pressure of numbers in St Mark's by moving some events into the Arsenale. Venetians, on the other hand, organise private masked and costumed celebrations, or gather in smaller squares. Consult the website for a full programme of events.

▶ *For Carnevale costume hire, see p154* Atelier Pietro Longhi, *p125* Banco Lotto N°10.

Palio delle Antiche Repubbliche Marinare

Bacino di San Marco. Vaporetto San Marco Vallaresso or San Zaccaria. **Date** *June or July.*

This competition takes place in Venice once every four years (next scheduled for 2019); in other years it happens in Amalfi, Genoa or Pisa. The 2000m race starts at the island of Sant'Elena and finishes at the Doge's Palace. Beforehand, 400-odd boats carrying costumed representatives of the four Marine Republics parade along the riva dei Sette Martiri and the riva degli Schiavoni.

Festa de San Pietro de Casteo

San Pietro, Castello. Vaporetto Giardini. **Date** *week of 29 June.*

The liveliest and most villagey of Venice's many local festivals is in celebration of San Pietro Martire. A week of events centres on the church green of San Pietro (*see p123*), where there are competitions, concerts, food stands and bouncy castles.

Festa di San Giacomo dell'Orio

Campo San Giacomo dell'Orio, Santa Croce. Vaporetto Rivadi Biasio or San Stae. **Date** *10 days in mid-late July.* **Map** *p146.*

Concerts, a barbecue and a charity raffle make up this local fair: it provides a great occasion to 'do as the Venetians do' in a truly beautiful campo (*see p157*).

♥ Festa del Redentore

Bacino di San Marco and Canale della Giudecca. **Date** *3rd weekend in July.*

The Redentore is the oldest continuously celebrated date on the Venetian calendar. At the end of a plague epidemic in 1576, the city commissioned Andrea Palladio to build a church on the Giudecca – Il Redentore (the Redeemer; *see p193*). Every July, a pontoon bridge is built across the canal that separates the Giudecca from Venice proper, so people can make the pilgrimage to the church. While the religious part of the festival falls on Sunday, what makes this weekend so special are the festivities on Saturday night. Boats of every shape and size gather in the lagoon between St Mark's, San Giorgio, the Punta della Dogana and the Giudecca, each holding merry-makers supplied with food and drink. This party culminates in an amazing fireworks display, from 11.30pm.

Ferragosto – Festa dell'Assunta

Date *15 Aug.*

If you want Venice without Venetians, this is the time to come, as everyone who can leaves the city. Practically everything shuts down and people head to the beach. There is usually a free concert in the cathedral of Santa Maria Assunta (*see p212*), on the island of Torcello, on the afternoon and evening of the 15th. Tourist offices (*see p306*) have more information.

Festa del Redentore fireworks

♥ Venice International Film Festival (Mostra Internazionale D'Arte Cinematografica)

Palazzo del Cinema, lungomare Marconi 90, Lido (041 521 8711, www.labiennale.org). Vaporetto Lido. **Date** *11 days in late Aug/ early Sept.*

See p236 Venice Film Festival.

Autumn

♥ Regata Storica

Canal Grande (www.regatastoricavenezia. it). **Date** *1st Sun in Sept.*

See p71 Rowing regattas.

Sagra del Pesce

Burano. Vaporetto 12. **Date** *3rd Sun in Sept.*

Fried fish and lots of white wine are consumed in this feast, in the *calli* between Burano's brightly painted houses (*see p208*), and around the church of San Martino Vescovo. This also marks the last regatta of the season, when rowers compete in the waters of Burano.

Sagra del Mosto

Island of Sant'Erasmo. Vaporetto 13 to Chiesa. **Date** *1st or 2nd weekend in Oct.*

This festival is a great excuse for Venetians to spend a day 'in the country' on the island of Sant'Erasmo (*see p211*), getting light-headed on the first pressing of wine. The salty soil does not lend itself to superior wine – which is why it's best to down a glass before the stuff has had much chance to ferment. Sideshows, grilled sausage aromas and red-faced locals abound.

Venice Marathon

Information: 041 532 1871, www. huaweivenicemarathon.it. **Date** *4th Sun in Oct.*

The marathon starts in the town of Stra, east of Padua, follows the Brenta Canal, and then winds through Venice to end on the riva Sette Martiri.

Festa di San Martino

Date *11 Nov.*

Kids armed with *mamma*'s pots and spoons raise a ruckus around the city, chanting the saint's praises and demanding trick-or-treat style tokens in return for taking their noise elsewhere. Horse-and-rider shaped San Martino cakes, coloured icing dotted with chocolate drops, sugar dragées and sweets, proliferate in cake shops.

Vogalonga p71

EVENTS

Festa della Madonna della Salute

Santa Maria della Salute, Dorsoduro. Vaporetto Salute. **Date** *21 Nov.*

In 1630-31, Venice was 'miraculously' delivered from the plague, which claimed almost 100,000 lives – one in three Venetians. The Republic commissioned a church from Baldassare Longhena, and his Madonna della Salute (literally, 'good health') was completed in 1687 (*see p182*). On this feast day, a pontoon bridge is strung across the Grand Canal from campo Santa Maria del Giglio to La Salute so that a procession led by the patriarch (archbishop) of Venice can make its way on foot from San Marco. Along the way, stalls sell cakes and candles for pilgrims to light inside the church. Then everybody eats *castradina* – cabbage and mutton stew – which tastes nicer than it sounds.

Winter

Christmas, New Year & Epiphany (La Befana)

Date *24 Dec-6 Jan.*

Venice's Yuletide festivities are low-key affairs. There are two or three notable events: fireworks in the Bacino di San Marco on New Year's Eve, the New Year's Day swim off the Lido (www.lidovenezia.it), and the Regata delle Befane on 6 January, a rowing race along the Grand Canal in which the competitors, all aged over 50, are dressed up in drag as *La Befana* – the ugly witch who gives sweets to good children and pieces of coal to bad ones.

Film

The excess of the international festival contrasts with the city's lack of viable cinemas

If you pitch up in town during the world's longest-running film festival in late summer, you might mistake Venice for cinema heaven. But outside the once-a-year jamboree, the scene is less exciting. The renaissance in 2012 of the Multisala Rossini cinema provided a little more choice for ardent cinemagoers, but many former picture palaces now house supermarkets: a pretty accurate reflection of local demand, with a diminishing population translating into decreasing numbers of moviegoers.

George Clooney arriving at the 74th Venice Film Festival

FILM

💙 Venice Film Festival

Palazzo del Cinema, lungomare Marconi 90, Lido (041 521 8711, www.labiennale.org). Vaporetto Lido. **Date** *11 days, starting late Aug/early Sept.* **Map** *p199.*

Founded in 1932, the annual Venice Film Festival (Mostra Internazionale d'Arte Cinematografica) is the oldest film festival in the world and remains one of the most prestigious. For 11 days in late summer the glitterati of the film industry, plus their entourage of press and fans, take over the Lido (*see p198*). The main venue is the marble-and-glass Palazzo del Cinema, where official competition screenings take place. Other screens can be found in the Palazzo del Casinò, the striking red box of the Sala Giardino and the 1,700 seater Palabiennale marquee.

The best film of the festival is awarded the *Leone d'Oro* – won by *The Shape of Water* (Guillermo del Toro) in 2017 – with other prizes for best director, actor and actress. Many screenings are open to the public, with tickets from as little as €5 (in 2017) available online until two days before the event; multi-ticket subscriptions are also available. Note that competition films are likely to sell out quickly. Further details, including a full programme of screenings, are available on the official Biennale website.

▶ *For other elements of the Biennale, see p121.*

Penelope Cruz and Javier Bardem at the 74th Festival

Where to go, what to see

Besides the festival at the beginning of September, when the Lido's bikini-clad hordes rub shoulders with journalists, photographers and a constellation of international stars, the only other ray of hope is **Circuito Cinema**, a city hall-backed film promotion initiative that runs and programmes a group of local arthouse cinemas.

The Circuito's cinemas include the **Giorgione Movie d'Essai**, **Multisala Astra** on the Lido and the **Multisala Rossini**, not far from campo Santo Stefano. See www.comune.venezia.it/cinema or www.venicemoviebook.it for details of others.

In Italy, the dubber is king, and the dearth of original-language films infuriates cinema lovers. The Giorgione, Rossini and Astra offer a limited selection of films in *versione originale*.

Associations

Circuito Cinema

Information: Palazzo Mocenigo, Santa Croce 1991, salizada San Stae (041 274 7140, www.comune.venezia.it/cinema). Vaporetto San Stae. **Map** *p146 G6.*

The Circuito Cinema operates as a publisher and as a cine-club organising a series of themed seasons and workshops. It also airs original-language films, mostly classics or arthouse movies. Its annual (July-June) CinemaPiù card (€35; €25 for students) gives discounts to all of Venice's cinemas. It can be bought from the Giorgione, Rossini and Astra cinemas (for all, *see below*).

Cinemas

Giorgione Movie d'Essai

Cannaregio 4612, rio terà dei Franceschi (041 522 6298). Vaporetto Ca' d'Oro. **No cards.** **Map** *p128 K6.*

This two-screener run by Circuito Cinema (*see above*) combines the usual fare with themed seasons and kids' films (on Saturday and Sunday at 3pm).

Multisala Astra

Via Corfù 9, Lido (041 526 5736). Vaporetto Lido. **No cards.** **Map** *p199.*

The council-run Astra is a two-screener usually offering the same fodder as the Giorgione (*see above*) a week before or after. During the Film Festival, the Astra is home to the Venice Film Meeting, which promotes locally made films.

Multisala Rossini

San Marco 3997A, salizada de la Chiesa o del Teatro (041 241 7274). Vaporetto Rialto or Sant'Angelo. **No cards.** **Map** *p82 H10.*

Besides a mix of big hits, smaller productions and retrospectives (and occasional screenings in *linga originale*), the very centrally located Rossini has a bar run by the Marchini dynasty (*see p102*), a restaurant and even an in-house supermarket.

Videotheques

Casa del Cinema – Videoteca Pasinetti

Palazzo Mocenigo, Santa Croce 1990, salizada San Stae (041 274 7140). Vaporetto San Stae. **Open** *Video archive 8.30am-1.30pm Mon-Fri. Shows 6pm, 9pm Tue, Fri.* **Admission** *by CinemaPiù card (€35), valid July-June. No cards.* **Map** *p146 G6.*

This council-run video archive was founded in 1991 to collect and conserve an incredible volume of audiovisual material concerning Venice, in all formats: feature film, TV documentary, newsreel, amateur video, and so on. More than 3,000 videos are kept here, and there's a screening room where brief film seasons are held.

Festivals

In these days of funding cuts, smaller film festivals struggle to survive – though the **Vittorio Veneto Festival** (www. vittoriofilmfestival.com), screening films for children and teenagers, is flourishing. However, the longest running and best-attended local cinema event is just over the border into the Friuli region, the **Silent Film Festival**.

Ca' Foscari Short Film Festival

Università Ca' Foscari Venezia, Dipartimento di Filosofia e Beni Culturali, Malcanton Marcorà, Dorsoduro 3484/D – 30123 (041 234 6244, http:// cafoscarishort.unive.it/)

This short-film festival, run by the students and staff of Ca' Foscari University, includes competitions, retrospectives and videos aimed at film students from around the world. The 2017 edition was held on 15-18 March in the Auditorium Santa Margherita.

Le Giornate del Cinema Muto

Information: Cineteca del Friuli, Palazzo Gurisatti, via Bini 50, Gemona (0432 980 458, www.giornatedelcinemamuto.it). **Date** *early Oct.*

At Europe's most prestigious silent movie festival, highlights include an international forum of musicians for silent movies, retrospectives and films such as the British documentary *The Battle of the Somme* (1916). Accreditation costs €65 (students under 26 €40) and allows unlimited viewings (except opening and closing nights). Non-accredited viewers pay €10 per screening during the day and €10-20 in the evening.

▶ *For a list of recommended films shot in Venice, see p310 Further Reference.*

Nightlife

Spritz-fuelled fun

Venice was once famous for endless partying; these days, you'll be hard-pressed to find much of a scene. There's hardly a dancefloor in the city – but then again, that's not what Venice is about. If you're happy to settle for drinks, chat and the occasional bout of live music in one of the city's late-night bars, fine; if you're after serious clubbing, you'll have to go further afield. A typical Venetian night out starts with a post-work and preprandial spritz (or three) in one of the bars around the Rialto market area, which might develop into a *giro de ombre* – a bar crawl Venetian-style. And for those still standing when the traditional *bacari* close, there's a network of late-opening bars hidden all over town – in particular on Cannaregio's 'party' fondamenta della Misericordia, or Dorsoduro's student headquarters of campo Santa Margherita.

Aperol spritz

Live music

Stringent noise pollution regulations and lack of adequate venues have effectively pulled the plug on large music events; recent years have seen waivers for **Carnevale** (*see p231*) and other summer events being introduced, then rescinded, as authorities bow to pressure from residents. Rock 'n' roll royals who do dates in Venice are usually confined to the very formal setting of one of the local theatres. There's better news for jazz heads as regular series of high-quality jazz and experimental music are organised by local cultural organisations such as **Caligola** (www.caligola.it).

Thanks to the tenacity of the handful of bar owners still willing to wrestle with red tape and persist in the face of party-pooper petitioning neighbours, it's still possible to play and hear live music in various *locali* around town. Venetian vibes tend to be laid-back, and these small, free gigs are almost always reggae, jazz or blues – with the occasional rock, Latino or world session. Clubs and venues on the nearby mainland draw bigger acts.

Club culture

For serious club culture, make for the mainland. In winter, a short bus or train ride to Mestre or Marghera (just across the bridge and well served by night buses) is all it takes to dance until dawn. In summer, most of the dance action moves out to the seaside resort of **Lido di Jesolo**, the place to be for house and techno, with a smattering of Latino.

Information and tickets

Day-to-day listings are carried by the two local papers, *Il Gazzettino* and *La Nuova Venezia*. For a fuller overview of concerts and festivals, with English translations, monthly listings magazine *Venews* (www.venezianews.it) and www.veneziadavivere.com/events is indispensable. Also keep your eyes peeled for posters advertising upcoming events. Tickets are usually available at the venue, but in some cases can be bought in advance at Venezia Unica outlets (*see p306*), or online via www.ticketone.it.

Unless specified, the bars listed below have no extra charge for music. Smoking is strictly forbidden in indoor public spaces, except in designated rooms with extraction systems.

▶ *Many of the drinking establishments listed in the various Explore chapters are also open well into the evening. Try, for example, the Skyline Bar in Giudecca, see p193.*

San Marco

▶ *See also p99* Bacarando in Corte dell'Orso.

Bacaro Jazz

San Marco 5546, salizada del Fontego dei Tedeschi (041 528 5249). Vaporetto Rialto. **Open** *noon-2am daily.* **Map** *p82 K8.*

Venice's most central late-night watering hole, Bacaro Jazz is a place to mingle with fellow tourists or foreign students rather than meet the locals. It hots up during happy hour (4-7pm), and the background jazz and wide range of killer cocktails keep the party going into the early hours.

Caffè Centrale

San Marco 1659B, piscina Frezzeria (041 88 76 642, www.caffecentralevenezia.com). Vaporetto San Marco Vallaresso. **Open** *7pm-1am Mon-Sat.* **Map** *p82 J11.*

Only the exposed bricks of the original 16th-century *palazzo*'s walls will remind you you're in Venice: this chic, contemporary restaurant and lounge bar is more New York or London. There's a studied air of coolness here, and the crowd that gathers for pre- and post-dinner *aperitivi* and cocktails is a sophisticated one. The cool spills into a dinner menu that would best be described as fussy, but the food is fresh (though not cheap) and vegetarians are catered for. Be prepared for fashion TV and music videos coming at you from screens all around the room.

Castello

Inishark

Castello 5787, calle del Mondo Novo (041 523 5300, www.inisharkpub.com). Vaporetto Rialto. **Open** *6pm-1.30am Tue-Sun.* **No cards. Map** *p108 L9.*

Tucked away in a small *calle* near Santa Maria Formosa, this Irish-style pub has the best Guinness on tap in town and great snacky food to soak up the black stuff. Though the friendly owners are Venetian through and through, the crowd that packs in here most nights is very international, with many coming for the four TV screens showing UK premier league, Italian Serie A, and major international football fixtures, plus key rugby matches.

Bacaro Jazz

Cannaregio

▶ *See also p136* Santo Bevitore *and p143* Al Timon.

Irish Pub
Cannaregio 3847, corte dei Pali già Testori (041 099 0916, www.theirishpubvenezia. com). Vaporetto Ca' d'Oro. **Open** *10am-2am Tue-Sun.* **Map** *p128 J6.*

Expats, locals and tourists of all ages prop up the bar in Venice's oldest Irish pub (previously known as the Fiddler's Elbow). Party-pooping neighbours have put a stop to the regular live music nights, but this is no deterrent to regulars, who pack the place out for the sports events shown on four plasma screens.

Paradiso Perduto
Cannaregio 2540, fondamenta della Misericordia (041 720 581, http:// ilparadisoperduto.wordpress.com). Vaporetto San Marcuola. **Open** *6pm-midnight Mon-Thur; noon-1am Fri, Sat; noon-midnight Sun.* **No cards.** **Map** *p128 H4.*

Probably the most famous Venetian haunt after Harry's Bar (*see p104*), this 'Paradise Lost' is well worth finding. Arty types of all ages take their places at the long *osteria* tables for the mix of seafood and succulent sounds (mainly jazz and salsa), which go live every Monday, and a surprising number of other nights, although the city's stringent noise regulations occasionally throw a spanner in the works.

San Polo & Santa Croce

▶ *See p151* Naranzaria.

Metricubi
San Polo 2003, campiello delle Erbe (www.metricubi.org). Vaporetto San Tomà. Check website and Facebook for events. **Map** *p146 G9.*

A cultural centre meeting all your intellectual needs, from 'philosophical spritz' evenings to concerts and lectures. An ARCI membership card is required and can be purchased on the door for €5, although the price might be waived for tourists.

Dorsoduro

▶ *See p177* Café Rosso *and p178* Impronta Café.

Piccolo Mondo
Dorsoduro 1056A, calle Contarini-Corfù (041 520 0371, 329 167 1250, www. piccolomondo.biz). Vaporetto Accademia. **Open** *11pm-4am daily.* **Admission** *€12 incl first drink.* **Map** *p170 F13.*

Called 'El Souk' in better days, this 'small world' remains one of the few places to dance in Venice proper. You may, therefore, find yourself on its dancefloor. If you do, you'll be mixing with ageing medallion men, lost tourists and foreign students so desperate to dance, they'll go anywhere.

Venice Jazz Club

*Dorsoduro 3102, fondamenta dei Pugni (340 150 4985, www.venicejazzclub.com). Vaporetto Ca' Rezzonico. **Open** 7pm-2am Mon-Wed, Fri, Sat. **Admission** €20 incl first drink. **Map** p170 D12.*

The intimate setting and nightly live music make this club, just behind campo Santa Margherita, a perfect place for a night out for fans of high-quality jazz. Concerts start at 9pm, and some food is served.

Lido di Jesolo

Most of Jesolo's clubs open at 11pm, but nobody who's anybody shows up until 1am. Save money (rather than face) by picking up flyers offering reduced entrance before 1am. The clubs listed below are perennial favourites.

Il Muretto

*Via Roma Destra 120, Lido di Jesolo (0421 371 310, www.ilmuretto.net). **Open** Mar-Sept 11pm-5am Wed, Fri, Sat, Sun. **Admission** €20-€50.*

The home of Italian house – and a Jesolo legend – Il Muretto has been going for over 40 years yet remains super-trendy. A mass of ecstatic youth floods the dancefloor for serious house music expertly spun by highly respected resident DJs and guests who are living legends in clubland: Rampling, Oakenfold, Kevorkian, Tenaglia and the Chemical Brothers, to name just a few.

In the know
Getting to Lido di Jesolo

The Lido di Jesolo bus (information at www.atvo.it) leaves from piazzale Roma, but it's more fun to get the double-decker *motonave* from San Zaccaria-Pietà, on the riva degli Schiavoni, to Punta Sabbioni and bus it from there. There are regular boats making the return journey, with a change at Lido between 1am and 6am. Note that if you drop before dawn, you'll need a lift or taxi (approximately €50) back to the boat stop at Punta Sabbioni as no buses link up with the boats during the night.

Terrazza Mare Teatro Bar

*Piazzetta Faro 1, Lido di Jesolo (0421 370336, www.terrazzamare.com). **Open** Apr-Sept 6pm-4am daily. **Admission** free-€10.*

This once-humble beach bar by the lighthouse is a restaurant and club, organising events in addition to club nights. With free entry (except special events), no heavy-handed bouncers or label-led dress code, the informal atmosphere attracts a mixed group of groovers, who flock here in their thousands.

Vanilla Club

*Via Buonarroti 15, Lido di Jesolo (0421 371648, 3382003300, www. vanilla.it). **Open** 11.30pm-5am Mon-Sat. **Admission** €10-€30.*

House, hip hop and R&B are the resident sounds in the Vanilla Club, located in the Acqualandia complex. There might also be a dash of disco sounds to boogie to under the palm trees.

Mestre & Marghera

Al Vapore

*Via Fratelli Bandiera 8, Marghera (041 930 796, www.alvapore.it). Train to Mestre, or bus 6 or 6/ from piazzale Roma. **Open** 7.30am-3pm, 6pm-2am Tue-Fri; 6pm-2am Sat, Sun. **Admission** free-€15 (incl 1st drink).*

This music bar has been putting on jazz, blues, soul and rock gigs for years and is very active on the local scene. Popular Jazz Buffet nights take place in the week, with funky DJ sets and a free buffet. At weekends, well-known Italian and international musicians perform on the tiny stage. There's no charge on Fridays, but drinks cost more. Over the summer months, Al Vapore moves to Estate Village.

Forte Marghera

*Via Forte Marghera 30. Tram to Forte Marghera (www.fortemarghera.it). **Open** 9am-midnight (later in summer) Tue-Sun, see website for special events. **Admission** free.*

Offering solace from the crowded swell of Venice in summer (although events continue year round), this cultural cooperative – a firm favourite with Venetians of all ages – boasts restaurants, bars, concerts and a deckchair-strewn waterfront lawn. The area, picturesquely arranged around an abandoned military fort, can be reached by crossing a field behind the tram tracks. It's also prime feeding ground for mosquitoes – bring strong repellent.

Sunspace/Beast Club

*Via Don Tosatto 9, Mestre (347 372 4863 mobile). Train or tram to Mestre, then bus 3. **Open** 11.30pm-4am Sat. **Admission** €15-€30.*

The first venue in the Venice region to specialise in hardcore techno; it plays host to big-name DJs and attracts well-heeled clubbers.

LGBT VENICE

Venice has everything and (next to) nothing for the gay traveller: enchanting, romantic, tolerant and indulgent, it's the perfect holiday venue… with hardly an LGBT-specific venue in sight. In the *centro storico* a quiet gay scene is tucked away in the private sphere: dinner parties or quiet drinks at the local *bacaro* define the way the city's gay community goes about its business. Buzzy Campo Santa Margherita (*see p174*) and the area around San Pantalon is the focal point for young Venetians. Its bars and *pizzerie* are all extremely busy during summer, and though it's not the cruisiest of places, it's certainly friendly. There's also plenty of evening life in the bars on the San Polo side of the Rialto bridge. **La Zucca** (*see p160*), ten minutes or so walk to the north-west, is one of Venice's most gay-friendly restaurants. Behind the Procuratie Nuove, by the Giardinetti Reali (turn right at the lagoon end of the piazzetta di San Marco), **Il Muro** is one of the city's oldest cruising institutions, but is no longer as popular as it once was. Rarely frequented from October to May, it can still pull a crowd during summer. But even with no one about, the place has a romantic charm all its own.

The summer provides more scope for fun, when gay visitors in large numbers descend on **Alberoni Beach** on the Lido for nude sunbathing and cruising. The dunes and pine forest are where the action is. If the weather's good, cruising starts as early as April, but if you enjoy being spoilt for choice, go for Saturdays and Sundays in July and August. (Take the B/ bus from Santa Maria Elisabetta to Alberoni Spiaggia, the last stop, then turn right and walk for about ten minutes.)

The Venice area's longest-running gay venue is in Mestre: **Metro** (Via Cappuccina 82B, 041 538 4299, www.clubmetrovenezia.it, 2 pm-2 am daily, €10-12 with Anddos membership) has a bar, a dry sauna, steam sauna, private rooms, darkroom and solarium. Massage and hydro-massage are also available. For a wider selection of venues, travel to Marghera or Padua.

▶ *For further information, see p302 LGBT.*

NIGHTLIFE

Venice Jazz Club

Performing Arts

There's more to Venice's cultural scene than Vivaldi

Looking back to the days – in the 18th and 19th centuries – when Venice boasted no fewer than 18 hugely active theatres with in-house playwrights churning out any number of works for an entertainment-hungry audience, you might think that contemporary Venice has become a backwater in the performing arts sector. But this town of fewer than 60,000 souls still boasts one of Europe's great opera houses, La Fenice, high-profile international festivals of the very latest in dance, theatre and music with the Biennale di Venezia, and a number of very serious musical research bodies staging some equally serious public events. At the other end of the scale, numerous commercial organisations cater to a less rigorous public happy to crown their rose-tinted Venetian idyll with costumed renditions of Vivaldi's greatest hits.

The season

Venice's theatre and dance season stretches from November to June – though La Fenice keeps on going for most of the year, closing only for August. Tourist-oriented classical music concerts are held all year. The summer coincides with the **Biennale di Venezia, Danza-Musica-Teatro** (*see p121*), which brings high-quality international productions and artists to perform contemporary theatre, dance and music in the city. Smaller theatre groups also take advantage of the summer temperatures from June onwards and move into Venice's open spaces. But the colder months are not without their serious attractions: look out for concerts held throughout the city during late December to provide some Christmas sparkle.

Information and tickets

Tickets for concerts and performances can usually be purchased at theatre box offices immediately prior to shows; the tourist information office near piazza **San Marco** (*see p306*) and **Venezia Unica** offices (*see p306*) sell tickets for 'serious' events; most travel agents and hotel receptions will obtain tickets for classical music concerts.

For high-profile or first-night productions at prestigious venues such as La Fenice, Teatro Carlo Goldoni, Teatro Malibran or Teatro Toniolo, the limited number of seats not taken by season-ticket holders will sell out days or even weeks in advance: tickets should be reserved at the theatres themselves or on their websites at least two weeks before performances.

Local newspapers *Il Gazzettino* and *La Nuova Venezia* carry listings of theatrical events, as does the bilingual monthly *Venews*.

THEATRE & OPERA

The popular *commedia dell'arte* offerings of playwrights Pietro Chiari and Carlo Gozzi – who went on to produce fairy-tale works including the original *Turandot* – were ousted from centre stage when the city's most enduringly popular playwright, Carlo Goldoni, came on the scene in the mid 18th century. A law student who ran away from school to join a band of travelling players, Goldoni reformed the genre by bringing to the stage his satirical observations, usually in dialect, of Venetians and their foibles. By the end of the 18th century, opera had become so popular in *La Serenissima* that, it's been calculated, almost 1,300 operas were produced in Venice in just

over a generation, and after the fall of the Republic, composers such as Donizetti, Bellini and Rossini regularly provided new works for the **La Fenice** opera house, which retains its preeminent position to this day.

The **Teatro Carlo Goldoni** in Venice and the **Teatro Toniolo** in Mestre tend to serve up standard theatrical fare. You can find more cutting-edge work in Venice's smaller theatres: the **Teatrino Groggia**; and the **Teatro Junghans** (www.accademiateatraleveneta.it), on the Giudecca, a theatre school that sometimes hosts productions by its own students, plus the occasional festival production. The **Teatro a l'Avogaria** explores the outer reaches of Venetian and Italian theatre, often using theatre for didactic purposes, while the **Centro Culturale Candiani**, in Mestre, puts on contemporary pieces. Many summer Biennale productions take place in theatre spaces created inside the Arsenale: the **Teatro alle Tese** and the **Teatro Piccolo Arsenale** (*see p251*).

Venues

Stages here tend to be multi-purpose, with **La Fenice** (*see p247*), for instance, hosting opera, dance and other performances, and the **Teatro Malibran** offering both classical music and ballet.

Centro Culturale Candiani

Piazzale Candiani 7, Mestre (041 238 6111, www.centroculturalecandiani.it). Bus 2 from piazzale Roma.

This 1970s arts centre in Mestre contains an auditorium, video library, exhibition space and outdoor arena. Al fresco performances are held from June to September. Entertainment ranges from Bach to contemporary classics, plus regular film screenings.

Teatrino Groggia

*Cannaregio 3161, Parco di Villa Groggia (041 524 4665, www.mpgcultura.it/ teatrino-groggia/). Vaporetto Sant'Alvise. No cards. **Map** p128 F1.*

Tucked away in the trees, this excellent little space in the northern part of Cannaregio has earned a firm following for its variety of multimedia performances, experimental music and drama, and shows for children in the beautiful garden.

Teatro a l'Avogaria

*Dorsoduro 1617, corte Zappa (041 099 1967, www.teatro-avogaria.it). Vaporetto Ca' Rezzonico or San Basilio. **Box office** 2.30-4.30pm daily. No cards. **Map** p170 C12.*

💙 La Fenice

*San Marco 1983, campo San Fantin (box office 041 24 24, information 041 786 511, www.teatrolafenice.it). Vaporetto Giglio. Box office 10am-5pm daily. Tours 9.30am-6pm daily (rehearsals permitting). Tickets €15-€300. Tours €10; €7 reductions. **Map** p82 H11.*

Venice's principal opera house – aptly named 'the phoenix' – has a long history of fiery destruction and rebirth. The 1792 theatre, designed by Giannantonio Selva, replaced the Teatro San Benedetto, which had burned down in 1774. Opera enjoyed huge popularity in Venice at the start of the 19th century and La Fenice was the focus of this enthusiasm, with famous composers, such as Donizetti, Bellini and Rossini, regularly providing the theatre with new works. Selva's building was itself destroyed by fire in 1836, but was rebuilt in the same style by the Meduna brothers. Besides

Verdi's *Rigoletto* and *La Traviata*, La Fenice hosted premières of Benjamin Britten's *The Turn of the Screw* and Igor Stravinsky's *The Rake's Progress*. In the 20th century, Luciano Berio and Venice's greatest modern composer, Luigi Nono, were commissioned to write for the opera house.

In 1996, another massive blaze broke out, courtesy of two electricians. After years of legal wrangling, the theatre was rebuilt and inaugurated in December 2003, reclaiming its position as one of the world's premier opera houses. La Fenice now offers opera, ballet and concert seasons, and its orchestra is one of the best in the country, but tickets don't come cheap. If you can't get a seat for a performance, explore the theatre on a tour (with audio guide; bookable at the box office). Hidden from view behind the ornate gilding and faux-Baroque plush are state-of-the-art technological innovations.

This experimental theatre (entry to which is by voluntary donation) was founded in 1969 by renowned director Giovanni Poli. It was at the Teatro a l'Avogaria that he continued the experimental approach he developed in the 1950s. Since his death in 1979, Poli's disciples have pressed on with his experiments, staging works by lesser-known playwrights from the 15th to 19th centuries.

Teatro Carlo Goldoni

San Marco 4650B, calle Carbonera (041 240 2011, www.teatrostabileveneto.it). Vaporetto Rialto. Map p82 J9.

The Goldoni serves up Venetian classics by its namesake, supplemented by 20th-century and more contemporary Italian pieces.

Teatro Malibran

Cannaregio 5873, calle dei Milion (041 965 1975, www.teatrolafenice.it). Vaporetto Rialto. Map p128 K7.

Inaugurated in 1678 as Teatro San Giovanni Crisostomo, this 900-seater was built on the site where Marco Polo's family *palazzo* once stood. The theatre now shares the classical music, ballet and opera season with La Fenice; in addition, it has its own chamber music season.

Teatro Toniolo

Piazzetta Battisti 1, Mestre (041 396 9222, box office 041 971 666, www. culturaspettacolovenezia.it/toniolo). Bus 2 or 7 from piazzale Roma.

Founded in 1913, the Teatro Toniolo serves up an assortment of performances, from vernacular favourites to contemporary plays. With its new stagings of Italian and foreign classics, musicals, cabaret, classical and pop music concerts, and contemporary dance and ballet, there is definitely something to suit all tastes.
▶ *For details of opera performances in Verona's Roman Arena, see p221 Opera in the Arena; for that city's Teatro Romano, see p220.*

CLASSICAL MUSIC

Venice has become a victim of its own musical tradition, with Vivaldi pouring out of its *scuole* and churches, usually performed by bewigged and costumed players. For many, experiencing Vivaldi in Venice is an absolute must. But more discerning music-lovers might feel somewhat Baroqued out by the predictable programmes performed by local groups, whose technical ability rarely goes beyond the so-so to fairly good range. Exceptions

are the **Venice Baroque Orchestra**, **Interpreti Veneziani** (*see p249* Choosing your Vivaldi), and the orchestra of **La Fenice** (*see p247*), one of the best in the country. As well as its opera and ballet seasons, La Fenice has at least two concert seasons a year. The **Teatro Malibran** shares the Fenice's programmes and also has its own chamber music season, with performances by the **Società Veneziana dei Concerti**. Mestre's **Teatro Toniolo** also has a symphony and chamber music season. Most other musical events take place in Venice's churches or *scuole*.

Churches, scuole & palazzi

In addition to the venues below, the **Basilica di San Marco** (*see p86*) holds a smattering of ceremonial concerts throughout the year, with the patriarch deciding who is to attend. Lovers of sacred music should aim to catch the sung Mass at St Mark's every Sunday at 9am or the Gregorian chant on the island of **San Giorgio** (*see p188*), also on Sunday at 11am.

Visiting music groups often come to town to give one-off, free performances in Venice's churches; look out for posters around town and check the local press for details.

Ateneo San Basso

San Marco 315A, piazzetta dei Leoncini (041 528 2825, www.virtuosidivenezia. com). Vaporetto San Marco Vallaresso. Shows 8.30pm Mon-Sat. Tickets €28; €22 reductions. No cards. Map p82 L10.

Just off St Mark's square, the Ateneo San Basso puts on the *Four Seasons* and other Vivaldi works – though not many.

Basilica dei Frari

San Polo, campo dei Frari (041 272 8611, www.basilicadeifrari.it/ calendario-concerti/). Vaporetto San Tomà. Map p146 E9.

The lofty Gothic Frari is one of the best venues in Venice for catching high-standard performances of sacred music. It has regular seasons in the autumn and spring; organ recitals and a number of free or low-cost afternoon concerts are held especially over Christmas and the New Year. If you go to one of the winter concerts, wrap up warm.
▶ *For further information on this magnificent basilica, see p162.*

Palazzo Barbarigo Minotto

San Marco 2504, fondamenta Duodo o Barbarigo (340 971 7272, www.musica palazzo.com). Vaporetto Giglio. Shows 8.30pm daily. Tickets €85. Map p82 H12.

Choosing Your Vivaldi

How to improve your listening pleasure

Chances are you won't be in Venice long before you're accosted by a costumed, bewigged (and often rather bedraggled) youth pushing a flyer for 'the' Vivaldi concert into your hand.

With its superb venues and unique atmosphere, Venice lends itself magnificently to early music – though in Venice this is all too often reduced to a quick romp through Vivaldi's *Four Seasons*. If you're going to indulge in a concert – and this *is* an indulgence, with few outfits offering tickets at less than €25, whatever the technical standard – you'll need to examine your priorities.

If you really want the whole costumed shebang, try **I Musici Veneziani**, who perform in the **Scuola Grande di San Teodoro** (*see p250*); if you're a true music buff, however, you may feel you're paying for the 'experience' rather than any musical finesse.

Performing beneath Carpaccio's dramatic painting of St Vitalis on his charger in the church of **San Vidal** (*see p102*), the **Interpreti Veneziani** are a serious musical ensemble, playing to a high standard. There's quite a bit of showmanship here too, with lots of cameraderie and high-fiving among performers at the end of movements. But they pack in the punters nightly, and most go away very happy.

To be absolutely sure to avoid disappointment, serious music aficionados should check out the programme at **La Fenice** (*see p247*) and the **Teatro Malibran** (*see p248*): besides the opera season at the former, there are numerous symphony and chamber music concerts throughout the year, and though getting tickets for these still requires forethought, it is easier than acquiring opera places.

If, on the other hand, you're happier to experience your early music while exploring Venice's *calli* in your own headphoned world, opt for a recording by the **Venice Baroque Orchestra** (www.venicebaroqueorchestra. it). Once upon a time, lucky music-lovers could catch this award-winning, globetrotting ensemble at the Scuola Grande di San Rocco. Nowadays you're more likely to catch them in the US or the Far East.

Formed in 1997 by conductor, harpsichordist, organist and Baroque scholar Andrea Marcon, the ensemble rediscovers neglected works of the Venetian Baroque, and performs them on period instruments. The group has won widespread acclaim for its performances of previously unpublished works by Claudio Monteverdi and Antonio Vivaldi, and for its revival of lost operas including Handel's *Siroe* (in 2000), *L'Olimpiade* by Baldassare Galuppi (in 2006) and the Venetian *serenata Andromeda liberata* (2004), which was composed at least in part by Vivaldi.

The orchestra's revolutionary playing technique does away with the mechanical, tinkly, so-called 'sewing machine' style that is usually the norm for Baroque music: it will make you feel as if you're hearing *The Four Seasons* for the very first time.

Teatro Malibran

Venice Open Stage

performs its Venetian Baroque and German Romantic repertoires several times a week – and also jazz evenings courtesy of the Venice Jazz Quartet.

La Pietà

Castello, riva degli Schiavoni (348 765 7154 mobile, www.ivirtuosiitaliani.eu, www. chiesavivaldi.it). Vaporetto San Zaccaria. **Shows** *8.30pm daily in season.* **Tickets** *€28; €23 reductions.* **Map** *p108 P11.*

I Virtuosi Italiani perform early music concerts in what must surely be the easiest sell in Venice: Vivaldi in the Vivaldi church. *See also p249.*

Santa Maria della Salute

Dorsoduro, campo della Salute (041 274 3928, basilicasalutevenezia.it/ programma/). Vaporetto Salute. **Shows** *3.30pm Mon-Fri.* **Map** *p170 J13.*

The basilica's magnificent 18th-century organ is played during vespers every week day.

San Vidal

San Marco 2862B, campo San Vidal (041 277 0561, www.interpretiveneziani.com). Vaporetto Accademia. **Shows** *9pm daily (8.30pm in winter).* **Tickets** *€29; €24 reductions.* **Map** *p82 G12.*

For highly professional renditions of Vivaldi and other mainly baroque favourites, visit the church of San Vidal (*see p102*), where the no-frills Interpreti Veneziani play to a backdrop of Carpaccio's image of San Vitale on a white horse over the high altar. Tickets can be purchased on the door, or at the Museo della Musica (*see p104*). *See p249* Choosing Your Vivaldi.

Scuola Grande di San Giovanni Evangelista

San Polo 2454, campiello della Scuola (041 718 234, www.scuolasangiovanni.it). Vaporetto San Tomà. **Shows** *9pm, days vary.* **Tickets** *Opera €30-€35; €25-€30 reductions. Concerts €25-30; €10-€20 reductions.* **Map** *p146 E8.*

This 14th-century *scuola*, with an imposing marble staircase and paintings by Tintoretto and Tiepolo, hosts concerts of ancient music played by Società Veneziana Concerti (venicechambermusic.org) and also by the Venetia Antiqua ensemble (www. venicemusicproject.it). Check the websites for occasional free concerts by visiting choirs and orchestras.

Scuola Grande di San Teodoro

San Marco 4810, salizzada San Teodoro (041 521 0294, www.imusiciveneziani. com). Vaporetto Rialto. **Shows**

In the beautiful surroundings of a 17th-century *palazzo*, performances include a variety of classic opera arias, Neapolitan songs and complete operas with few instruments and a piano to accompany the singers. During the evening, the small audience follows the performers around the salons of the *palazzo*, from the frescoed Sala Tiepolo on to the bedroom for the more intimate 'love duets'.

Palazzetto Bru Zane

San Polo 2368, campiello Forner (041 521 1005, www.bru-zane.com). Vaporetto San Tomà. **Shows** *vary.* **Tickets** *€15; €5 reductions.* **Map** *p146 E8.*

Stuccoed and frescoed Palazzo Bru Zane is home to the Centre for French Romantic Music, a busy research and performance institute which hosts concerts, operas, seminars and special musical events for children where under-12s go free and their parents pay €10. There are free tours of the *palazzo* every Thursday, at 2.30pm (Italian), 3pm (French) and 3.30pm (English). Check the website for programme details.

Palazzo delle Prigioni

Castello 4209, ponte della Paglia (328 712 3431 mobile, www.collegiumducale. com). Vaporetto San Zaccaria. **Shows** *9pm daily.* **Tickets** *€29; €20 reductions.* **Map** *p108 M11.*

Just over the Bridge of Sighs from the Doge's Palace, the prisons host concerts by the Collegium Ducale Orchestra – which

Arts Festivals

A packed calendar of performances

Biennale di Venezia, Danza-Musica-Teatro

041 521 8711, www.labiennale.org. Date Dance mid-late June. Theatre July-Aug. Music Oct. Tickets prices vary.

Venice's Biennale festival umbrella has expanded its dance, music and theatre department and enriched the city's cultural offering as a result. The international programme is staged in two spectacular venues inside the Arsenale – the **Teatro Tese** and the smaller **Teatro Piccolo Arsenale** – and in squares and venues around the city. There are also workshops and a host of side events.

Festival dei Matti

338 860 3921, www.festivaldeimatti.org. Venues various. Date late May.

Organised by the Cooperativa Con-tatto, the Festival dei Matti ('of the Crazies') explores madness in a themed programme that looks at the creative and communicative potential of mental illness of all kinds and degrees. Plays, debates and workshops are held in venues including the Teatrino Palazzo Grassi, the Teatrino Groggia and others.

Festival Galuppi

041 241 0899, www.festivalgaluppi.it. Venues various. Tickets €25; €20 reductions. Date late Aug-mid Oct.

This festival is dedicated to the Venetian composer Baldassarre Galuppi. Listen to 18th-century classical music in otherwise inaccessible venues, such as the islands of San Francesco del Deserto and Lazzaretto Nuovo. Tickets can be bought at venues, or through Venezia Unica (*see p306*).

Le Giornate Wagneriane

Associazione R Wagner, Ca' Vendramin Calergi, Cannaregio 2040, campiello Vendramin (041 276 0407, 338 416 4174). Venues various. Date Nov-Dec.

Wagner is the star of a series of world-class concerts organised by the Associazione R Wagner; the Giornate Wagneriane also includes conferences on the great man, and visits to the house he occupied while in Venice. Concerts are free, but get tickets in advance: call or email arwv@libero. it. Venues used in the past have included Palazzo Bru Zane (*see p250*) and La Fenice (*see p247*).

Venice Open Stage

Dorsoduro, campazzo San Sebastiano (www. veniceopenstage.org/). Vaporetto San Basilio or Zattere. Tickets free. Date June-July. Map p170 B12.

Run by Venice's IUAV university, this outdoor festival brings together productions from drama schools for ten days of spectacle and experimentation.

8.30pm daily. Tickets €34-€46; €26 reductions. Map p82 K9.

If your heart is set on performers in wigs, head for the Scuola Grande di San Teodoro, where the local I Musici Veneziani orchestra dishes up Vivaldi and a medley of opera arias.

Other music venues

Fondazione Cini

Isola di San Giorgio (041 271 0229, www.cini. it). Vaporetto San Giorgio. Map p190 N14.

The foundation draws on its impressive archives to organise music seminars, workshops, masterclasses and concerts of rare or neglected music. Concerts are held either at the Fondazione HQ on San Giorgio or in the Squero of San Giorgio (www.boxol. it/auditoriumlosquero) or at Palazzo Cini (*see*

p186). Just turn up at the venues in time for the concerts, which are free.

▶ *For more about the Cini Foundation, see p194.*

DANCE

Most dance events are limited to the summer months, when the **Biennale** (*see p121*) provides contemporary performances. The **Teatro Toniolo** and **Centro Culturale Candiani** also have fairly mainstream contemporary dance offerings. The seasons at **Teatro La Fenice** and **Teatro Malibran** always include classical ballet features. In the summer, tango aficionados can watch or even join performances in campo San Giacomo dell'Orio, on the steps of the station or in front of the Salute basilica (www.tangoaction.com).

Understand

Support (Lorenzo Quinn, 2017)

History

Desolate lagoon to city state

Venice's origins were nothing if not ignominious: in the fifth century AD, rampaging barbarians forced inhabitants of the towns in the far north-east of the Italian peninsula to flee for their lives on to the sandy banks of a desolate lagoon. In the city's earliest days, that scared and scattered community eked out a living by trading in salt and fish. It's all the more wondrous, therefore, that this would develop into the Most Serene Republic of Venice, one of Europe's most powerful city-states: a republic with a rock-solid system of government that flourished for over a millennium, and a maritime power that wielded almost total control over the shipping routes of the eastern Mediterranean for six centuries. Envied for its luxurious extravagance, hated for its insolent self-assurance, Venice was the exotic odd-piece-out in the patchwork of Europe.

The Translation of the Body of St Mark to the Basilica (c1260)

Life on the lagoon

Until the collapse of the Roman Empire in the fifth century AD, the islands of the Venetian lagoon hosted only transient fishing hamlets. The nearby cities on the mainland, on the other hand, were among the most prosperous in Roman Italy. With the final disintegration of any semblance of security in the late sixth century, there was a larger influx of population to the marshes.

These population movements were meant to be temporary, but as economic life on the mainland collapsed, the lagoon islands came to be thought of as permanent homes. They offered enormous potential in the form of fish and salt – basic necessities. Once settled in the lagoon, the fugitives could also enjoy the relative peace and tranquility that would be denied to the peoples of mainland Europe for centuries to come.

Enormous public works were necessary almost from the start to shore up and consolidate the islands of the lagoon (*see p209* Mud Houses). Huge amounts of timber had to be cut down and transported here. The trunks were sunk deep into the mud as foundations for the mainly wooden buildings of the island villages. And above all, the mainland rivers, which threatened to silt up the lagoon, had to be tamed and diverted.

And yet this battle against nature helped to unite the early lagoon dwellers into a close-knit community and eventually into a republic that was to become one of the strongest and most stable states in European history. The fight against the sea never ended. Even in the 18th century, when the French army was advancing on the lagoon and the Venetian Republic was living its decline and fall, the government invested its last resources in the construction of the *murazzi*, the massive sea walls that run between the Lido, Pellestrina and Chioggia.

Eastern promise

In 552, Byzantine Emperor Justinian I was determined to reconquer Italy from the barbarians. His first object was the city of Ravenna. But his troops were confronted with an almost insurmountable problem: they had made their way overland, via the Dalmatian coast on the eastern side of the Adriatic, but were blocked by the barbarian Goths who controlled the mainland to the north of Venice. The only way they could attack and take Ravenna was to bypass the Goths, crossing the lagoon.

Already by this time, the lagoon communities had adopted a practice that was to be the keynote of Venetian diplomacy for 1,250 years: staying as far as possible from, and (where possible) profiting by, other people's quarrels. Justinian's request presented a dilemma: helping him would be seen as a declaration of war against the Ostrogoths in Ravenna, with whom the lagoon communities had reached a comfortable modus vivendi, assuring safety on the mainland for their traders. Yet the Eastern emperor was offering vast monetary and political rewards for transporting his troops.

The communities eventually threw in their lot with Byzantium. Justinian conquered Ravenna and marched on to Rome. From this time on the communities of the lagoon became vassals of the Eastern Empire; Venice would remain technically subject to the Byzantine emperors until considerably later than the Sack of Constantinople – an attack led by Venetians – during the Fourth Crusade in 1204.

It was not until 697, under the growing threat of the barbarian Lombards who then controlled the mainland, that the communities scattered around the lagoon – now officially recognised by Byzantium as a duchy – decided to convert their fragile confederation into a stronger, more centralised state. In the course of this year (or maybe not: some have dismissed the story as a Venetian myth), they elected one Paoluccio Anafesto to be their first doge, as the dukes of Venice became known. Yet right from the beginning *il doge* was very different from the other feudal strongmen of Europe.

Plan of Venice (Ignazio Danti 1536-1586)

St Mark

Evangelist in sausage wrapping

'History records no more shameless example of body snatching, nor any of greater long-term significance', remarked John Julius Norwich in describing how the relics of St Mark found their way to Venice.

As Italy's settlements began to grope their way out of the Dark Ages, a city's status was linked significantly, if not exclusively, to its religious associations: possession of significant relics conferred kudos. Rome was top of the pile, with the body of Jesus' right-hand-man St Peter. But an evangelist's remains represented an enviable windfall too: for a young republic keen to raise itself from the sludgy marshlands on which it lay, getting hold of such sought-after spoils would mean being able to compete with long- established European political and economic centres.

Venice already had a patron saint – Theodore. And the Byzantine emperor had graciously donated the remains of John the Baptist's father, St Zacharias, which were hosted in one of the city's earliest churches (San Zaccaria, *see p114* – the remains lie in the second chapel on the right). Their importance was immediately overshadowed in the year 828, however, when two of the city's merchants, Rustico di Torcello and Buono di Malamocco, convinced (or bribed) the custodians of St Mark's body in Alexandria to entrust it to them, lining the case in which it was secreted with pork to avoid closer

scrutiny by the city's Muslim authorities – an episode depicted in a mosaic in St Mark's cathedral (*see p86 & p255*).

However much Venetians like to claim Mark as their own, the saint's link to the city is tenuous at best. There is very little reliable historical information surrounding the evangelist's life; much of what we 'know' is no more than foundation myth and folklore. Lagoon dwellers gave (and still give) much credence to the story that an angel appeared to St Mark as he sailed past the island of Rialto, revealing to him that he would eventually be laid to rest on those shores. (The angel's opening gambit – *pax tibi Marce, evangelista meus;* peace to you Mark, my evangelist – is inscribed on countless carvings of the open book held by St Mark's symbol, the winged lion, around the city. His reported follow-up – *hic requiescet corpus tuum;* here your body will rest – is omitted.)

A far better claim to ownership is made by Coptic tradition. Mark, born in modern-day Libya, is believed to have founded the Christian church in Egypt when he settled in Alexandria in the second half of the first century AD. It was there that he met his sorry end: not yet willing to relinquish their pagan gods, the city's inhabitants tied him to a horse and dragged his body through the city's streets for two days.

In the first application of a system that would be honed into shape over centuries (*see p96* Machinery of State), the doge was elected for life by a council chosen by an assembly that represented all the social groups and trades of the island communities. Technically, therefore, he was elected democratically, although the strongest groups soon formed themselves into a dominant oligarchy. Yet democracy of a kind survived in the system of checks and balances employed to ensure that no single section of the ruling elite got its hands on absolute power.

The first ducal power struggle took place in 729. The doge in question, Ipato Orso, achieved the duchy's first outstanding military victory when he dislodged Lombard forces from Ravenna. Success, though, went to Orso's head, and he attempted to transform the doge's office into a hereditary monarchy. Civil war racked the lagoon for two years, ending when a furious mob forced its way into Orso's house and cut his throat. Troubles continued with the

two succeeding doges: both were accused of tyranny, and were not only deposed and exiled but also ceremonially blinded.

Civil strife, commercial strength

The lagoon dwellers were becoming a commercial power to be reckoned with in the upper Adriatic, the eastern Mediterranean, the Black Sea and North Africa. Craftsmen were sent abroad to Dalmatia and Istria to study the art of shipbuilding; they learned so swiftly that by the seventh century the construction and fitting out of seagoing vessels had become a thriving industry.

Mercantile expansion and technical advances went hand in hand, as tradesmen brought back materials and techniques from afar – especially the Middle and Far East, where technical and scientific culture was far in advance of the West.

In 781, Pepin, son of the Frankish king Charlemagne, invaded Italy and attacked the Lombards. Wariness of mainland struggles still dominated the duchy's policy and it played for time, unsure whether to sacrifice the alliance with Byzantium to this new and powerful player on the European scene. In the end, however, Pepin's designs on Istria and Dalmatia – part of the Venetian sphere of influence – caused relations to turn frosty. Exasperated by the duchy's fence-sitting, Pepin attacked its ally Grado on the mainland, taking all the mainland positions around Venice, and besieging the lagoon communities from the sea.

In the mid eighth century the confederation had moved its capital from Heraclea in the northern lagoon to Malamocco on the Adriatic coast, where it was at the mercy of Frankish naval forces. In 810, a strong leader emerged in the form of an admiral, Angelo Partecipazio. He abandoned the besieged capital of Malamocco, moving it almost overnight to the island archipelago of Rialto.

Next he ordered his fleet to head out of the lagoon to attack Pepin's ships, then feign terror and retreat. In hot pursuit, the deep-keeled Frankish ships ran aground on lagoon sandbanks; the locals, with their knowledge of deep-water channels, picked the crews off with ease: thousands were massacred.

After his great victory against the Franks, Partecipazio was elected doge. During his reign, work began on a ducal palace on the site of the current one, and the confederation of islands that made up the lagoon duchy was given the name 'Venetia'. Around the same time, the flourishing city of Torcello began to decline, as the surrounding lagoon waters silted up and malarial mosquitoes took over.

The making of myths

It was also around this time that Venice set about embroidering a mythology worthy of its ambitions. After Venetian merchants stole the body of St Mark (*see p257*) from Alexandria and brought it back with them to their city – traditionally said to be in the year 829 – the city's previous patron, the Byzantine St Theodore, was unceremoniously deposed and the Evangelist – symbolised by a winged lion – set up in his place. A shrine to the saint was erected in the place where St Mark's basilica (*see p86*) would later rise.

Angelo Partecipazio's overwhelming success in both military and civic government led to another tussle for power. Before he died in 827, he made certain that his son Giustiniano would succeed him. When Giustiniano died two years later, his younger brother Giovanni was elected doge, despite dissent and jealousy from rival

The crusades presented Venice with its greatest opportunity yet for expanding trade routes while reaping a profit

families. It was a measure of Partecipazio's importance that his surname was to feature repeatedly in the ducal roll of honour over the next century.

Blind cunning

The development of the vast Venetian empire grew out of the mercantile pragmatism that dominated Venetian political thinking. They embarked upon territorial expansion for two main reasons: to secure safe shipping routes and to create permanent trading stations. Harassed by Slav pirates in the upper Adriatic, the Venetians established bases around the area from which to attack the pirate ships: gradually they took over the ports of Grado and Trieste, then expanded along the coastlines of Istria and Dalmatia. In some cases, Venetian protection against pirates was requested; in others, 'help' arrived unbidden.

With the coast well defended, the Venetians rarely bothered to expand their territories into the hinterland. There was, for many centuries, a certain mistrust of *terraferma*; Venetian citizens were not even allowed to own land outside the lagoon until 1345.

The crusades presented Venice with its greatest opportunity yet for expanding trade routes while reaping a profit. Transporting crusaders to the Holy Land became big business for the city. More importantly, the naïve crusaders were easy prey for the professional generals – the *condottieri* – who commanded Venice's army of highly trained mercenaries: the eager defenders of the faith were, as often as not, exploited to extend and consolidate the Venetian empire.

Never was this more true than in the case of the Fourth Crusade, which set off from Venice in 1202 to reconquer Jerusalem. The Venetian war fleet was under the command of Doge Enrico Dandolo (*see p259*), who, though 80 and completely blind, was a supremely cunning leader, outstanding tactician and accomplished diplomat. Other European crusader leaders were persuaded to take time out to conquer the strategic Adriatic port of Zara, thus assuring Venice's

Enrico Dandolo

The scourge of Byzantium

A brilliant, charismatic tactician and leader of men to some, a wily, ruthless, cynical manipulator to others, Venice's Doge Enrico Dandolo remains a resonant figure in Venetian history, perfectly reflecting that mix of heroism and pragmatism that made *La Serenissima* a political and mercantile power to be reckoned with.

Born in or around 1107, Dandolo came from a long-lived line of Venetian patricians, with a jurist father and a prelate uncle who overshadowed him until he was well into his 60s. But this gave Enrico time to hone his diplomatic acumen, and to sharpen his intense – some say pathological – dislike for the eastern Christian empire of Byzantium. By the time he was elected doge in 1192 – at around 85 – he was spoiling for a fight.

His first recorded contacts with the powerful empire came in 1171-72, when he accompanied Doge Vitale Michiel II on what was meant to be a punitive raid after Emperor Manuel Comnenus had – as part of his juggling alliances with Italian powers – confiscated the goods of the 20,000-odd Venetians living in his realm. The campaign was a disaster: plague struck the 120 Venetian ships, which not only were routed by the Byzantines but also brought the disease back to Venice with them. The doge was killed by an angry mob; Dandolo was sent back to Constantinople the following year to try to negotiate a settlement.

It was around this time that the Venetian lost his sight. There's no evidence to support the popular tale that it was the Emperor Manuel who had his eyes put out. And cataracts seem unlikely as portraits of him in very old age show him clear-eyed. Whatever the cause of his blindness, he didn't let the disability stop him.

Dandolo was handed a chance for a vendetta on a plate when the Fourth Crusade requested help with transport for a seaborne attack on the Muslim city of Cairo. Venice acquiesced, but levied a huge charge that placed the mainly French crusaders heavily in her debt. This, in turn, gave Dandolo immense bargaining power once the force set out in 1202. The stated aim of the crusaders may have been to defeat the Muslim infidel who had defiled the Holy Places, but Dandolo soon turned the force into an avenging host, persuading it first to descend on the (Christian) town of Zara in Dalmatia, which had dared to ally itself with Hungary against Venice, and then on Constantinople itself. Pope Innocent III had given his blessing to the Crusade but expressly forbade any attack on the eastern Christian capital of Constantinople, a magnificent city of half a million people, which he dreamed of reuniting with western Christendom in one all-conquering Christian empire. Dandolo hid the pope's fulminations from most of the crusaders and personally led the attack on and siege of the city.

In April 1204 the crusaders finally broke through Constantinople's massive walls and subjected the city to three days of carnage, burning and looting, extracting such punishment that the rift between the Roman and Orthodox church remained unbridgeable ever after. The pope excommunicated the crusaders, but Dandolo returned triumphant to Venice with far more than the 150,000 silver marks demanded in ransom, plus unimaginable artistic booty, including the four bronze horses that now grace the facade of St Mark's basilica.

The following year the indefatigable nonagenarian set off on another military campaign in Bulgaria, but this proved too much for him. In an ironic twist, he died peacefully in Constantinople, the city he had trashed, and was buried in the great church, then mosque, of Hagia Sophia, where a plaque still commemorates him.

ARRIGO DANDOLO

Da un dipinto di scuola Veneziana

control of much of the Dalmatian coast. Even more surprisingly, they let themselves be talked into attacking Constantinople.

Venice's special relationship with the Eastern Empire had always had its ups and downs. In 1081 and 1082, Venice had done the Byzantine emperor a favour when it trounced menacing Normans in the southern Adriatic. But, in 1149, Venice's trading privileges were withdrawn in disgust at Venetian arrogance during a siege of Corfu.

As the Fourth Crusade set out, Dandolo saw that this was an ideal opportunity to remove the Byzantine challenge to Venetian trade hegemony once and for all. He pulled the wool over his fellow crusaders' eyes, with the apparently noble argument that the Eastern emperor must be ousted and replaced by someone willing to reunite the eastern Orthodox and western Roman churches.

They acquiesced, but there was nothing noble about the brutal, bloody, Venetian-led sacking of Constantinople on 13 April 1204, nor about the pillaging that followed. The Venetians looted the city's greatest treasures, including the celebrated quartet of antique bronze Greek horses that was transported back to Venice and placed above the entrance of St Mark's basilica. Innumerable other artefacts – jewellery, enamels, golden chalices, statuary, columns, precious marbles and much more – were plundered: they are now part of the fabric of Venice's *palazzi* and churches.

But the booty was only a minor consideration for the Venetians and their pragmatic doge: the real prize was the one handed out when the routed Byzantine empire was carved up. The Venetians were not interested in grabbing huge swathes of territory that they knew they couldn't

defend. This was left to the French and German knights, who, indeed, lost it within a few decades. Putting their intimate knowledge of eastern trade routes to excellent use, the Venetians hand-picked those islands and ports that could guarantee their merchant ships a safe passage from Venice to the Black Sea and back. These included almost all the main ports on the Dalmatian coast, certain strategic Greek islands, the Sea of Marmara and a number of strategic Black Sea ports.

For many years after the conquest of Constantinople, Venetian ships could sail from Venice to Byzantium without leaving waters controlled by their city. Venice marked the turn of events by conferring a new title on its doge: *Quartae Partis et Dimidiae Totius Imperii Romaniae Dominator* – Lord of a Quarter and Half a Quarter of the Roman Empire.

Age of uprisings

In 1297, in what came to be known as the *Serrata del Maggior Consiglio* (Great Council Lockout), the leaders of the Venetian merchant aristocracy decided to limit entry to the Grand Council to those families which had held a seat in the *maggior consiglio* in the previous four years, or to descendants of those who had belonged at any point since 1172. Under these rules, only around 150 extended families were eligible for a place, but the number of council members leapt to some 1,200.

Up-and-coming clans were understandably indignant at the thought of being forever excluded from power and from a coveted place in the *Libro d'oro* – the Golden Book – of the Venetian aristocracy. In 1310, a prosperous merchant, Baiamonte Tiepolo, harnessed the discontent in a

Riva degli Schiavoni (Leandro Bassano, 1595)

rebellion against the aristocratic oligarchy. Had Tiepolo's standard-bearer not been felled by a loose brick knocked out of place by an old lady watching the shenanigans from her window, the uprising may have succeeded. However, as it was, his troops fled in panic, the uprising was savagely crushed, and the much-feared Council of Ten was granted draconian powers. An extensive network of spies and informers was set up to suppress any future plots.

In 1354, Doge Marino Faliero made a bid to undermine the powers of the Venetian oligarchy while increasing and consolidating his own powers as a permanent hereditary leader. This plot, too, was mercilessly suppressed and Faliero was beheaded.

The Council of Ten – along with the Venetian Inquisition that was also established after the Tiepolo plot of 1310 – wielded its special powers most effectively after the Faliero incident, ensuring that this was the last serious attempt to attack the principle of rule by elite. It was at this time that lion's-head postboxes first appeared at strategic points around the city: Venetians were encouraged to drop written reports of any questionable activity that they noticed through their marble mouths.

Lavish love and luxury

While Venice's mercantile power was at its zenith from the 13th to the 15th centuries, vast fortunes were amassed and lavished on building and decorating great *palazzi* and churches. It was at this time that the city took on the architectural form still visible today. For sheer luxury, Venice's lifestyle was unequalled anywhere else in Europe.

In the 14th and 15th centuries Venice was one of the largest cities in Europe, with an estimated population of between 150,000 and 200,000. International visitors were generally astounded by *La Serenissima*'s legendary opulence and phenomenal economic dynamism.

When ships set sail from Venice for the Middle East, their holds were crammed with Istrian pine wood, iron ore, cereals, wool, and salted and preserved meats. These were traded for textiles, exotic carpets, perfumes, gold and silverware, spices, precious stones of all kinds, ivory, wax and slaves; with a virtual monopoly on all these much sought-after commodities, Venice was able to sell them on to the rest of Europe's moneyed classes at enormous profit.

The Venetian aristocracy liked to live in comfort. 'The luxury of any ordinary Venetian house,' wrote one traveller in 1492, 'is so extraordinary that in any other city or country it would be sufficient to decorate

International visitors were generally astounded by La Serenissima's legendary opulence and phenomenal economic dynamism

a royal palace.' The Venetians were also investing huge amounts of money in their summer villas on the mainland, designed and decorated by the leading Veneto architects and painters.

Venetians lavished the same kind of attention on their appearance. Fortunes were spent on the richest textiles and jewellery. Venetian women were famous for the luxury of their clothing, of their furs and of their fabrics woven with gold and silver thread. Their perfumes and cosmetics were the envy of all Europe, as were the beauty and charm of the courtesans who dominated the social and cultural life of the city.

So dedicated were Venetians to the cult of love and earthly pleasures, that the Patriarch, Venice's cardinal, was compelled to issue orders forbidding the city's nuns from going out on the town at night. Sumptuous festivals of music, theatre and dance were almost daily occurrences during these wild times. The visit of a foreign ruler, a wedding or funeral of a member of the aristocracy, a religious festival, a naval or military victory, or delivery from an epidemic – all these were excuses for public celebrations. The city's foreign communities – Jews, Armenians, Turks, Germans, French and Mongols, many of them permanent residents in this truly cosmopolitan city – would also celebrate their national or religious feast days with enormous pomp.

Despite the wealth of the city and the full employment created by its many trades and industries (at full stretch, the shipyard was capable of launching one fully equipped ship every day), life was not easy for the city's poorest residents, who lived in damp, filthy conditions. Epidemics of disease were also frequent; indeed, it is estimated that more than half the city's population died in the Black Death of 1348-49. Social tension and discontent were rife.

Genoese jealousy

Meanwhile, the enormous wealth of the Venetian Republic and its rapidly expanding empire inevitably provoked jealousy among the other trading nations of the Mediterranean – above all in the powerful

Venice's Sestieri

Dividing up the city

Most of the towns and cities of the Italian mainland were happy to follow the example of the ancient Romans, slicing themselves into *quartieri* (quarters) which would have been delineated by the main axis roads the *cardo* and *decumanus* – that intersected each other at the city centre. Ever original, Venice opted to set itself apart with *sestieri* (sixths) – topological divisions that still characterise the city today.

Historians squabble about who was responsible for the breakdown. Some say that the *sestieri* date from the very earliest settlements in these marshy lagoon islands – unlikely, given that the inhabitants were few and that power, when it stabilised, lay in Torcello (*see p212*) and Malamocco (*see p198*), only shifting to what we now call Venice in the ninth century. Some argue that ninth-century Doge Orso Partecipazio created the *sestieri* as soon as he had moved his base to Rivoalto – now known as Rialto. Still others say it was the need to raise taxes for waging war on the Byzantine Emperor Manuel Komnenus that led Doge Vitale Michiel II to carve the city into more

manageable, runnable administrative divisions in 1171. Unwieldy and difficult to pin down, the *sestieri* nonetheless reflect Venice's largely impenetrable topography. To make orientation even more difficult, street names are considered decorative or descriptive – many, for example, are called *calle drio la chiesa* (street behind the church) or *calle forner* (bakery street) – and house numbers relate to the *sestiere* and not to the street. In Castello, the largest *sestiere*, numbers begin at one and go up to almost 7,000, often with inexplicable leaps from one front door to the next. If this seems complicated, you have to wonder how they managed before 1798, when the Austrians arrived to instill 'order' into the vanquished city-state: until then, there had been no numbers at all.

Locals and guidebooks will tell you that the *sestieri* are symbolised in each gondola's *ferro* (prow decoration), where six prongs – the six *sestieri* – point forward and a seventh – Giudecca (part of the *sestiere* of Dorsoduro) – points back. There's no historic documentation for this... but why doubt a good story?

Gondola's *ferro*

city state of Genoa, Venice's main rival for trade with the East.

In 1261, the Genoese had clashed with the Venetians when the former obliged the Byzantine emperor by helping to evict Venice's high-handed merchants from Constantinople. Skirmishes between the two Italian powers continued throughout most of the 14th century, regularly flaring up into periods of open warfare, and often resulting in disastrous defeats for Venice.

By 1379, the situation had become desperate for *La Serenissima*. The Genoese fleet and army had moved into the upper Adriatic and, after a long siege, had taken Chioggia, at the southern end of the lagoon. From here the Genoese attacked and occupied much of the lagoon, including the passage to the open sea. Venice was under siege and began to starve.

Then, in 1380, the city worked another of its miracles of level-headed cunning. Almost the whole of the Genoese fleet was anchored inside the fortified harbour of Chioggia. Vittor Pisani, the admiral of the Venetian fleet, ordered hundreds of small boats to be filled with rocks. Panicked by a surprise Venetian attack on the mouth of the port, the Genoese failed to notice that the small boats were being sunk in the shallow port entrance, preventing any escape. The tables had been well and truly turned, and Venice besieged the trapped Genoese fleet until it was forced to surrender unconditionally. Genoa's days as a great naval power were over, and Venice exulted.

Ironically, however, this victory was to spell the beginning of the end for *La Serenissima*. For although the Republic had reached the climax of its prosperity and had re-acquired its supremacy in the East, concentrating its energies on fighting Genoa was to prove a costly mistake. Venice's leaders badly underestimated the threat posed by the emergence of the Turks as a military power in Asia Minor and the Black Sea area. Convinced – wrongly and ultimately fatally – that diplomacy was the way to deal with the Ottoman threat, Venice turned its attention to conquering other powers on the Italian mainland.

Mainland expansion

For centuries, Venice had followed a conscious policy of steady neutrality towards the various powers that had carved up the Italian mainland. Europe's political upheavals from the end of the 12th century to the end of the 14th century put paid to that neutrality. The bitter rivalry between Venice and the other Italian maritime states, especially Pisa and Genoa, inevitably brought it into conflict with their mainland allies: the Pope, the Scaligera dukes of Verona and a succession of Holy Roman emperors.

The defeat of the vast Scaligera empire (which included much of the Venetian hinterland) by Count Gian Galeazzo Visconti of Milan in 1387 brought the Milanese much too close to the lagoon for comfort. All-important trade routes through northeastern Italy, across the Alps and into northern Europe beyond were threatened. Venice began a series of wars that led to the conquest of Verona (*see p218*) and its enormous territories in 1405, and also of near neighbours Padua (*see p216*) and Vicenza (*see p222*).

By 1420, Venice had annexed Friuli and Udine; by 1441, *La Serenissima* controlled Brescia, Bergamo, Cremona and Ravenna. The land campaign continued until 1454, when Venice signed a peace treaty with Milan. Though Ravenna soon slipped from Venice's grasp, the rest of the Republic's immense mainland territories were to remain more or less intact for almost 300 years.

The Portuguese spice things up

Even as Venice expanded into the mainland, events were conspiring to bring its reign as a political power and trading giant to a close.

In 1453, the Ottoman Turks swept into Constantinople, and Venice's crucial trading privileges in the former Byzantine Empire were almost totally lost. In 1487, Vasco da Gama rounded the Cape of Good Hope; in 1489, he became the first European to reach Kolkata by sea, shattering Venice's monopoly on the riches of the East. The arrival of Portuguese ships laden with spices and textiles in Portuguese ports caused a sensation in Europe and despair in Venice. The Venetians hastily drew up plans to open a canal at Suez to beat the Portuguese at their own game, but the project came to nothing. Instead, cushioned by the spoils and profits of centuries and exhausted by 100 years of almost constant military campaigning, the city sank slowly over the next two centuries into dissipation and decline.

That decline, naturally, was glorious. For most of the 16th century few Venetians behaved as if the writing were on the wall. Such was the enormous wealth of the city that the economic fall-out from the Turks' inexorable progress through the Middle East went almost unnoticed at first. Profits were not as massive as before, but the rich remained very rich and the setbacks in the East were partly counter-balanced by exploitation of the newly acquired *terraferma* territories.

Francesco Morosini (1619-1694)

Turkish delight

Its coffers almost empty and its mainland dominions left in tatters, Venice was now forced to take stock of the damage that was being done by the Turks.

In 1497, as the Ottomans stormed through the Balkans, *La Serenissima* had been obliged to give up several Aegean islands and the port of Negroponte; two years later, it lost its forts in the Peloponnese, giving the Turks virtually total control of the southern end of the Adriatic. And though Venice was jubilant about securing Cyprus in 1489 – won by pressuring the king's Venetian widow Caterina Cornaro into bequeathing control of the island – the acquisition involved the Republic in almost constant warfare to keep the Turks away from this strategically vital strip of land.

In 1517, Syria and Egypt fell to the Turks; by 1529 the Ottoman Empire had spread across the southern Mediterranean as far as Morocco. The frightened European powers turned to Venice for help repulsing the common foe. But mistrust of the lagoon republic by its new allies was deep and, in their determination to keep Venice from deriving too much financial profit from the war against the Turks, the campaign itself was botched.

In 1538, a Christian fleet was trounced at Preveza in western Greece; in 1571, Venice led a huge European fleet to victory against Turkish warships in the Battle of Lepanto, in what is now the Gulf of Corinth. But despite the self-glorifying propaganda campaign that followed, it became apparent that the Turks were as strong as ever. In a treaty signed in 1573, Venice was forced ignominiously to hand over Cyprus, its second-last major possession in the eastern Mediterranean. (Crete, the final one, held out until 1669.)

Trade deficit

By the 17th century, Venice was no longer under any illusion about the gravity of its crisis. The Savi alla Mercanzia (state trading commission) noted on 5 July 1610 that 'our commerce and shipping in the West are completely destroyed. In the East only a few businesses are still functioning and they are riddled with debt, without ships and getting weaker by the day. Moreover, and this must be emphasised, only a small quantity of goods is arriving in our city, and it is becoming increasingly difficult to find buyers for them. The nations which used to buy from us now have established their businesses elsewhere. We are facing the almost total annihilation of our commerce.'

Venice was down but not quite out. Between 1681 and 1687, Francesco Morosini,

As revenue gradually declined through the 16th century, spending on life's little pleasures increased, producing an explosion of art, architecture and music. Titian, Tintoretto, Veronese and Giorgione were at work in the city. Palladio, Sanmicheli and Scamozzi were changing the face of architecture and *litterati* dazzled with their wit and learning. *La Serenissima* rang with music.

On the mainland, however, Venice's arrogant annexation of territory had not been forgotten by the powers that had suffered at her hands. When Venice took advantage of the French invasion of Italy in the final years of the 15th century to extend its territories still further, the Habsburgs, France, Spain and the papacy were so incensed that they clubbed together to form the League of Cambrai, with the sole aim of annihilating Venice.

They came very close to doing so. One Venetian military rout followed another, a number of Venetian-controlled cities defected, and others that did not were laid waste by the hostile forces. Only squabbling within the League of Cambrai stopped Venice itself from being besieged. By 1516, the alliance had fallen to pieces and Venice had regained almost all its territories.

As revenue gradually declined through the 16th century, spending on life's little pleasures increased

the brilliant strategist then in command of the Venetian fleet, reconquered much of the territory taken by the Turks, including Crete and the Peloponnese. But these moments of glory, celebrated with colossal pomp in Venice itself, were invariably short-lived.

Exhausted by debts and the sheer effort of its naval campaigns, the Venetian Republic lacked the resources needed to consolidate its victories. By 1718, it was struggling to keep its head above water as the Austrians and Turks forced it to cede most of its gains in the humiliating Treaty of Passarowitz.

By the time the Venezia Trionfante café (now Caffè Florian; see p98) opened for business in piazza San Marco in 1720, the Republic was virtually bankrupt; its governing nobility had grown decadent and politically inert. But decadence was good for the city's growing status as the party capital of Europe. Aristocratic women of all ages and marital states were accompanied in their gadding by handsome young *cisibei* (male escorts), whose professions of chastity fooled nobody. Masked nuns were a common sight at the city's gambling houses and theatres; church officials who tried to confine nuns to the convent by the church of San Zaccaria would be met with a barrage of bricks.

Priests too were not slow to join in the fun: composer-prelate Antonio Vivaldi's supposed affairs with members of his famous female choir were well publicised. And though Giacomo Casanova, the embodiment of sexual excess, never actually donned a cassock, he had been a promising student of theology before he realised where his true vocation lay.

Throwing in the cap

Bankrupt, politically and ideologically stagnant and no longer a threat to its former enemies, Venice directed its final heroic efforts against the forces of nature. As Napoleon prepared to invade Venice in 1797, the city was spending the meagre funds left in its coffers on building the *murazzi*, the vast stone and marble dyke designed to protect the city from the worst ravages of unpredictable Adriatic tides. On 12 May 1797, the last doge, Lodovico Manin, was deposed by the French, who, even before the Republic bowed to the inevitable and voted itself out of existence, had handed control over to Austria. Manin gave his doge's cap to the victors, saying, 'Take this, I don't think I'll be needing it any more.'

In 1805, Napoleon absorbed Venice back into his Kingdom of Italy. Until 1815, when the French emperor's star waned and Venice once again found itself under Austrian control, Napoleon's Venetian plenipotentiaries were given free rein to dismantle churches, dissolve monasteries and redesign bits of the city, including the wide thoroughfare now known as via Garibaldi and its adjoining public gardens.

The last spark of Venice's independent spirit flared up in 1848, when lawyer Daniele Manin (no relation of the last doge) led a popular revolt against the Austrians. An independent republican government was set up, holding out against siege for five heroic months. It was doomed to failure from the outset, however, and the Austrians were soon firmly back in the saddle, keeping their grip on this insignificant backwater until 1866, when a weakened Austria, badly beaten on other fronts by the Prussians, handed the city over to the newly united kingdom of Italy.

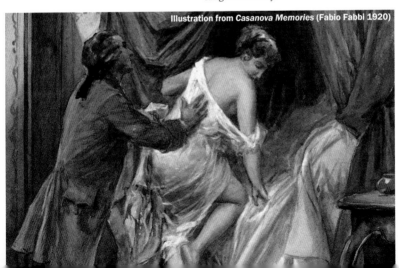
Illustration from *Casanova Memories* (Fabio Fabbi 1920)

Architecture

Competitive construction against the odds

Think of the least likely place to build a successful city and Venice ticks all the boxes: marshy islands in a salt lagoon, buffeted by winds and at the mercy of tides, with no fresh water and only the most difficult means of communication. The earliest structures, set on wooden piles driven deep into the mud and created by nameless local master masons, were things of elegance and grace. Later, the technical challenges – and of course a surplus of fabulously wealthy patrons in this trade-and-art superpower – drew the greatest architects from elsewhere too: early Renaissance master Mauro Codussi from Bergamo; Vicenza-based Andrea Palladio; Tuscan-born Jacopo Sansovino. A sense of practicality mixed with a love of extravagant, competitive show led to the construction of family *palazzi* that were a perfect mix of business hub and desirable residence.

When decline set in, former glories flaked, chipped, peeled and began subsiding into the muddy lagoon. But even in its decay Venice remained peerlessly beautiful – a unique gem to be cherished and preserved in its watery setting.

Scala Contarini del Bòvolo, *p102*

Medieval and Byzantine

Venetian architecture began in Torcello, where the cathedral of **Santa Maria Assunta** (*see p212*), founded in 639, is the oldest surviving building on the lagoon. It has been remodelled since then – notably in the ninth and 11th centuries – but still retains the simple form of an early Christian basilica.

Next door, the 11th-century church of **Santa Fosca** (*see p212*) has a Greek cross plan – also found in **San Giacomo di Rialto** (*see p148*), considered to be the earliest church in Venice proper. The portico of Santa Fosca exhibits a feature that recurs in the first-floor windows of 12th-century townhouses on the Grand Canal: stilted arches, with horseshoe-shaped arches atop slender columns.

That the history of Venetian architecture can be charted by following the development of the arch is understandable in a city built on mud, where load-bearing capabilities were a prime consideration. In the latter part of the 13th century, the pure, curved Byzantine arch began to sport a point at the top, under the influence of Islamic models. An early example of this can be seen in the heavily restored **Albergo del Selvadego** in calle dell'Ascensione (San Marco). Soon this point developed into a fully fledged ogee arch – a northern Gothic trait.

Meanwhile, the **Basilica di San Marco** (St Mark's basilica; *see p86*) was continuing to evolve. A makeshift chapel for holding St Mark's relics was replaced in 832 by a church modelled on the Church of the Apostles in Constantinople; that burned down, to be replaced with the one we see today.

The main body of the current church, with its Greek cross plan surmounted by five domes, dates from the 11th century; but it was embellished extensively over the next four centuries. Two humbler 12th-century churches, **San Giacomo dell'Orio** (*see p157*) and **San Nicolò dei Mendicoli** (*see p173*), both feature squat, detached bell towers – a key feature of the Veneto-Byzantine style.

In the 14th and 15th centuries, the city's own Arab-tinged version of Gothic came into its own

Gothic and late Gothic

In the 14th and 15th centuries, Venetian architecture developed an individual character unmatched before or since. It was at this time that the city's own Arab-tinged version of Gothic came into its own. By the mid 14th century, the ogee arch (two concave-convex curves meeting at the top) had sprouted a point on the inside of its concave edge – producing the cusped arch, which distributes the forces pressing down on it so efficiently that the Victorian art critic John Ruskin decreed that 'all are imperfect except these'.

By the beginning of the 15th century, this basic shape had been hedged around with elaborate tracery and trefoils (clover-shaped openings) and topped with Moorish-looking pinnacles in a peculiarly Venetian take on the flamboyant Gothic style, which reached its apotheosis in the façades of the **Palazzo Ducale** (*see p92*) and the **Ca' d'Oro** (*see p130*) – both completed by 1440.

Outside of St Mark's, church architecture reflected the traditional building styles of the large religious orders that commissioned the work: the cavernous brick monuments of **Santi Giovanni e Paolo** (1430; *see p111* and the **Frari** (1433; *see p162*) are classic examples of, respectively, the Dominican and Franciscan approaches. Both have a Latin cross plan, a large rose window and a generous sprinkling of pinnacles.

More individual are churches such as **Santo Stefano** (*see p102*), with its wooden ship's-keel roof, and the **Scuola Vecchia della Misericordia** (*see p140*), with its ogee windows and Flemish-style roof gable. Both involved the collaboration of Giovanni and Bartolomeo Bon, who also worked on the Ca' d'Oro.

Majestic Grand Canal palaces (*see p68*) continued to indulge the yen for elaborate tracery windows, but behind the façade the structure went back centuries. The Venetian *palazzo* was not only a place of residence; it was also the family business headquarters; the internal division of space reflects this, with loading and storage space below a magnificent first-floor piano nobile. On the roof there was often a raised wooden balcony or *altana*: in a city where space was always at a premium, private courtyards were the preserve of the very wealthy indeed.

Early Renaissance

Venetians were so fond of their own gracefully oriental version of Gothic that they held on to it long after the new classicist orthodoxy had taken over central Italy. For the second half of the 15th century, emergent Renaissance forms existed alongside the Gothic swansong. Sometimes they merged or clashed in the same building, as in the church of **San Zaccaria** (*see p114*), which was begun by Antonio Gambello in 1458 in the pure northern Gothic style but completed by Mauro Codussi in the Renaissance idiom he was then elaborating.

Next to nothing is known about Codussi's background, save that he may have trained under Giovanni Bon. In 1469, he was appointed *protomagister* (works manager) for the church of **San Michele** (*see p202*). Within ten years he had completed the first truly Renaissance building in the city. The austere Istrian marble façade with its classical elements has something Palladian about it, though the curves of the pediment and buttresses are pure Codussi, adapted from a late Gothic model.

San Zaccaria

Lombardesque style

Codussi took over a number of projects begun by Pietro Lombardo, who represents the other strand of early Renaissance architecture in northern Italy. This was based on the extensive use of inlaid polychrome marble, Corinthian columns and decorated friezes. Lombardo's masterpiece is **Santa Maria dei Miracoli** (*see p134*), but he also designed – with his sons – the lower part of the façade of the **Scuola Grande di San Marco** (*see p115*), with its trompe l'oeil relief. The Lombardesque style was all the rage for a while, producing such charmers as tiny, lopsided **Ca' Dario** (1487-92) on the Grand Canal.

High Renaissance

Codussi's influence lingered into the 16th century in the work of architects such as Guglielmo dei Grigi and Scarpagnino, both of whom have been credited with the design of the **Palazzo dei Camerlenghi** (1525-28; *see p148*). Around this time, the construction in piazza San Marco of the **Procuratie Vecchie** and the **Torre dell'Orologio** (for both, *see p97*), both to designs by Codussi, demonstrated that in the centre of civic power, loyalty to the myth of Venice tended to override architectural fashions.

It was not until the late 1520s that something really new turned up, courtesy of Jacopo Sansovino, a Tuscan sculptor. Perhaps it was the influence of his new-found friends Titian and the poet Pietro Aretino that secured him the prestigious position of *protomagister* of St Mark's only two years after his arrival, despite his lack of experience; Sansovino went on to create a series of buildings that changed the face

of the city. He began to refine his rational, harmonious Renaissance style in designs for the church of **San Francesco della Vigna** (begun in 1532; *see p112*) and **Palazzo Corner della Ca' Grande** (*see p78*), Venice's first Roman-style *palazzo*.

But it was in piazza San Marco that Sansovino surpassed himself. **La Zecca** (*see p97*) – the state mint – with its heavy rustication and four-square solidity, is a perfect financial fortress. The **Biblioteca Marciana** (completed in 1554, also known as the Libreria Sansoviniana; *see p91*) is his masterpiece, disguising its classical regularity beneath a typically Venetian wealth of surface detail. The little **Loggetta** at the base of the Campanile (*see p85*) showed that Sansovino was capable of a lightness of touch.

Palladian pre-eminence

Michele Sanmicheli built the imposing sea defences on the island of Le Vignole, and two hefty Venetian *palazzi*, the **Palazzo Corner Mocenigo** (1559-64) in campo San Polo and the **Palazzo Grimani di San Luca** (1556-75) on the Grand Canal.

But it was another out-of-towner, Andrea Palladio (*see p270*), who would set the agenda for what was left of the 16th century. The man who invented the post-Renaissance found it difficult to get a foothold in a city that valued flexibility above critical rigour. But he did design two influential churches: **San Giorgio Maggiore** (begun in 1562; *see p122*) and the **Redentore** (1577-92; *see p193*). The church of **Le Zitelle** (*see p192*) was built to Palladio's plans after the architect's death.

Palladio's disciple, Vincenzo Scamozzi, designed the **Procuratie Nuove** (*see*

Andrea Palladio

Classical motifs for an influential new style

Arguably the most influential figure in Western architecture, Andrea Palladio had an unremarkable start. He was born in Padua on 30 November 1508 and baptised Andrea di Pietro della Gondola. His father apprenticed him at the age of 13 to Giovanni da Porlezza, a stone carver in Vicenza. Recognising his talent, the workshop put up the money for Andrea's guild entrance fee. He learned to design and carve church altars, tombs and architectural elements, many commissioned by local nobility. While working on a villa on the outskirts of Vicenza between 1530 and 1538, he met its owner, Count Giangiorgio Trissino, the wealthy leader of a group of Humanist intellectuals dedicated to reviving classical culture.

This chance meeting was to change the course of Western architecture. Trissino set about turning Andrea into a worthy heir to Vitruvius, the ancient architect whose treatise De Architectura underpinned the return to classical models in the Italian Renaissance. He also gave Andrea a more suitable name: 'Palladio' resonated with classical associations, and was the name of a helpful angel in Trissino's epic poem *Italia liberata dai goti* ('Italy Liberated from the Goths'). Trissino also gave Palladio time off and funds to study Roman antiquities in Verona and Padua, and took him to Rome

three times between 1540 and 1550. Palladio studied, measured and sketched all the major classical remains, as well as the buildings and plans of Renaissance greats throughout Italy. In 1554, he published Le *antichità di Roma* (*The Antiquities of Rome*), a sort of proto-guidebook.

Palladio's early patrons were part of the Trissino circle, who provided both work and intellectual stimulation after Trissino died in 1550. Among these enlightened Vicentine nobles were Pietro Godi, whose **Villa Godi Valmarana ora Malinverni** (*see p223*) was Palladio's first independent commission, completed by 1542 and one of his most radical, pared-back designs. The Barbaro brothers encouraged Palladio to create one of his masterpieces, the **Villa Barbaro a Maser** (1550-57; *see p223*). Another patron, Girolamo Chiericati helped give the architect his first big break, in 1549: restructuring Vicenza's town hall (the **Basilica Palladiana**; *see p224*) which established Palladio as one of the leading architects of his day.

Palladio also benefited from good timing. In the 16th century, the Venetian government insisted that nobles build villas on the *terraferma* (mainland) in order to boost agricultural production and increase *La Serenissima*'s control over the countryside. Commissions for villas were thus plentiful

Basilica del Santissimo Redentore

throughout the Veneto. In 1570, Palladio moved to Venice, to become unofficial chief architect, with prominent churches such as **San Giorgio Maggiore** (see p195) and the **Redentore** (see p193) reinforcing his fame. His influential treatise, *I quattro libri dell'architettura* (*The Four Books of Architecture*, 1570), spread his name further.

The pared-back design for which Palladio became so famous was certainly inspired by Roman and Greek architecture, but was never copied from it; Palladio used classical motifs, creating a style that defined elegance. The most recognisable feature of his buildings is the use of the Greco-Roman temple front as a portico; equally innovative were the dramatic high-relief effects on façades. The floor plans usually emphasised a strong central axis and symmetrical wings, with room proportions determined mathematically to create harmonic spaces, typically with high ceilings. Though always unmistakably his, each of Palladio's buildings is startlingly different – from the stark simplicity of **Villa Pisani** (1540) at Bagnolo di Lonigo to the vast complexity of the statue-crowned Palazzo Chiericati (now the **Museo Civico**; see p225) in Vicenza.

In his day, Palladio's domestic villa architecture largely overshadowed his other accomplishments. His country residences uniquely combined both a working farmhouse and elegant country retreat, with much of the decoration serving a function: the gracious entrance ramp at the **Villa Emo** (see p223) was also intended as a platform for threshing grain.

Palladio's designs also encompassed other practical functions: stables, cellars, granaries and dovecotes were located within the compounds and were intrinsic to the villa as a whole. Never ostentatious, overbearing in size or using costly materials, they made subtle statements through a dignified classical vocabulary, harmony of proportions both external and internal, and a human scale. Palladio's inventiveness and sensitivity extended to the aspect and location of villas, which he regarded as highly important in their function as an antidote to the stresses of urban life. Building near a river or canal was recommended; as well as allowing easy access by boat, water guaranteed cool breezes during the hot summer months, irrigated the gardens and, not incidentally, 'will afford a beautiful prospect'. Palladio's style would be copied throughout Europe for centuries.

p84). At the same time, Antonio Da Ponte was commissioned to design a stone bridge at the **Rialto**, in 1588, after designs by Michelangelo and Palladio had been rejected.

Baroque

The examples of Sansovino and Palladio continued to be felt well into the 17th century. It wasn't until the arrival of Baldassare Longhena in the 1620s that Venice got twirly bits in any abundance. Longhena was a local boy who first made his mark with the Duomo in Chioggia. But it was with the church of **Santa Maria della Salute** (see p182) that he pulled out all the stops. Commissioned in 1632, and 50 years in the making, this highly theatrical church dominates the southern reaches of the Grand Canal.

Longhena was also busy designing a series of impressive *palazzi*, including the huge Grand Canal hulk of **Ca' Pesaro** (1652; see p155). He also designed the façade of the **Ospedaletto** (1667-74; see p114), with its grotesque telamons. It was a taste of things to come: the overwrought façade continued to develop in the 1670s, extending from the exuberance of the **Gli Scalzi** (see p131) and **Santa Maria del Giglio** (see p104) – both by Longhena's follower Giuseppe Scalzi – to the bombast of **San Moisè** (see p104), a kitsch collaboration between Alessandro Tremignon and sculptor Heinrich Meyring.

Neoclassicism

During the 18th-century decline, limp variations on Palladio and Longhena dominated the scene. Domenico Rossi adorned Palladian orders with swags and statuary in the façades he designed for the churches of **San Stae** (1709-10; see p158) and the **Gesuiti** (1715-28; see p182).

Sumptuous palaces continued to go up along the Grand Canal; one of the last was the solid **Palazzo Grassi** (see p101), built between 1748 and 1772. It was designed by Giorgio Massari, who was also responsible for **La Pietà** (see p120) – the Vivaldi church – the oval floorplan of which strikes a rare note of originality. The **Palazzo Venier dei Leoni** – now home to the Peggy Guggenheim Collection (see p183) – also dates from the mid 18th century. Funds ran out after the first storey, giving Venice one of its most bizarrely endearing landmarks.

Giannantonio Selva's **La Fenice** opera house (1790-92; see p247) was one of the Serene Republic's last building projects. Napoleon's arrival in 1797 marked the destruction of many churches and convents, but also began a series of clearances that

The city became an architectural sacred cow, untouchable by the unclean hand of innovation

allowed for the creation of the city's first public park, the **Giardini pubblici** (*see p118*), and the nearby thoroughfare now known as **via Garibaldi**. Piazza San Marco took on its present-day appearance at this time too, when the Procuratie Vecchie and Nuove were united by the neoclassical **Ala Napoleonica**.

Under the Austrian occupation (1815-66), restoration replaced construction, and a railway bridge linking Venice to Mestre (1841- 42) was built, ending the city's isolation.

In his influential book the *Stones of Venice* (1853), John Ruskin set out to discredit 'the pestilent art of the Renaissance' in favour of 'healthy and beautiful' Gothic. Such was his clout that the city became an architectural sacred cow, untouchable by the unclean hand of innovation. Instead, Venice began to recreate its Gothic and Byzantine past, with exercises such as the **Palazzo Franchetti**, a 15th-century edifice at the north-eastern foot of the Ponte dell'Accademia that was redesigned in neomedieval style (1878-82).

One of the city's most elegant neo-Gothic works is the **cemetery of San Michele** (1872-81). Another landmark from the period is the **Molino Stucky** (1897-1920; *see p192*), a flour mill on the Giudecca designed in Hanseatic Gothic style by Ernest Wullekopf. The turn of the 20th-century was also a boom time for hotels, with the **Excelsior** on the Lido (1898-1908) setting the eclectic, Moorish-Byzantine agenda.

Modernity catches up

Venice's modern architecture is limited. To date, only locally born modernist Carlo Scarpa (1906-78; *see p273* Scarpa in Venice) has created a body of work: the entrance and garden patio of the **Biennale gardens** (1952; *see p121*), the **Negozio Olivetti** (1957-58; *see p97*) in piazza San Marco, the entrance lobby of the IUAV architecture faculty near piazzale Roma and the ground-floor reorganisation of the **Museo Querini Stampalia** (1961-63; *see p112*). Scarpa's student, Mario Botta, has recently overhauled the top-floor exhibition rooms of this last establishment.

The 1970s and '80s brought one or two adventurous public housing projects around outlying areas of the city or lagoon, such as Giancarlo De Carlo's low-income housing on the island of Mazzorbo (1979-86). A new high-tech airport terminal by local architect Giampaolo Mar was inaugurated in summer 2002 and the 70-hectare (170-acres) **Parco di San Giuliano**, designed by Boston-based urban planner Antonio Di Mambro, opened on the mainland by Mestre in 2004. Vittorio Gregotti and others worked on the revamp of industrial areas in north-western Cannaregio, including a former slaughterhouse that now houses the university's economics faculty. Milan's Cino Zucchi reworked the Venetian idiom in housing built around the former Junghans factory on the Giudecca. Japanese superstar Tadao Ando refurbished **Palazzo Grassi** (*see p101*) and the **Punta della Dogana** (*see p185*).

After years of controversy, delays, staggering over-spending and a long litany of other woes, the **Ponte della Costituzione** – by Spain's Santiago Calatrava and known invariably to locals as the ponte di Calatrava – was inaugurated in 2008, sans the requisite disabled access (since added, in the shape of a strange bubble that crosses the canal on the outside of the structure). But this fourth bridge over the Grand Canal, linking the railway station and the key road transport hub at piazzale Roma, continues to bring more troubles in its wake: in 2013 city hall announced that it was sueing the Calatrava studio for the extra cost of its various shortcomings.

Other recent projects have met a variety of fates.

Work on a massive extension of the hopelessly overcrowded **cemetery island of San Michele** by London-based architect David Chipperfield entered its second phase in 2015, despite outrage the previous year that white stone tombs in the first-stage area were developing dark stains and emitting foul smells.

A plan by fashion designer Pierre Cardin to build a futuristic skyscraper – the Palais Lumière – in Mestre appeared (mercifully) to have been shelved until Mayor Luigi Brugnaro dusted it off to give it further thought in 2016. No final decision has been announced.

A deafening silence hangs about the **Venice Gateway** hotel and convention complex near the airport, a typically outré project by Canadian-American architect Frank Gehry which appears to have drowned in a sea of red tape.

Scarpa in Venice

A true Venetian architect

A Venetian born and bred, save for a few years spent in his youth in nearby Vicenza, Carlo Scarpa (1906-78) was one of Italy's most highly regarded architects – without even qualifying as an architect until just before his death.

Utterly imbued with the textures of the lagoon city, he worked with wood and glass (he was creative director of the Venini glassmaker from 1933 to 1947), stone and concrete to blend his very modern designs into the context of his native city. The results are dotted all around Venice.

With the restoration and reopening of the **Negozio Olivetti** (Olivetti showroom, 1957-58; *see p97*) in piazza San Marco, one of Scarpa's most remarkable gems has been returned to the city, thanks to the FAI (www.fondoambiente.org), Italy's equivalent of Britain's National Trust.

In his restyling (1961-63) of the ground floor of the **Fondazione Querini Stampalia** (*see p112*), Scarpa ran water from the canal outside, bringing it into an indoor space of travertine and games with levels, then through a garden courtyard of deceptive simplicity. His too is the wooden bridge leading across to one of the Foundation's entrances.

Despite his lack of academic qualifications, Scarpa had a close relationship with Venice's universities, teaching interior design at the IUAV (the architecture & design university) from the late 1940s until his death. For IUAV he designed the main entrance (Santa Croce 191, campazzo dei Tolentini), and comprehensively overhauled the IUAV Fondazione Masieri annexe (Dorsoduro 3900, calle del Remer). For **Ca' Foscari**, Venice's

other university, he designed the entrance to the Arts faculty (Dorsoduro 1686, campo San Sebastiano); and revamped (1935-37) the ground floor of the main university premises (Dorsoduro 3246, calle Foscari; you can take a good look over coffee or a meal at the university's canteen, open 8am-7pm Mon-Fri, 8am-1pm Sat during term time). His wooden Baratto lecture theatre there (1955-56) burned down but was rebuilt in 1979 to his specifications.

The architect left his mark on the **Biennale gardens** (*see p121*), designing what was once the main ticket booth (1952), the Venezuelan pavilion (1956) and a sculpture garden (1952). He was also responsible for the plinth (1968) for Augusto Murer's Partigiana sculpture by the Giardini vaporetto stop.

Between 1945 and 1959, he pottered away at the **Gallerie dell'Accademia** (*see p180*), modernising and upgrading in a series of interventions of such delicacy that you'll need to look closely to notice them. (The gallery's new rooms, designed by his son Tobia and opened to the public in 2014, are far less subtle.)

There's more of Scarpa's work to be seen around the Veneto region, including the dramatic **Castelvecchio** (*see p220*) makeover in Verona and the Antonio Canova sculpture museum in Possagno. Scarpa died after falling down a flight of stairs in Japan, but was buried – according to his wishes – standing, wrapped in winding sheets like a medieval knight, in a corner of his extraordinary Brion-Vega tomb in San Vito d'Altivole, near Treviso.

ARCHITECTURE

Istituto Universitario Architettura Venezia

Art

A treasure house of painting from the Renaissance to the present day

The lagoon city's unique atmosphere figures largely in its art. From the late Middle Ages until the mid 18th century, artists of the highest calibre, inspired by the unique colours and light of this unlikely smattering of overcrowded islands in a desolate lagoon, left their mark around the city. The result today is an anomaly: an extraordinary concentration of artistic treasures, of which the city's dwindling population is still inordinately, possessively proud.

Though little art is made in Venice these days, the city's very particular relationship with the art world continues. The 2009 inauguration of the contemporary gallery at the Punta della Dogana means that Venice's concentration of 20th- and 21st-century art is almost as important as its Renaissance glories. For a damp town buffeted by threatening tides, Venice is truly a unique and precious repository of art.

Processione della Vera Croce a Piazza San Marco (Gentile Bellini 1496)

Art in situ

A key element in the effectiveness of Venetian painting is that many great pictures remain in the buildings for which they were painted. Leave the madding crowd at San Marco behind, and you'll soon come across superb pictures in obscure churches: glowing altarpieces and pulsating canvas *laterali* (paintings for side walls of chapels). Seeing these pictures in their original sites reveals how aware painters were of the relation of their works to the surrounding architecture, light and existing artwork.

Yet, exceptionally, the paintings also relate to the physical context of Venice itself. What makes Venetian painting distinctive – the decorated surfaces, asymmetry, shimmering light effects and, above all, warm tonalities – can also be found in the lagoon environment. Renaissance Venice's visual culture encompassed the richness of Islamic art and Byzantine mosaics, the haphazard arrangement of streets and canals with their strong shadows, and light experienced through haze or reflected off moving water.

The end of anonymity

Venetian church interiors were once covered with frescoes; the damp climate means that very few of these earliest works survive today. The official history of Venetian painting begins in the 1320s with the first painter to emerge from medieval anonymity, **Paolo Veneziano** (c1290-1362), who worked in egg tempera and gold leaf on wood panel. He championed the composite altarpiece, which would become one of the key formats of Venetian painting. His polyptychs, such as *The Coronation of the Virgin* in the Accademia Gallery (*see p180*), were ornately framed, compartmentalised works featuring sumptuous fabrics, a preference for surface decoration and pattern over depth, and a stiffness derived from Byzantine icons. A love of drapery and textile patterns proved to be a Venetian constant, still visible in Veronese's paintings in the 16th century and even beyond that in Tiepolo's 18th-century works.

Although many painters worked in Venice in the century after Paolo Veneziano, the next major legacy was that of a team, **Giovanni d'Alemagna** (John of Germany) and his brother-in-law **Antonio Vivarini**, active in the mid 15th century. Their three altarpieces in San Zaccaria (dated 1443, *see p114*), one in San Pantalon (*see p176*) and an imposing canvas triptych in the Accademia demonstrate the transition from Gothic to Renaissance.

Although Italian art historians give precedence to Antonio, the sudden decline in the quality of his works after Giovanni's death in 1450 suggests that his partner was the brains behind the operation. Antonio's younger brother, **Bartolomeo Vivarini**, who ran the family workshop from the 1470s until about 1491, learned Renaissance style

Blessing of Saint Mark (Bartolomeo Vivarini, 1474)

Jacopo, Giovanni and Gentile

The Bellinis and the Venetian Renaissance

Jacopo Bellini (1400-1470) had good reason to be proud of his sons: **Gentile** (1429-1507) and **Giovanni** (1430-1516) are synonymous with Venetian Renaissance art. But their father also played a crucial role. A pupil of Gentile da Fabriano, and familiar with the most prominent artists of the very early Italian Renaissance, Jacopo brought back to his native Venice styles and techniques (including the use of oil paint rather than tempera) that would determine the development of art at this remarkable period for the city.

In a flourishing workshop that would also include Andrea Mantegna, who married a Bellini daughter, Jacopo and his acolytes broke away from the art of the late Middle Ages, gradually exchanging the stiff style adopted from Byzantine icons for a softer, more natural one.

If Giovanni is the Bellini brother considered more highly today, Gentile was perhaps more successful during his lifetime, appointed as the official portrait painter to the doges and given key diplomatic tasks too. In 1479 he was sent to Constantinople as Venice's cultural representative to the court of Sultan Mehmed II, whose portrait he painted. But it

is as a chronicler of life in Venice that Gentile fascinates most today. Immense canvases painted for the Doge's Palace have been destroyed by fire. But his two scenes from the *Miracle of the Relic of the Holy Cross* (1496-1500), now in the Accademia (see *p180*) are packed with minute, charming details – each of which tells its own particular story about life in 15th-century Venice.

Giovanni Bellini's lasting appeal is due, arguably, to his extraordinary way with colour. Using oils in a way no one before him had mastered so well, he created hues and moods that broke the mould of Italian painting. The 1505 altarpiece of San Zaccaria church (see *p114*) is a case in point. The warmth and the contrasts, the delicacy and humanity of the subjects in this *Sacra conversazione* are a total break with the past.

Giovanni's novel approach set off ripples that would continue to widen through the Venetian Renaissance and beyond: through pupils such as Sebastiano del Piombo, the enigmatic Giorgione and the great colourist Titian, Giovanni's influence was lasting and profound.

ART

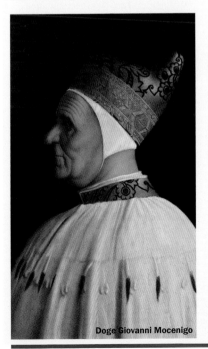

Doge Giovanni Mocenigo

Madonna with Child (Giovanni Bellini)

from both painting and sculpture, as seen in the lapidary figures in the altarpiece (1474) in the Cappella Corner of the Frari (*see p162*).

By the next generation, the main players had become more clearly defined. From around 1480, **Giovanni Bellini** directed the dominant workshop in Venice. Most of Bellini's sizeable output, stretching from the late 1450s until his death in 1516, was painted on wood panel rather than the newer canvas. The important group of early Bellini devotional pictures in the Museo Correr (*see p90*) and the many variations on the Madonna and Child theme in the Accademia show how varied and moving these subjects could be.

Equally impressive is Bellini's magnificent series of altarpieces. In these he perfected the subject of the *Sacra conversazione* (Sacred Conversation), where standing saints flank a seated figure, usually the Virgin Mary, within a setting that evokes the gold mosaics and costly marbles of the Basilica di San Marco (*see p86*). The inner glow afforded by the new medium of oil paint allowed Bellini to model his figures with an astonishing delicacy of light and shadow. One can follow his progress through a series of altarpieces that remain in situ: in Santi Giovanni e Paolo (*see p111*), the Frari, San Zaccaria and San Giovanni Crisostomo (*see p133*).

Giovanni's elder brother, **Gentile Bellini**, enjoyed even greater official success: from 1474 until his death in 1507 he directed the decoration of the Palazzo Ducale (*see p92*), replacing crumbling frescoes with huge canvases. He also performed a diplomatic role for the Venetian government, travelling to Constantinople in 1479 to paint for the Ottoman sultan. Although his Palazzo Ducale canvases were destroyed by fire in 1577, his *Procession in Piazza San Marco* (1496), now in the Accademia, shows his ability to depict sumptuous public spectacle with choreographic verve.

Three painters born in the second half of the 15th century, and who were active in the 16th, are worth seeking out. **Cima da Conegliano** (c1459-1517) offers a stiffer style than Bellini, depicting figures standing in dignified repose against crisp landscapes.

Cima's best altarpieces, in the Accademia, and at San Giovanni in Bragora (*see p123*), the Madonna dell'Orto (*see p140*) and the Carmini (*see p176*), all demonstrate a mastery of light.

Vittore Carpaccio (c1465-1525) specialised in narrative works for the *scuole* (*see p115* Scuole Stories). Two intact cycles from around 1500 are among the treasures of Venetian painting: the grand St Ursula cycle in the Accademia and that of St George and St Jerome in the intimate Scuola di San Giorgio degli Schiavoni (*see p123*). **Lorenzo Lotto** (c1480-1556) spent much of his career outside Venice. His best altarpieces in the city, in the Carmini and Santi Giovanni e Paolo, combine an uncanny accuracy – in rendering landscape or cloth, for example – with a deeply felt spirituality. His impressive portraits, such as the *Portrait of a Youth*, in the Accademia, employ an unusual horizontal format.

Secular subjects

At the beginning of the 16th century, Venetian painting took a dramatic turn. Three of Bellini's pupils – Giorgione, Sebastiano del Piombo and Titian – experimented with new secular subject matter and new ways of handling paint. **Giorgione** (c1477-1510) remains one of the great enigmas of art. No other reputation rests on so few surviving pictures. The hard contours and emphasis on surface pattern seen in earlier Venetian painting have softened in his work, and for the first time the atmosphere becomes palpable, like damp lagoon air. Two haunting pictures in the Accademia, *La Tempesta* and *La Vecchia*, may be deliberately enigmatic, more concerned with mood than story. It can be argued that the modern concept of the painting was born in Venice soon after 1500. For the first time, three conditions that we now take for granted were met: these works were all oil on canvas, painted at the artist's initiative, and not intended for a specific location.

Sebastiano del Piombo (c1485-1547) left his mark with a similar emphasis on softened contour and tangible atmosphere. His major altarpiece, which was painted around 1507 and can still be seen in San Giovanni Crisostomo, shows a *Sacra conversazione* in which some of the figures are seen in profile, rather than head on, and hidden in shadow. Even more exciting is a set of standing saints painted as organ shutters, now in the Accademia, which show an unprecedented application of thick paint (*impasto*).

It can be argued that the modern concept of the painting was born in Venice soon after 1500

Bellini and del Piombo

Showdown at the altars

A fascinating showdown can be seen in San Giovanni Crisostomo (*see p133*), where the elderly **Giovanni Bellini** outshone his former pupil **Sebastiano del Piombo**, some 50 years his junior. Sebastiano struck first, around 1507, with the high altarpiece (*below left*), boldly setting the central figure of St John Chrysostom in profile and immersed in shadow. He contrasted the saint with a particularly lyrical John the Baptist (note how the scroll winding around his staff mimics the turning of the saint's body and the drapery

swirls). Not to be outdone, Bellini's 1513 altarpiece in the right chapel (*below right*) includes similar chessboard paving and a twisting St Christopher, clearly critiquing Sebastiano's Baptist. The central figure is presented as a seated geriatric holding a tome, literally facing off against his rival's prototype. Bellini made sure viewers knew that this was not the work of a young trendy: he signed and dated the painting prominently near Christopher's knee.

Titian and Tintoretto

Events conspired to boost the early career of **Titian** (Tiziano Vecellio, c1488-1576) when, in the space of only six years (1510-16), Giorgione fell victim to the plague, Sebastiano del Piombo moved to Rome and Giovanni Bellini passed away. Titian soon staked his claim with a dynamic *Assumption of the Virgin* (1518) for the high altar of the Frari. There he dominated the enormous space by creating the largest panel painting in the world.

The lagoon city is the place to appreciate in situ the nearly 70-year span of the master's religious work. These include a second, glorious altarpiece in the Frari (the *Madonna di Ca' Pesaro*), the virile St

Christopher fresco in the Palazzo Ducale and the ceiling paintings in the sacristy of the Salute (*see p182*).

For a decade (c1527-39), Titian had a true rival in **Pordenone** (c1483-1539), a painter of muscular figures engaged in violent action. Now, for the first time in decades, Pordenone's work can be appreciated in Venice. The recently restored *Saints Christopher and Martin* in the church of San Rocco (*see p164*) shows an urgent style that had great appeal. Even more interesting is the confrontation in the church of San Giovanni Elemosinario (*see p152*), where Pordenone's bulging figures on the right altar square off against the soft contours of Titian's high altar. Yet, once again, Titian found his road cleared of obstacles when his adversary suddenly died.

By the 1560s, in works such as the extraordinary *Annunciation* in San Salvador (*see p99*), Titian's handling of paint had become so loose that his forms were not so much defined by contours as caressed into being. Line was replaced by quivering patches of warm colouring.

Contemporaries swore that the old artist painted as often with his fingers as with the brush. Nowhere is this tactile quality more apparent than in Titian's final painting, a *Pietà* originally intended for his tomb, and now in the Accademia. Left unfinished at his death during the plague of 1576, this picture summarises the Venetian artistic tradition, with its glittering mosaic dome and forms so dissolved as to challenge the very conventions of painting.

Instead of mourning Titian's death, Jacopo Robusti (c1518-94) – better known as **Tintoretto** – probably breathed a sigh of relief. Though he rose to fame in the late 1540s, he had to wait until he was 58 years old before he could claim the title of Venice's greatest living painter. Yet Tintoretto was canny enough to learn from his rival. He supposedly inscribed the motto 'The drawing of Michelangelo and the colouring of Titian' on the wall of his studio.

Tintoretto's breakthrough work, *The Miracle of the Slave* (1548), now in the Accademia, offered a brash attempt at

Paintings by Tintoretto, Four Doors Room, Palazzo Ducale, from 1578.

this synthesis, combining Michelangelo's confident muscular anatomies with Titian's glistening paint surface. Borrowing the figure types and violent compositions of Pordenone, Tintoretto's aggressive and tumultuous canvases marked the end of the decorative narrative painting tradition perfected by Carpaccio.

As Ruskin noted in *The Stones of Venice* (1851), Tintoretto, unlike Titian, is an artist who can be appreciated only in Venice.

Among the dozens of works in his home town, the soaring choir paintings in the Madonna dell'Orto (c1560) or the many canvases at the Scuola Grande di San Rocco (*see p166*), executed in 1564-87, amaze in their scale and complexity,

notably his wall-sized Crucifixion (1565). His many workshop assistants, including two sons and a daughter, allowed him to increase production to unprecedented levels. Tintoretto went even further than Titian in the liberation of the brush stroke. The tradition of bravura handling that goes from Rubens to Delacroix to De Kooning begins with the action painters of 16th-century Venice.

Paolo Veronese (1528-88) made his impact in Venice with a love of rich fabrics and elegant poses that contrasts with Tintoretto's agitated figures. Veronese's savoir faire is best seen in the overpopulated feasts he painted for monastery refectories, such as the *Feast in the House of Levi*, now in

the Accademia. His wit can be seen in one of the few great 16th-century mythological paintings remaining in Venice: *The Rape of Europa*, in the Palazzo Ducale, with its leering, slightly comical bull. His supreme ensemble piece is in San Sebastiano (*see p173*), a church that features altars, ceilings, frescoes and organ shutters all painted by Veronese, as well as the artist's tomb.

Venetian painting was also practised outside Venice: **Jacopo Bassano** (c1510-92) was an artist based in a provincial centre who kept pace with the latest innovations. Alhough his work is best seen in his home town, Bassano del Grappa, a number of canvases in the Accademia and an altarpiece in San Giorgio Maggiore (*see p195*) display characteristic Venetian flickering brush work and dramatic chiaroscuro.

With the following generation, the golden age of Venetian painting drew to a close. The prolific **Palma il Giovane** (c1548-1628) created works loosely in the style of Tintoretto. His finest pictures, such as the *Crucifixion* in the Madonna dell'Orto or those in San Giacomo dell'Orio (*see p157*) or the Oratorio dei Crociferi (*see p141*), all date from the 1580s.

After the deaths of Veronese and Tintoretto, the pressure was gone and the quality of Venetian art took a nosedive, as can be seen at San Giovanni Elemosinario, now open after decades *in restauro*.

Outsized canvases by painters active at the end of the 16th century crowd the church's walls but the aforementioned small altarpieces by Titian and Pordenone, executed more than half a century earlier, dominate the space.

Baroque and Rococo

In the following years, Baroque in Venice was represented largely by out-of-towners (**Luca Giordano**, whose restored altarpieces adorn the Salute) or by bizarre posturing (**Gian Antonio Fumiani**'s stupefying canvas ceiling in San Pantalon). Exaggerated light effects ruled the day. It was only at the beginning of the 18th century that Venetian painting experienced a resurgence.

Giambattista Piazzetta (1683-1754) produced a ceiling painting in Santi Giovanni e Paolo and a sequence of altarpieces – particularly those in Santa Maria della Fava (*see p114*), the Gesuati (*see p182*) and San Salvador – all demonstrating restrained elegance and a muted palette.

Giambattista Tiepolo (1696-1770), the greatest painter of the Venetian rococo, adapted the zigzag scheme introduced by Piazzetta for use with warm pastel colours. In his monumental ceilings in the Gesuati, the Pietà (*see p120*) and Ca' Rezzonico (*see p175*), Tiepolo reintroduced frescoes on a large scale after more than two centuries of canvas ceilings. Perhaps the most satisfying place in which to study his work is the upper room of the Scuola Grande dei Carmini (*see p176*), where the disproportionately low ceiling provides a close-up view of his technique. The dazzling Tiepolo was only

Punta della Dogana and Santa Maria dell Salute (Canaletto, 1730-45)

Gallerie dell'Accademia

one of a number of important artists at work in 18th-century Venice, including his own son, **Giandomenico Tiepolo** (1727-1804).

Though frequently his father's assistant, Giandomenico can be seen at his independent best in an eerie cycle of *14 Stations of the Cross* in San Polo (*see p152*). **Gaspare Diziani** (1689-1767) deserves credit for three gorgeous ceiling canvases on the life of St Helen in the former meeting room of the Scuola del Vin (wine merchants' confraternity), entered through the church of San Silvestro (*see p153*). Above all, the essence of the Venetian rococo is to be found in the sites where architecture, sculpture and painting were employed to form a unified whole: the Gesuati, Santa Maria della Fava, San Stae (*see p158*) and the furnished rooms of Ca' Rezzonico.

In the 18th century, collectors provided a constant demand for portraits and city views. A female artist, **Rosalba Carriera** (1675- 1757), developed a refined portrait style using pastels. **Canaletto** (1697-1768) and **Guardi** (1712-93) offered views of Venice.

The popularity of these landscape paintings as Grand Tour souvenirs means that although examples exist in the Accademia and Ca' Rezzonico, both artists are seen at their best in Britain. A different aspect of 18th-century painting, and perhaps Guardi's masterpiece, can be seen in the astonishingly delicate *Stories of Tobias* (1750-53) decorating the organ loft in the church of Angelo Raffaele (*see p172*). Pietro Longhi (1702-85) created amusing genre scenes that gently satirised the social life of his day; they can be enjoyed in the Museo della Fondazione Querini Stampalia (*see p112*).

Patrons, not producers

By the time of Napoleon's conquest in 1797, Venetian painting, like Venetian military power, was a spent force. Over the following 200 years, however, Venice's unique setting and lavish collections have been a magnet for foreign visitors, including artists.

Venice now exhibits painters, rather than producing them. The city's contemporary art scene is increasingly vibrant, with a handful of smaller players and three major institutions: the prestigious Biennale (*see p121*); the Peggy Guggenheim Collection (*see p183*), which has expanded and is flourishing; and the extraordinary Palazzo Grassi–Punta della Dogana nexus (*see p101* and *p185*).

Although attention is currently focused on the contemporary, Venice's incomparable artistic heritage had a boost when, after ten years' work, to a design by Tobia Scarpa (son of Carlo, *see p273*), the Grandi Gallerie dell'Accademia finally saw the light of day in December 2013. The ground floor of the present Accademia building – used by the city's fine arts school from 1807 to 2003 – has been converted into additional galleries so that nearly 650 works (instead of the previous 400) can be displayed, many of them specially restored for the opening.

Plan

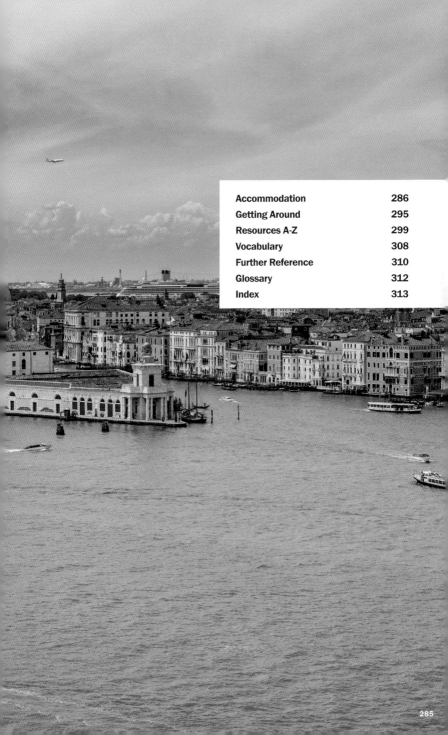

Accommodation

A day-trip to Venice just won't do. To appreciate the city's 24-hour magic, you have to fall asleep to the sound of gondoliers crooning and awake to the very particular bouncing echo of footsteps rushing along a narrow *calle*.

If horror tales of hair-raising prices are a deterrent, remember, this is a Jekyll and Hyde city: even the most expensive places will slash prices in the low season. Of course, peak times still pull in visitors in their thronging millions. As well as summer, Carnevale, big regattas, key Biennale events and important religious festivities including Christmas and Easter will push up prices. Outside of these times, you'll find that the Lagoon City is refreshingly quiet and relatively cheap – to sleep in, at least.

The scene

Venice's accommodation sector continues to change and expand. Some of this is retrenching: at the Gritti Palace (*see p291*) for example, a massive revamp some years ago has reduced the number of rooms, but ramped up the luxury quotient still further.

Small continues to be beautiful, and chic B&Bs proliferate: CimaRosa (*see p293*) is one of the best. But off-piste locations are also proving popular, with some of the most uncharacteristic out on the islands of the lagoon.

Where to stay

Venice is divided into six *sestieri* plus outlying islands, Giudecca being the closest of these. Though you'll be hard pushed to tell where one ends and the next begins, a closer look reveals that each has its own particular feel.

Plush hotels and tourist action centre around St Mark's square and the riva degli Schiavoni: many first-timers feel that

In the know
Price categories

Our price categories are based on hotels' standard prices (not including seasonal offers or discounts) for one night in a double room with en suite shower/bath. Breakfast is included unless otherwise stated. Given the potential for off-season discounts, it's always worth trying to negotiate a better deal.

Luxury	€500+
Expensive	€250-500
Moderate	€150-250
Budget	up to €150

being right in the thick of it is best, but the crowd thronging outside the front door can tarnish that pampered feel.

Remember that Venice is small and wherever you are, you'll never feel far from the sightseeing action. On the right bank of the Grand Canal, in the *sestieri* of Dorsoduro, Santa Croce and San Polo, there are chic little hideaways for those who seek style without the glam trappings. Moving away from the hub at St Mark's square, Castello and Cannaregio also harbour good options in their refreshingly residential *calli* and *campi*.

Our categories

Venice is a city of immense accommodation price swings: the same room that costs €500 in high season, or during a crowd-pulling festival or event, might plummet to €150 in the late November doldrums; and even mid-range options at around €200 will be on offer at €75 a night or less when wintry weather drives less hardy souls from the lagoon city.

For this reason, placing hotels under category headings is as difficult as it is misleading. As a general rule of thumb, however, Luxury means a double room in mid-season will start at €500 and stop at nothing; 'Expensive' means it will cost from €250 up to €500 per night; 'Moderate' means €150-€250, and 'Budget' will come in at below €150.

Whatever agency or booking site you use to find your accommodation, don't presume that it's offering the best price. Always check

Palazzo Abadessa *p292*

The Tourist Tax

What you need to know

Like most destinations in Italy, Venice levies a tourist tax (*imposta di soggiorno*) on visitors, which must be paid over and above the lodging rates when you stay in any hotel or rented accommodation. It is charged separately from your room bill and should be paid in cash, so bear that in mind when checking out. Tourist tax rates vary by type of accommodation, season and age.

In low season, the tax for those staying in a one-star hotel in island Venice is 70c per adult per day (30c ages 10-16) while a five-star hotel charges €3.50 (€1.70). In high season the rate is €1 (50c) in a one-star and €5 (€2.50) in a five-star. Under-tens are not charged. The tax is charged for a maximum five days in any given establishment.

hotel websites carefully and look out for special deals. It's often cheaper to book directly with the selected establishment.

Getting to your hotel

Reaching your hotel in this labyrinthine city can be a challenge. Ask for very clear directions, which should include the nearest vaporetto (ferry) stop, campo (square) or church. Alternatively, ask for GPS coordinates – but bear in mind that if you plan to rely on your smartphone to get you there, you should download a map on to your device before arriving: Venice's 4G signal can disappear unexpectedly in places.

If you have mobility problems and/or don't fancy dragging your suitcase over too many bridges with steps, ask whether your hotel of choice has a *porta d'acqua* (canal-side entrance) where a water taxi can pull right up to reception.

Facilities for the disabled are scarce in Venetian hotels, partly due to the nature of the buildings. Many establishments are spread over several floors but do not have lifts; always check first. *See p300* for information on disabled travel in Venice.

What you will (and won't) get

In general, room prices include breakfast. Except in more upmarket hotels, 'breakfast included' means a continental breakfast of tea/coffee, pastries and, if you're lucky, yoghurt and/or fruit: don't expect a full cooked meal, and be aware that what's on offer varies wildly in freshness and generosity. If it's unclear whether or not you'll be given breakfast as part of your room rate, avoid surprises by asking when you book.

Most room prices also include Wi-Fi. Don't be surprised, though, if thick walls and meandering corridors make for a shaky signal.

Most hotels will charge more for rooms with canal or lagoon views. As some canals are muddy

La Calcina *p293*

backwaters, and others are major highways with a constant procession of bellowing gondoliers (not so good for light sleepers), it pays to ask exactly what this water view consists of.

By law Italian hotels cannot provide irons in rooms, though some may have an ironing room for guests' use, or press clothes on request. The electric kettle is not a piece of equipment considered vital by Italians, so don't presume that it will feature in your hotel room.

Don't be surprised if thick walls and meandering corridors make for a shaky wifi signal

Self-catering

If you're travelling as a family or group, or staying for an extended period, an apartment with kitchen facilities might prove a sensible option. Beside the usual plethora of AirBnB offerings, many of Venice's hotels are adding apartments to their repertoire.

Among hotels listed in this guide, La Calcina (*see p293*), the Bauer group's Villa F (*see p291*), AD Place (*see p292*) and Corte di Gabriela (*see p292*) have self-catering facilities.

The websites www.viewsonvenice.com and www.veniceapartment.com are also good resources for finding an apartment.

CimaRosa Boutique B&B *p293*

Luxury
Aman Grand Canal Venice

San Polo 1364, calle Tiepolo Baiamonte (041 270 7333, www.aman.com). Vaporetto San Silvestro. **Rooms** *24.* **Map** *p146 F6.*

Aman's Venetian outpost is exactly what you'd expect of this Far Eastern hotel group: utter luxury, immaculate service and exceptional style. The hotel is housed in palazzo Papadopoli, the only building on the Grand Canal with two private gardens; the count-owner of the *palazzo* still lives on the top floor and often sweeps in to lend an aristocratic Venetian air – which is just as well because one complaint that could be levelled at the hotel is that it's much like any Aman hostelry anywhere in the world. The restaurant serves Italian and Asian cuisine. The bedrooms and suites are exercises in pared-back luxury: one has frescoes by GB Tiepolo; another has a magnificent fireplace designed by Sansovino.

The Bauer Venezia

San Marco 1459, campo San Moisè (041 520 7022, www. bauervenezia.com). Vaporetto San Marco Vallaresso. **Rooms** *210.* **Map** *p82 H8.*

This Venetian accommodation classic a stone's throw from St Mark's square is a hotel of different parts, spreading from a rather brutal 1930s building on campo San Moisè to a glorious antique *palazzo* with Grand Canal frontage. Appearances are deceptive, and the newer extension conceals vast halls inside, where marble, gold and black detailing give the place the air of a grand art deco ocean liner. The water-facing Il Palazzo, on the other hand, offers plusher, more traditional opulence. There are views to remember at breakfast, which is served either at canal-level, or on the Settimo Cielo (seventh heaven) terrace. The Bauer empire extends across the water to the Giudecca, where accommodation options Palladio Spa and Villa F back on to a gorgeous garden.

Belmond Hotel Cipriani

Giudecca 10, fondamenta San Giovanni (041 240 801, www. hotelcipriani.com). Hotel launch from San Marco Vallaresso vaporetto stop, or Vaporetto Zitelle. **Rooms** *95.* **Map** *p190 G2.*

Set amidst verdant gardens, the Cipriani has superb facilities as well as a private harbour for your yacht and a better-than-average chance of rubbing shoulders with an A-list film star, especially during the film festival (*see p236*) when many make this their base. Rooms are as luxurious and well appointed as you'd expect in this category. If this seems too humdrum, take an apartment in the neighbouring 15th-century Palazzo Vendramin, with butler service and private garden. Facilities include tennis courts, a pool, a sauna, a spa, a gym and a fine-dining restaurant designed by Adam Tihany. There's a motorboat to San Marco, but many guests never even leave the premises.

Gritti Palace

San Marco 2467, campo Santa Maria del Giglio (041 794 611, www.thegrittipalace.com). Vaporetto Giglio. **Rooms** *82.* **Map** *p82 G8.*

With much fanfare, the Gritti Palace reopened in 2013 after a massive makeover that reduced the number of rooms and suites but upped the already considerable luxury quotient, while adding some handy 21st-century conveniences such as a state-of-the-art concrete lining for the ground floor, so that guests checking in during *acqua alta* (high water) will no longer have to do so with the lagoon lapping around their knees. The air of old-world charm and nobility about this 15th-century *palazzo* now feels fresher, with superb Rubelli fabrics replacing fittings that had become frayed over the decades, and every piece of antique furniture restored and polished. Refined and opulent, adorned with luscious bathroom treats and fresh flowers, each room is uniquely decorated; one is lined with antique floor-to-ceiling mirrors. If you want a canal

or campo view, specify when booking: some rooms overlook a dingy courtyard. Breakfast, or just an *aperitivo* on the vast canal terrace, is an experience in itself.

Metropole

Castello 4149, riva degli Schiavoni (041 520 5044, www. hotelmetropole.com). Vaporetto San Zaccaria. **Rooms** *67.* **Map** *p108 L8.*

Of all the grand hotels that crowd this part of the riva, the Metropole is arguably the most characterful. The owners' museum-level collection of antiques and curios are dotted in the sumptuous public rooms – which have a deliciously exotic, decadent air – and through the varied bedrooms, which vary from slightly gloomy classic doubles to glorious suites shimmering with mosaics and marbles. In winter, tea and cakes are served in the velvet-draped *salone*; in summer, guests relax in the pretty garden to the sound of water trickling in the fountain. There are views over the lagoon (for a hefty supplement), the canal or on to the garden. The hotel's Met restaurant has one Michelin star and prices to match.

Palazzo Venart

Santa Croce 1961, calle Tron (041 523 3784, www.palazzovenart. com). Vaporetto San Stae. **Rooms** *18.* **Map** *p146 G6.*

New for 2016, five-star Palazzo Venart gives guests all the antiques, brocades and sparkling chandeliers of classic Venetian hotel tradition, but places them in a boutique hotel context, with very friendly service and a pretty garden leading down to the Grand Canal to boot. The 18 rooms are equally sumptuous but each has its own feel and colour scheme; the coloured marbles in the huge (for Venice) bathrooms are extraordinary. A low glassed-in structure in the palm- and magnolia-filled courtyard is home to Glam, the latest addition to superchef Enrico Bartolini's empire and Venice's hottest new restaurant opening. Hotel guests' breakfast is served here.

Expensive
AD Place

*San Marco 2557A, fondamenta
della Fenice (041 241 3234, www.
adplacevenice.com). Vaporetto
Giglio. **Rooms** 12 + 7 apartments.
Map p82 G8.*

Tucked away on a quiet canal
behind the La Fenice opera
house, 12-room AD Place mixes
a friendly atmosphere with great
service in bedrooms and public
spaces, which revel in a wild
combination of candy-stripe
colours and baroque touches.
Rooms (spread over four floors
with no lift) vary in size: some
of the standard rooms are fairly
small but the top floor suite, with
its canopied bed in the master
bedroom, is suitable for families,
as is a ground-floor room that is
wheelchair-adapted. The hotel's
private water entrance means
you can get straight here by water
taxi. The glorious roof terrace is a
great place to watch the sun set.
AD Place has recently expanded
its self-catering side, bringing to
seven (three of them opening in
2017) the number of its elegant-
with-a-twist apartments sleeping
up to six people. In low season,
the hotel slips into the moderate
category.

Al Ponte Antico

*Cannaregio 5768, calle
dell'Aseo (041 241 1944, www.
aponteantico.com). Vaporetto
Rialto. **Rooms** 7. **Map** p128 H5.*

With its padded reception desk,
festooned curtains and lashings
of brocade in public spaces
and most of the bedrooms, the
family-run Al Ponte Antico takes
the traditional Venetian hotel
decor idiom and turns it into
something over-the-top, Louis
Quinze-ish and faintly decadent:
a pleasant change from the
prudish norm. In a 16th-century
palazzo on the Grand Canal, with
views over the Rialto Bridge, Al
Ponte Antico's exquisite little
balcony overlooks the water,
as do some doubles and suites.
Owner-manager Matteo Peruch
will make you feel totally at home
from the moment you arrive, and
the breakfasts here are famous
and feted.

Ca' Maria Adele

*Dorsoduro 111, rio terà dei
Catecumeni (041 520 3078, www.
camariaadele.it). Vaporetto
Salute. **Rooms** 14 + mini-
apartment. **Map** p170 G9.*

Situated in the shadow of the
basilica of Santa Maria della
Salute, Ca' Maria Adele marries
sumptuous 18th-century
Venetian decadence with modern
design, with some Moorish
elements and a host of quirky
tongue-in-cheek details thrown
in. Brothers Alessio and Nicola
Campa preside attentively over
a main hotel of 12 luxurious
bedrooms, five of which are
themed; the red and gold Doge's
Room is voluptuous, the Sala
Noire ultra-sexy. There's an
intimate sitting room on the
ground floor with chocolate
brown faux-fur on the walls and
black pony-skin sofas, plus a
Moroccan-style roof terrace for
sultry evenings. Breakfast can
be consumed in bed or in any of
the hotel's public spaces. Next
door at number 113 are two more
splendid rooms, which can be
booked as a private suite: and 50
metres from the mother ship is
the equally delightful MiniPalace
where a private terrace overlooks
San Giorgio Maggiore and
the Salute. Service is deft
but discreet.

Corte di Gabriela

*San Marco 3836, calle degli
Avvocati (041 523 5077, www.
cortedigabriela.com). Vaporetto
Sant'Angelo. **Rooms** 10, plus 2
apartments. **Map** p82 F7.*

Corte di Gabriela marries classic
Venetian frescoes and stucco
with some molto-mod design
details to produce a very stylish
four-star boutique handily
placed in a quiet street near
campo Santo Stefano (*see* p101).
Obliging, well-informed staff
preside over a pretty courtyard
and a warmly red living room
complete with grand piano and
a little bar. Spacious bedrooms
come with iPads and kettles; the
bathrooms are large and chic.
The breakfast is a rich feast of
home-baked goodies. Two self-
catering apartments located near
the hotel are perfect for groups
or families. Corte di Gabriela is

towards the lower end of this
price range.

Palazzo Abadessa

*Cannaregio 4011, calle Priuli
(041 241 3784, www.abadessa.
com). Vaporetto Ca' d'Oro.
Rooms 15. **Map** p128 H4.*

A beautiful, shady walled
garden is laid out in front of this
16th-century *palazzo*, which is
filled with antiques, paintings
and silver, and where the
prevailing atmosphere is that
of an aristocratic private home
(which it is), restored and opened
to guests. Service is charming
but discreet. A magnificent
double stone staircase leads to
the impressive bedrooms, all of
which are beautifully appointed
with richly coloured brocade-
covered walls, and some of which
are truly vast. Beware, however:
the three low-ceilinged doubles
on the mezzanine floor are rather
cramped. Bathrooms tend to be
on the small side. In low season,
prices at this lovely place fall
into the affordable end of the
'moderate' category, especially if
you book ahead.

Palazzo Stern

*Dorsoduro 2792A, calle del
Traghetto (041 277 0869, www.
palazzostern.com). Vaporetto
Ca' Rezzonico. **Rooms** 24. **Map**
p170 D8.*

Built in the early 20th century in
eclectic pastiche style, Palazzo
Stern is now home to this elegant
hotel. A magnificent wooden
staircase leads up to rooms done
out in classic Venetian style in
pale shades. Pricier rooms have
views over the Grand Canal but
the standard doubles at the back
face towards a lovely garden.
There's a view that stretches
across the city to the Dolomites
from the rooftop terrace, where
there's a jacuzzi for guests' use.
A wonderful breakfast terrace
overlooks the canal.

Moderate
Al Ponte Mocenigo

*Santa Croce 2063, fondamenta
Rimpetto Mocenigo (041 524
4797, www.alpontemocenigo.
com). Vaporetto San Stae. **Rooms**
15 + 8 + 6. **Map** p146 F4.*

This delightful hotel, which has its own little bridge on a quiet canal near campo San Stae, has expanded recently into two nearby structures, taking the number of rooms and suites to 29. It remains, however, one of Venice's best-value accommodation options. It has tastefully decorated mod-Venetian rooms – some in a luscious shade of deep red, others in rich gold – and well-appointed bathrooms, not to mention Wi-Fi access throughout, a bar, a Turkish bath, a pretty courtyard garden and genuinely charming owners – Walter and Sandro – who manage to be warm and laid-back in just the right ratio. This hotel is at the less expensive end of the moderate price range, becoming remarkably budget in low season.

La Calcina
Dorsoduro 780, fondamenta delle Zattere (041 520 6466, www.lacalcina.com). Vaporetto Accademia or Zattere. Rooms 29. Map p170 E9.

La Calcina is a perennial favourite – Victorian critic John Ruskin opted to stay here – but remains great value at quieter moments. The open vistas of the Giudecca canal provide the backdrop for meals taken on the terrace of this hotel, a view shared by the bedrooms at the front of the building. With an air of civilised calm, La Calcina is one of the best-value hotels in its category. Rooms have parquet floors, 19th-century furniture and a refreshingly uncluttered feel; one single is without private bath. There is an *altana* (suspended roof terrace), and a number of suites and self-catering apartments are available in adjacent buildings.

CimaRosa Boutique B&B
Santa Croce 1958, calle Tron (www.cimarosavenezia.com). Vaporetto San Stae. Rooms 5. Map p146 G6.

The supremely stylish B&B in the quiet northern Santa Croce district has just five beautiful rooms, their colours picking up the hues of the city. On the ground floor, the water of

the Grand Canal laps outside the windows of a chic but comfortable living room where breakfast is served. Upstairs, a kitchenette has tea- and coffee-making equipment plus a fridge to keep your wine cool. Three of the bedrooms overlook the canal. Owner-manager Brittany and her architect husband created this Venetian home-from-home; her all-female team cossett guests through their stay. Book early because returnee guests fill the place up quickly.

Locanda Novecento
San Marco 2683-4, calle del Dose (041 241 3765, www.novecento. biz). Vaporetto Giglio. Rooms 9. Map p82 F8.

This home-from-home with a gently exotic edge is a real pleasure to come back to after a hard day's sightseeing, especially when it's warm enough to relax in the delightful little garden. With its friendly, helpful staff, and reading and sitting rooms, Novecento is a very special place to stay. Wooden floors, ethnic textiles, oriental rugs, Indonesian furniture and individually decorated rooms make a refreshing change from the ubiquitous pan-Venetian style. Art shows are regularly mounted in the public rooms.

Locanda Orseolo
San Marco 1083, corte Zorzi (041 520 4827, www.locandaorseolo. com). Vaporetto Rialto or San Marco Vallaresso. Rooms 15. Map p82 H7.

This wonderfully welcoming *locanda* has beamed ceilings, painted wood panelling, leaded windows and rich colours; there's even a tiny water entrance. The immaculate bedrooms are ranged over three floors (there's no lift) and are furnished in a fairly restrained Venetian style. Choose between a canal view (which can be noisy) or quieter rooms overlooking the square. Breakfast is exceptionally generous. The team that runs the place bend over backwards to ensure their guests are happy. This delightful hotel is fiendishly difficult to find: go through the iron gate almost opposite the church in

campo San Gallo, bear left into a smaller campo and you'll see the sign.

Oltre il Giardino
San Polo 2542, fondamenta Contarini (041 275 0015, www. oltreilgiardino-venezia.com). Vaporetto San Tomà. Rooms 6. Map p146 E6.

Tucked away at the end of a *fondamenta* and accessed through a *giardino* (garden), this attractive villa was once owned by Alma Mahler, widow of the composer Gustav. Today, host Lorenzo Muner welcomes guests to this stylish yet homely hotel. Going against the deep-hued, brocaded Venetian grain, Oltre il Giardino's neutral/pastel shades and wood floors provide the backdrop for a mix of antique furniture, contemporary objets and unexpected splashes. Subtly colour-themed bedrooms vary considerably in size; the large suites and junior suites can be equipped with beds in their living room, and are perfect for groups or families. All are equipped with LCD TVs, robes, slippers and luxurious bath goodies.

Budget
B&B San Marco
Castello 3385L, fondamenta San Giorgio degli Schiavoni (041 522 7589, 335 756 6555, http://www. realvenice.it/smarco_index. htm). Vaporetto San Zaccaria. Closed Jan; 2wks Aug. Rooms 3. Map p108 L7.

One of the few Venetian B&Bs that come close to the British concept of the genre, Marco Scurati's homely apartment lies just behind San Giorgio degli Schiavoni. Two of the three cosy, antique-filled bedrooms share a bathroom and so work particularly well as a suite for a family or group; the other is en-suite. Marco and his wife Alice serve breakfast in their own kitchen and guests are treated very much as part of the family.

Generator
Giudecca 86, fondamenta delle Zitelle (041 877 8288, http:// generatorhostels.com). Vaporetto Zitelle. Beds 240. Map p190 F2.

ACCOMMODATION

Venice's once-dowdy youth hostel has undergone the Generator treatment, emerging with some hip decor, infinitely more inviting public spaces, a lively nightlife scene and a restaurant. There are double, triple and quad rooms suitable for families, and dorms sleeping up to 16 people, some of which are women-only. Though prices are low when the city's quiet, they do follow the trend elsewhere and rise sharply at busy times; breakfast and other meals are extra. People travelling on a tight budget should factor in the cost of a *vaporetto* pass, because most of what you'll be wanting to visit is over the water.

Hotel Rio
Castello 4358, campiello Santi Filippo e Giacomo (041 520 8222, www.hotelriovenezia.com). Vaporetto San Zaccaria. **Rooms** *18.* **Map** *p118 M10.*
Spread over four adjoining buildings and dotted around narrow corridors, the 18 rooms of the Rio are surprisingly chic and comfortable after a recent makeover. Friendly young staff and services such as beverage-making equipment in a small common room compensate for downsides such as tiny bathrooms. Some rooms sleep up to four people. The hotel's position is perfect for intense sightseeing, just minutes away from St Mark's square and very handy for a busy *vaporetto* stop.

San Samuele
San Marco 3358, salizada San Samuele (041 520 5165, www. hotelsansamuele.com). Vaporetto San Samuele or Sant'Angelo. **Rooms** *10.* **Map** *p82 E7.*
Flowers cascade from the window boxes of this delightful, friendly little hotel in an excellent location. The spotlessly clean rooms have a simple, sunny aspect and the welcome is always warm. The San Samuele is several notches above most of its fellow one-star establishments, although both the single rooms and one of the doubles have bathrooms in the corridor, and walls are rather thin. There's free Wi-Fi throughout and staff are always ready with well-informed advice and recommendations. Plans are afoot to add further 'superior' rooms upstairs, all with air-con. San Samuele is very popular, so book well in advance. Breakfast is not included, though there's a coffee machine in reception for guests, and a fridge to keep your supplies in.

Silk Road
Dorsoduro 1420E, calle Cortelogo (388 119 6816, www. silkroadhostel.com). Vaporetto San Basilio. **Rooms** *5.* **Map** *p170 C9.*
Sparse, basic but well placed and extremely clean, Silk Road offers four-bed women's, men's and mixed dorms, plus one double room. There are good-sized lockers for all in the dorms, and the kitchen – where owner Alex will spontaneously cook up meals for guests from time to time – is equipped with a big fridge and other facilities. The vibe is convivial, and lone women travellers will feel totally safe.

Venice Certosa Hotel
Isola della Certosa (041 277 8632, hotel.ventodivenezia.it). Vaporetto Certosa. **Rooms** *18.*
Facing across the lagoon towards the eastern end of Castello and a short hop from Venice proper on the 4.1/4.2 *vaporetto*, this bright, modern hostel/hotel on the quiet island of Certosa (*see p210*) has a pine forest on one side and a forest of masts on the other – and a large percentage of yachties from the neighbouring marina occupying its clean, simple rooms. There's a night shuttle service from the city centre, and a restaurant for those times when you can't face another lagoon crossing. The hotel lies somewhere between the budget and moderate range.

Generator *p293*

Getting Around

ARRIVING & LEAVING

By air
Low-cost carriers fly visitors to Venice through Venice, Treviso and Verona airports. National carriers fly principally to Venice, although some have services to Verona.

Venice Marco Polo Airport
Switchboard 041 260 6111, flight & airport information 041 260 9260, www.veniceairport.it.
You can get a bus or taxi (*see below*) to piazzale Roma, but you may find that the **Alilaguna boat service** (041 240 1701, www.alilaguna.it) drops you nearer your hotel. The dock is seven minutes' walk from arrivals; porter service costs €5 per bag. Various Alilaguna services call at San Marco, Rialto, Fondamenta Nove, Guglie, Zattere, Ca' Rezzonico, Sant'Angelo, San Stae, Zitelle, San Zaccaria, Arsenale, Lido, Bacini, Ospedale, Murano Colonna and Madonna dell'Orto vaporetto stops, as well as the Mulino Stucky Hilton on the Giudecca island, and at the Stazione Marittima cruise ship terminal: check which is handiest for your final destination. Main services are hourly, others less frequent. Tickets (€15 to Venice, the Lido or the Stazione Marittima) can be purchased at Alilaguna's counter in the arrivals hall or on board. Allow 70 mins to San Marco.

Two **bus** companies operate services from the airport. The slower bus 5, run by **ACTV** (041 272 2111, timetable information 041 24 24, www.actv.it), travels between the airport and piazzale Roma, leaving every 15 mins; journey time 25-30 mins. Tickets (€8; €15 return) can be purchased

at the machine next to the bus stop at the airport, or at any ACTV/ Hellovenezia ticket office; discounted fares are available when purchased together with tourist transport passes; *see p296.*

The quicker, non-stop bus service (20 mins) between the airport and piazzale Roma is run by **ATVO** (0421 594 671/672, www.atvo.it). Buy tickets (€8; €15 return) from the ATVO counter at the airport, or at their piazzale Roma office. You may also be able to just pay the driver directly if you have exact change.

A regular **taxi** from the airport to piazzale Roma costs €40 and takes about 20 mins. You can pay in advance by credit card in the arrivals hall at the **Cooperativa Artigiana Radio Taxi** desk (041 59 64).

The most luxurious way to reach the centre is by **water taxi**. **Consorzio Motoscafi Venezia** (041 522 2303) charges from €100 for the half-hour crossing. *See p297* Water taxis.

Sant'Angelo Airport
(Treviso) *0422 315 111, www.trevisoairport.it.*
ATVO (0422 315 381, www.atvo.it) bus services run between the airport and Venice's piazzale Roma to coincide with flights – if the flight arrives late, the bus will wait. The journey takes about 70 mins, and costs €12 one way, €22 return (valid for ten days). Buses from piazzale Roma to Treviso airport leave ridiculously early, so ensure your timely arrival.

Alternatively, there are **trains** between Treviso and Venice (35 mins), with connections between the airport and station by bus or taxi (**Taxi Padova**, 049 651 333); **ACTT** (0422 32 71)

bus 6 does the 20-minute trip at frequent intervals throughout the day and costs €1.30.

Valerio Catullo Airport
(Verona) *045 809 5666, www.aeroportoverona.it.*
A **bus** (0458 057911) runs every 20 mins to Verona train station, from 5.35am to 11.10pm. The 20-minute journey costs €6 (pay on board). For transport between Verona and Venice, *see p221.*

Major airlines
Alitalia *89 20 10, www.alitalia.com.*
British Airways *199 712 266, www.britishairways.com.*
Easyjet *848 887 766, www.easyjet.com.*
Ryanair *(Treviso Airport) 895 895 8989, www.ryanair.com.*

By train
The **Trenitalia** website (www.trenitalia.com) gives exhaustive information on rail timetables, in English as well as Italian. Tickets can be booked through the website with a credit card; you'll receive an email with a barcode and a booking code, either of which should be presented (on your smartphone, tablet, computer and so on, or in a print-out) to inspectors on board the train. Trenitalia's national rail information and booking number is 892 021 (24hrs daily). Press 1 after the recorded message, then say 'altro' to speak to an operator (who may not speak English). Tickets can also be purchased at the station (*see below*) or at travel agents around the city bearing the Trenitalia logo.

The slowest trains are prefixed **R** (Regionale) or **RV** (Regionale Veloce) and are remarkably cheap; **IC** (Intercity) trains are slightly faster and cost a little more. **Frecce** high-speed trains are more expensive still, though there are large discounts to be had if you book online and well in advance: you will be given a reserved seat number when you book on Frecciarossa and Frecciargento trains.

If you have a regular railways-issued ticket, you must **validate** it in the machines on the platform before boarding or face a fine; if you forget, locate the inspector as soon as possible to waive the fine.

The private train operator **Italo** (www.italotreno.it) also runs high-speed services from Venice's Santa Lucia to Rome, Florence, Bologna, Naples, Padua and Salerno. It's worth checking the website, as prices can be competitive.

▶ *For details of trains to/from Padua, Verona and Vicenza, see p217, p221 and p225.*

Stazione di Venezia Santa Lucia *Vaporetto Ferrovia.* **Open** *Information 7am-9pm daily. Tickets 6am-9pm daily.* **Map** *p128.*

This is Venice's main station. Most trains arrive here, though a few will only take you as far as Mestre on the mainland; if so, change to a local train (every ten minutes or less during the day) for the short hop across the lagoon. Tickets can be bought from the counters in the main hall (all major credit cards accepted) or from vending machines throughout the station (For other options, *see above.*)

By bus
Long-distance buses to Venice all arrive at piazzale Roma.

By car
Prohibitive parking fees make cars one of the least practical modes of arrival, and you certainly won't want your car in the city (*see p298* Driving). Many Venetian hotels offer their guests discounts at car parks, and VeneziaUnica (*see p306*) has special offers too. Main car parks (all open 24hrs) are listed below.

Autorimessa Comunale
Santa Croce 496, piazzale Roma (041 272 7301, avm.avmspa.it/it/content/autorimessa-comunale-0). Vaporetto Piazzale Roma. **Rates** *€26 per 24hrs or part thereof.* **Map** *p146.*

Marco Polo Park Venice *Marco Polo Airport (041 260 3060, www.veniceairport.it). Bus 5 from piazzale Roma, or free shuttle bus from main entrance of Venice airport.* **Rates** *from €5.50/day (discounts for longer periods).*

Parking Stazione *Viale Stazione 10, Mestre (041 938 021). Bus 2 from piazzale Roma or train to Mestre station.* **Rates** *€16/day.*

Venezia Tronchetto Parking
Isola Nuova del Tronchetto 1 (041 520 7555, www.veniceparking.it). Vaporetto Tronchetto. **Rates** *€3/ hr; €21/day.*

PUBLIC TRANSPORT

Public transport – including vaporetti (water buses) and local buses – in Venice itself and in some mainland areas is run by **ACTV** (www.actv.it). **ATVO** (0421 594 671, www.atvo.it) runs more extensive bus services to numerous destinations on the mainland.

Information
Venezia Unica's extremely helpful call centre (041 2424) provides information on vaporetto and bus schedules. Its outlets at many vaporetto stops sell tickets and **Venezia Unica** passes (*see p306*) which allow users to buy multiple services and access them all through one ticket. If you're lucky, you can also pick up one of the free transport timetable booklets, but these are published at the start of the season and tend to run out swiftly; timetables are posted at all vaporetto stops.

The free VeneziaUnica app has real-time transport information and can be downloaded from Google Play or the iTunes store.

Vaporetti
Venice's vaporetti (water buses) run to a very tight schedule, with sailing times for each line marked clearly at stops. Strikes sometimes occur, but are always announced in advance; look out for notices posted inside vaporetto stops bearing the title *sciopero* (strike). Services are also curtailed and rerouted for Venice's many rowing regattas; these disruptions are also announced with posters in vaporetto stops.

Regular services run from about 5am to around midnight, after which a frequent night service (N) operates.

Taking a boat in the wrong direction is all too easy. Remember: if you're standing with your back to the station and want to head down the Grand Canal, take Line 1 (slow) or Line 2 (faster) heading left.

Not all passenger ferries are, strictly speaking, vaporetti. A **vaporetto** is larger, slower and more rounded in shape, and has room for 230 passsengers; older boats have outside seats at the front that are much sought-after. These vessels follow routes along the Grand Canal.

The **motoscafo** is sleeker, smaller (160 passengers) and has outside seats only at the back. It runs on routes encircling the island. **Motonave** are large double-decker steamers, taking 600-1,200 passengers, and cross the lagoon to the Lido.

A **single trip** by vaporetto costs €7.50 (valid for 75 mins on multiple boats); a **shuttle journey** (ie one stop across the Grand Canal, the hop across to the Giudecca, or from Sant'Elena to the Lido) is €5. Passes for **24hrs** (€20), **36hrs** (€25), **48hrs** (€30), **72hrs** (€40) or **1 week** (€60) are also available and can be purchased as part of a Venezia Unica package (*see p306*). Tickets and passes can be bought from *tabacchi* (*see p305*) and at Venezia Unica counters at many vaporetto stops; stops without ticket counters have automatic ticket-dispensing machines. Once you're on board, you can only buy single tickets.

Tickets must be validated prior to boarding the vaporetto, by swiping them in front of the machines at the entrance to the jetty. Note that for multiple journey tickets you need only stamp your ticket once, at the start of the first journey.

Traghetti

The best way to cross the Grand Canal when you're far from a bridge is to hop on a *traghetto*. These unadorned *gondole* are rowed back and forth at fixed points along the canal. At €2 (70c for resident travel card holders), this is the cheapest gondola ride in the city – Venetians make the short hop standing up.

Traghetti ply between the following points:

Santa Sofia–Pescheria
7.30am-8pm Mon-Sat; 8.45am-7pm Sun. **Map** *p128 J7.*

Riva del Carbon–Riva del Vin
8am-12.30pm Mon-Sat. **Map** *p82 J9.*

Ca' Garzoni–San Tomà *7.30am-8pm Mon-Sat; 8.30am-7.30pm Sun.* **Map** *p82.*

San Samuele–Ca' Rezzonico
7.45am-12.30pm Mon-Sat. **Map** *p170 F10.*

Santa Maria del Giglio–Santa Maria della Salute *9am-6pm daily.* **Map** *p170 H13.*

Punta della Dogana–Vallaresso *9am-2pm daily.* **Map** *p82 K12.*

Buses

ACTV buses operate to both Mestre and Marghera on the mainland, as well as serving the Lido, Pellestrina and Chioggia.

Services for the mainland depart from piazzale Roma (*see map p146*). From midnight until 5am, buses N1 (leaving every 30 mins) and N2 (leaving every hour) depart from Mestre for piazzale Roma, and vice versa. There are also regular night buses from the Lido (departing at least hourly) to Malamocco, Alberoni and Pellestrina.

Bus tickets, costing €1.50 (also available in blocks of ten tickets for €14), are valid for 75 mins, during which you may use several buses, though you can't make a return journey on the same ticket. They can be purchased from ACTV/ Venezia Unica ticket booths (*see p306*) or from *tabacchi* (*see p305*) anywhere in the city. They should be bought before boarding the bus and then stamped on board.

WATER TAXIS

Water taxis are hugely expensive: expect to pay €100 from the airport (*see p295*) directly to any single destination in Venice, and more for multiple stops. The minimum possible cost for a 15-minute trip from hotel to restaurant is €60, with most journeys averaging €110 once numbers of passengers and baggage have been taken into account. In all cases, tariffs are for five people or less, with each extra passenger charged €10 up to a maximum of ten people. Between

the hours of 10pm and 7am, there is a surcharge of €10.

Taxi pick-up points can be found at piazzale Roma, outside the train station, next to the Rialto vaporetto stop, and next to San Marco-Vallaresso vaporetto stop, but it's more reliable to call and order yourself. Pre-booking through the **Motoscafi Venezia** website can give discounts on some routes. Avoid asking your hotel to book a taxi for you, as they frequently add a 10% mark-up. Beware of unlicensed taxis, which charge even more than authorised ones. The latter have a black number on a yellow background.
Consorzio Motoscafi Venezia
041 240 6711, 522 2303, www. motoscafivenezia.it. **Open** *24hrs daily.*

GONDOLAS

For an overview of gondola trips in Venice, *see p63* Gondolas. Official gondola stops can be found at (or near) the following locations:

Fondamenta Bacino Orseolo **Map** *p82 K11.*
Riva degli Schiavoni *in front of the Hotel Danieli.* **Map** *p82 M11.*
San Marco Vallaresso *vaporetto stop.* **Map** *p82 K12.*
Santa Lucia *railway station.* **Map** *p128 D6.*
Piazzale Roma *bus terminus.* **Map** *p146 B7.*

Traghetto near ponte di Rialto

Water taxi

**Santa Maria del
Giglio** *vaporetto stop.* **Map**
p82 H13.
Piazzetta San Marco *jetty.* **Map**
p82 M11.
Campo Santa Sofia *near Ca'
d'Oro vaporetto stop.* **Map**
p128 J6.
San Tomà *vaporetto stop.* **Map**
p146 F10.
Campo San Moisè *by the Hotel
Bauer.* **Map** *p82 K12.*
Riva del Carbon *at the southern
end of the Rialto Bridge, near the
vaporetto stop.* **Map** *p82 J9.*

Fares
These are set by the **Istituzione
per la Conservazione
della Gondola e Tutela del
Gondoliere** (Gondola Board; 041
528 5075, www.gondolavenezia.
it). Prices are €80 for 30 mins and
€40 for each additional 20 mins
during the day (8am-7pm), and
€100 for 40 mins, €50 for each
additional 20 mins, at night
(7pm-8am). Prices are for six
passengers or fewer; having your
own personal crooner will push
the fare up. In the event that a
gondolier tries to overcharge you
– and it does happen: be prepared
to stick to your guns – complain to
the Gondola Board.

DRIVING

Driving is an impossibility in
Venice: even if your vehicle was

capable of going up and down
stairs and squeezing through
the narrowest of alleyways, it
wouldn't be legal for you to do
so. Instead, you'll need to park
on the outskirts and walk or use
alternative means of transport.
   You can drive on the Lido, but
there aren't many places to go.
A car ferry (route 17) leaves from
the Tronchetto ferry stop for Lido
San Niccolò every 50 mins and
the cost is determined by the
size of your car, starting at €26
per car, plus a regular vaporetto
ticket (*see p199*) per person.

Car breakdowns *(Automobile
Club d'Italia) 803 116.*
CCISS traffic news *1518.*

Car hire
It's only worth hiring a car if
you are planning to visit the
Veneto countryside or travel
further afield. If you decide to
rent a car, motorcycle or moped
while in Italy, make sure you pay
the extra charge to upgrade to
comprehensive insurance cover.

Avis *041 523 7377, www.
avisautonoleggio.it.*
Europcar *041 523 8616, www.
europcar.it.*
Hertz *041 528 4091, www.
hertz.it.*
Maggiore National *041 523
7377, www.maggiore.it.*

Mattiazzo *041 522 0884, www.
mattiazzo.it.* Chauffeur-driven
limousine hire.

Parking
For a list of car parks, *see p296.*

CYCLING

Bicycles are banned – and otiose
– in Venice itself, but are a great
way of exploring the Lido (*see
p196*) or Sant'Erasmo (*see p211*).

Cycle hire
Lido on Bike *Gran Viale 21B,
Lido (041 526 8019, www.
lidoonbike.it).* **Open** *Mar-Sept
9am-7pm daily.* **Rates** *€5/1.5hr;
€9/day.*
Venice Bike Rental *Gran
viale Santa Maria Elisabetta
79A, Lido (041 526 1490, www.
venicebikerental.com).* **Open**
Mar-Oct 8.30am-8pm daily.
Rates *€4/hr; €9/day. No cards.*

WALKING

Much of your Venetian
sightseeing will be done on
foot. Be aware that there are
over 400 bridges, all with steps.
For etiquette tips and how to
traverse Venice when it floods,
see p67 Walk Like a Venetian. For
tour guides, *see p307.*

Resources A-Z

Travel Advice

For up-to-date information on travel to a specific country – including the latest on safety and security, health issues, local laws and customs – contact your government's department of foreign affairs. Most have websites with useful advice for would-be travellers.

Australia
www.smartraveller.gov.au

Republic of Ireland
foreignaffairs.gov.ie

Canada
www.voyage.gc.ca

UK
www.fco.gov.uk/travel

New Zealand
www.safetravel.govt.nz

USA
www.state.gov/travel

ACCIDENT & EMERGENCY

For ambulance, police or fire services, call the **Numero Unico Emergenze** 112.

Medical emergencies

For urgent medical advice from local health authority doctors during the night, call 041 238 5600 in Venice and on the Lido, and 041 238 5631 in Mestre (8pm-8am Mon-Fri; 10pm Sat-8am Mon). The following hospitals have 24-hour casualty departments (*pronto soccorso*):

Ospedale dell'Angelo *Via Tosatto, Mestre (041 965 7111). A huge hospital on the outskirts of Mestre.*

Ospedale Civile *Castello 6777, campo Santi Giovanni e Paolo (041 529 4111, casualty 041 529 4516). Vaporetto Ospedale. Map p108 N6.* Housed in the 15th-century Scuola di San Marco (*see p115*), Venice's main civic hospital has helpful staff and doctors who are quite likely to speak English.

Other emergencies

Thefts or losses should be reported immediately at the nearest police station (either the Polizia di Stato or Carabinieri; *see p304*). Report the loss of your passport to the nearest consulate or embassy (*see p301*). Report the loss of credit cards or travellers' cheques to your credit card company (*see p303*).

ADDRESSES

Postal addresses in Venice consist of the name of the *sestiere* (district) plus the house number. With only this information, you will probably never reach your destination. For convenience, we have also given the name of the *calle* (street) or *campo* (square) etc, where each place is located. But finding your way around remains a challenge, especially as matters are sometimes complicated by there being an official Italian and several unofficial Venetian dialect names in use for the same location. When asking for directions, make sure you ascertain the nearest vaporetto stop, church, large square or other easily identifiable local landmark.

AGE RESTRICTIONS

Buying/drinking alcohol 18.
Driving 18.
Sex (hetero- & homosexual) 14.
Smoking 16.

CLIMATE

Venice's unique position gives the city a bizarre mix of weather conditions. During the winter, high levels of humidity often make winter days seem colder than their average few degrees above zero, and summer days become humid as soon as the thermometer rises above 25°C (77°F).

Strong north-easterlies in winter, coming off the snow-covered Alps (snow in the city is rare) have bone-chilling effects but make the weather crisp and clear, with blue skies and great views. In the still summer months, high humidity can make it stiflingly hot; a warm southerly wind called the *scirocco* makes the heat more intense.

Autumn and spring are generally mild, with occasional pea-soup fog. August and November are the rainiest months, while *acqua alta* is mainly an autumn and winter event.

CONSUMER

Tourism-related complaints are handled by Tourist Mediation Counter (phone 041 2424).

CUSTOMS

If you arrive from an EU country you are not required to declare goods imported into or exported from Italy as long as they are for personal use.
For people arriving from non-EU countries the following limits apply:
• 200 cigarettes or 100 cigarillos or 50 cigars or 250g of tobacco.
• 1l of spirits or 2l of wine.
• one bottle of perfume (50ml), 250ml of eau de toilette.
• gift items not exceeding €430 (€150 for children under 15). Anything above these limits will be subject to taxation at the port of entry. For more information, call customs

(*dogana*) at Marco Polo Airport on 041 269 9311 or consult www.agenziadoganemonopoli.gov.it. If you are not an EU citizen, remember to keep your official receipt (*scontrino*) as you are entitled to a rebate on IVA (sales tax) paid on purchases of personal goods costing more than €155, as long as they leave the country unused and are bought from a shop that provides this service. Make sure there's a sign displayed in the window, and also ask for the form that you'll need to show at customs on departure. For more information about customs, see the Italian government website, **www.agenziadoganemonopoli.gov.it**, which has a section in English.

DISABLED

With its narrow streets, 400-plus stepped bridges and lack of barriers between canals and pavements, this city is no easy task for anyone with impaired mobility or vision to negotiate. But with determination and forward planning, Venice is far from impossible, and recent efforts to make the city more negotiable for disabled travellers have helped.

Start your research on the city council website, **www.comune.venezia.com**. Type '*Venezia accessibile*' into the search box; once you reach the page, you'll find the English option button. Here you'll find itineraries and a useful map of barrier-free zones; at the time of writing, the map still showed long-removed stairlifts previously installed on some bridges.

VeneziaUnica (041 2424, www.veneziaunica.it) also provides information and shows itineraries without barriers, as well as hosting a helpful FAQ section on its 'Accessible Venice' pages.

Alilaguna (www.alilaguna.it) services between the airport and Venice proper can carry wheelchairs, as can most vaporetti: these will move you between bridge-free areas of the city in an enjoyable fashion. Staff will help you on and off the boats, and ensure that assigned areas are available; if they're

short-tempered at peak times, don't take offence – they're like that with everyone. Tickets for wheelchair users cost €1.50 for 75 mins; if you have an *accompagnatore*, s/he travels free.

Transport

Public transport is one area where Venice scores higher than many other destinations, as standard vaporetti and *motonavi* have a reasonably large, flat deck area and there are no steps or steep inclines on the route between quayside and boat, enabling easy travel along the Grand Canal, on lines 1 and 2. Lines that circle the city use *motoscafi*; some of their older models have not yet been adapted to accommodate wheelchairs, although the onboard ACTV personnel are unerringly helpful. The vaporetto lines that currently guarantee disabled access (though peak times should be avoided if possible) are 1, 2, LN and N. Some of the buses that run between Mestre and Venice also have wheelchair access. For further details, consult the Accessible Venice site; for train- or plane-related information, phone

Trenitalia (199 303 060) or **Marco Polo Airport** (041 260 9260).

DRUGS

Anyone caught in possession of any quantity of drugs of any kind will be taken before a magistrate. There is no distinction between possession for personal use and intent to supply. All offenders are therefore subject to stiff penalties, including lengthy prison sentences. Foreigners can expect to be swiftly deported. Couriering or dealing can land you in prison for up to 20 years.

ELECTRICITY

Italy's electricity system runs on 220/230V. To use British or US appliances, you will need two-pin adaptor plugs: these are best bought before leaving home, as they tend to be expensive in Italy and are not always easy to find. If you do need to buy one here, try any electrical retailer (look for *Casalinghi*, *Elettrodomestici* or *Ferramenta* in the yellow pages).

Climate

Average temperatures and monthly rainfall in Venice

	High (°C/°F)	Low (°C/°F)	Rainfall (mm/in)
January	6/42	-1/30	58/2.3
February	8/47	1/33	54/2.1
March	12/54	4/39	57/2.2
April	16/61	8/46	64/2.5
May	21/70	12/54	69/2.7
June	25/77	16/61	76/3.0
July	28/82	18/64	63/2.5
August	27/81	17/63	83/3.3
September	24/75	14/58	66/2.6
October	18/65	9/49	69/2.7
November	12/53	4/40	87/3.4
December	7/44	0/32	54/2.1

EMBASSIES & CONSULATES

There are a handful of diplomatic missions in Venice. But for most information, and in emergencies, you will probably have to contact offices in Rome or Milan. There is no longer a British Consulate in Venice; for assistance, refer to the duty officer at the Milan consulate. There is a US Consular Agency in Venice, open by appt only (041 541 5944). Citizens of other countries should refer to http://embassy.goabroad.com/.

Consulates in Milan
Australia *02 7767 4200.*
Ireland *02 5518 7569.*
New Zealand *02 7217 0001.*
South Africa *02 885 8581.*
United Kingdom *06 4220 2431.*
United States *02 290 351.*

Embassies in Rome
Australia *06 852 721.*
Canada *06 85444 2911.*
Ireland *06 585 2381.*
New Zealand *06 853 7501.*
South Africa *06 8525 4262.*
United Kingdom *06 4220 0001.*
United States *06 46741.*

HEALTH

The *pronto soccorso* (casualty department) of public hospitals provides free emergency treatment for travellers of any nationality. The public relations department of Venice's **Ospedale Civile** (041 529 4588) can provide general information on being hospitalised in Venice. EU citizens are entitled to reciprocal medical care if they have an EHIC (European Health Insurance Card) card, which, in the UK, can be applied for online (www.dh.gov.uk) or by post using forms that you can pick up at any post office. For minor treatments, take your EHIC card with you to any doctor for a free consultation. Drugs they prescribe can be bought at pharmacies (*see below*) at prices set by the health ministry. Tests or appointments with specialists in the public system (*Sistema sanità nazionale*, SSN) are charged at fixed rates (*il ticket*) and a receipt issued.

Non-EU citizens should review their private health insurance plans to see if expenses incurred while travelling are covered. If not, some form of travel health insurance is strongly advised (*see p301* Insurance).

Contraception & abortion
Condoms are on sale near the checkout in supermarkets, or over the counter at chemists. The contraceptive pill is freely available with a prescription at any pharmacy. *Consultori familiari* (family-planning clinics) are run by the local health authority; EU citizens with an EHIC card (*see left*) are entitled to use them, paying the same low charges for services and prescriptions as locals. Non-EU citizens may use the service and, depending on their insurance plan, claim refunds. The *consultori* are staffed by good gynaecologists – book ahead for a visit. Abortions are legal when performed in public hospitals.

Dentists
Dental treatment in Italy is expensive; your insurance may not cover it. For urgent dental issues, go to the **Ambulatorio Odontostomatologico** at the Ospedale Civile (*see p299*).

Hospitals
See p299 Accident & emergency.

Opticians
Most opticians will do emergency repairs on the spot.

Punto Vista (Elvio Carraro) *Cannaregio 1982, campiello Anconeta (041 720 453). Vaporetto San Marcuola.* **Open** *9am-1pm, 3.30-7.30pm Mon-Sat.* **Map** *p128 B2.*

Pharmacies
Pharmacies (*farmacie*), identified by a green or red cross above the door, are run by qualified chemists who will dispense informal advice on, and assistance for, minor ailments, as well as filling prescriptions. Over-the-counter drugs are much more expensive in Italy than in the UK

or US. They can be purchased in some larger supermarkets.

Most chemists are open 9am-12.30pm, 3.45-7.30pm Mon-Fri and 9am-12.45pm Sat. A small number remain open on Sat afternoon, Sun and at night on a duty rota system, details of which are posted outside every pharmacy.

Most pharmacies carry homeopathic medicines, and will check your blood pressure. If you require regular medication, bring adequate supplies with you. Ask your GP for the generic rather than the brand name of your medicine: it may be available in Italy under a different name.

Water
Forget *Death in Venice*-style cholera scares: tap water here is regularly checked, safe to drink and tastes good. Fountains throughout the city provide a constant source of free tap water.

ID

You are legally obliged to carry photo-ID with you at all times. Hotels will ask for an identification document when you check in, but they should take the details and return the ID to you immediately.

INSURANCE

EU nationals are entitled to reciprocal medical care in Italy, provided they are in possession of a European Health Insurance Card (EHIC; *see left*). Despite this provision, short-term visitors from all countries are advised to get private travel insurance to cover a broad number of eventualities (from injury to theft). Non-EU citizens should always ensure that they take out comprehensive medical insurance with a reputable company before leaving home. Visitors should also take out adequate property insurance before setting off for Italy. If you rent a car, motorcycle or moped, make sure that you pay the extra for full insurance and sign the collision damage waiver before taking off in the vehicle. It's also worth checking your home insurance first, as it may already cover you.

INTERNET & WI-FI

Most hotels, of all standards, offer Wi-Fi. Very few now charge for it, but to avoid surprises, it's best to enquire before you use. A city-wide Wi-Fi service is accessible for a fee through VeneziaUnica (*see p306*). However, you will find no shortage of cafés and bars offering free Wi-Fi. If you opt to use an internet café, you will be asked to present ID to conform with anti-terrorism laws.

LANGUAGE

Although Italian is the official language, some locals speak the Venetian dialect, too; this is also used interchangeably with Italian for local place names, which can be confusing. English is spoken by staff in hotels, at major sights and in all but the most spit-and-sawdust restaurants, but a smattering of Italian will help you get the most from your trip. *See also p308* Vocabulary. For details of language schools, *see p305* Study.

LEFT LUGGAGE

Marco Polo Airport *Arrivals hall, ground floor, behind the bar (041 260 5043).* **Open** *5am-9pm daily.* **Rates** *€6 per item per day. No cards.*
Piazzale Roma bus terminus *041 523 1107.* **Open** *6am-9pm daily.* **Rates** *€7 per item per day. No cards.* **Map** *p146 B9.*
Santa Lucia railway station *041 785 670.* **Open** *6am-11pm daily.* **Rates** *€6 per item per 5hrs; 90¢ every additional hour from 6am to midnight, 40¢ every additional hour after midnight. No cards.* **Map** *p128 C6.*

LEGAL HELP

If you are in need of legal advice, your first stop should always be your consulate or embassy (*see p301*).

LGBT

The national gay rights group **ArciGay** (www.arcigay.it) sponsors activities, festivals, counselling and AIDS awareness. In Venice, the city council's **Osservatorio LGBT** keeps a weather eye out for acts of discrimination or intolerance around the lagoon and posts news of any LGBT-related events and initiatives on its blog queervenice.blogspot.it (Italian only). **Anddos** (www.anddos. org) membership (€10-17) is often needed to enter gay venues in Italy; it can be purchased at the door, though many venues will waive the requirement for tourists. In a city so used to, and tolerant of, an immense diversity of travellers, you'll be hard pressed to find a hotel that *isn't* gay-friendly. That said, there are some clear favourites, including **Al Ponte Mocenigo** (*see p292*) and **San Samuele** (*see p294*). Others include **B&B Fujiyama** (Dorsoduro 2727A, calle lunga San Barnaba, 041 724 1042, www.fujiyama.life), **Alle Guglie B&B** (Cannaregio 1308, calle del Magazen, 320 360 7829, www. alleguglie.com) and the **Molino Stucky Hilton** (Giudecca 810, fondamenta San Giacomo, 041 272 3311, www.molinostuckyhilton. com).

LIBRARIES

Most of the libraries listed below have online catalogues. For assistance with in-depth research at the national level consult the **Servizio bibliotecario nazionale** website (www.sbn.it). In most cases, you will need ID and/or a letter of presentation to use these libraries; they do not lend books to non-members.

Archivio di Stato *San Polo 3002, campo dei Frari (041 522 2281, www.archiviodistatovenezia. it). Vaporetto San Tomà.* **Open** *8.10am-5.50pm Mon-Fri.* **Map** *p146 E9.* The state archives house all official documents relating to the administration of the Venetian Republic, and a host of other historic manuscripts. Material must be

requested between 8.10am and 1pm Mon-Fri.
Archivio Storico delle Arti Contemporanee (ASAC) *Padiglione Centrale ai Giardini di Castello, calle Paludo Sant'Antonio (041 521 8939, www.labiennale.org/ it/asac). Vaporetto Giardini.* **Open** *10am-5pm Tue-Fri.* **Map** *p108 V14.* Located inside the Biennale gardens, at the eastern end of Castello, this is the archive of the Venice Biennale contemporary art festival (*see p121*).
Biblioteca Centrale IUAV *Santa Croce 191, fondamenta Tolentini (041 257 2315, http://sbd.iuav. it/). Vaporetto Piazzale Roma.* **Open** *9am-11.45pm Mon-Fri (from 2pm 1st Mon of mth).* **Map** *p146 C9.* The library of one of Italy's top architecture faculties has a vast collection of works on the history of architecture, town planning, art, engineering and social sciences.
Biblioteca Fondazione Giorgio Cini *Isola di San Giorgio Maggiore (041 271 0255, www. cini.it). Vaporetto San Giorgio.* **Open** *9am-6pm Mon-Fri.* **Map** *p190 N14.* The Giorgio Cini Foundation houses libraries that are dedicated to art history, Venetian history, literature, theatre and music.
Biblioteca Fondazione Scientifica Querini Stampalia *Castello 5252, campo Santa Maria Formosa (041 271 1411, www.querinistampalia. org). Vaporetto Rialto or San Zaccaria.* **Open** *10am-midnight Tue-Sat; 10am-7pm Sun.* **Map** *p108 M9.* A collection with an emphasis on all things Venetian. *See also p112.*
Biblioteca Museo Correr *San Marco 52, piazza San Marco (041 240 5211, www.visitmuve.it). Vaporetto San Marco Vallaresso.* **Open** *8.30am-1.30pm Mon, Wed, Fri; 8.30am-5pm Tue, Thur.* **Map** *p82 K11.* This small library contains prints, manuscripts and books about Venetian history and art history.
Biblioteca Nazionale Marciana *San Marco 7, piazzetta San Marco (041 240 7211, www.marciana.venezia. sbn.it). Vaporetto San Marco Vallaresso.* **Open** *8am-7pm*

Mon-Fri; 8am-1.30pm Sat. **Map p82 L11.** The city's main public library has medieval manuscripts and editions of the classics dating from the 15th century.

Ca' Foscari Cultural Flow Zone *Dorsoduro 1392, Zattere (041 234 5811, www.unive. it/cfz). Vaporetto Zattere.* **Open** *9am-midnight Mon-Fri; 9am-8pm Sat; 2pm-midnight Sun.* **Map p170 E11.** This modern space functions as a cultural centre dedicated to promoting exchange amongst students.

LOST PROPERTY

Your mislaid belongings may end up at one of the *uffici oggetti smarriti* listed below. You could also try the police (*see p304*), or get in touch with **Veritas**, the city's rubbish collection department (041 729 1111).

ACTV *Santa Croce, piazzale Roma c/o Garage comunale AVM (041 272 2179). Vaporetto Piazzale Roma.* **Open** *7am-7.30pm daily.* **Map p146 B9.** Items found on vaporetti or buses.

Comune (City Council) *San Marco 4136, riva del Carbon (041 274 8225). Vaporetto Rialto.* **Open** *9am-1pm Mon-Fri.* **Map p82 J9.**

FS/Stazione Santa Lucia *(041 78 55 31).* Staff hand over all lost and found items to the Comune of Venice (*see above*).

Marco Polo Airport *Arrivals Hall (WFS and GH Venezia 041 260 9228; AVIA Partner 041 260 9226/7, lost objects 041 260 9260). Bus 5 to Aeroporto.* **Open** *WFS and GH Venezia 10am-12.30pm; 2-6pm. AVIA Partner 10am-1pm; 3-6pm.*

MEDIA

For useful websites, *see p311.*

Daily newspapers (national and international)

Sometimes lengthy, turgid and featuring indigestible political stories, Italian newspapers can be a frustrating read. On the plus side, they are delightfully unpretentious and happily blend serious news, leaders by globally known commentators, and well-written, often surreal, crime and human-interest stories. Sports coverage in the dailies is extensive and thorough. There are also the mass-circulation sports papers *Corriere dello Sport, La Gazzetta dello Sport* and *Tuttosport.* The *Financial Times, Wall Street Journal, USA Today, International New York* and most European and (usually) UK dailies can be found on the day of issue at newsstands around town as well as online.

Corriere della Sera *www. corriere.it.* To the centre of centre-left, this solid, serious but often dull Milan-based daily is good on crime and foreign news.

La Repubblica *www.repubblica. it.* Centre-ish, left-ish La Repubblica is good on the Mafia and the Vatican, and comes up with the occasional scoop on its business pages.

Il Sole-24 Ore *www.ilsole24ore. com.* This business, finance and economics daily has a great arts supplement on Sun.

Daily newspapers (local)

Il Gazzettino *www.gazzettino. it. Il Gazzetino* is one of Italy's most successful local papers. It provides national and international news on the front pages and local news inside, with different editions for towns around the Veneto region.

La Nuova Venezia *http:// nuovavenezia.gelocal.it.* This popular, small-circulation daily – known to Venetians as La Nuova – contains lively editorials, crime stories, local news and event listings.

Magazines

Panorama (roughly centre right; www.panorama.it) and *L'Espresso* (centre left-ish; http:// espresso.repubblica.it/) provide a general round-up of the week's events, while *Sette* and *Venerdì* – respectively the colour supplements of *Corriere della Sera* (Thur) and *La Repubblica* (Fri) – have nice photos, though the quality of the journalism often leaves much to be desired.

For *Hello!*-style scandal, try *Gente* and *Oggi* with their weird mix of sex, glamour and religion, or the generally execrable scandal sheets *Eva 3000, Novella 2000* and *Cronaca Vera. Internazionale* (www. internazionale.it) provides an excellent digest of interesting bits and pieces gleaned from around the world the previous week.

But the biggest-selling magazine of them all is *Famiglia Cristiana*, which alternates Vatican line-toeing with Vatican baiting, depending on the state of relations between the Holy See and the idiosyncratic Paoline monks who produce it. It's available from newsstands or in most churches.

Radio

Radio Venezia *(FM 92.4)* Pop music, pop music, pop music. Did we mention pop music?

Radio Capital *(FM 98.5)* Heavy on advertising, but generous with information on city events and news. 1980s and '90s classics with a sprinkling of current hits.

Radio Padova *(FM 103.9)* Popular chart music and concert information for the Veneto area.

Television

Italy has six major networks (three are owned by the state broadcaster **RAI**, the other three belong to Silvio Berlusconi's **Mediaset** group). Dancing girls, variety shows, music and beauty competitions predominate. The standard of news and current affairs programmes varies. Television in the Veneto is now digital.

MONEY

Italy's currency is the euro (€). There are euro banknotes of €5, €10, €20, €100 and €200, and coins worth €1 and €2 as well as 1¢ (*centesimo*), 2¢, 5¢, 10¢, 20¢ and 50¢. Notes and coins from any euro-zone country are valid.

Banks & ATMs

Most banks (*banche*) have cash dispensers accepting cards

with the Maestro, Cirrus or Visa Electron symbols; the daily withdrawal limit is usually €250.

Most banks are open 8.20am-1.20pm and 2.45-3.45pm Mon-Fri. All banks are closed on public holidays and work reduced hours the day before a holiday, usually closing at 11am.

Changing money

The best exchange rates are to be had by withdrawing cash from ATMs. The exchange rates and commissions for currency transactions at banks vary greatly, but most offer more generous rates than bureaux de change (*cambio*). Travellers' cheques are almost a thing of the past: many banks no longer accept them and those that do charge large commissions.

Note that anywhere with a 'no commission' sign will probably offer dire exchange rates. There is no longer an American Express office in Venice.

Travelex *San Marco 5126, riva del Ferro (041 528 7358, www. travelex.it). Vaporetto Rialto.* **Open** *9.30am-6.45pm Mon-Sat; 9am-5pm Sun.* **Map** *p82 J9.* Cash and travellers' cheques exchanged. MasterCard and Visa cardholders can also withdraw cash – but note that you will need your passport or other valid photo ID. **Other locations** San Marco 142, piazza San Marco (041 277 5057); Marco Polo Airport arrivals (041 269 8271).

Lost or stolen cards

Report lost credit or debit cards to your issuing bank.

Tax

For information on reclaiming IVA (VAT or sales tax), *see p300.*

OPENING HOURS

Food shops traditionally close on Wed afternoon; non-food shops on Mon morning. In practice, larger shops are open six or even seven days a week, as are smaller ones at busier times of the year. Note that ticket offices often shut an hour (or even more) before

final closing time. *See also p303* Banks & ATMs, *p301* Pharmacies, *p304* Postal services, and *p304* Public holidays.

POLICE

For emergencies, *see p299.*

Both the (nominally military) **Carabinieri** and the **Polizia di Stato** deal with crimes and emergencies of any kind. If you have your bag or wallet stolen, or are otherwise made a victim of crime, go as soon as possible to either force to report a *scippo* ('bagsnatching'). A *denuncia* (written statement) of the incident will be made for you. Give police as much information as possible, including your passport number, holiday address and flight numbers. The *denuncia* will be signed, dated and stamped with an official police seal. It is unlikely that your things will be found, but you will need the *denuncia* for making an insurance claim.

Carabinieri *Castello 4693A, campo San Zaccaria (041 27411). Vaporetto San Zaccaria.* **Map** *p108 N10.*
Polizia di Stato *Questura Santa Croce 500, piazzale Roma (041 271 5511, http://questure. poliziadistato.it/Venezia). Vaporetto Piazzale Roma.* **Map** *p146B7.*

POSTAL SERVICES

Italy's postal service (www.poste. it) is generally reliable. Postage supplies – such as large mailing boxes and packing tape – are available at most post offices; stamps can be bought at post offices and *tabacchi* (*see p305*). Each district has its own sub-post office, open 8.20am-1.45pm Mon-Fri, 8.20am-12.45pm Sat.

Italy's standard postal service, *posta prioritaria*, gets letters to their destination within 48hrs in Italy, three days for EU countries and four or five for the rest of the world. A letter of 20g or less in Italy costs 85¢, within the EU €1, and to the rest of the world €2.20 or €2.90 (Oceania). Express and parcel post services are also available).

Postboxes are red and have two slots: *Per la città* (for Venezia, Mestre and Marghera), and *Tutte le altre destinazioni* (all other destinations).

Posta Piazzale Roma *Santa Croce 511, fondamenta Santa Chiara (041 244 6811). Vaporetto Piazzale Roma.* **Open** *8.20am-7.05pm Mon-Fri; 8.20am-12.35pm Sat.* **Map** *p146 B8.*

PUBLIC HOLIDAYS

On official public holidays (*giorni festivi*), public offices, banks and post offices are closed. So, in theory, are shops – but in tourism-oriented Venice, this rule is often waived. Some bars and restaurants may observe holidays: if in doubt, call ahead. You won't find much open on Christmas Day and New Year's Day.

Public transport is reduced to a skeleton service on 1 May, Christmas Day and New Year's Day, and may be rerouted or curtailed for local festivities, especially those including regattas (*see p71*); details are posted at vaporetto stops and at the bus terminus in piazzale Roma.

Holidays falling on a Sat or Sun are not celebrated on the following Mon. By popular tradition, if a public holiday falls on a Tue or Thur, many people will also take the Mon or Fri off as well, a practice known as *fare il ponte* ('doing a bridge').

New Year's Day (*Capodanno*) 1 Jan
Epiphany (*Befana*) 6 Jan
Easter Monday (*Pasquetta*)
Liberation Day (*Festa della Liberazione*) and patron saint's day (*San Marco*) 25 Apr
Labour Day (*Festa del Lavoro*) 1 May
Assumption (*Ferragosto*) 15 Aug
All Saints' Day (*Ognissanti*) 1 Nov
Festa della Salute (*Venice only*) 21 Nov
Immaculate Conception (*L'Immacolata*) 8 Dec
Christmas Day (*Natale*) 25 Dec
Boxing Day (*Santo Stefano*) 26 Dec

RELIGION

Mass (*messa*) times vary from church to church and are posted by front doors and in the free leaflet, *Un'ospite di Venezia*. Services are usually held between 9am and 11am and again at 6.30pm on Sun (7.30pm in St Mark's basilica; *see p86*); most churches have Mass on Sat at 6pm. The church of San Zulian (*see p99*) has Mass in English at 11.30am on Sun throughout the year. Listed below are the non-Catholic denominations in the city.

Anglican
St George's *Dorsoduro 729A, campo San Vio (041 520 0571). Vaporetto Accademia.* **Services** *Holy Eucharist 10.30am Sun.* **Map** *p170 G13.*

Greek Orthodox
San Giorgio dei Greci *Castello 3412, ponte dei Greci (041 522 5446, www.istitutoellenico. org). Vaporetto San Zaccaria.* **Services** *9.30am, 10.30am Sun.* **Map** *p108 P10.*

Jewish
Synagogue *Cannaregio, campo del Ghetto Vecchio (041 715 012, www.jvenice.org). Vaporetto Guglie.* **Services** *after sunset Fri; Sat am.* **Map** *p128 E4.*
For security reasons, those wishing to attend services at the synagogue must call in advance or present themselves, with ID, to the main office of the Jewish Community (at the synagogue).

Lutheran
Chiesa Evangelica Luterana *Cannaregio 4448, campo Santi Apostoli (041 524 2040, www.kirche-venedig.de). Vaporetto Ca' D'Oro.* **Services** *10.30am 2nd & 4th Sun of mth.* **Map** *p128 K7.*

Methodist & Waldensian
Chiesa Valdese *Castello 5170, fondamenta Cavagnis (041 522 7549, www.chiesavaldese. org). Vaporetto Rialto or San Zaccaria.* **Services** *11.30am Sun.* **Map** *p108 M8.*

Muslim
There is currently no official mosque in central Venice.

SAFETY & SECURITY

Venice is, on the whole, an exceptionally safe place at any time of day or night, and violent crime is almost unknown. Lone women should steer clear of dark alleyways (as far as is possible in labyrinthine Venice) late at night, though they are more likely to be harassed than physically attacked.

Bag-snatchers are a rarity, mostly because of the logistical difficulties of making a quick getaway. However, pickpockets operate in crowded thoroughfares, especially around San Marco and the Rialto, and on public transport, so make sure you leave passports, plane/train tickets and at least one means of getting hold of money in your hotel room safe.

If you are the victim of theft or other serious crime, contact the police (*see p304*).

SMOKING

Smoking is banned anywhere with public access – including bars, restaurants, stations, offices and on all public transport – except in clearly designated smoking rooms.

Tabacchi
Tabacchi or *tabaccherie* (identified by a white T on a black or blue background) are the only places in Italy where you can legally buy tobacco products. They also sell stamps, telephone cards, individual or season tickets for public transport, lottery tickets and the stationery required when dealing with bureaucracy.

Most of Venice's *tabacchi* pull their shutters down by 7.30pm. If you're gasping for nicotine late in the evening or on Sun, you will have to try one of the automatic cigarette vending machines in campo Santa Margherita, piazzale Roma, next to the train station, on strada Nova near Ponte della Guglie and near Santi Apostoli, fondamenta della Misericordia, calle dei Fabbri, although these only 'open' at 9pm to prevent sales to minors.

STUDY

Studying at either of Venice's two main universities is likely to involve lectures and exams in Italian, making a good knowledge of the Italian language a prerequisite. However, there are some exceptions, especially at the more international IUAV. To find out about entrance requirements, consult the faculty websites of the **Istituto Universitario di Architettura di Venezia** (IUAV; www.iuav.it) or the **Università degli Studi di Venezia Ca' Foscari** (www.unive.it), both in English.

Both universities run exchange programmes and participate in the EU's Erasmus scheme. The **Venice International University** (041 271 9511, www. univiu.org) is a consortium of 15 universities and agencies. Students registered at one of the member universities (see the website for a list) are eligible to apply for VIU undergraduate activities. There are also masters and PhD programmes available for foreign students.

Italian courses are available at several language schools in the city, including **Istituto Venezia** (www.istitutovenezia.com) and **Venice Italian School** (www. veniceitalianschool.com).

TELEPHONES

Dialling & codes
Italian landline numbers must be dialled with their prefixes, even if you're phoning within the local area. Numbers in Venice and its province begin **041**; numbers in Padua province begin **049**; in Vicenza they begin **0444**; in Verona **045**.

Numbers generally have seven or eight digits after the prefix; some older ones have six, and some switchboards five. If you try a number and can't get through, it may have been changed to an eight-digit number. Check the directory (*elenco telefonico*) or with directory enquiries (see below).

Numeri verdi ('green numbers') are free and start 800 or 147. Numbers beginning 840 and 848 are charged at a nominal rate. These numbers can be called from within Italy only, and some are available only within certain regions. Mobile phone numbers always begin with a 3.

When calling an Italian landline from abroad, the whole prefix, including the 0, must be dialled; so, to call a number in Venice from the UK, dial 00 39 041... . To make an **international call** from Venice dial 00, then the country code (+44 for the UK; +1 for the USA), then the area code (usually without the initial 0) and the number.

Mobile phones

Standard European handsets will work in Italy, but your service provider may need to activate international roaming before you leave. There are no longer roaming charges within the EU, but you should always check exactly what your contract allows (in terms of calls, texts, minutes and data usage) to avoid unexpected charges. Tri-band US handsets should also work; check with the manufacturer.

If your phone is not locked to your home SIM card/service provider, you can buy an Italian pay-as-you-go SIM card available from mobile phone shops for around €10, allowing you to make cheaper calls within Italy. In theory you have to provide an Italian tax code to purchase one of these; in practice, many vendors will waive this requirement.

Operator services

You can call 1254 for **directory enquiries** but charges for information are steep. Instead, get the information for free at www.1254.it or www.paginebianche.it.

Public phones

There are a few public phones in Venice along the tourist routes, but many are out of service. Those that remain operate only with phone cards (*schede telefoniche*) and/or major credit cards.

Phonecards costing €2.50, €5 and €7.50 can be bought at post offices, *tabacchi* (*see p305*) and some newsstands.

TIME

Italy is one hour ahead of London, six ahead of New York, eight behind Sydney and 12 hours behind Wellington.

TIPPING

There are no hard and fast rules on tipping in Italy, though Venetians know that foreigners tip generously back home, and expect them to be liberal. Some upmarket restaurants (and a growing number of cheaper ones) will add a service charge to your bill: ask *il servizio è incluso*? If not, leave whatever you think the service merited (Italians leave 5-10%). Bear in mind that all restaurants include a cover charge (*coperto*) – a quasi-tip in itself.

TOILETS

Public toilets (*servizi igienici pubblici*) are numerous and relatively clean in Venice, but you have to pay (€1.50) to use them, unless you have invested in the appropriate Venezia Unica package (*see below*). Follow blue and green signs marked WC. By law, all cafés and bars should allow anyone to use their facilities; however, many Venetian bar owners don't. The website https://wctoilettevenezia.com/ has a map of public toilets in the city and an associated app: Bagni a Venezia.

TOURIST INFORMATION

Information

Both the official tourist board's website, www.veneziaunica. it, and the extremely helpful call centre (041 2424) have useful information for visitors, including transport timetables, events listings and a host of other information, in English and Italian. There's also a free VeneziaUnica app in English. Several free publications – available at tourist offices and in some bars –provide

supplementary information. There's also *Un'ospite di Venezia* (*A Guest in Venice*), a bi-weekly bilingual booklet compiled by hoteliers. For details of upcoming events, consult the local press (*see p303*) and look out for posters plastered on walls across the city.

Venezia Unica *San Marco 71F, piazza San Marco (041 2424, www.veneziaunica.it). Vaporetto San Marco-Vallaresso.* **Open** *9am-7pm daily.* **Map** *p82 K11.*
The official City of Venice tourist service provides information on sights and events, a list of hotels and walking itineraries with maps for sale. It also issues and adds services to the Venezia Unica City Pass (*see below*). Staff will put you in touch with registered guides and give details of guided tours (*see p307*). Tickets for special events are sold at some offices. In addition to the branches listed here, there are outlets (generally open 8am-8pm daily) at the following vaporetto stops: Tronchetto, Piazzale Roma, Ferrovia, Rialto, San Marco-Vallaresso, San Marco-San Zaccaria, Fondamenta Nove, Lido. **Other locations** Santa Lucia railway station (7am-9pm daily); Marco Polo Airport Arrivals Hall (8.30am-7pm daily); Piazzale Roma Garage ASM (7.30am-7.30pm daily).

Venezia Unica City Pass
This all-in-one pass is available from Venezia Unica outlets in the city (*see above*) or online at www.veneziaunica.it (not easy to navigate but worth the effort). It combines access to public transport with admission to tourist attractions, tickets for cultural events and many other useful services, including the two museum passes and Chorus church pass (*see p65*), city-wide Wi-Fi, use of public toilets, transport to and from the airport, car parks (*see p296*), guided tours and audio-guides. The Pass allows you to select and pay for only the services you require, and the total price is slightly less than if you'd bought everything separately. If you buy online, you will be sent a code which you will need in order to collect your City Pass from a

Venezia Unica outlet in the city. Additional services can be added online or in person at any time.

Other passes
For the museum and Chorus passes, *see p65*. Travellers aged between 6 and 29 should consider buying the **Rolling Venice** card (€6), which allows you to purchase a three-day travel pass for €22 instead of the usual €40, and gives discounts at many sights, shops and restaurants.

Guided tours
Venezia Unica provides information on guides by language and area, or try the following:
Context *www.contexttravel. com/cities/venice*. **Rates** *vary*. The university professors and experts at Context take groups of visitors (maximum six) on customised and/or themed tours.

Cooperativa Guide Turistiche
041 520 9038, www. guidevenezia.it. **Rates** *€140 for half-day tour, for up to 30 people; €4 for every extra person. No cards*. This cooperative offers made-to-measure tours in English and other languages. In high season, book at least a week in advance.

Guide to Venice *328 948 5671 mobile, www.guidetovenice.it*. **Rates** *€50-€70/person*. Historian Martino Rizzo specialises in tours of the islands, including cruises on traditional boats such as the Nuovo Trionfo. He also runs tours of Venice itself.

See Venice *349 084 8303, www. seevenice.it*. **Rates** *from €70-80/ hr*. Luisella Romeo organises tours of sights, a range of interesting themed visits and shopping tours.

Venice with a Guide *www. venicewithaguide.com*. **Rates** *€150 for 2hrs or €30/person*. Ten qualified multilingual guides.

VISAS

For EU citizens, a passport or a national identity card valid for travel abroad is sufficient. Non-EU citizens must have full passports. Citizens of the US, Canada, Australia and New Zealand do not need visas for stays of up to 90 days. In theory, visitors are required to declare their presence to the local police within a few days of arrival, unless they are staying in a hotel, where this will be done for them. In practice, you will not need to report to the police station unless you decide to extend your stay and you apply for a *permesso di soggiorno* (permit to stay).

Vocabulary

Italian is pronounced as spelled. Stresses usually fall on the second-last syllable; a stress on the final syllable is indicated by an accent.

There are three 'you' forms: the formal singular *lei*, the informal singular *tu*, and the plural *voi*. Masculine nouns and accompanying adjectives generally end in 'o' (plural 'i'), female nouns and their adjectives end in 'a' (plural 'e').

Venetian

The distinctive nasal Venetian drawl is more than just an accent: locals have their own vocabulary too. Venetians tend to ignore consonants, running vowels together in long diphthongs (explaining how *vostro schiavo* – 'your servant' – became *ciao*.) *Xè* is pronounced '*zay*'; *gò* sounds like 'go' in 'got.' For more, visit www.veneto.org/language.

Pronunciation

Vowels

a *as in* a**sk**
e *like* **a** *in* **a**ge *(closed e) or* **e** *in* s**e**ll *(open e)*
i *like* **ea** *in* **ea**st
o *as in* h**o**tel *(closed o) or in* h**o**t *(open o)*
u *as in* b**oo**t

Consonants

c *before a, o or u – like* **c** *in* **c**at
c *before an e or an i – like the* **ch** *in* **ch**eck (**sh** *as in* **sh**ip *in Venetian*)
ch *like* **c** *in* **c**at
g *before a, o or ui – like* **g** *in* **g**et
g *before an e or an ii – like the* **j** *in* **j**ig
gh *like the* **g** *in* **g**et
gl *followed by an ii – like* **lli** *in* mi**lli**on
gn *like* **ny** *in* ca**ny**on
qu *as in* **qu**ick
r *always rolled*
s *two sounds, as in* **s**oap *or* ro**s**e
sc *before an e or an ii – like the* **sh** *in* **sh**ame
sch *like the* **sc** *in* **sc**out
z *two different sounds, like* **ts** *or* **dz**

Useful phrases

hello and goodbye *ciao (used informally in other parts of Italy; in all social situations in Venice)*
good morning, hello *buongiorno*
good afternoon, good evening *buonasera*
please *per favore, per piacere*
thank you *grazie*
you're welcome *prego*
excuse me *mi scusi (polite), scusami (informal) scusime/me scusa*
I'm sorry *mi dispiace/me dispiaxe*
I don't understand *non capisco, non ho capito/no gò capío*
do you speak English? *parla inglese?*
open *aperto/verto*
closed *chiuso*
when does it open? *quando apre?*
it's closed *è chiuso/xè serà*
what's the time? *che ore sono?*
do you have a light? *hai d'accendere?/ti gà da accender, ti gà fógo?*

Transport

car *macchina*
bus *autobus*
taxi *tassì, taxi*
train *treno*
plane *aereo*
stop (bus/vaporetto) *fermata*
station *stazione*
platform *binario*
tickets biglietto, biglietti
one way *solo andata*
return *andata e ritorno*
I'd like a ticket to... *Vorrei un biglietto per...*

Communications

phone *telefono*
mobile phone *cellulare*
postcard *cartolina*
stamp *francobollo*
email *(messaggio di) posta elettronica*

Directions

entrance *entrata*
exit *uscita*
where is...? *dov'è...?/dove xè?*
(turn) left *(giri a) sinistra*
(it's on the) right *(è sulla/a) destra*
straight on *sempre dritto*
could you tell me the way to...? *mi può indicare la strada per...?*
is it near/far? *è vicino/lontano?*

Eating & drinking

▶ *For other words and phrases associated with Venetian food and drink, see p43 The Venetian Menu.*

I'd like to book a table for four at eight *vorrei prenotare una tavola per quattro alle otto*
that was poor/good/delicious *era mediocre/buono/ottimo*
the bill *il conto*
I think there's a mistake in this bill *credo che il conto sia sbagliato*
is service included? *è incluso il servizio?*

Accommodation

I'd like to book a single/ twin/double bedroom *vorrei prenotare una camera singola/doppia/matrimoniale*
I'd prefer a room with a bath/shower/ window over the courtyard/canal *preferirei una camera con vasca da bagno/doccia/ finestra sul cortile/canale*

Shopping

shop *negozio/botega*
how much does it cost/is it? *quanto costa?, quant'è?/quanto xè?*
do you accept credit cards? *si accettano le carte di credito?*
do you have small change? *ha delle monete?*
I'd like to try on the blue sandals/black shoes/brown boots *vorrei provare i sandali blu/le scarpe nere/gli stivali marroni*
I take (shoe) size *porto il numero...*
I take (dress) size *porto la taglia...*
it's too loose/too tight/just right *mi sta largo/ stretto/bene*

a litre *un litro*
100 grams of *un etto di*
200 grams of *due etti di*
one kilo of *un kilo di*

Days & times

Monday *lunedì*
Tuesday *martedì*
Wednesday *mercoledì*
Thursday *giovedì*
Friday *venerdì*
Saturday *sabat*
Sunday *domenica*

yesterday *ieri*
today *oggi/ancùo*
tomorrow *domani*
morning *mattina*
afternoon *pomeriggio*
evening *sera*
this evening *stasera*
night *notte*
tonight *stanotte*

Numbers

0 *zero;* **1** *uno;* **2** *due;* **3** *tre;* **4** *quattro;* **5** *cinque;* **6** *sei;* **7** *sette;* **8** *otto;* **9** *nove;* **10** *dieci;* **11** *undici;* **12** *dodici;* **13** *tredici;* **14** *quattordici;* **15** *quindici;* **16** *sedici;* **17** *diciassette;* **18** *diciotto;* **19** *diciannove;* **20** *venti;* **21** *ventuno;* **22** *ventidue;* **30** *trenta;* **40** *quaranta;* **50** *cinquanta;* **60** *sessanta;* **70** *settanta;* **80** *ottanta;* **90** *novanta;* **100** *cento;* **1,000** *mille;* **2,000** *duemila*

Further Reference

BOOKS

Non-fiction

Paolo Barbaro *Venice Revealed: an Intimate Portrait*
Fascinating facts on the city's physical structure.

Francesco Da Mosto
Francesco's Venice
Coffee-table guide by a scion of an aristocratic Venetian family.

Robert Davis & Garry Marvin *Venice: the Tourist Maze*
A well-documented study of Venice's role as a tourist mecca.

Deborah Howard *The Architecture of Venice*
Howard's Architecture is the definitive account.

WD Howells *Venetian Life*
US consul's (1861-65) account of Venetian life before mass tourism.

Peter Humfrey *Painting in Renaissance Venice*
Informative and compact enough to carry with you.

Frederick C Lane *Venice: a Maritime Republic*
The best single-volume scholarly history of Venice.

Mary Laven *Virgins of Venice: Broken Vows and Cloistered Lives in the Renaissance Convent*
The title says it all.

Michelle Lovric *Venice: Tales of the City*
Compendium of writers on Venice.

Damiano Martin *The Da Fiore Cookbook*
How to cook like they do at Da Fiore (*see p159*).

Mary McCarthy
Venice Observed
Witty account of Venetian art.

Jan Morris *Venice*
Impressionistic history.

John Julius Norwich *A History of Venice; Paradise of Cities*
Engagingly rambling.

John Pemble *Venice Rediscovered*
On the 19th-century obsession with things Venetian.

David Rosand *Painting in 16th-Century Venice*
Read before your trip.

John Ruskin *The Stones of Venice*
Ruskin's hymn to the Gothic.

Gary Wills *Venice: Lion City*
Fascinating blend of history and art criticism.

Fiction & literature

Lord Byron *Childe Harold's Pilgrimage; Beppo*
Venice as a dream (Harold) and at Carnevale (Beppo).

Giacomo Casanova *My Life*
The great seducer's escapades in mid 18th-century Venice.

Michael Dibdin *Dead Lagoon*
Aurelio Zen returns to Venice.

Ernest Hemingway *Across the River and into the Trees*
Could have been titled 'Across the Canal and into the Bar'.

Henry James *The Wings of the Dove*
Melodrama couched in elegant prose.

Donna Leon *Acqua Alta (and many others)*
Series featuring detective commissario Guido Brunetti.

Thomas Mann *Death in Venice*
Disease, decadence, indecision, voyeurism.

Ezra Pound *The Cantos*
Full of abstruse Venetian details.

William Rivière *A Venetian Theory of Heaven*
Novel set among the English community in Venice.

William Shakespeare *The Merchant of Venice; Othello*
The bard's Venetian offerings.

Sally Vickers *Miss Garnett's Angel*
Elderly English lady's staid life is overturned by angelic encounters.

FILM

Casanova
(Lasse Halstrom, 2005)
Heath Ledger plays a sugary no-sex-please version of the legendary lover.

The Comfort of Strangers
(Paul Schrader, 1990)
Based on an Ian McEwan novel.

Death in Venice
(Luchino Visconti, 1971)
Dirk Bogarde chases a boy around cholera-plagued Venice.

Don't Look Now
(Nicholas Roeg, 1973)
Chilling tale of a couple in Venice after the death of their daughter.

Eve
(Joseph Losey, 1962)
Budding novelist meets temptress.

The Merchant of Venice
(Michael Radford, 2004)
Al Pacino is Shylock in this star-studded adaptation.

Senso
(Luchino Visconti, 1954)
Tale of sadism and passion.

The Tourist
(Florian Henckel, 2010)
Jolie and Depp in schlocky
thriller-comedy.

MUSIC

Lorenzo Da Ponte *(1749-
1838)* Penned libretti for
Mozart's *Marriage of Figaro, Don
Giovanni* and *Così fan tutte*.

Andrea Gabrieli *(c1510-
1586)* Organist of St Mark's
basilica, Gabrieli senior's
madrigals were Venetian
favourites.

Giovanni Gabrieli *(c1556-
1612)* composed sacred and
choral music, particularly
motets; *In ecclesiis* is perhaps his
masterpiece.

Antonio Vivaldi *(1678-
1741)* There's no escaping his
Four Seasons in Venice.

WEBSITES

www.agendavenezia.org
Comprehensive cultural events
listings for the city (English).

www.aladinofferte.it
Ads for everything from flats for
rent to *gondole* for sale.

www.meetingvenice.it
Hotel booking service for city
and surrounds, plus news on
events and tourist attractions
(English).

www.venetia.it
History, useful phone numbers
and links (English).

www.venezia.net
Apartment rentals to
information on hiring a
Carnevale costume (English).

www.venezianews.it
Information-packed magazine:

music, film, theatre, art
and sports listings, plus
interviews and features (Italian
and English).

www.veneziaunica.it
Essential site for pre-booking
transport and services (English;
see also p306).

APPS

Eat Italy Tips for foodies
(English).

hitide Venice Instant info on
tides and *acqua alta* (English).

Tap Venice Eating Essential
guide to snacking and dining
(English).

**Telegraph Travel Guide–
Venice** Handy maps and tips
(English).

Venezia Unica Real-time
vaporetto and events info
(English).

Glossary

A

amphitheatre (*ancient*) an oval open-air theatre.

apse large recess at the high-altar end of a church.

B

baldachin canopy supported by columns.

Baroque artistic period from the 17th-18th centuries, in which the decorative element became increasingly florid, culminating in the rococo (*qv*).

barrel vault a ceiling with arches shaped like half-barrels.

basilica ancient Roman rectangular public building; rectangular Christian church.

Byzantine Christian artistic and architectural style drawing on ancient models developed in the fourth century in the Eastern empire and through the Middle Ages.

C

campanile bell tower.

campo Venetian for *piazza* or square.

capital head of a column, generally decorated according to classical orders (*qv*).

caryatid column carved in the shape of a female.

chiaroscuro from Italian *chiaro* (light) and *scuro* (dark); juxtaposition of light and shade to bring out relief and volume.

cloister courtyard surrounded on all sides by a covered walkway.

coffered ceiling decorated with sunken square or polygonal panels.

cupola dome-shaped roof or ceiling.

E

ex-voto an offering given to fulfil a vow; often a small model in silver of the limb/organ/loved one cured as a result of prayer.

F

fan vault vault formed of concave semi-cones, meeting at the apex; it has the appearance of four backwards-leaning fans meeting.

festoon painted or carved swag or swathe decorated with fruit and/or flowers.

fresco painting technique in which pigment is applied to wet plaster.

G

Gothic architectural and artistic style of the late Middle Ages (from the 12th century), of soaring, pointed arches.

Greek cross (church) in the shape of a cross with arms of equal length.

grisailles painting in shades of grey to mimic sculpture.

I

iconostasis rood screen; screen in Eastern-rite churches separating the nave from the sanctuary.

intarsia form of mosaic made from pieces of different-coloured wood; also know as **intaglio**.

L

Latin cross (church) in the shape of a cross with one arm longer than the other.

loggia gallery open on one side.

lunette semi-circular surface, usually above window or door.

M

Mannerism post-High Renaissance style of the later 16th century; characterised in painting by elongated, contorted human figures.

monoforate with one opening (cf biforate, triforate, polyforate *qv*), usually used of windows.

N

narthex enclosed porch in front of a church.

nave main body of a church; the longest section of a Latin cross church (*qv*).

O

ogival (arches, windows etc) curving in to a point at the top.

opus sectile pavement made of (usually) geometrically shaped marble slabs.

orders classical rules governing the proportions of columns, their entablatures and their **capitals** (*qv*), the most common being the less ornate Doric, the curlicue Ionic and the Corinthian, which is decorated with stylised leaves.

P

palazzo large and/or important building (not always a palace).

pendentives four concave triangular sections on top of piers supporting a dome.

piano nobile showiest floor of a *palazzo* (*qv*), containing mainly reception rooms with very high ceilings.

pilaster column-shaped projection from a wall.

polyforate with more than one opening (cf monoforate).

polyptych painting composed of several panels (cf dyptych with two panels, triptych with three).

porphyry hard igneous rock ranging from dark green to dark purple; this latter was most commonly used, and known as *rosso antico*.

presbytery the part of a church containing the high altar.

R

reredos decorated wall or screen behind an altar.

rococo highly decorative style fashionable in the 18th century.

Romanesque architectural style of the early Middle Ages (c500 to 1200), drawing on Roman and Byzantine (*qv*) influences.

rusticated masonry blocks with deep joints between them used to face buildings or monuments.

S

sarcophagus (*ancient*) stone or marble coffin.

stele upright slab of stone with decorative relief sculpture and/or commemorative inscription.

T

transept shorter arms of a Latin cross church (*qv*).

trilobate with three arches.

triumphal arch arch in front of an apse (*qv*), usually over the high altar.

trompe l'œil decorative painting effect to make surface appear three-dimensional.

Index

Photo credits

Credits

Crimson credits
Authors Clara Marshall, Anne Hanley, Luisa Grigoletto
Editors Clara Marshall, Chiara Barbieri, Anna Norman
Proofreader Liz Hammond
Layouts Patrick Dawson, Emilie Crabb, Mihaela Botezatu
Cartography Gail Armstrong, Simonetta Giori

Series Editor Sophie Blacksell Jones
Production Manager Kate Michell
Design Mytton Williams

Chairman David Lester
Managing Director Andy Riddle

Advertising Media Sales House
Marketing Lyndsey Mayhew
Sales Joel James

Photography credits
Front cover oriontrail/iStock.com
Back cover left Viacheslav Lopatin/Shutterstock.com; centre Renata Sedmakova/Shutterstock.com; right Christian Mueller/Shutterstock.com
Interior Photography credits, *see p319.*

Publishing information
Venice City Guide 8th edition
© TIME OUT ENGLAND LIMITED 2018
January 2018

ISBN 978 1 780592 49 7
CIP DATA: A catalogue record for this book is available from the British Library

Published by Crimson Publishing
21d Charles Street, Bath, BA1 1HX (01225 584 950, www.crimsonpublishing.co.uk) on behalf of Time Out England.

Distributed by Grantham Book Services
Distributed in the US and Canada by Publishers Group West (1-510-809-3700)

Printed by Replika Press Pvt. Ltd., India.